D1367105

Attention Deficit Disorders and Hyperactivity in Children

PEDIATRIC HABILITATION

series editor ALFRED L. SCHERZER

Cornell University Medical Center
New York, New York

Attention Deficit Disorders and Hyperactivity in Children

edited by

Pasquale J. Accardo
St. Louis University School of Medicine
St. Louis, Missouri

Thomas A. Blondis
University of Chicago Pritzker School of Medicine
Chicago, Illinois

Barbara Y. Whitman
St. Louis University
St. Louis, Missouri

Marcel Dekker, Inc.   New York • Basel • Hong Kong

ISBN: 0-8247-8429-4

This book is printed on acid-free paper.

MARCEL DEKKER, INC.
270 Madison Avenue, New York, New York 10016

Current printing (last digit):
10 9 8 7 6 5 4 3 2 1

PRINTED IN THE UNITED STATES OF AMERICA

Such an assumption then requires an expanded medical model to carry out appropriate interdisciplinary team diagnosis and treatment. Related behavioral pathology and emotional problems (comorbidity) are interpreted as secondary and often preventable phenomena. The child with attentional deficits with or without hyperactivity whose habilitation is exclusively in the hands of a single discipline remains very much at risk to become a long-term treatment failure.

Our effort is the outcome of ongoing work with children with attentional disorders and their families at the Knights of Columbus Developmental Center at Cardinal Glennon Children's Hospital, St. Louis, Missouri. The Center and its work exist only because of the continued generous support of Columbian Charities of Missouri. The typing of many parts of this book and the final cutting and pasting of the pieces were accomplished with the invaluable assistance of Terry Gardner and Patricia Bennett. The Division of Biomedical Communications of St. Louis University School of Medicine completed most of the artwork and photographic plates. Judith DeCamp and Janet Overton, production editors at Marcel Dekker, Inc., and Dr. Alfred Scherzer, the series editor, have been helpful and supportive throughout.

Pasquale J. Accardo
Thomas A. Blondis
Barbara Y. Whitman

REFERENCES

Stancin, T., Christopher, N., Coury, D. (1990). Reported practices of pediatric residents in the management of attention-deficit disorder. *Am. J. Dis. Child. 144*: 1329-1333.

Zametkin, A.J., Nordahl, T.E., Gross, M., King, A.C., Semple, W.E., Rumsey, J., Hamburger, S., Cohen, R.M. (1990). Cerebral glucose metabolism in adults with hyperactivity of childhood onset. *N. Engl. J. Med. 323*:1361-1366.

Contents

Contributors

Pasquale J. Accardo, M.D. Professor of Pediatrics, St. Louis University School of Medicine, and Director of the Knights of Columbus Developmental Center, Cardinal Glennon Children's Hospital, St. Louis, Missouri

Thomas A. Blondis, M.D. Assistant Professor, Section of Developmental Pediatrics, Department of Pediatrics, University of Chicago Pritzker School of Medicine; Attending Physician, Wyler Children's Hospital; La Rabida Children's Hospital; and Woodlawn Maternal and Child Health Clinic, Chicago, Illinois

Arnold J. Capute, M.D., M.P.H. Associate Professor of Pediatrics, The Johns Hopkins University School of Medicine, and Director of Training, The Kennedy Institute, Baltimore, Maryland

Dana S. Clippard, M.Ed. Learning Skills Specialist, Communication Disorders Unit—Rusk Rehabilitation Center, University of Missouri, Columbia, Missouri

Karen J. Cunningham Assistant Professor, Eastern Illinois University, Charleston, Illinois

Larry W. Desch, M.D. Assistant Professor, Department of Child Health (Pediatrics), University of Missouri—Columbia Medical School, Columbia, Missouri

Carol A. Haake, Ed.D. Instructor, Department of Pediatrics, St. Louis University School of Medicine, and Director of Special Education, Knights of Columbus Developmental Center, Cardinal Glennon Children's Hospital, St. Louis, Missouri

Desmond P. Kelly, M.B., Ch.B. Assistant Professor of Pediatrics, Department of Pediatrics, Southern Illinois University School of Medicine, Springfield, Illinois

Jill D. Morrow, M.D. Post-Doctoral Fellow in Developmental Pediatrics, Department of Pediatrics and Adolescent Medicine, St. Louis University School of Medicine, and Knights of Columbus Developmental Center, Cardinal Glennon Children's Hospital, St. Louis, Missouri

Lizette Peterson, Ph.D. Professor, Department of Psychology, University of Missouri, Columbia, Missouri

Nancy J. Roizen, M.D. Assistant Professor and Section Chief, Section of Developmental Pediatrics, Department of Pediatrics, University of Chicago Pritzker School of Medicine; Attending Physician, Wyler Children's Hospital; and La Rabida Children's Hospital, Chicago, Illinois

Dana J. Scroggs Speech and Language Pathologist, Communication Disorders Unit—Rusk Rehabilitation Center, University of Missouri, Columbia, Missouri

Carla Smith, M.S.W. Social Worker, Knights of Columbus Developmental Center, Cardinal Glennon Children's Hospital, St. Louis, Missouri

Jeffrey H. Snow, Ph.D. Assistant Professor and Pediatric Neurophychologist, Department of Pediatrics, University of Arkansas for Medical Sciences, Little Rock, Arkansas

Mark Stein, Ph.D. Assistant Professor of Clinical Psychiatry and Pediatrics, Director of the Hyperactivity, Attention, and Learning Problems Clinic, University of Chicago Pritzker School of Medicine, Chicago, Illinois

Jean M. Thomas, M.D., M.S.W. Assistant Professor of Child and Adolescent Psychiatry, Assistant Professor of Pediatrics, St. Louis University School of Medicine, and Director of the Department of Child and Adolescent Psychiatry, Cardinal Glennon Children's Hospital, St. Louis, Missouri

Monica H. Ultmann, M.D. Assistant Professor, Department of Pediatrics, St. Louis University School of Medicine, and Division of General Academic Pediatrics and Knights of Colombus Developmental Center, Cardinal Glennon Children's Hospital, St. Louis, Missouri

Barbara Y. Whitman, Ph.D.   Associate Professor, Departments of Social Services and Pediatrics, St. Louis University, and Director of Family Services and Family Studies, Knights of Columbus Developmental Center, St. Louis, Missouri

1

The Misdiagnosis of the Hyperactive Child

Pasquale J. Accardo
St. Louis University School of Medicine, St. Louis, Missouri

Barbara Y. Whitman
St. Louis University, St. Louis, Missouri

> *"The only thing I know for sure is this: a horse's head is finally unknowable to me. Yet I handle children's heads—which I must presume to be more complicated, at least in the area of my chief concern. . . . In an ultimate sense I cannot know what I do in this place—yet I do ultimate things. Irreversible, terminal things. I stand in the dark with a pick in my hand, striking at heads!"*
>
> [Shaffer, 1982]

> *"Principia essentialia rerum sunt nobis ignota."*
>
> [Thomas Aquinas]

In the present work hyperactivity is viewed not in isolation but rather as part of the larger entity "Attention Deficit Hyperactivity Disorder" (ADHD). The conformity to the APA's Diagnostic and Statistical Manual (DSM-III-R) [American Psychiatric Association, 1987] terminology, however, in no way implies acceptance of the APA's underlying etiological and prognostic nihilism. Rather, the neurobehavioral syndrome of ADHD is understood as occupying a place on the spectrum and continuum of pediatric developmental diagnoses that result from diffuse chronic central nervous system impairment and that entertain cerebral palsy and autism as the paradigmatic neurodevelopmental disorders. The clinical approach to hyperactive children thus requires a familiarity with the entire range of brain damage from the most severe to the mildest degrees.

It would be an over simplification to interpret recent research trends as signaling a return to the older lumped category of minimal brain dysfunction (MBD). What they do indicate is the failure of a psychosocial dimensional trait clustering approach to impose any kind of clinical sense on this complex area of dysfunction in children. In an expanded conceptualization of minimal cerebral palsy, the motor disorder is not viewed as the major disability [Capute and Accardo, 1991]; rather, cognitive and perceptual deficits are considered the most handicapping aspects for most degrees of cerebral palsy: and it is the almost inexplicable refusal to adequately allow for an overlap on the level of 50% to 75% between ADHD and learning disabilities [Accardo et al., 1990] that seriously impairs the clinical relevance of much research in the ADHD field. If, furthermore, one considers attentional deficit as a specific type of learning disorder, the degree of overlap only increases. Ignorance of this primary neuropediatric association between ADHD behaviors and cognitive deviance has caused the literature to be flooded with confusing and inconclusive studies of secondary associations with depression, conduct disorder, and oppositional behavior. The history of our evolution to this sorry state of affairs can only be sketched in the briefest outline, but two culpable disciplines must be singled out for the greatest blame: pediatrics, for refusing to encourage the level of clinical expertise in developmental disabilities that might have ameliorated the present situation; and special education, for persistently failing to adequately recognize and understand the most basic distinctions among academic underachievement, school failure, learning disability, ADHD, and other behavioral and psychopathological diagnoses. The resolution to many of these problematic areas certainly lies outside the competance of education; and pediatric medicine, in turn, has not taken up the challenge of adequate communication with education. (Other disciplines are excused from greater culpability only because of their more peripheral involvement.)

HISTORY

The prehistory of disorders of attention and activity in children rivals their recent history in its confusion. Prior to Still's classic 1902 series of lectures describing children who were fidgety, restless, inattentive, and disobedient to a pathologic degree and who exhibited both choreiform movements and minor congenital anomalies, there is little of strict scientific import. However, in 1845 a pediatrician, Dr. Heinrich Hoffman, published a rhymed children's book that chronicled the behavioral misadventures of Slovenly Peter, Cruel Frederick, and Fidgety Philip. This popular work went through numerous editions [Rodin and Key, 1989] and was translated into English by, among others, Mark Twain. "Strüwwelpeter" in the title [Hoffman, 1845] is often translated as "straw Peter" but is more accurately "shaggy-headed," a possible reference to the electric hair commonly found in hyperactive children as a minor dysmorphic feature. Attentional disorders ranging from impetuosity to extreme fixation were described as tempermental variations in 1500 by Pico della Mirandola [1930]. Many of the stereotypic behaviors of the English Punch and the Italian marionette Punchinello are quite descriptive of ADHD children. More primitive societies institutionalized such socially disruptive behavior in rituals such as the rain dance of the Zuñi Indians, a Pueblo tribe. The Plains Indians had secret societies of clowns, "mud heads," called koyemshi, "delight makers" [Lowrie, 1954]. And behind these structures lurked the prevasive "trickster myth" [Radin, 1972] that in many ways recalls the untreated ADHD adolescent and adult.

Finally, the prehistory of a given disorder should always attempt to identify its patron saint. The child therapist Caryll Houslander often intoned, "St. Peter, dear saint of impulses, pray for me that I may stop cutting off peoples' ears" [Ward, 1988]. But perhaps a better choice, from an organic/genetic perspective, would be St. John the Baptist who gave one of the earliest reports of fetal hyperactivity: "the babe leaped in her womb" [Luke 1:41]—this combined with a later career marked by persistent impulsivity and a degree of social inappropriateness.

A chronology of the modern history of *brain damage* is outlined in Appendix I. The paradigm of brain damage or an organic explanation for deviant behavior or delayed cognition has never, rumors to the contrary, been disproven. The debate remains part of the larger philosophical question of nature versus nature (Table 1), and most, if not all, of the relevant data are quite susceptible to reinterpretation by the opposing school. Both sides reluctantly admit the existence of extreme (albeit rare) cases that support the alternative hypothetical framework, both give lip service to complex neurobehavioral entities requiring a multidisciplinary approach that allows adequate input from all perspectives,

Table 1   Two Paradigms

	Organic	Non-Organic
Etiology	Fixed individual differences: genetic organic biochemical	Changeable, interactional environment: child-rearing practices parent-child dyad family psychopathology
Natural history	Neurobehavioral manifestations of brain problems are coextensive with life cycle. Altered neuronal substrate is permanent. Environment, interactions, and expectations can be modified.	Behavioral symptoms are manifestations of the current situation and tend to be isolated to a specific age group. Environment, interactions, and expectations can be modified. No allowance is made for permanent neuronal substrate.
Prognosis	Irreversibly pessimistic	Conditionally optimistic
Philosophy	Human nature is definable although not necessarily defined; this reflects a limited range of potentials that can be widened or narrowed within certain limits.	There is no fixed human nature. We can define human nature any way we choose. There are no limitations on human potential.
Determinants:	Nature Determinism Predestination Materialist	Nurture Free will Grace Idealist

The deterministic/pessimistic facets of the organic hypothesis are not actually required by the model.

but both then quickly shift to a level of practice that is predominantly undisciplinary and often unsuccessful in the long term.

CLINIMETRICS

The differential diagnosis of attentional deficit problems in the clinical setting is admittedly difficult. In the absence of an objective and pathognomonic marker, research into both diagnosis and its dependent variable, outcome, for ADHD provides a ready example of the contradictory results that can be obtained from state versus trait approaches. (The statistical algorithm for most factor analytic studies of questionnaires will usually exclude symptoms of high specificity and low sensitivity. Thus reported visual and auditory hallucinations are exceedingly rare but highly diagnostic of psychosis and schizophrenia; these symptoms are very useful to the clinician but not often included on mental health checklists.) The dichotomy goes deeper than the usual discrepancy between clinical experience and research design [Goldbloom, 1984; Susser, 1984]. The interface between behavioral neurology and minimal central nervous system dysfunction requires a more complex model than those presumed in the literature. The assumption that because one end of a correlation can be measured with seeming objectivity that the other variable is readily susceptible to similarly exact metricization flies in the face of clinical sensibility. For example, in the early 1970s a number of researchers "disproved" the clinical impression of an association between soft neurological signs and learning disabilities. The strength of such studies was to introduce an advanced refinement to the standardized eliciting of such soft signs; their weakness lay in their simplistic (by modern interpretations) understanding of learning disability. A full defense of the wisdom of the clinician will not be undertaken here [see Feinstein, 1987], but three specific problem areas will be highlighted: (1) an overreliance on questionnaires as opposed to clinical diagnosis, (2) the confusion of the continuity hypothesis with an irrational consistency and, finally, (2) the contribution of missed and misunderstood diagnoses and misunderstandings of hyperactivity to the development of a mythological condition—hyporitalinemia—with its attendant treatment failures.

The Questionnaire Quandary

Using a Bayesian approach [Howson and Urbach, 1989] to decision analysis, Bergman and Pantell [1984] assumed a 3% prevalence for hyperactivity and an instrument with a 95% true-positive rate and a 10% false-negative rate. (Table 2, column 1). The probability that hyperactivity would really be present in a child so identified by this hypothetical test was only 0.227. Using research data on one of the Conners scales [Schacter et al., 1986], hypothetical prevalence rates for hyperactivity of 1% and 10% actually yielded lower posterior probabilities (Table 2, column 2) that, in turn, were not strikingly different from the results obtained by flipping a coin to decide whether a child were

Table 2   Bayes Theorem Applied to Hyperactivity Diagnosis

	1	2		3	
P(T/D)	0.95	0.64	0.64	0.5	0.5
P(D)	0.03	0.01	0.10	0.01	0.10
P(T)	0.126	0.353	0.379	0.5	0.5
P(D/T)	0.227	0.018	0.169	0.01	0.10

P(T/D), true-positives (sensitivity); P(D), prevalence (hypothetical); P(T), true-positives & false positives; P(D/T), posterior probability = P(T/D) × P(D)/P(T). (see text for futher explanation).

hyperactive (Table 2, column 3). The accepted practice of utilizing such scales in the absence of clinical judgment would be quite analogous to diagnosing mental retardation with nothing but an IQ score. Even though it may be possible to distinguish normal from hyperactive children by refined statistical analyses of the co-occurrence of such symptoms as inattention, impulsivity, and overactivity [Gittelman, 1988], the pursuit of such discriminatory capability makes no clinical sense without an accompanying diagnosis. Such diagnosis can only be performed by skilled clinicians and not by a score derived from a questionnaire completed by any number of untrained observers. Fairly striking neurobehavioral syndromes such as autism and Tourette's sundrome are apparently capable of being missed by skilled professionals [Volkmar et al., 1985], and both these conditions would probably score in the ADHD range on most behavioral questionnaires.

The above is not meant to argue against the clinical use of questionnaires to either aid in diagnosis or monitor therapeutic effectiveness. It simply highlights the complete inadequacy of such instruments to replace the complex process of diagnosis and strongly calls into question the results of research studies that utilize such questionnaires as their sole criterion. Behavioral neurology can only suffocate amid a welter of such "correlation coefficients between fuzzies" [Cohen, 1976].

Continuity and Discontinuity

The earliest descriptions of minimal brain dysfunction (MBD) recognized one striking characteristic that both confused observers but also qualitatively distinguished these children's immature behaviors from other normal and abnormal patterns—inconsistency. This pathologic variability allowed some observers to see only a normal child who occasionally misbehaved and others to see only different degrees of abnormality. It allowed some parents and professionals to focus on the normal behavior sometimes exhibited and presume that only a lack of motivation prevented the child from behaving appropriately all the time. It further allowed some of these parents and professionals to generate all sorts of interesting psychodynamic and sociological hypotheses and submit these children to a wide variety of interventions with, at best, limited and short-term success. That there are environmental, situational, and motivational variables that impact on ADHD children's behavior is undeniable. It is the clinician's job to both allow for these and to assess the contribution of biological variation to the evolution of problematic child behavior patterns. While an organic component implies a fixed and unchanging substrate for a developmental disorder, this in no way requires the disability to exhibit identical symptomatology in all settings and at all ages. The area of learning disabilities overlaps to a large extent with ADHD and provides a useful example of the kind of variable expression characteristic of most disorders of attention and learning in children.

Many different attempts at classifying *learning disabilities* (LD) have been proposed but none has become universally accepted. One approach that is very useful as a first-order approximation is provided by the dichtomy between sequential and simultaneous processing [Brown and Aylward, 1987; Shinn-Strieker, 1986]. *Sequential learning* is logical, stepwide, and analytical, with a strong bias toward verbal and memory skills. *Simultaneous learning* is holistic, gestalt, and synthetic, with a strong orientation toward non-verbal, pictorial, and insight strategies. (This division only loosely resembles that between left- and right-brain functions.) If one examines the variations in task content for elementary, secondary, and postsecondary curricula, one finds a constantly alternating emphasis on first simultaneous and then sequential learning (Figure 1).

Mild discrepancies between a given child's sequential and simultaneous skills often reflect nothing more than a preferential learning style and would be insufficient to cause any academic difficulties. More significant deficits in one type of information processing create a cognitive imbalance that can be compensated in varying degrees by these children's strengths in the opposite type of learning as well as by their ability to learn and develop other coping strategies. When the discrepancy reaches a degree of severity that cannot be compensated for, the child begins to experience academic difficulty and ultimately school failure. The location of this point is dependent on IQ (brighter

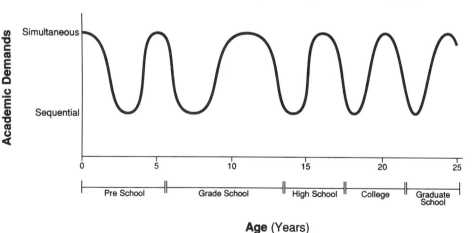

Figure 1   Cyclical variations in academic demands over time. Phases where recognition and comprehension (simultaneous tasks) predominate are followed by phases in which rote memory (a sequential task) is emphasized [modified from Accardo et al., 1989].

children are more likely to successfully compensate on their own for longer periods of time), the severity of the deficit, the competitiveness and academic demands of the school, the individual teacher's instructional style and personality, class size and structure, the supportiveness of the family and home environment, coexisting emotional diagnoses in the child, and numerous other biomedical and psychosocial factors. It is certainly true that in the absence of any processing deficit some children will fail because of a combination of these other factors. This does not free the clinician from the responsibility of identifying all significant determinants of academic problems. Most professionals subscribe to an oversimplified interpretation of LD and categorically attribute it to a single etiology; poor motivation is probably the most commonly blamed culprit.

The complex interaction between factors that contribute to LD is only heightened by the observation that a fixed processing deficit does not need to demonstrate its presence at any given age: the LD child will not necessarily appear LD in a grade that does not tap his deficit areas, and screening psychometric procedures will not always be able to accurately diagnose such problems. A fixed neurodevelopmental deficit does not always and everywhere reveal itself: the organic substrate is continuous but is perceived in a variable and evolving symptom constellation. The ADHD that frequently accompanies LD only confuses the presenting picture [McGee and Share, 1988]. This complexity is so frustrating that many educators have come to doubt the existence of LD [Algozzine and Ysseldyke, 1986; Ysseldyke et al., 1982]. Many confusing test behaviors reflect this overlap: ADHD students perhaps more than LD students demonstrate a tendency to miss easy items and then pass more difficult ones in a graded series. Difficulties on the Wepman are probably more related to attentional rather than auditory discrimination problems. It would be a misinterpretation of these uneven performances to attribute erratic learning to motivational and compliance factors—i.e., "Could do better if he tried" [Ounsted, 1982].

Misdiagnosing and Misunderstanding the Hyperactive Child

Cat breeders and owners have long been able to identify the brain-damaged kitten who impels himself along as if he could walk through walls, and continues to do so into adulthood. It seems to have taken medicine a bit longer to realize that parent and teacher reported hyperactivity does in fact exist and has both quantitative [Porrino et al., 1983] and qualitative [Schworm and Birnbaum, 1989] characteristics. That researchers were able to miss these objectives realities for almost two decades represents an interesting methodological critique from the perspective of clinical commonsense.

In the earlier MBD literature the role of hyperactivity was overplayed. More recent attempts to place hyperactivity in the perspective of attentional disorders have suffered from vacillation on the part of the American Psychiatric Association as to whether to code separately for the presence of hyperactivity. In the presence of ADHD there are conflicting views on the importance of such hyperactivity as an individual symptom. Frank and Ben-Nun [1988] described an increased incidence of cognitive abnormalities with hyperactivity, while Accardo et al. [1990] noted a decrease in learning disabilities when hyperactivity accompanied the ADHD. Hyperactivity remains an organism-specific variable [Gandour, 1986] whose diagnostic importance awaits clarification.

If one is trying to unravel the complex interrelationships among hyperactivity, ADHD, LD, and emotional disorders, all these categories will need to be addressed simultaneously. Thus almost all right brain deficit syndrome children exhibit attentional deficits in addition to their learning disorder [Voeller, 1986], and follow-up studies on adult outcomes for LD children suggest a higher incidence of psychopathology for nonverbal LD profiles [Spreen, 1988 a and b]. Most studies investigate the association between emotional diagnoses and ADHD *or* LD but not both.

Focusing on the wrong symptom—hyperactivity or emotional disorder—will lead to the wrong treatment—stimulant medication or psychotherapy. Treating an incomplete diagnostic profile is gambling with outcome. Given the differential that needs to be considered (Table 3), the typical assessment process tends to be cursory. The fairly large number of variables that can significantly impact on diagnosis, treatment, and outcome tend to be ignored (Table 4) simply because individual disciplines assume their irrelevance. The disparate views on stimulant medication can provide an example for much of the illogicality that pervades the approach to the ADHD child.

Stimulant medication should never be the first treatment approach to ADHD and should never represent the only intervention for ADHD, but these restrictions are compatible with the further recommendation that stimulant medication should almost always be given a trial in ADHD children, and this trial should be integrated into a total therapeutic program. To be pro or anti the use of stimulant medication in ADHD makes about as much sense as being for or against the use of antibiotics in infections diseases. Many abscesses could be treated by antisepsis, heat, nutrition, rest, analgesia, and incision and drainage without antibiotics. The routine employment of antibiotics with attendant risks of idiopathic, allergic, or even potentially fatal anaphylactic reactions (approximately 1 in 40,000 for penicillin) could then be avoided and the evolution of resistant strains of microorganisms not encouraged. It is well known that overreliance on antibiotics tends to decrease the use of other anti-infective techniques, such as hand washing. But the true opposite of *overuse* is not underuse but *appropriate use*, and the inappropriate use of stimulant medication for ADHD children takes many forms.

Table 3   Some Conditions that Need To Be
Differentiated from ADHD

Normal behavior
Mental retardation
Hyperthyroidism
Autistic disorder
Plumbism
Choreiform (neostriatal) syndrome (e.g., craniopharyngioma)
Wittmaack-Ekbom syndrome
von Recklinghausen disease (neurofibromatosis)
Acathisia
Clumsy child syndrome
Debilité du Dupré
Gilles de la Tourette syndrome
Briquet syndrome
Psycho-organic syndrome (POS)
Neurodegenerative disorders
Childhood depression
Maternal depression
Multiple personality disorder (MPD)
Chaotic unstructured home environment
Specific learning disability
Developmental disorder of language

It should be readily apparent from the selection of items in this list
that neither a questionnaire nor a single professional discipline would
be sufficient to yield an accurate diagnosis. In our own studies we were
surprised to find that parental depression and childhood depressive
symptomatology were not significantly higher in ADHD children [Accardo et al., 1990]. That this presumed association needs to be reexamined
has already been suggested in the work of Richters and Pellegrini [1989].

Despite the fact that a significant proportion of ADHD children do not
respond to any medication, while others respond to only one or several of
the drugs available, many physicians consider the trial of a single drug at a
single dosage to be adequate, and the ineffectiveness of generic equivalents
is not widely recognized. Transient symptoms noted at the start of therapy
are often misinterpreted as unacceptable side effects. Many children are maintained on part-time dosages that allow their attentional behaviors to ride an
emotional roller coaster. (Such an irrational dependence on short-acting
stimulants accounts for a large part if not all of the reported advantages of
the longer acting tricyclic antidepressants.) Medication errors could be multiplied indefinitely, but basically most of them stem from a poor understanding of the complex nature of the disorder being treated along with an incomplete data base for both diagnosis and follow-up. A well-constructed, cohesive
treatment program requires parental understanding and a clear idea on the

Table 4 Sample Factors that Need To Be Allowed for in the Diagnosis, Treatment, and Outcome of ADHD and Specific Learning Disabilities

Biological	Cognitive	Behavioral
Age	IQ	Inattention
Neurological	Scatter	Impulsivity
Motor coordination	Simultaneous versus sequential	Hyperactivity
Graphomotor skills	processing	Remorse
Soft signs	Syndromes (patterns of psy-	Anxiety disorder
Seizures	chometric soft signs)	Depression
EEG	Learning Disability	Adjustment disorder
Evoked potentials, BEAM	Dyslexia	Conduct disorder
CT, MRI, PET	Dyscalculia	Oppositional disorder
	Written language	Enuresis
Dysmorphology	Disarticulation	Temporal course
Microcephaly	Developmental disorder of	Age at onset
Short stature	language	Syndromes
Syndromes	Grade	Autism
Neurofibromatosis	Retention	Tourette
Fetal alcohol	Special education	
Perinatal risk factors	Grades	
Fetal activity	Learning profile	
Failure to thrive		
Genetics		
Family history		
Fragile X chromosome		
Family psychopathology		
Child abuse/neglect		
Drug responsiveness		
Stimulants (at least 8 combi-		
nations possible)		
Other drugs		

The complex interactions between these variables are difficult to imagine. For example, to the three major stimulants used in treatment, some ADHD children respond to none, some to one, some to two, and some to all three. With regard to just one class of drugs, therefore, we have a potential minimum of eight neurochemically distinct subgroups. The child's response to such medication is, of course, assessed with a placebo, double-blind control for each drug, starting at a low dosage, titrated through toxicity, and repeated after a several-month drug vacation. This pattern is then matched against all the other variables such as a detailed psychoeducational profile and emotional complications over time. The temporal course of all these factors is frequently ignored. As noted earlier, LD is not simply present or absent. When these children are behaviorally described as having "good and bad days," this is an oversimplification. They have good and bad half days, hours, and weeks or months—as one mother reported, even good and bad minutes. More recently, some parents are describing good and bad years. This cyclical variation affects even drug responsiveness: a child whose behavioral management, family environment, special educational services, and all other obviously relevant variables remain the same will one year be an excellent drug responder and the next year be unresponsive. Lest it be thought that the earlier responsiveness represent a fluke, a year or two later, positive responsiveness will return. Variability, inconsistency, is the hallmark of the ADHD syndrome. Problem-solving is ongoing, and fluctuations should not be unthinkingly attributed to school, family, or physician mistakes or presumed primary emotional disorders.

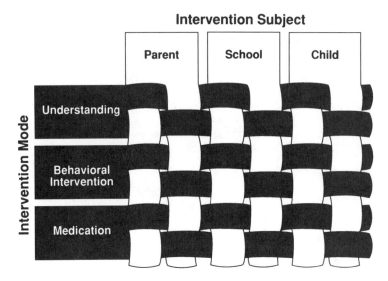

Figure 2   In subject-treatment interactions, the first level of intervention is understanding. Parents who do not understand the biological nature of ADHD will have their unrealistic expectations and undeserved guilt negatively impact on the degree of success anticipated from appropriate behavior management provided by therapists who remain similarly uninformed about the complex nature of the disorder they are treating. School teachers who strongly favor or oppose the use of medication go beyond their professional competence and represent an obstacle to the ADHD child's habilitation. Separate from the limitations to understanding presented by the child's age, the failure of involved adults to adequately comprehend the nature of the ADHD child's disability severely restricts their ability to provide the consistent support the child needs.

professional's part of the origin and manifestations of ADHD symptomatology (Figure 2). Behavioral management techniques that involve the whole family will be less effective in the absence of such understanding, and both are needed to optimize any positive effects of medication. The inappropriate use of medication without adjunctive behavioral treatment [Kelleher et al., 1989] is due to the high and mostly unreimbursed cost for such therapy [Kwasman, 1989] as well as a definite shortage of experienced therapists willing to spend time on simple behavior managment as opposed to more interesting emotional disorders of childhood.

CONCLUSION

There is no doubt that behavioral questionnaires are better than nothing; however, that is probably the only thing they are better than. They have all the limitations inherent in instruments that rely on untrained, biased observers to make difficult judgments on complex behaviors. The reliance on questionnaires is itself biased in that it presumes a specific discipline's approach to the diagnosis and treatment of childhood disorders. The frequent need to shore-up such results with other information often conceals the fact that the most important diagnostic data comes from these other sources. In our clinic two-thirds of all children referred with chief complaints of inattention and hyperactivity qualified for a diagnosis of ADHD. Two out of three nonprofessional guesses were correct; the error rate of one out of three is extremely high, but it would take an absurdly poor screening instrument to perform worse. Using the Diagnostic Interview Schedule for Children (DISC), Lindgren [1989] reported an underdiagnosis of ADHD in the elementary school-age population (4.8% instead of 6.1%). There is also little doubt that some children are misdiagnosed as ADHD. Questionnaires will not compensate for a lack of clinical skill.

The necessary clinical expertise must cover the full spectrum of neurodevelopmental disorders. The presence of ADHD, LD, or both reflects a fixed underlying central nervous system deficit. The expression of the ADHD or LD can be extremely variable depending on the demands placed upon the child. It is sociologically true but neurologically false to say, for example, that dyslexia did not exist in preliterate societies. In this context the question of whether ADHD or LD comes first is not only irrelevant but betrays a fundamental misunderstanding of their common organic etiology. Translation into therapeutic implications reveals this misunderstanding as unfortunate indeed.

The use of stimulant medication in ADHD is frequently inappropriate: overuse, underuse, misuse, abuse. And in this it traces the same course as ADHD itself: overdiagnosed, underdiagnosed, misdiagnosed, and, probably worst of all, incompetely diagnosed. And incompletely understood. The referral of an ADHD child with emotional symptomatology to psychiatry in place of completing a full psychoeducational battery for LD testifies to this incompleteness. ADHD subsumed the isolated symptom of hyperactivity but remains itself incomplete with regard to coexisting learning and language disorders that represent far more than an accidental association.

APPENDIX I

The Modern History of Brain Damage

The items included in this chronology go beyond the typically narower confines of brain dysfunction [sources include Accardo, 1989; Mettler, 1947; Waites 1989 a and b]. They reflect a broader but specific model of developmental disabilities as representing a spectrum and continuum of chronic neurological dysfunction [Capute and Accardo, 1991]. A wealth of valid clinical observations in many of the older entries in this chronology still await a place in modern theoretical formulations that achieve their rigor by excluding a lot that is relevant. Brain damage no longer implies perinatal asphyxia. Obstetrics is exonerated from blame for most developmentally poor outcomes, concomitantly, further advances in prenatal care cannot be expected to have a significant impact on lowering the incidence of such developmental disabilities.

Chronology

1741	Nicholas Andry (1658-1742) publishes *L'orthopedie ou l'art de prevenir et de corriger dans les enfants les difformites du corps* with a complete absence of operative techniques; prevention through an understanding of normal neuro-orthopedic development is stressed.
1745	Carl Linnaeus (1707-1778) describes a case of aphasia.
1747-1749	Jacob Rodrigues Pereire (1715-1780) demonstrates the educability of congenital deaf mutes.
1753	James Lind (1716-1794) identifies a deficiency of citrus fruits (vitamin C) as causing scurvy and recommends lemon juice as a preventive treatment.
1762	Jean Jacques Rousseau's *Emile* romanticizes the education of youth.
1784	Michael Underwood (1737-1820) describes poliomyelitis in his *Treatise on the Diseases of Children*.
1787	Dietrich Tiedemann (1748-1803) publishes his "Observations on the mental development of a child."
1800-1806	Jean Marc Gaspard Itard (1774-1838) works with "the wild child," Victor, using techniques from Pereire and ideas from Rousseau. He basically invents special education and behavioral psychology.
1805	Heinrich Pestalozzi (1746-1827) introduces scientific psychology into early education.
1806	Philippe Pinel's *A Treatise on Insanity* tries to distinguish permanent cognitive defects from more treatable psychiatric diagnoses.
1812	Johann Christian Reil (1759-1813) mentions cases compatible with cerebral palsy.

1924	J. Gerstmann describes a syndrome of parietal lobe dysfunction leading to finger agnosia, right-left disorientation, dysgraphia, and dyscalculia.
1925	Arnold Gesell publishes *The Mental Growth of the Pre-School Child: A psychological Outline of Normal Development from Birth to the Sixth year, Including a System of Developmental Diagnosis.*
	Samuel Torrey Orton offers "strephosymbolia" as a more suitable term than "congenital word blindness" and suggests the dysfunction is not uncommon in schoolchildren. *Arch Neurol Psychiatry 14*:581.
	Lewis M. Terman (1877-1956) begins his study of gifted children.
1926	George Minot and William Murphy discover the beneficial effects of liver in pernicious anemia.
1926-1927	E. D. Bond, G. E. Partridge, "Post-encephalic behavior disorders in boys and their management in a hospital" *Am J Psychiatry 6*:25-103.
1928	Samuel Torrey Orton, "A physiological theory of reading disability and stuttering in children" *New Engl J Med 199*:1046-1052.
1929-1930	Worster-Drought and Allen in a series of three papers present the syndrome of congenital auditory imperception (congenital word deafness) with an excellent historical review and summary in the last paper. *J. Neurol Psychopathology.*
1931	N. H. M. Burke, "Stigmata of degeneration in relation to mental deficiency," *Proc Roy Soc Med 24*:413-428.
1932	Allen discusses speech defects that are apparently congenital in origin and says "true idioglossia is associated only with inability to appreciate the meaning of word-sounds . . . " *Br J Dis Children 24*:98.
1934	A. Følling discovers the metabolic defect in phenylketonuria.
	E. Kahn and L. H. Cohen, "Organic drivenness—a brain stem syndrome and an experience" *New Engl J Med 210*:748-756.
1937	Charles Bradley reports a positive effect of amphetamines on hyperactivity in "The behavior of children receiving benzedrine" *Am J Psychiatry 94*:577-585.
	Hiram Houston Merritt and Tracy Putnam discover Dilantin's efficacy in the treatment of epilepsy.

1937   *Reading, Writing and Speech Problems in Children* is a summary of Orton's concepts and experiences with language disability in children. Congenital word blindness, strephosymbolia, and specific reading disability are noted to be synonymous. Norton: New York.

1938   Lauretta Bender's *A Visual Motor Gestalt Test and Its Clinical Use* (American Orthopsychiatry Association Research Monographs, No. 3) introduces a perceptual motor task as an indicator of both organic brain damage and emotional psychopathology.

1939   Harold Skeels and Harold Dye challenge the stability of the IQ based on the effects of differential stimulation by caretakers with mental retardation.

1941   Alfred Strauss and Heinz Werner distinguish between exogenous and endogenous mental retardation. The exogenous form will later be referred to as the Strauss Syndrome or the brain-damaged child syndrome.

1942   Alfred Strauss and Heinz Werner, "Disorders of conceptual thinking in the brain-injured child" *J Nervous Mental Dis 96*:153-172.

Kurt Goldstein publishes *Aftereffects of Brain Injuries in War.*

1943   Leo Kanner first describes "Autistic disturbances of affective contact."

Grace M. Fernald, *Remedial Techniques in School Subjects*. New York: McGraw-Hill.

1945   First successful use of exchange transfusion to treat erythroblastosis fetalis by Harry Wallerstein.

1947   Arnold Gesell (1880-1961) and Catherine S. Amatruda *Developmental Diagnosis: Normal and Abnormal Child Development: Clinical Methods and Pediatric Applications*. New York: Paul B. Heober.

Alfred Strauss & Laura Lehtinen *Psychopathology and Education of the Brain Injured Child*. New York: Grune & Stratton.

Lauretta Bender introduces the term "soft neurological signs" in "Childhood Schizophrenia: clinical study of one hundred schizophrenic children" *Am J Orthopsychiatry 17*:40-46.

1948   Temple Fay proposes that infant motor development is best interpreted according the epigenetic law: ontogeny recapitulates phylogeny. This will become the basis for patterning therapy.

Kurt Goldstein, *Language and Language Disturbances.*

Heinz Werner, *The Comparative Psychology of Mental Development.*

1949   Lauretta Bender describes "Psychological problems of children with organic brain disease" *Am J Orthopsychiatry 19*:404-415.

        Henry Bakwin reports on "Cerebral damage and behavior disorders in children" *J Pediatr 34*:371-381.

        L. S. Penrose, *The Biology of Mental Defect*.

1950   "Specific dyslexia (congenital word blindness): A clinical and genetic study" by Bertil Hallgren. The beginning of the change from word blindness to specific dyslexia. A genetic study suggesting the syndrome follows a monohybrid autosomal dominant pattern of genetic inheritance. *Acta Psychiatra Neurol Scand*, Suppl. 65.

1952   Allen's "The history of congenital auditory imperception" is presented in *New Zeal Med J 51*:239.

1954   "A research approach to reading retardation" by R. D. Rabinovitch discusses primary reading disability and secondary reading problems, reviews emotional problems caused by reading failure, and presents an argument for remedial language training.

1955   Alfred Strauss and Newell Kephart, *Psychopathology and Education of the Brain-Injured Child*. Vol. 2.

1956   Benjamin Pasamanick introduces the concept of a continuum of reproductive casualty.

        "A neurological appraisal of familial congenital word blindness" by Arthur Drew is a study of word blindness in three generations, indicating a dominant mode of inheritance. *Brain 79*:445.

        Lauretta Bender, *Psychopathology of Children with Organic Brain Disorders*. Springfield, IL: Charles C Thomas.

1957   Templin presents clinical research findings in the language areas of articulation of speech sounds, sound discrimination ability, structure of the sentence, and vocabulary. *Certain Language Skills in Children*. Minneapolis: University of Minnesota Press.

        Maurice Laufer and Eric Denhoff, "Hyperkinetic behavior syndrome in children." *J Pediatrics 50*:463-473.

1959   Jerome Lejeune reports the first example of a human autosomal aberration in Down Syndrome.

        H. F. R. Prechtl and C. J. Stemmer introduce the choreiform syndrome (Ein choreatiformes syndrom bei kindern. *Wiener Medizinische Wochenschrift 19*:1-9.

        Bronson Crothers and Richmond Paine described *The Natural History of Cerebral Palsy* (Cambridge, Massachusetts: Harvard University

Press) with a focus on the associative deficits that complicate the neuromotor disability.

Hilda Knobloch and Benjamin Pasamanick describe the "Syndrome of minimal cerebral damage in infancy" *J Am Med Assoc 170*:1384-1387.

1960   The Doman-Delacato phylogenetic retraining or patterning therapy for brain-damaged, mentally retarded, mentally deficient, cerebralpalsied, emotionally disturbed, spastic, flaccid, rigid, epileptic, autistic, athetoid, hyperactive, and dyslexic children is presented in *J Am Med Assoc*.

Newell Kephart's *The Slow Learner in the Classroom* stresses the importance of motor training.

1961   E. M. Taylor describes the effects of brain damage on psychological testing in children. *Psychological Appraisal of Children with Cerebral Defects*. Cambridge, Massachusetts: Harvard University Press.

1962   Richmond, S. Paine, "Minimal chronic brain syndromes in children." *Dev Med Child Neurology 4*:21-27.

Norman Geschwind proposes a neuroanatomical substrate (the angular gyrus) for dyslexia.

1963   Martin Bax and Ronald MacKeith question the conceptualization of *Minimal Cerebral Dysfunction*.

1964   B. Bateman introduces the discrepancy model for "Learning disabilities—yesterday, today, and tomorrow." *Exceptional Children 31*: 167-177.

Marianne Frostig introduces her "Developmental Tests of Visual Perception" and a training program to correct the deficiencies uncovered.

Developmental Dyslexia by Macdonald Critchley is timely, informative, erudite and now a classic.

1965   S. S. Gubbay, E. Ellis, J. N. Walton, and S. D. M. Court "Clumsy children. A study of apraxic and agnosic defects in 21 children." *Brain 88*:295-312.

1966   Alexander Luria's *Higher Cortical Functions in Man* is based on his experiences with Russian head injuries in World War II.

Sam D. Clemens, *Minimal Brain Dysfunction in Children: Terminology and Classification*. Public Health Service Publication, No. 1415.

Hilda Knobloch and Benjamin Pasamanick "Prospective studies on the epidemiology of reproductive casualty" *Merrill-Palmer Quart 12*:27-43.

1967   Herbert Cohen, Lawrence Taft, M. S. Mahadeviah, and Herbert Birch show "soft neurological signs" to independently relate to age, IQ, diagnosis, and severity in "Developmental changes in overflow in normal and aberrantly functioning children." *J. Pediatr. 71*:39-47.

Doris Johnson and Helmer Mykellbust introduce a psychoneurological definition of *Learning Disabilities: Educational Principles and Practice.* New York: Grune & Stratton.

E. Lenneberg summarizes research supporting the organic basis of language development. *Biological Foundations of Language.* New York: John Wiley.

William M. Cruickshank, *The Brain Injured Child in Home, School and Community.*

1968   World Federation of Neurology meets at Texas Scottish Rite Hospital and adopts the following definition of developmental dyslexia: "A disorder manifested by difficulty in learning to read despite conventional instruction, adequate intelligence, and socio-cultural opportunity. It is dependent upon fundamental cognitive disabilities which are frequently of constitutional origin."

Mary Waldrop emphasizes the correlation between hyperactivity and minor physical anomalies.

Alexander Thomas, Stella Chess, and Herbert Birch describe the difficult child in *Temperament and Behavior Disorders in Children.* New York University Press.

S. A. Kirk, J. J. McCarthy, and W. D. Kirk introduce the Illinois Test of Psycholinguistic Abilities (ITPA).

Linus Pauling coins the term "orthomolecular medicine" to sanitize the use of megavitamin therapy for schizophrenia, autism, hyperactivity, mental retardation, learning disabilities, and the common cold.

1970   Critchley's *Aphasiology* describes the "preverbitum" as the processes of thought that immediately precede the act of speaking or writing. Preverbitum may be defined as the complex silent thinking processes that immediately precede exteriorization and is of necessity formulated, disciplined, and coordinated so as to serve as a communicative act. Unlike inner speech, it must proceed to the stage of conforming with accepted grammatical usages.

1971   Paul Wender popularizes the concept of congenital hypoampheta-
       minemia. *Minimal Cerebral Dysfunction in Children.* New York:
       Wiley Interscience.

       Stella Chess reports autistic disorder as behavioral teratology conse-
       quent on congenital rubella.

       Elena Boder describes three atypical reading-spelling patterns: dys-
       phonetic, dyseidetic, and alexic.

       A. Towbin "Organic causes of minimal brain dysfunction. Perinatal
       origin of minimal cerebral lesions" *J Am Med Assoc 217*:1207-1214.

1972   Marian De Meyer's group begins to publish a series of papers explod-
       ing the emotional/interactional etiology of autism.

       Jean Ayres' "Southern California Sensory Integration Test Battery"
       promotes the use of occupational therapy to treat learning disabilities.

       Wolf Wolfensberger, *Normalization: The Principle of Normalization
       in Human Services.* Toronto: National Institute on Mental Retardation.

1973   Benjamin Feingold claims hyperactivity and a spectrum of behavioral
       and cognitive disorders are secondary to the ingestion of salicylates,
       food colors and additives, and other low molecular weight substances.

       Education for All Handicapped Children Act (PL 94-142) enacted.

1974   R. M. Adams, J. J. Kocsis, and R. E. Estes "Soft neurological signs
       in learning-disabled children and controls." *Am J Dis Child 128*:614-
       618.

1975   P. Schrag and D. Divoky's *The Myth of the Hyperactive Child* (New
       York: Pantheon Books) represents the introduction of uninformed
       polemics into an extremely complicated area of medical treatment.

1979   H. L. Needleman's group suggests that subclinical lead toxicity con-
       tributes to disorders of attention and learning.

       Marcel Kinsbourne and Paula Caplan describe a subgroup of ADHD
       children (usually girls) as "overfocussed children" in *Children's
       Learning and Attention Problems.* Boston: Little, Brown.

1982   Fenfluramine is reported to be effective in the treatment of autism.

REFERENCES

Accardo, P. J. (1989). William John Little (1810-1894) and cerebral palsy in the nineteenth century. *J. Hist. Med. Allied Sci. 44*:56-71.
Accardo, P. J.; Blondis, T. A.; and Whitman, B. Y. (1990). Disorders of attention
and activity level in a referral population. *Pediatrics 85*:426-431.

Accardo, P. J.; Haake, C.; and Whitman, B. Y. (1989). The learning disabled medical student. *J. Dev. Behav. Pediatr. 10*:253-258.

Algozzine, B., and Ysseldyke, J. E. (1986). The future of the LD field: screening and diagnosis. *J. Learn. Disab. 19*:394-398.

American Psychiatric Association (1987). *Diagnostic and Statistical Manual.* 3rd ed., rev. Washington, D.C.: American Psychiatric Association.

Bergman, D. A., and Pantell, R. H. (1984). The art of science of medical decision making. *J. Pediatr. 104*:649-656.

Brown, F. R., III, and Aylward, E. H. (1987). *Diagnosis and Management of Learning Disabilities: An Interdisciplinary Approach.* Boston: College-Hill.

Capute, A. J., and Accardo, P. J., eds. (1991). *Developmental Disabilities in Infancy and Childhood.* Baltimore: Paul H. Brookes.

Cohen, J. D. (1976). Is there a greater incidence of color-vision deficiencies in learning-disabled children? *Clin. Pediatr. 15*:518-522.

Feinstein, A. R. (1987). *Clinimetrics.* New Haven: Yale University Press.

Frank, Y., and Ben-Nun, Y. (1988). Toward a clinical subgrouping of hyperactive and nonhyperactive attention deficit disorder. *Am. J. Diseases Child. 142*:153-155.

Gandour, M. J. (1986). Activity level as a dimension of temperament in toddlers: Its relevance for the organismic specificity hypothesis. *Child. Dev. 60*:1092-1098.

Gittelman, R. (1988). The assessment of hyperactivity: The DSM-III approach. In L. M. Bloomingdale and J. A. Sergeant, eds. *Attention Deficit Disorder: Criteria, Cognition, Intervention.* Oxford: Pergamon Press, pp. 9-28.

Goldbloom, R. B. (1984). Science and empiricism in pediatrics. *Pediatrics 73*:693-698.

Hoffman, H. (1845). *Der Strüwwelpeter: Oder lustige geschichten und drollige bilder.* Leipzig: Insel-Verlag.

Howson, C., and Urbach, P. (1989). *Scientific Reasoning: The Bayesian Approach.* LaSalle, Illinois: Open Court.

Kelleher, K. J., Hohmann, A. A., and Larson, D. B. (1989). Prescription of psychotropics to children in office-based practice. *Am. J. Diseases Child. 143*:855-859.

Kwasman, A. (1989). Management of attention deficit. *Clin. Pediatr. 28*:336.

Lindgren, S. (1989). Quoted in: Diagnosis of hyperactivity by primary care MDS. *Pediatr News 23*(8):15.

Lowie, R. H. (1954). *Indians of the Plains.* New York: McGraw-Hill.

McGee, R., and Share, D. L. (1988). Attention deficit disorder-hyperactivity and academic failure: Which comes first and what should be treated? *J. Am. Acad. Child. Adolesc. Psychiatry 27*:318-325.

Mettler, C. C. (1947). *A History of Medicine.* Philadelphia: Blakiston.

Ounsted, C. (1982). Could do better if he tried. In Apley, J., and Ounsted, C., eds. *One Child.* London: William Heinemann Medical Books, pp. 48-53.

Pico della Mirandola, Gianfrancesco (1930). *On the Imagination.* Trans. Harry Caplan. New Haven: Yale University Press.

Porrino, L.; Rapoport, J. L.; Ismond, D.; Sceery, W.; Behar, D.; and Bunney, W. (1983). Twenty-four hour motor activity in hyperactive children and controls. *Arch. Gen. Psychiatry 40*:681-687.

Radin, P. (1972). *The Trickster: A Study in American Indian Mythology.* New York: Schocken Books.

Richters, J., and Pellegrini, D. (1989). Depressed mothers' judgments about their children: An examination of the depression-distortion hypothesis. *Child Dev. 60*: 1068-1075.

Rodin, A. E., and Key, J. D. (1989). Straw Peter Syndrome. *Medicine Literature and Eponyms: An Encylopedia of Medical Eponyms Derived from Literary Characters*. Malabar, Florida: Robert E. Krieger Publishing, pp. 299-301.

Schachar, R.; Sandberg, S.; and Rutter, M. (1986). Agreement between teachers' ratings and observations of hyperactivity, inattentiveness and defiance. *J. Abnorm. Child Psychol. 14*:331-345.

Schworm, R. W., and Birnbaum, R. (1989). Symptom expression in hyperactive children. *J. Learn. Disab. 22*:35-40, 45.

Shaffer, P. (1982). *Equus*. In *The Collected Plays*. New York: Harmony Books, pp. 402, 476.

Shinn-Strieker, T. (1986). Patterns of Cognitive Style in Normal and Handicapped Children. *J. Learn. Disabil. 19*:572-576.

Smith, J. D., and Nelson, D. G. K. (1988). Is the more impulsive child a more holistic processor? A reconsideration. *Child Dev. 59*:719-727.

Spreen, O. (1988). *Learning Disabled Children Growing Up: A Follow-up into Adulthood*. Oxford: Oxford University Press.

Spreen, O. (1988). Prognosis of learning disability. *J. Consult. Clin. Psychol. 56*: 836-842.

Still, G. F. (1902). The Coulstonian Lectures on some abnormal psychical conditions in children. *Lancet 1*:1008-1012, 1077-1082, 1163-1168.

Susser, M. (1984). Causal thinking in practice: Strengths and weaknesses of the clinical vantage point. *Pediatrics 74*:842-849.

Voeller, K. K. S. (1986). Right-hemisphere deficit syndrome in children. *Am. J. Psychiatry 143*:1004-1009.

Volkmar, F. R.; Hoder, E. L.; and Cohen, D. J. (1985). Inappropriate uses of stimulant medications. *Clin. Pediatr. 24*:127-130.

Waites, L. (1989). *Select Annotated Bibliography of Dyslexia*. Dallas: Texas Scottish Rite Hospital.

Waites, L. (1989) *Select Bibliography of Oral Language Disorders and Phonology (Congenital Aphasia, Idioglossia, Congenital Word Deafness, and Congenital Auditory Imperception)*. Dallas: Texas Scottish Rite Hospital.

Ward, M. (1988). *Caryll Houselander: That Divine Eccentric*. Westminster, Maryland: Christian Classics.

Ysseldyke, J. E.; Algozzine, B.; Shinn, M. R.; and McGue, M. (1982). Similarities and differences between low achievers and students classified learning disabled. *J. Spec. Ed. 16*:73-85.

Background

2

The "Expanded" Strauss Syndrome: MBD Revisited

Arnold J. Capute

The Johns Hopkins University School of Medicine, Baltimore, Maryland

> *"De una causa bien pueden proceder dos effectos contrarios. [Two contradictory effects may well proceed from a single cause.]"*

The Strauss syndrome denotes the neurobehavioral cluster first described in the 1930s by Alfred E. Strauss, a psychologist who studied the characteristics of brain-injured adolescents and young adults [Strauss and Lehtinen, 1947; Strauss and Kephart, 1955]. Prior to this, Hohman had reported a similar neurobehavioral profile in victims recovering from von Economo's encephalitis [Hohman, 1922]. This behavioral pattern was also noted in other brain-injured cohorts who had sustained nonspecific, generalized cerebral injury through gunshot wounds, head injuries, and other conditions affecting the brain. Subsequently the components of this syndrome were also exhibited by children with hyperactivity, attentional problems, and learning disabilities. This almost pathognomonic neurobehavioral profile includes (1) an attentional spectrum aberration ranging from short attention span to perseveration, (2) an activity spectrum peculiarity varying from hyperactivity to hypoactivity or listlessness associated with (3) easy distractibility and (4) emotional lability with or without temper tantrums.

THE CLINICAL TRIAD

To appreciate the clinical implications of this neurobehavioral profile readily apparent in developmental disabilities (and more specifically in children with attention deficit hyperactivity disorder [ADHD]), one must first recognize the fact that when neurons are destroyed, dysfunction occurs in three main developmental "streams": (1) motor, (2) central processing (language and visuomotor or problem-solving), and (3) behavior. Thus, the three dimensions of attention deficit and learning disabilities (Figure 1) include (1) a motor dysfunction spectrum ranging from incoordination and clumsiness to outright significant motor impairment (cerebral palsy) represented by a motor quotient below 50 [Capute and Shapiro, 1985]; (2) a central-processing (cognitive) dysfunction, usually highlighted by a significant visuomotor (problem-solving)-language dissociation or intra-ability deviancy; and (3) a fairly typical neurobehavioral profile (Strauss syndrome).

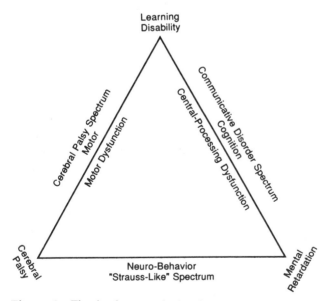

Figure 1   The developmental triangle.

One can equate the motor spectrum dysfunction with a minimal or mild subclinical cerebral palsy. The motor spectrum dysfunction involves a deviancy or nonsequentialness in motor milestone appearance. Minimal or mild subclinical cerebral palsy involves a mild degree of motor delay but with a motor quotient of greater than 50.

The evident central-processing (cognitive) dysfunction can be referred to as minimal brain dysfunction (MBD) or minimal cerebral dysfunction (MCD) to highlight the associated perceptual disorder.

The Strauss spectrum, or neurobehavioral profile, will vary in intensity according to the severity of the cognitive disarray produced by the underlying brain injury. Furthermore, the characteristics will change over time with cerebral maturation and vary with the further development of the cognitive abilities of the infant, child, or adolescent.

"Expanded" Strauss Syndrome

The Strauss syndrome profile becomes exaggerated or "expanded" when one includes mental retardation, especially when the mental retardation is associated with a superimposed communicative disorder as reflected by a performance (problem-solving)-language disparity or significant intra-ability deviance, which is found when one goes from mild cognitive limitations to more severe ones.

The usual behavioral characteristics are transformed into more ritualistic stereotypic behavioral patterns such as head banging, body rocking, hand flapping, or waving hands in front of the eyes/face. In addition, the short attention span is present to such a degree that eye contact is difficult to maintain; perseveration is so exaggerated, it is commonly misinterpreted as a high degree of interest in a particular object or action. Some of these activities such as head banging or slapping of the face may well develop into self injurious behavioral mannerisms.

As yet, it is not known whether this increase in the intensity of the profile is a direct result of increased general brain damage or, more specifically, the involvement of more localized lesions, which results in a greater magnitude of the accompanying communicative disorder. The terms "minimal" or "mild" cerebral palsy, "minimal brain dysfunction," and "minimal brain damage" were used in the 1940s and 1950s [Denhoff and Feldman, 1981] but were frequently refuted because it was felt that the brain pathology did not exist (perhaps the means available did not detect the subtleties of brain injury). Recent advances in the neurosciences can detect abnormalities within the neurotransmitter system and neurocytoarchitectural damage. It is anticipated that we will be returning to the terminology of MBD as definitive techniques become more readily available for the study of brain pathology and dysfunction.

When this behavioral pattern occurs within the *cerebral palsy* population, it is modified, frequently less intensified, because of the physical limitations of the child due to the severe delay in motor coordination, which is further impaired by such orthopedic deformities as contractures, hip dislocations, scoliosis, or wheelchair confinement.

Children with *autism* exhibit these behavioral manifestations in the most extreme form, and the profile expression is again subject to the developmental level at which the child is functioning. Leo Kanner basically described the Strauss syndrome in its most profound state in children with "early infantile autism" [Kanner, 1943]. The cardinal characteristics of autism actually represent this neurobehavioral profile but with a more specific cluster of the "expanded" form: "lack of eye contact" due to an extraordinarily short attention span, "preservation of sameness" due to the child's having significantly better visuomotor skills coupled with a relatively better visual memory, "delayed echolalia" due to a (relatively) "excellent" rote memory with ability to sustain and repeat certain expressions for a long period of time, and "pronominal reversals" in which the child uses *you, me,* and *I* indiscriminately. Kanner had singled out a cohort of autistic children who had language skills no better than those of an average 24-30 month-old child (at 24 months, children first use the pronouns *you, me,* and *I* in an indiscriminate fashion; discriminate use takes place at 30 months of age). Kanner also highlighted the echolalia evident in this syndrome. In normal development, echolalia is present at 7 or 8 months of age as syllable imitation; between 18 and 24 months of age, echolalia becomes word and phrase repetition; it becomes more pronounced at 2 years of age and disappears by 30 months of age. Echolalia should never be present to a significant degree, but if it is or if it persists past 30 months of age, a receptive language disorder should be suspected.

It is interesting to note that in Kanner's original cohort of 11 children, the "pronominal reversals" and "echolalia" disappeared during the preadolescent years—a reflection of the severity of language dysfunction present.

The Motor Spectrum

Motor dysfunction is maximal in cerebral palsy with these infants and children functioning at a motor quotient less than half of expectancy. This motor spectrum concept can be better understood if one were to divide this spectrum into clinical and subclinical forms: the clinical form represented by the significant motor impairment present in children with cerebral palsy; the subclinical, mild form represented by children who are clumsy. On the one hand, children with cerebral palsy are significantly limited in sports activities because of their motor handicap [Scherzer and Tscharnuter, 1982]; those with the milder form of motor impairment are found in the preschool language disabled or school-age learning disorder populations. One observes that these "minimal cerebral palsied" infants become children unable to participate in games that are physically competitive, although these children can play at team positions requiring lesser degrees of motor adroitness. They might be represented "clinically" by the right fielder, second baseman, bat boy, or bench warmer. However, since our society does not hold motor functioning in high esteem, clumsiness in motor skills (motor quotients between 50 and 70, i.e., mild, subclinical cerebral palsy) is generally accepted. If motor skills were mandated for scholastic or job attainment, children with "subclinical" motor impairment would be clinically recognized on the cerebral palsy spectrum; but society places minimal physical demands upon clumsy children, so there is little interference with educational or vocational placement. However, some children may escape genetically based motor clumsiness by the motor area being spared due to specificity that can occur with involvement of the cognitive areas alone.

In infancy the presence of exaggerated primitive reflexes, a delay in their suppression, or a poor quality exhibited by emerging postural (equilibrium and righting) reactions can be indicative of later motor imperfections. The poor quality of postural reactions can be elicited in the school-age child by having tasks performed requiring equilibrium and righting skills. These include tandem walking, maintaining balance with the eyes closed and arms extended, and standing on one foot. Furthermore, one might categorize the minimal and mild subclinical forms of cerebral palsy as (1) the "choreiform" syndrome with both choreic movements and athetotic positioning, (2) the "diplegic" syndrome manifested by early toe walking and later knock-kneed positioning of the lower extremities, and (3) the "hemiplegic" syndrome with asymmetrical neurodevelopmental signs and symptoms.

The preceding motor constellations may be used to clinically screen for the presence of underlying associated cognitive and neurobehavioral disorders. Motor cues are commonly utilized in practice for the detection of significant mental retardation and may also be used to detect milder forms of developmental disability.

Each aspect of the triangle, again, represents a spectrum of involvement resulting in overlapping disabilities. Motor dysfunction shows the relationship among cerebral palsy, ADHD, and learning disabilities. These minor motor signs are frequently referred to as "soft" or subtle signs and are not indicative of an intracerebral catastrophic event. They are quite prevalent in children with learning disabilities. However, in cerebral palsy, due to the fact that "hard" signs, which are indicative of an intracerebral catastrophe, are also present, "soft" signs are overshadowed and frequently not looked for. It should be obvious that there is little reason to examine for soft signs in the presence of hard ones.

The preceding description of motor dysfunction exemplifies the principle that when one developmental area is involved (motor), one should look for other areas of involvement as well (cognitive, neurobehavioral). With brain injury, all three of the above described dimensions are usually involved to some degree.

Cognitive Profiles

On the cognitive side of the triangle, one notes a learning disability spectrum, actually a communicative one, going from the "mild" form such as ADHD with learning disability to a profound chaotic or perverted communicative disorder represented by the autistic-like manifestations previously described. One might claim that these autistic-like children represent a perversion of communication since they do not use language as a functional communicative skill. The mild side of this spectrum features "deviant" development represented psychometrically by a dissociation between performance and verbal items on tests such as the WISC-R. More important than the dissociation is the deviancy or unevenness noted with the psychometric profile commonly referred to as exhibiting "variability" or "scattering." The pediatrician will note this variability in carrying out certain visuomotor or problem-solving tasks and when recording language acquisition. While the WISC-R is excellent for diagnosing mental retardation with significant below-average intellectual functioning in a global fashion, it becomes merely a screening tool for learning disabilities with wide variability in the verbal and performance areas. Remember there is no one IQ for any person, especially those with a communicative or learning disability. As one proceeds along the spectrum of communicative disorders or learning disabilities, variability becomes so extensive and erratic that clinicians are often confused by the splintered skills that are evident. "Echolalia," for example, is mystifying since expressive language appears to be better than receptive language, and "What comes out of the computer can never be better than what goes into it." Since echolalic talk does not include comprehension, such chaotic psychometric profiles can be misleading. Professionals have a tendency to look at the numbers rather than the social and adaptive skills that this group of children possesses. As the spectrum moves toward mental retardation it gives rise to the pseudo-issue of autism "with" and "without" mental retardation or autism with or without some portion of the WISC-R approaching "normal." Also, as one approaches the more distorted side of the spectrum, the more chaotic the communicative disorder and the more "expanded" the Strauss syndrome manifestations.

Whether this "expanded" version is due to a greater degree of brain injury, to a greater dissociation between language and problem-solving skills, or to both, remains open for scientific investigation. In "early infantile autism" as described by Kanner, children had problem-solving abilities significantly better than their language ones. Again, many of his autistic patients had their "pronominal" reversals and "echolalia" disappear between 5 and 6 years of age, demonstrating that language development was indeed progressing much slower than normal.

Temporal Dimension

In addition to the above-mentioned quantitative aspects of the Strauss syndrome (going from the mild/moderate forms of learning disabilities to the severe/perverted forms in the autistic syndromes), its presence can be noted in a temporal fashion initially detected in intrauterine life and continuing through infancy, early and late childhood, to preadolescence, and adolescence (Figure 2).

Fetal Period   Clinical determinants of fetal well-being are presently subjective, with the mother noting the quality and quantity of fetal movements, relating them to daily activities including feeding, sleeping, and moving about. Intrauterine activity can be either sustained for long periods or take place at unusual times such as during maternal sleep or rest. Hypoactivity reflects a paucity or decrease in fetal movements. Spontaneous or sound-provoked movements can be used as a means of assessing fetal well-being. "Kick-charts" are available for quantifying fetal movements of increased or decreased frequency to be reported to the obstetrician. Quantitative and qualitiative measures of fetal activity to objectively establish fetal well-being can be generated from such noninvasive techniques as sonography. In addition to the subjective study of fetal motility, sound or vibratory stimuli can also be investigated for assessing fetal status. Fetal hypoactivity has been associated with mental retardation, and fetal hyperactivity relates to later ADHD [Accardo et al., 1990].

Neonatal/Infant Period   During the neonatal and infant years, an infant "Strauss-like" behavioral profile, indicative of central nervous system insult, can be evident. Manifestations include colic (usually lasting more than 2 months and exhibiting an atypical temporal pattern), night/day confusion, and excessive crying or irritability. And then there is the "extra good" or overly quiet infant who has to be awakened for feeding. While one can associate the Strauss syndrome with "terrible two" behaviors, their manifesta-

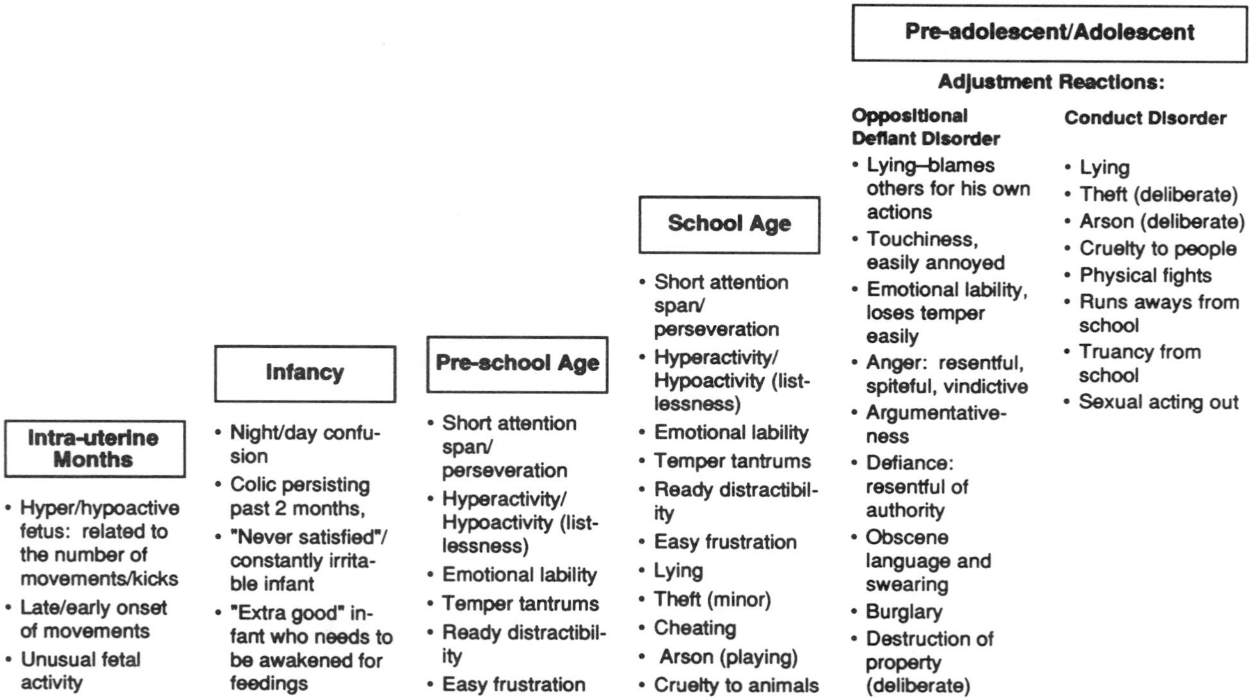

Pre-adolescent/Adolescent

Adjustment Reactions:

Oppositional Deflant Disorder

- Lying—blames others for his own actions
- Touchiness, easily annoyed
- Emotional lability, loses temper easily
- Anger: resentful, spiteful, vindictive
- Argumentativeness
- Defiance: resentful of authority
- Obscene language and swearing
- Burglary
- Destruction of property (deliberate)

Conduct Disorder

- Lying
- Theft (deliberate)
- Arson (deliberate)
- Cruelty to people
- Physical fights
- Runs aways from school
- Truancy from school
- Sexual acting out

School Age

- Short attention span/perseveration
- Hyperactivity/Hypoactivity (listlessness)
- Emotional lability
- Temper tantrums
- Ready distractibility
- Easy frustration
- Lying
- Theft (minor)
- Cheating
- Arson (playing)
- Cruelty to animals

Pre-school Age

- Short attention span/perseveration
- Hyperactivity/Hypoactivity (listlessness)
- Emotional lability
- Temper tantrums
- Ready distractibility
- Easy frustration

Infancy

- Night/day confusion
- Colic persisting past 2 months,
- "Never satisfied"/constantly irritable infant
- "Extra good" infant who needs to be awakened for feedings

Intra-uterine Months

- Hyper/hypoactive fetus: related to the number of movements/kicks
- Late/early onset of movements
- Unusual fetal activity

Figure 2 The Temporal Dimension of the Expanded Strauss Syndrome.

tions do differ since the physiological hyperactivity noted at 2 years of age is goal-oriented, while the pathological hyperactivity of the Strauss syndrome is nongoal oriented and impulsive, if not compulsive, in origin.

An infant Strauss profile may reflect sympathomimetic nervous system manifestations that are clinical markers for underlying central nervous system dysfunctioning.

Preschool/School-Age Periods   Infant Strauss profile transforms to the more typical preschool form around 4 or 5 years of age. By this time, the child is usually hyperactive (but at times hypoactive or listless), is readily distractible, demonstrates emotional lability, has developed temper tantrums, and is easily frustrated. These characteristics usually persist into the early school years with a further modification of the neurobehavioral profile as other features become highlighted. These other features include lying, stealing, and cheating—behaviors that require a higher level of cognition than exists in the preschool child. One might say that children with ADHD and learning disability begin to become "con artists" as a defense mechanism. While some researchers include fire-setting and cruelty to animals as part of this profile, others question whether these superimposed manifestations represent emotional overlays requiring counseling.

Adolescent Outcomes   One of the most pertinent questions for professionals managing children with learning disabilities and attentional disorders is whether the qualitative or quantitative aspects of the Strauss syndrome correlate with later drug addiction, alcohol ingestion, or other sociopathic entities. The Strauss syndrome, particularly the "expanded" form, also transforms into future conduct disorders of children and adolescents.

The expanded Strauss profile can be followed sequentially and clinically quantified from fetal life through infancy, the preschool and school-age years, and into the preadolescent and adolescent years (Figure 2). During the preschool and school years particularly (with the attendant further development of cognitive function and certain situational demands), this syndrome is clinically expressed as the more traditional adjustment reactions of the preadolescent and adolescent years. These various neurobehavioral clusters are misidentified as the conduct and oppositional deviant disorders. For example, the stealing witnessed in the early preschool years is limited to minor infractions such as taking money from mother's pocketbook or perhaps pocketing some candy at the neighborhood store with later progression in the adolescent years to burglary and car theft. Another example is the progression from stepping on the tail or roughly shoving an animal pet aside in the early school years to aggressiveness, physical fighting, and more deliberate cruelty to animals in the adolescent years. This temporal continuity of the Strauss syndrome lends itself to early intervention with the distinct pos-

sibility of instituting early preventative measures to modify or perhaps eliminate many of the adjustment reactions of adolescents that serve as a prelude
to alcohol and drug ingestion as well as more serious criminal infractions.

With the availability of noninvasive neuroradiologic techniques to study
cerebral organization, as well as biochemical neurotransmitters as markers
for various behavioral manifestations, a better appreciation of the expanded
Strauss syndrome is developing. Also as more recognition is given to the neurobehavioral symptoms being of organic origin, it becomes more plausible to
place increasing emphasis on neuropharmacological approaches to treatment,
with mental health counseling playing an important but adjunctive role.

REFERENCES

Accardo, P. J., Tomazic, T., Morrow J., and Whitman, B. Y. (1990). Fetal activity
level in developmental disabilities. *Pediatr. Res.* (abstr).

Capute, A. J., Shapiro, B. K. (1985). The motor quotient method for the early detection of motor delay. *Am. J. Dis. Child. 139:*940.

Denhoff, E., Feldman, S. A. (1981). *Developmental Disabilities: Management through
Diet and Medication.* New York: Marcel Dekker.

Hohman, L. B. (1922). Post encephalic behvavior disorders in children. *Johns
Hopkins Hosp. Bull. 380:*372.

Kanner, L. (1943). Autistic disturbances of affective contact. *Nervous Child 2:*217.

Scherzer, A. L., Tscharnuter, I. (1982). *Early Diagnosis and Therapy in Cerebral
Palsy: A Primer on Infant Development Problems.* New York: Marcel Dekker.

Strauss, A. A., Kephart, N. C. (1955). *Psychopathology and Education of the Brain-
Injured Child.* Vol. 1. New York: Grune and Stratton.

Strauss, A. A., Lehtinen, L. E. (1947). *Psychopathology and Education of the Brain-
Injured Child.* New York: Grune and Stratton.

3

The Roots of Organicity: Genetics and Genograms

Barbara Y. Whitman

St. Louis University, St. Louis, Missouri

"Accidents will occur in the best-regulated families."

[Dickens, *David Copperfield*]

AN EPIGENETIC PUZZLE

Current epidemiologic estimates of the prevalence of attention deficit hyperactivity disorder (ADHD) in children under 18 years of age range between 3% and 10% [Lambert et al., 1981; Szatmari et al., 1989]. The disorder is developmentally, psychologically, academically, and socially disruptive to affected children and their families. Until recently, ADHD was viewed as a transient, benign although sometimes intense, behavioral disturbance of prepubertal children. Current studies document multiple increased comorbidity risks for ADHD children and many social and psychiatric sequelae for ADHD adults [Munir, 1987; Weiss, 1985]. As the facade of benignness disintegrates, the search for etiology intensifies. Evidence strongly supports familial transmission for ADHD with a probable genetic heritability component.

Researching genetic influences on complex neurobehavioral disorders such as ADHD is neither simple nor direct. Methodological issues combined with complicated and elusive multifactorial genetic mechanisms challenge the most committed investigator. Similar research efforts with other behavioral disorders [e.g., Reich et al., 1975] have generated several sophisticated mathematical models to unravel these genetic complexities. Yet, "none of the substantive issues in [behavioral] genetic epidemiology is clarified by mathematical rigor or computational elegance" [Norton, 1982].

This chapter examines the genetic epidemiology of ADHD as it is currently understood. The data will need to be transdisciplinary, encompassing findings from genetics, epidemiology, developmental medicine, and psychiatry. Piecing together the "epigenetic puzzle" [Gottesman, 1982] is analogous to assembling a complex jigsaw puzzle. The pieces must be turned over, examined, the border framed, and the picture assembled through a careful fitting together of the pieces. To form the borders of the ADHD genetic puzzle, we turn to the first sequential steps of a behavioral genetic investigation.

BORDERING THE GENETIC JIGSAW PUZZLE

The search for genetic influences in ADHD is hampered by a clinical heterogeneity due in part to (a) a lack of precise diagnostic criteria and (b) a lack of confirmatory technologies. Thus research depends on behavioral diagnoses that yield clumsy, complex, unstable, and often overdetermined phenotypes that in turn can dilute or even mask heritability associations. ADHD has many symptoms (e.g., variable attention, fluctuating memory, increased activity level, impulsivity, distractability, impaired sleep patterns, and emotional lability) and much diversity in the way individual symptoms are expressed in any given individual. Since the diagnosis is compiled from a symptom complex, a few children may display all symptoms, while others display less; and some symptoms will exhibit greater severity than others. Certain symptoms may also be found in other disorders and not be specific to ADHD, whereas a few symptoms may be specifically and causally related to the ADHD itself. The more closely related the defining symptoms are to the underlying mechanism of the disorder, the more informative the genetic analysis will be [Pennington and Smith, 1988]. Positive results from even coarsely defined phenotypes may nonetheless be meaningful.

Although less than perfect, the standardization of diagnostic criteria for ADHD in the Diagnostic and Statistical Manual III [American Psychiatric Associations, 1980] allows a more indepth evaluation of its genetic epidemiology while at the same time pointing the way to refining the genotype. With this coarse type, yet lacking a specific diagnostic gold standard, the data supporting a genetic etiology must be robust both conceptually and methodologically. This robustness is accomplished through a sequential series of methodological approaches that include: (a) evidence of aggregation in biologically related individuals, (b) twin studies, (c) adoption studies, and (d) statistical linkage modeling. We will review these methods and the data from relevant investigations in order.

Familiarity/Aggregation

The first step in the search for genetic influences is a test of familiarity—whether or not there is an increased occurence of the disorder among family members of affected individuals when compared to the incidence among family members of a similar person not affected by the disorder. If genetic mechanisms are at work, the data should yield an aggregation or increased incidence of the disorder in the relatives of the index case compared to that found in the family of the unaffected control. Further, that aggregation should decrease proportionally as the closeness of familial relationships decreases (i.e., siblings versus cousins). The primary technique for this research is the construction of a family genogram or pedigree followed by a close examination of the genogram for both excessive family prevalence and an aggregation pattern compatible with genetic transmission.

The family genogram is a standardized format for drawing a family tree that records information about family members and their relationships [McGoldrick and Gerson, 1985]. Genograms display family information graphically and in a way that quickly and concisely provides a gestalt of complex family information. When family data are presented in genogram format, the presence and aggregation of behavioral disorders becomes readily apparent. Figure 1A shows a genogram obtained during a routine clinic evaluation for the presence of minor neurological dysfunction. Compare this genogram with that of a family whose presenting difficulty was "rule out Prader-Willi" (a single-occurence genetic insult) (Figure 1B). Similarly, compare Figure 1A with a genogram of the family of a boy whose presenting difficulty was behavior problems when his father had recently been diagnosed as having Huntington's chorea (a known autosomal dominant genetic disorder (Figure 1C)). The concept of aggregation is clearly apparent with these comparisons. Both Prader-Willi syndrome and Huntington's Chorea are confirmable by laboratory tests. Diagnosing behavior disorders requires the reporting of a number of individual symptoms beyond a threshold. The difficulty inherent in such a task for complex behavior disorders is obvious. Thus even in the initial stages of a genetic investigation, the genogram mapping is fraught with difficulty.

There are two basic approaches to collecting the data necessary to construct a family genogram: the family-study method and the family-history method. *Family-study* methods require direct interviews of all family mem-

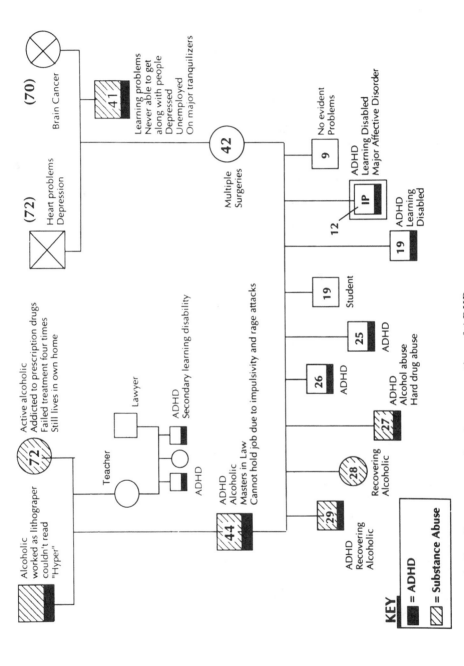

Figure 1A Family genogram showing aggregation of ADHD.

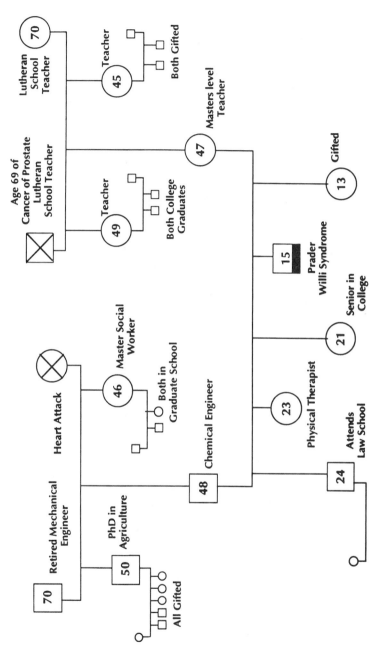

Figure 1B Family genogram showing aggregation of Prader-Willi syndrome.

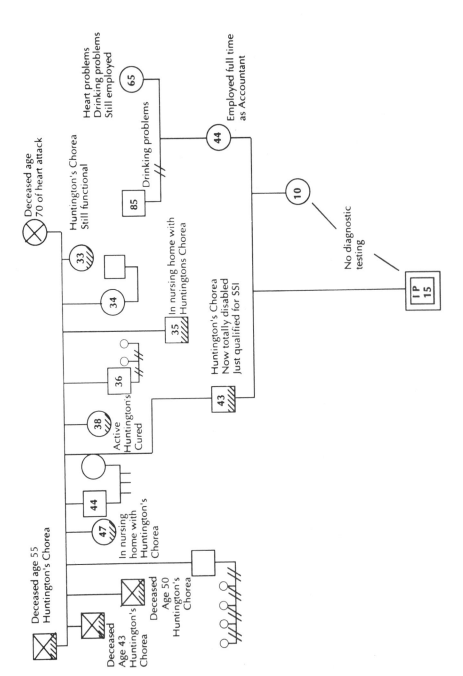

Figure 1C Family genogram showing aggregation of Huntington's chorea.

bers regarding the presence or absence of the disorder(s) in question; *family-history* methods utilize information about relatives obtained indirectly from the index patient or other family members. So the two basic approaches are the family-study method of direct reporting frought with all the biases inherent in that method, versus the family-history methods, which is a judgment report about someone by someone else with all the biases inherent in that method of data collection. Thus each method reflects directly the difference between asking someone about himself versus asking someone else about his behaviors, symptoms, thoughts, or feelings; and each of these two methods has built in advantages and disadvantages [Andreasen et al., 1977; Weissman, 1986]. Family-study methods are cost and labor intensive. While initially less expensive, the family-history method is likely to significantly underestimate the presence of a given disorder in a pedigree and to be biased toward those most severely affected [Thompson et al., 1982]. Its cost is thus in missed data. Both methods suffer from a lack of construct validity in poorly defined disorders. Disregarding cost factors, family-study methods are superior for a number of reasons. However, a degree of reliance on the family history is often unavoidable when some family members cannot be interviewed due to unavailability, death, or refusal to participate.

These methodological problems become even more acute when the disorder in question is a disorder of childhood. Even when the luxury of direct interview of all family members is possible, the data from adults regarding their status as children is diluted by both the passage of time, the accuracy of the adults' memory, and their initial perception of themselves as children. Since most children do not describe (or perceive) themselves as hyperactive or failing to concentrate unless the environment has communicated those labels or descriptors to them, the presence of a disorder can still be missed. Further, since standardized diagnostic criteria are a recent event, many adults positive for the disorder by today's diagnostic criteria may not recognize themselves as such due to having received a different diagnostic label as a child.

Despite these limitations, an increased prevalence of ADHD is consistently documented in the biological relatives of ADHD probands as compared to that found in unaffected children [Morrison and Stewart, 1971; Cantwell, 1972; Welner et al., 1977; Stewart et al., 1980; Morrison, 1979; Biedermin et al., 1986; Cantwell, 1988].

Although the documentation of familial aggregation is a necessary first step in a genetic search, familial aggregation alone is insufficient to assert genetic heritability. Aggregation can result from shared culture and expectations and from common environmental factors such as infection, diet, or stress. To unequivocally establish the presence of genetic influences, and the attendant mode and magnitude of recurrence risks, additional research steps are needed. Again, in the absence of a biochemical marker, the next steps involve twin and adoption studies.

Twin Studies

Twin studies rest on the assumption that monozygotic (MZ) twins resulting from the splitting of a single fertilized egg are genetically identical. Differences between two individuals with identical genetic makeup could result from subsequent genetic mutation or significantly different environmental influences (not limited to but including child rearing, infections, and the like). Because postfertilization genetic mutation is extraordinarily rare, differences between identical twins are safely assumed to result from environmental factors. Fraternal or dizygotic (DZ) twins that result from the simultaneous fertilization of two separate eggs are genetically no more similar than any two siblings born of the same parent. Differences between DZ twins thus derive from both genetic and environmental influences. Where DZ twins are more alike than serially born siblings, the increased likeness is explained by their shared environment. When comparing MZ with DZ twins in a genetic search, rate differences for a suspected genetic trait are examined. To the extent that MZ twins are more alike on the index trait than DZ twins, that difference in alikeness is attributed to the fact that MZ twins are genetically identical whereas DZ twins share only half their genetic material. When reared in a common environment, MZ twins should be more alike (i.e., more frequently affected) than DZ twins, DZ twins more alike than serially born siblings, and siblings more alike than nonrelated persons in the rate of occurrence of genetically determined traits or disorders.

To rule out the influence of common environment, this proportionally decreasing relationship should hold even when the twins are separated early in life and raised in different environments. When reared apart, the degree of similarity reflects the degree of genetic identity. If the trait is due solely to genetic factors, then MZ twins reared apart should have the same disorder 100% of the time. If the trait is totally environmentally determined, then the twins should not have the trait (disorder) with any greater frequency than any two children raised in dissimilar environments.

Twin studies have been used extensively in the study of schizophrenia and alcoholism. Extensively, however, is a relative term: the number of MZ and DZ twin pairs reared apart is, in and of itself, small; and the number of twin pairs who (1) have been reared apart, (2) have any given disorder, and (3) are available for study is even smaller. Those twin studies that have looked specifically at ADHD confirm the presence of a genetic influence [Lopez, 1965]. However, such studies remain hampered by a number of methodological difficulties that do not yet allow absolute confirmation of a genetic diathesis.

Adoption Studies

A separate methodology that has been used frequently in the study of behavioral heritability is the study of affected children adopted out of their biological family. If a trait is genetic, these children should resemble their biological relatives more closely than they do their adoptive relatives. Conversely, a study of the biological families of affected adopted children should yield higher prevalence rates for the disorder then prevalence rates found in the family into which they were adopted. Similarly unaffected adopted children should have lower prevalence rates in their biological families than affected adopted children.

While logically sound, there are a number of subtle biases that can creep in during the execution of these studies. First, it must be determined that the adoptive family does not carry the disorder in question. Since adoption agencies frequently seek to match children with families along a number of often genetically determined dimensions such as color, temperament, family background, and the like, it is possible that such placement methods might also select for companion or correlated (if not so desirable) traits. Unless the research design is controlled by a sampling methodology, true genetic linkages could be masked by common environmental factors based on selective adoptive placement methods.

Second, the availability and cooperation of biological relatives who are contacted a number of years after a child has been given up for adoption, and the reliability and validity of the data they provide, raises problems not only of methodology but also of legality and ethics. A number of studies using this methodology have been conducted in countries such as Denmark and Sweden that maintain a national health registry [e.g., Goodwin et al., 1973, 1974; Bohman, 1978; Cloninger et al., 1981]. Such registers are not yet readily accepted in the United States. Adoption records are usually considered closed and inviolate except in rare circumstances. Despite that, a number of studies using these methods (or a very close approximation) conclude that ADHD exhibits a genetic diathesis. The biological families of ADHD children exhibit a significantly higher rate of childhood ADHD among first- and second-degree relatives than do their adoptive families [Cunningham et al., 1975; Cadoret et al., 1975; Morrison and Stewart, 1973; Alberts-Corush et al., 1986].

Genetic-Linkage Methods

Genetic-linkage studies employ known genetic markers in combination with a template statistical algorithm to test whether two genes (the marker and the trait in question) co-occur together in a nonrandom fashion, thus indicating proximity on the same chromosome. If a trait can be shown to be linked to a known genetic marker locus, it is inferred that a major gene for that trait is located on the same chromosome as the marker [Smith et al., 1983]. Genetic-linkage maps are constructed by studying family histories and statistically measuring the frequency with which the two traits are linked or inherited together. These studies, then, depend both on having discovered a linked marker and on the available statistical methodology.

Until recently, the technology for determining marker traits was rudimentary. Advances in molecular genetics, particularly those based on recombinant DNA methodologies, now allow a more complete construction of human gene maps. Simply stated, a genetic library of known genetic fragments is being created. These fragments, restriction fragment length polymorphisms (RFLP), are then used to search (a process called *probing*) a given chromosome for either a match or a complement. If either is found, then that portion of the chromosome is labeled or mapped. Using such methods, the genetic predisposition for Huntington's chorea has been localized to abnormalities on chromosome 4 [McGuffin, 1987]. As more of these RFLP probes are isolated and applied in marker studies, our map of the normal and abnormal chromosome/gene composition increases in precision. As of mid 1985, there were at least 900 of these marker probes [McGuffin, 1987].

While these methods ultimately promise a direct mapping of the gene locus for ADHD, they more immediately offer a complement of marker sites for studying family genograms and for constructing a family genetic map by way of the statistical pathway known as *linkage analysis*. This methodology pairs the trait in question with marker traits in the search for family transmission but does so by analogic mathematical modeling rather than direct laboratory study. Such models have documented a linkage between dyslexia and chromosome 15 [De LaChapelle, 1985] and have strongly suggested a link between Tourette's syndrome and chromosome 18 abnormalities [Comings et al., 1986; Donnai, 1987; Handelin, 1986].

Co-Morbidity—An Oblique Pathway to the Heritability of ADHD

That ADHD has a strong genetic component seems well documented by family study methods. A clearer specification of the genetic mode of transmission must evolve as the diagnostic picture and syndrome subtypes are clarified. A closer look at the substance of the genetic puzzle pieces is now in order. Returning to our analogy, the substance of the genetic jigsaw picture is not a single snapshot but rather a collage of research snapshots taken at different points in time and from different angles. Figure 2 gives an overview of these various research points of view. A more intensive look at the substance of each snapshot follows.

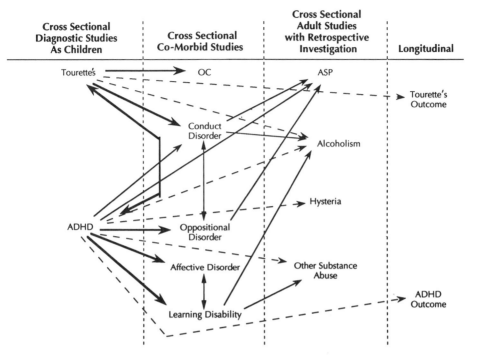

Figure 2 Research approaches to ADHD co-morbidities. OC, obsessive compulsive disorder; ASP, antisocial personality.

Co-morbidity studies represent a cross-sectional picture of ADHD children as they have been systematically studied for the consistant presence of other disorders cooccurring with the ADHD. This systematic co-occurrence is termed "co-morbidity." While, the presence of specific co-morbidities in ADHD children has long been noted, it was not until standardized inclusion and exclusion diagnostic criteria for a number of childhood behavior disorders as specified by the APA—via DMS-III, 1980, and DSM-IIIR, 1987— were specified that this clinical suspicion could be confirmed. ADHD children are more likely to display severe behavior disorders including conduct disorder and oppositional disorder of childhood, to be subject to major affective disorders (either unipolar or bipolar), and to develop other neuropsychological disorders including learning disabilities, tics, and Gilles de la Tourette syndrome. Conversely, studies of other disorders (such as Tourette's syndrome) have yielded evidence that ADHD is a separate co-morbid risk for that disorder [Comings and Comings, 1984; Sverd et al., 1988].

As is the case with family-aggregation data, two general questions must be asked: (1) Is this co-morbidity real in the sense that these disorders quan-

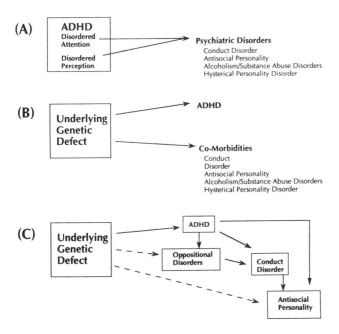

Figure 3 Causal models of ADHD co-morbidities. (A) Dysfunction in basic psychological processes comprising ADHD lead to the development of a particular set of psychiatric difficulties. (B and C) Models of co-morbidity based on presumption of a common genetic defect: (B) direct rise; (C) rise through evolutionary paths.

titatively occur together significantly beyond the rate found in a general population? and (2) What are the causal pathways for these co-occurrences? Earlier thinking advocated a causal model that dysfunction in basic psychological processes (e.g., attention, perception) in ADHD children led to the development of a particular set of psychiatric difficulties (see Figure 3A). Recently, this model has been challenged by the hypothesis of co-morbidity based on a common genetic defect (see Figure 3 B and C). However, since not all children with ADHD develop one or more associated disorders, it remains unclear whether those that do are a distinct, and possibly a more severely affected, subgroup. Further, since those investigators reporting the co-occurence of ADHD with other behavior disorders tend to be separate from those investigators studying the co-morbidity of ADHD with mood disorders and separate still from those studying ADHD and neuropsychological dysfunction such as Gilles de la Tourette syndrome, integrative collaboration to more fully explore these associations has yet to be conducted.

One striking exception is a study of the association of ADHD with conduct disorder, oppositional disorder, and major depressive disorder in both current ADHD index cases and first degree relatives (parents and siblings). Biederman et al. [1986] found significantly higher rates of oppositional disorder and conduct disorder in both ADHD probands and their relatives than in a group of matched controls and postulated a familial vulnerability of common genetic origin.

Commonality of Parental Pathology

A different genetic snapshot in our collage includes a number of studies that look at the families (particularly the parents) of ADHD children for the systematic presence of other disorders. Recall that until recently, it was thought that children outgrew ADHD, so investigations of families and parents of ADHD children had focused only on current health status with regard to the presence of other disorders and only occasionally looked for the historical presence of ADHD. From this point of view a number of well-designed studies suggest that male adult parents of ADHD children have a significantly higher rate of two psychiatric diagnoses: antisocial personality (ASP) and alcoholism. Female adult parents of ADHD children are more frequently diagnosed with hysteria (Briquet's syndrome or somatization disorder) [Cantwell, 1972; Morrison, 1980]. A different set of studies suggests higher rates of affective disorders as well [Biederman et al., 1987]. As with the previously reported family aggregation studies, this data needs to be scrutinized with methodologies that can separate environmental from genetic components—particularly the adoption/separation studies. Morrison and Stewart [1971] supplemented their original report with a follow-up study designed to approach this question and found adult behavioral disorders (ASP, alcoholism, and hysteria) far more prevalent among the biologic relatives of ADHD children than among their adoptive parents.

A reverse approach was used by Cadoret et al. [1986]. In this study, parents of children adopted away were classified as psychiatrically disturbed or normal, and the diagnostic status of the adopted children then pursued. When the parental psychiatric diagnosis was ASP, there were significantly more children with ADHD noted that in other parental diagnostic categories or in psychiatrically normal biological parents.

The genetic components of alcoholism (and to a lesser extent ASP) are well documented. The clustering of these disorders among the parents of ADHD children has led some authors to speculate a common underlying genetic pathway.

Deviant Adults Look Back

If ADHD is genetically related to adult psychiatric outcomes, then a cross-sectional look at diagnosed adults should yield developmental histories that include an increased prevalence of ADHD. Several authors have investigated this hypothesis in an adult population engaged in treatment for alcoholism [Tarter et al., 1977; Goodwin et al., 1975; Wood et al., 1983]. Using multiple sources of data, a ten-fold increased prevalence (33% as opposed to 3%) of childhood ADHD was identified in this population. In addition, Wood et al. [1983] noted that for many adult alcoholics, the attentional disorder continued to have an impact on their lives as reflected by hyperactivity and attentional deficits and at least two of the following: an inability to complete tasks efficiently, a short or quick temper, prominent affective lability, impulsivity, and abnormally poor or low stress tolerance. Similar findings (but of somewhat lesser magnitude) were reported with opiate addicts [Eyre et al., 1982; Shuckit et al., 1978].

While increased ADHD is reported in substance abusers, it is not universal in this population. From the other side of the coin, the question can be raised, Is a psychiatric diagnosis and substance abuse the inevitable outcome of this childhood disorder? To investigate that question, longitudinal follow-up studies of a previously diagnosed ADHD population are needed. The following section reviews some first attempts.

Hyperactive Boys Grown Up

Given the greater prevalence of ADHD in males, it is not surprising that research to date has been weighted heavily toward looking at outcomes for males. One report of 101 males between the ages of 16-23 [Mannuzza et al., 1988] noted that 48% of the previously diagnosed hyperactive group qualified for a non-ADHD DSM-III diagnosis. This number represented a two-fold increase over the rate in a matched control group. In addition, the authors report a clustering of diagnoses within the ASP and substance-abuse categories. An earlier report by Morrison included 21 females as well as 27 males and a matched control group. Again a significantly increased prevalence of psychiatric disorders with a clustering in the ASP and substance-abuse groups (particularly alcoholism) was noted. Unfortunately, a closer analysis of the females was lacking.

Such psychopathology, however, is not an inevitable outcome. Greenfield et al., [1988] described two subgroups of ADHD outcomes in adulthood. The first group was characterized by an absence of appreciable alcohol use, antisocial behavior, and emotional problems. The second group was characterized by the presence of these difficulties. These authors interpret the differences as due to the presence of continuing symptoms. Two additional, if not contrasting, explanations can be offered. First, children with ADHD who, in addition, have co-morbidity for conduct disorder and oppositional disorder appear to have far worse adult outcomes that those without such co-morbidity. Second, for those who do not demonstrate co-morbidity but who run into behavioral skirmishes as adolescents (e.g., experimenting with recreational drugs, legal infractions), these skirmishes appear to escalate in more rapid and more severe fashion than their nondiagnosed age peers in similar situations. Thus the findings seem to suggest that adult outcomes are due, at least in part, to the severity of the original disordered status (presence or absence of accompanying psychiatric diagnoses) as well as to an interaction between continuing symptoms and the environment. Even adults with more positive outcomes are not symptom free; they appear rather to have managed around their symptoms more effectively and to have avoided falling prey to certain environmental hazards. Again, outcome data specific to females are lacking.

THE PIECES ASSEMBLED

The assembly of a complex jigsaw is always slower at the beginning. As some of the pieces are used, the probabilities for the remaining pieces being correctly placed increases, and progress (usually) accelerates. A look at the current assembly of the ADHD genetic puzzle is reflected in Figure 4. ADHD appears to be both familial and genetic, and perhaps on a spectrum that includes Tourettes and/or conduct disorder as its most severe form; accompanied frequently by learning disabilities and evolving over time. There appear to be at least three subgroups of ADHD: (1) those with Tourettes as a more severe form of ADHD or conduct disorder or both; (2) those children with a dual diagnosis of ADHD and learning disability; and, finally, (3) a group with no significant co-morbidities. Adult outcomes appear to reflect continuing problems, but the severity of these problems is a direct reflection and evolution of the earlier disordered status.

At least two of the common co-morbidity diagnoses for these children have solid evidence for a dysfunctional gene locus: the learning disability spectrum (at least with regard to dyslexia) has been located on C15, while Tourettes has been located on C18. While suggesting a single major locus for these disorders, there is still much that is unknown including the mode of transmission, and the nature of the high rate of co-morbidity for these disorders if in fact they arise from separate genetic origins. Nonetheless, there appears to be a genetic spectrum from which ADHD derives. Until more complete cytogenetic findings are available, we must continue to pursue these statistical searches.

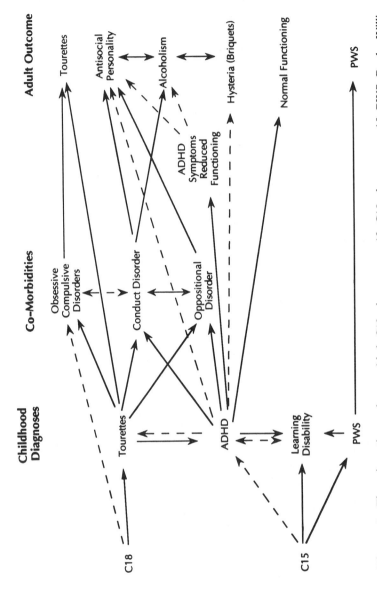

Figure 4 The epigenetic puzzle assembled. C18, chromosome 18; C15, chromosome 15, PWS, Prader-Willi syndrome.

Nonetheless, recent cytogenetic findings give rise to speculation regarding both the current genetic understandings and the direction of future research into the genotype of ADHD. Most notably are the chromosome abnormalities underlying Prader-Willi syndrome, a disorder characterized by hypotonia, obesity, and mental retardation. Since 1981, the origins of this disorder have been attributed to a Q11-13 deletion on the proximal arm of C15. Recently, however, it was discovered that if that deletion occurred on the paternal contribution to the C15 pair, PWS resulted; while if the deletion was present on the maternal contribution to the C15 pair, the phenotypic expression that results is Angelman syndrome rather than PWS. PWS can also occur in a child with a complete C15 pair; however, that pair consists of a maternal heterodysomy, which represents a complete deletion of the paternal C15 and a complete duplication of a normal maternal C15. The phenotype of these children has yet to be fully delineated but they are clinically within the PWS spectrum, although they appear to be somewhat different from those with a simple deletion.

Perhaps the differential expression of ADHD and other of its common co-morbid disorders reflects a similar cytogenetic picture. Until such findings are available, research must continue at the current macro level with intervention designed to alleviate the symptomatic expression of the various subgroups and to anticipate a possible evolutionary illness pattern with ongoing need for intervention services.

REFERENCES

Alberts-Corush, J., Firestone, P., Goodman, J. (1986). Attention and impulsivity characteristics of the biological and adoptive parents of hyperactive and normal control children. *Am. J. Orthopsychiatry 56*:413-423.

American Psychiatric Association (APA) (1980) *Diagnostic and Statistical Manual of Mental Disorders.* 3rd ed. (DSM-III). Washington, D.C.: American Psychiatric Association.

American Psychiatric Association (APA) (1987). *Diagnostic and Statistical Manual of Mental Disorders.* 3rd ed. rev. (DSM-III-R). Washington, D.C.: American Psychiatric Association.

Biederman, J., Munir, K., Knee, D., Habelow, W., Armentano, M., Autor, S., Hoge, S., Waternaux, C. (1986). A family study of patients with attention deficit disorder and normal controls. *J. Psychiatric Res. 20*:263-274.

Biederman, J., Munir, K., Knee, D., Armentano, M., Autor, S., Waternaus, C., Tsuang, M. (1987). High rate of affective disorders in proband with attention deficit disorder and in their relatives: A controlled family study. *Am. J. Psychiatry 144*:330-333.

Bohman, M. (1978). Some genetic aspects of alcoholism and criminality: A population of adoptives. *Arc. Gen. Psychiatry 35*:269-276.

Cadoret, R., Cunningham, L., Loftus, R., Edwards, J. (1975). Studies of adoptees from psychiatrically disturbed biologic parents. *Pediatrics 87*:301-306.

Cadoret, R. Troughton, E., O'Gorman, T., Haywood, E. (1986). An adoption study of genetic and environmental factors in drug abuse. *Arch. Gen. Psychiatry. 43*:1131-1136.

Cantwell, D. (1972). Psychiatric illness in the families of hyperactive children. *Arch. Gen. Psychiatry 27*:414-417.

Cantwell, D. (1988). Families with attention deficit disordered children and others at risk. *J. Chem. Depend. Treat. 1*:163-186.

Cloninger, C. R., Bohman, M., Sigvardsson, S. (1981). Inheritance of alcohol abuse: Cross-fostering analysis of adopted men. *Arch. Gen. Psychiatry 36*:861-868.

Comings, D., Comings, B. (1984). Tourette's syndrome and attention deficit disorder with hyperactivity: Are they genetically related? *J. Am. Acad. Child Psychiatry 23*:138-146.

Comings, D. E., Comings, B. G., Dietz, G., Muhleman, D., Okada, T. A., Sarinana, F., Simner, R., Sparkes, R., Crist, M., Stock, D. (1986). Linkage studies in Tourette syndrome. *Am. J. Hum. Gen. 39*:A151.

Cunningham, L., Cadoret, R. J., Loftus, R., Edwards, J. E. (1975). Studies of adoptees from psychiatrically disturbed biological parents. *Br. J. Psychiatry 126*: 534-549.

De La Chapette, A. (1985). Mapping hereditary disorders. *Nature 317*:472-273.

Donnai, D. (1987). Gene location in Tourette syndrome. *Lancet 3*:627.

Eyre, S., Rounsaville, B., Kleber, H. (1982) History of childhood hyperactivity in a clinic population of opiate addicts. *J. Nervous Mental Dis. 170*:522-529.

Gittelman, R., Mannuzza, S., Shenker, R., Bonagura, N. (1985). Hyperactive boys almost grown up. *Arch. Gen. Psychiatry 42*:937-947.

Goodwin, D. W., Schulsinger, F., Hermansen, L., Guze, S. B., Winokur, G. (1973). Alcohol problems in adoptees raised apart from alcoholic biologic parents. *Arch. Gen. Psychiatry 28*:238-242.

Goodwin, D. W., Schulsinger, F., Hermansen, L., Guze, S., Winokur, G. (1975). Alcoholism and the hyperactive child syndrome. *J. Nervous Mental Dis. 160*:349-353.

Goodwin, D. W., Schulsinger, F., Moller, N., Hermansen, L., Winokur, G., Guze, S. B. (1974). Drinking problems in adopted and nonadopted sons of alcoholics. *Arch. Gen. Psychiatry 31*:164-169.

Gottesman, I. L., Shields, J. (1982). *Schizophrenia: The Epigenetic Puzzle.* New York: Cambridge University Press.

Greenfield, B., Hechtman, L., Weiss, G. (1988). Two subgroups of hyperactives as adults: Correlations of outcome. *Can. J. Psychiatry 33*:505-508.

Handelin, B. (1986). *Report of the Genetic Workshop on Tourette Syndrome, April 1986, Washington, D.C.* New York: The Tourette Syndrome Association.

Lambert, M. N., Sandoval, J., Sansone, D. (1981). Prevalence of hyperactivity and related treatments among elementary children. In *Psychosocial Aspects of Drug Treatment for Hyperactivity,* (Gadow, K., and Loney, J., eds. Colorado: Westview Press, pp. 249-294.

Lopez, R. (1965). Hyperactivity in twins. *Can. Psychiatric Assoc. J. 10*:421.

Mannuzza, S., Klein, R., Bonagura, N., Konig, P., Shenker, R. (1988). Hyperactive boys almost grown up. *Arch. Gen. Psychiatry 45*:13-18.

McGoldrick, M., Gerson, R. (1985). *Genograms in Family Assessment*. New York: W. W. Norton.

McGuffin, P. (1984). Genetic influences on personality, neurosis and psychosis. In *Scientific Principles of Psychopathology*, McGuffin, P., Shanks, M. F., Hodgson, P., eds. London: Grune and Stratton, pp. 191-226.

McGuffin, P. (1987). The new genetics and childhood psychiatric disorder. *J. Child Psychol. Psychiatry 28*:215-222.

Morrison, J. (1979). Diagnosis of adult psychiatric patients with childhood hyperactivity. *Am. J. Psychiatry 136*:955-958.

Morrison, J. (1980). Adult psychiatric disorders in parents of hyperactive children. *Am. J. Psychiatry 137*:825-827.

Morrison, J., Stewart, M. (1971). A family study of the hyperactive child syndrome. *Biol. Psychiatry 3*:189-195.

Morrison, J., Stewart, M. (1973). The psychiatric status of the legal families of adopted hyperactive children. *Arch. Gen. Psychiatry 28*:888-891.

Munir, K., Biederman, J., Knee, D. (1987). Psychiatric comorbidity in patients with attention deficit disorder: A controlled study. *J. Am. Acad. Child Adoles. Psychiatry 26*:844-848.

Norton, N. (1982). *Outline of Genetic Epidemiology*. New York: Karger, p.

Pennington, B., Smith, S. (1988). Genetic influences on learning disabilities: An update. *J. Consult. Clin. Psychol. 56*:817-823.

Reich, T., Cloninger, C. R., Guze, S. B. (1975). The multifactorial model of disease transmissions: I. Description of the model and its use in psychiatry. *Brit. J. Psychiatry 127*:1-10.

Schuckit, M. A., Petrich, J., Chiles, J. (1978). Hyperactivity: Diagnostic confusion. *J. Nervous Mental Dis. 166*:79-87.

Smith, S., Kimberling, W., Pennington, B., Lubs, H. (1983). Specific reading disability: Identification of an inherited form through linkage analysis. *Science 219*: 1345-1347.

Stewart, M. S., DeBlois, C. S., Cummings, C. (1980). Psychiatric disorder in the parents of hyperactive boys and those with conduct disorder. *J. Child Psychol. Psychiatry 21*:283-292.

Sverdt, J., Curley, A., Jandorf, L., Volkersz, L. (1988). Behavior disorder and attention deficits in boys with Tourette syndrome. *J. Am. Acad. Child Adolescent Psychiatry 27*:413-417.

Szatmari, P., Offord, D., Boyle, M. H. (1989). Ontario child health study: Prevalence of attention deficit disorder with hyperactivity. *J. Child Psychol. Psychiatry Allied Disciplines 30*:219-230.

Tarter, R. E., McBride, H., Buonpane, N., et al. (1977). Differentiation of alcoholics: Childhood history of minimal brain dysfunction, family history and drinking pattern. *Arch. Gen. Psychiatry 34*:761-768.

Thompson, W. D., Orvaschel, H., Prusoff, B., Kidd, K. (1982). An evaluation of the family history method for ascertaining psychiatric disorders. *Arch. Gen. Psychiatry 39*:53-58.

Weiss, G., Hechtman, L., Milroy, T., Perlman, T. (1985). Psychiatric status of hyperactives as adults: A controlled prospective 15-year follow-up of 63 hyperactive children. *J. Am. Acad. Child Psychiatry 24*:211-220.

Weiss, G., Hechtman, L., Perlman, T., Hopkins, J., Wener, A. (1979). Hyperactives as young adults. *Arch. Gen. Psychiatry 36*:675-681.

Weissman, M., Merikangas, K., John, K., Wickramaratne, P., Pursoff, B., Kidd, K. (1986). Family-genetic studies of psychiatric disorders. *Arch. Gen. Psychiatry 43*:1104-1116.

4

Neurochemical Aspects of Attention Deficit Hyperactivity Disorder

Larry W. Desch

University of Missouri, Columbia, Missouri

> *"The beauty of neurometapsychopharmacology is that it predicts any outcome and cannot be invalidated by any findings."*
>
> [Wender, 1984]

There continues to be considerable debate concerning the description, causation, and treatment of childhood attention deficit disorder with or without hyperactivity. This chapter is primarily concerned with what has been described about the neurochemical and neurophysiological aspects of the attention deficit hyperactivity disorder (ADHD). Despite significant progress over the last 50 years much controversy continues regarding the neurochemistry of behavior and attention. It is without a doubt that neurotransmitters are involved in the symptomatology of ADHD. However, much uncertainty remains as to whether this is a primary neurochemical disorder or is secondary to behavioral changes that cause subsequent changes in neurotransmitters and their interactions. For the purpose of this chapter, the more likely hypothesis, that changes in neurotransmitters are the primary etiology, will be accepted. Theories based on this view will be discussed and contrasted and possible neuropathological etiologies for changes in neurotransmitters will be briefly explored. Finally, directions for future research and treatments that may be more specific to the neurochemical abnormalities will be outlined.

Historical Review

That neurotransmitters can effect behavior has been known for nearly a century. Abel [1901] and Elliott [1904] were able to demonstrate the behavioral effects of adrenalin-like substances. These were large stimulatory effects noted with various types of laboratory animals. Von Euler [1948] discovered norepinephrine acting as a transmitter of electrical responses within the brain. Prior to this elucidation of the location of neurotransmitter substances, it had been noted by Bradley [1937] that amphetamines could cause a "striking" behavior improvement in children who had behavior disorders and hyperactivity.

Following these early reports a succession of research studies were done to try to clarify the action of stimulants on the central nervous system (CNS) and later to determine whether they play a role in the pathophysiology of ADHD. Primarily, the influence of the catecholamines, dopamine and norepinephrine, have been investigated.

RESEARCH TECHNIQUES

To understand the abnormal neurochemistry that might be taking place in children with ADHD, basically two research approaches have been used. The first of these is the study of various bodily fluids for the presence of metabolites of catecholamines in children before or during stimulant treatment. The second method is to design specific pharmacological probes that may be actual drug treatments—some type of metabolite or anti-metabolite or a neurotransmitter. These two approaches have been the predominant ones used to describe and verify different hypotheses regarding the neurochemistry of ADHD.

Pharmacological Probes

One major difficulty in evaluating many of the animal studies in research on ADHD, especially those studies using pharmacological probes, is the realization that the doses of stimulant medications that decrease activity levels in children are approximately 1/10 that which will inhibit activity in rats. However, this dosage discrepancy was recently dealt with by Robbins and Sahakian [1979] who present evidence that species which had greater body weight often had a greater sensitivity to drug doses when a comparison was made on a mg/kilogram basis. Most recent animal research has used appropriate amounts of stimulants; however, confusion has resulted in the past when unexpected or contrary results were reported based on research done with inappropriate dosages.

As with most of our understanding regarding the pathophysiology of brain functioning, simple hypotheses about ADHD have been discarded, for the most part, only to be replaced by those that are seemingly more complex. As the diversity of what is called ADHD is clarified, it is possible that for some children a simple neurochemical explanation can be found. However, it is likely that the complex neurochemical interactions are the more common.

A number of studies have looked at the levels of catecholamines and their metabolites in urine, plasma, platelets, and cerebrospinal fluid (CSF) in untreated children with ADHD compared to controls. Many of these studies are inconclusive or contradictory (see Table 1). A recent review of Zametkin and Rapoport [1987] has critiqued the design flaws of many of these quantitative studies. In summary, it has thus far been found that there are no significant differences between levels of catecholamines or their metabolites in nontreated children with ADHD compared to those in normal control children. However, this is not to say that some differences may not actually exist that could be proven by carefully designed large studies. Essentially, these past studies have mainly evaluated selected metabolites of norepinephrine, dopamine, and serotonin. Norepinephrine is metabolized to 3-methoxy-4-hydroxyphenylglycol (MHPG), dopamine to homovanillic acid (HVA), and serotonin to 5-hydroxy-indolacetic acid (5-HIAA) (see Figures 1 and 2). However, from these inconclusive studies a number of specific theories have arisen.

NOREPINEPHRINE THEORIES

In his catecholamine hypothesis, Kornetsky [1970] saw norepinephrine as the major precipitating factor for the hyperkinetic behavior observed with ADHD. He theorized that giving children with ADHD a stimulant such as amphetamine worked by binding to post-synaptic norepinephrine receptors and therefore reducing the neurotransmission of noradrenaline.

Metabolic Studies

Urinary catecholamine studies have focused mainly on levels of the norepinephrine metabolite MHPG but such work has led to inconsistent results. Most studies have found less urinary MHPG in ADHD children than control subjects [e.g., Shekim et al. 1977, 1983]. No differences, however, were found by Rapoport et al. [1978] and Wender et al. [1971]; and Khan and

Table 1 CSF, Blood, and Urine Metabolities in Control and ADHD Children

Investigators	Subjects		Fluid	Metablite	Findings
	ADHD	Control			
Shetty and Chase [1976]	24	6	CSF	HVA, 5HIAA	No difference in HVA, 5HIA
Shaywitz et al. [1977a]	6	16	CSF	5HIAA	No difference in 5 HIAA
Rapoport et al. [1974a]	35	19	Serum	NE	No difference in NE
Bhaganan et al. [1975]	11	11	Serum	5HT	Decreased 5HT in ADDH
Ferguson et al. [1981]	49	11a	Serum	NE	No difference in NE
Coleman [1971]	25		Whole Blood	5HT	Decreased 5HT in ADDH
Irwin et al. [1981]	55	38b	Platelets	5HT	No difference in 5HT
Rapoport et al. [1974a]	17	75	Platelets	5HIAA	No difference in 5HIAA
Wender et al. [1971]	9	6	Urine	HVA	No difference
Shekim et al. [1983]	9	9	Urine	HVA	No difference
Shekim et al. [1983]	9	9	Urine	MHPG	Decreased MHPG in ADDH
Yu-cun and Yu-feng [1984]	73	51	Urine	MHPG	Decreased MHPG in ADDH
Shekim et al. [1979]	15	13	Urine	MHPG	Decreased MHPG in ADDH
Khan and DeKirmenjian [1981]	10	10	Urine	MHPG	Increased MHPG in ADDH
Wender et al. [1971]	9	6	Urine	MHPG	No difference in ADDH
Rapoport et al. [1978]	13	14	Urine	MHPG	No difference in ADDH
Rapoport et al. [1978]	13	14	Urine	Dopamine	No difference in ADDH
Rapoport et al. [1978]	13	14	Urine	NE	Increased in ADHD

aNormal values.
bYoung adults.
(Adapted from Zametkin and Rapoport, 1987.)

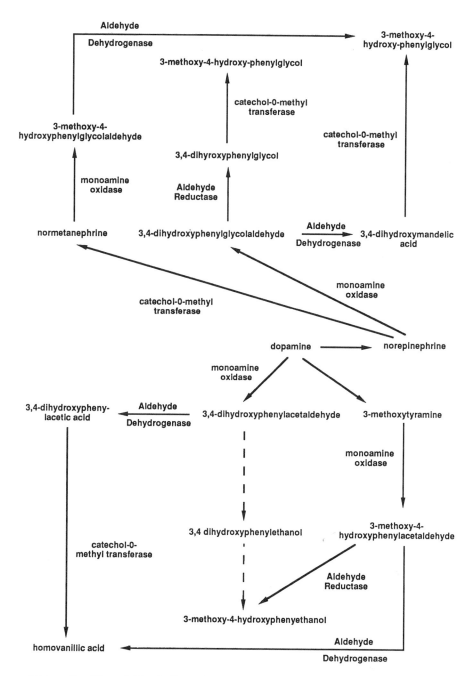

Figure 1 (Upper) Metabolism of norepinephrine. Dopamine is converted to nore-pinephrine through oxidation by dopamine-β-hydroxylase. (Lower) Metabolism of dopamine. Dopamine that is not converted to norepinephrine is rapidly metabolized by monoamine oxidases.

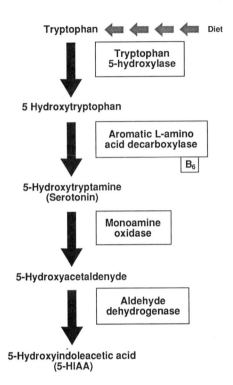

Figure 2   Metabolism of serotonin. Monoamine oxidase play a role in regulation of this neurotransmitter.

DeKirmenjian [1981] found *increased* urine MHPG in ADHD. However, some of these MHPG urinary studies may have been flawed because of a prolonged depression of MHPG from previous stimulant medication [Zametkin et al., 1985]. In nearly all of this research a period of "wash-out" (more than 2 weeks) was not performed so that the extremely variable depression of MHPG levels among subjects and between studies may thus be partially explained.

Further research is needed to determine whether there really is a difference between urinary MHPG levels in untreated children with ADHD compared to those in normal subjects. If MHPG levels are truly decreased in children with ADHD this may reinforce the hypothesis of decreased norepinephrine activity or levels.

Pharmacological Studies

There are several lines of pharmacological research that support a norepinephrine theory. It has been shown by at least three studies [Brown et al., 1981;

Shekim et al., 1977; Zametkin et al., 1984] that dextro-amphetamine decreases urinary excretion of MHPG, which has lead to the inference that norepinephrine metabolism is altered by this stimulant. Shekim et al. [1979] tested subjects who were shown to be clinically responsive to amphetamines for urinary output of MHPG and demonstrated a decrease in this metabolite after treatment.

Shen and Wang [1984] showed in a controlled study that ADHD children had 20% lower levels of urinary MHPG; and, those that responded to Ritalin (methylphenidate) showed a further 20% decrease. Methylphenidate has been shown by numerous animal studies to effect primarily the noradrenergic system.

According to a study by Zametkin et al. [1985], however, there may be no significant effect of methylphenidate on MHPG excretion. They have concluded that the most important consideration that must be addressed when evaluating the results of studies in which peripheral metabolites (e.g, urinary) are measured is that any change may reflect either a true drop at the synapse or a "compensatory" drop because of an actual increase at the synaptic level.

In contrast to these studies, however, recent investigation by Murphy [1989] using fenfluramine, a serotonin antagonist, demonstrated large decreases in urinary and plasma MHPG, but was accompanied by minimal or no behavioral improvements. Therefore, a reduction in norepinephrine metabolism does not always lead to behavioral changes.

Monoamine oxidase (MAO) inhibitors have also been shown to decrease the metabolism of catecholamines. The two types of MAO's are different in their effects, with MAO-A mainly affecting norepinephrine and MAO-B related to dopamine metabolism. In relationship to the norepinephrine hypothesis of ADHD, a study done by Rapoport et al. [1985] showed significant behavioral improvement after the MAO inhibitors clogyline or tranylcypromine were given, both of which inhibit norepinephrine metabolism.

A study by Rapoport and colleagues [1985] used alternatives to stimulants in order to try a different pharmacological probe technique. This study used desipramine, a tricyclic antidepressant that inhibits norepinephrine uptake at the synapse with subsequent increased norepinephrine turnover. Desipramine has no known dopaminergic effect. Improvements in behavior ratings were found but what was *not* shown was improved attention based on the use of a continuous performance task. In a related study, Donnelly et al. [1986] found a reduction in urinary MHPG with acute desipramine treatment, with a net increase in sympathetic activity despite the decrease in norepinephrine metabolism. The main mechanism of action of desipramine was interpreted as increase of norepinephrine *availability* at nerve terminals (see Figure 3).

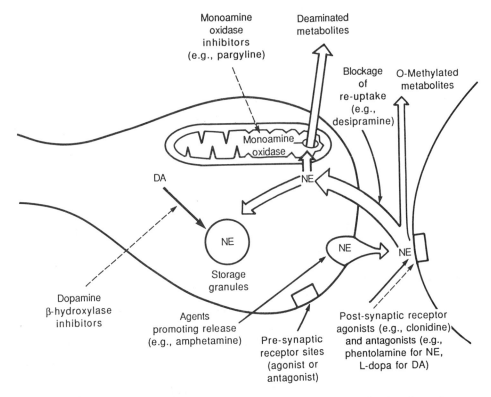

Figure 3 Diagram of a catecholamine synapse. Probable sites of action for various drugs mentioned in this chapter are shown. Similar activities occur with dopamine containing neurons, except that dopamine is not β-hydroxylated (see Fig. 1). [Adapted from Antelman and Caggiula, 1977.]

In these related studies, this research group presents evidence felt to be indicative of a norepinephrine system defect being responsible for the ADHD symptomatology. However, since they did not show an improvement in attention in the desipramine study, it seems unlikely that the norepinephrine system by itself could be wholly responsible for the clinical characteristics of ADHD. Most likely, with ADHD there may be several closely linked but still somewhat separate systems that are involved, each of which has a different response to interruptions of or enhancements to either dopamine or norepinephrine metabolism.

Deficiencies of the Theory

More appears to be involved with the various pathways than changes reflected solely by altering levels of norepinephrine metabolites. This is in spite of significant correlations between the neurochemical responses and clinical improvement. A recognition of other possible explanations is especially important since ADHD children may excrete normal or low levels of MHPG prior to treatment, which would seem to indicate that there may be qualitative and quantitative differences that exist prior to treatment.

DOPAMINE HYPOTHESIS

There appear to be definite neurophysiological differences in the responders and nonresponders to various psychostimulants. These differences may relate to the various findings of different researchers. Wender [1971] suggested on the basis of some preliminary neurochemical studies that children with ADHD could be subdivided into two groups—those who have decreased dopamine and those with decreased norepinephrine metabolism. The previous section addressed the noradrenergic hypothesis and several studies that relate to this hypothesis as well as a few that seem to refute it. This section will address the evidence for a "dopamine hypothesis."

The study of dopamine system functioning in children with ADHD began with an animal model [Shaywitz et al., 1976]. In that study, after brain dopamine was depleted in developing rats, they subsequently demonstrated increased motor activity.

Pharmacological Studies

Over the years, a number of dopaminergic stimulators of postsynaptic dopamine receptors have been tried as therapeutic agents (see Figure 3) including piribidel, amantadine, and L-Dopa. These drugs would be expected to increase the overall effect of the dopaminergic system; however, when administered to children with ADHD, no significant clinical improvements were noted.

On the other hand, drugs that inhibit dopamine metabolism may have some effect. Results of a 1983 study using the MAO-B pargyline (a dopamine oxidase inhibitor) demonstrated that behaviors much improved following the use of this drug [Wender et al., 1983]. Unfortunately, there were many unpleasant side effects, with the use of this drug.

There is indirect evidence, however, for a simple dopamine hypothesis. Shaywitz et al. [1982] demonstrated treatment effects of methylphenidate on serum prolactin and growth hormone levels. These hormonal effects can best be explained by an action of methylphenidate on the lower hypothalamic dopaminergic pathways. Shaywitz et al. [1977] also found decreased CSF HVA compared to controls in boys with hyperactivity who had responded to stimulant medications. However, another study, by Shetty and Chase [1976], did not find any baseline differences between hyperactive controls and children. Both of these studies may be faulted in that they had very few experimental subjects.

Deficiencies of the Dopamine Hypothesis

A line of evidence that is discouraging to a simple dopamine hypothesis is the moderate degree of effectiveness of the antipsychotics haloperidol, chlorpromazine, and thioridazine in low doses. However, these drugs have some weak noradrenergic blocking activities in addition to their dopamine antagonistic properties [Windsberg and Yepes, 1978].

There have been several studies that have looked at the effects of dopamine blockade by contrasting high or low doses of tranquilizers such as haloperidol or thioridazine. In a study done by Werry and Aman [1975], which compared the effects of methylphenidate to haloperidol, the methylphenidate-treated group did much better on attentional measures using a continuous performance task. A group treated with low-dose haloperidol, however, did show significant improvement in behavior ratings. A study by Gittelman-Klein et al. [1976] evaluated the combination of thioridazine and methylphenidate compared to the effects of giving each of these drugs singly or to giving a placebo. In that study, the groups with methylphenidate either alone or in combination with thioridazine had significantly better teacher ratings of behavior than the thioridazine alone or placebo groups. There did not appear to be any decreased effects due to any dopaminergic blockade from the low-dose thioridazine.

A much stronger dopaminergic block can be achieved by the use of haloperidol, however, and a study by Levy and Hobbes [1988] did demonstrate some effect from a dopaminergic blockade. Haloperidol was given singly and in combination with methylphenidate in a placebo-controlled trial. A number of measures of attention were used by the continuous performance task (CPT) results are perhaps the most telling. The use of haloperidol by itself decreased the continuous performance results; if haloperidol was given before methylphenidate, no improvement in attention, including the CPT, was noted.

In order to understand the implications of this type of research, it is important to reconsider in a new way the results of the study by Rapoport et al. [1985] that was described previously. In that study, the use of the drug desipramine did not demonstrate any improved attention or vigilance based on the lack of improvement on CPT. Using this comparison as a basis for the hypothesis, it appears likely that some features of ADHD (e.g., motor overactivity) are probably pathophysiologically based in abnormalities of norepinephrine function, other features, in this case vigilance and attention (e.g., as that with CPT) are probably dopaminergic functions.

Interestingly, since haloperidol actually worsened vigilance and attention, this suggests to some researchers, such as Levy and Hobbes [1988], that even though behavioral improvement may occur with the use of tricyclics, the "cognitive" improvements do not occur. Levy and Hobbes also believe that such results lend credence to a critical stimulation of a "dopaminergic component" that causes the improved cognition in children with ADHD following stimulant drugs such as methylphenidate. Although there remains some minimal support for a simple dopamine system malfunction as the etiology for ADHD, a unitary theory seems increasingly unlikely based on the multitude of studies that have demonstrated conflicting evidence. At the very least, other mechanisms appear to be at work.

SEROTONIN THEORIES

In the past several decades it has become recognized that another neurotransmitter, serotonin, may have a small role in the etiology of the behavior problems seen with ADHD. Many children with ADHD also exhibit aggressiveness, and a number of studies have demonstrated both increased activity and increased aggressiveness in serotonin depleted animals. Two early investigations in children with hyperactivity demonstrated decreased platelet serotonin [Coleman, 1971; Bhagauan et al., 1975]; however, this finding of decreased serotonin was not replicated in later studies [Rapoport et al., 1974; Ferguson et al., 1981]. The latter study actually demonstrated increased serotonin values. Urine and CSF studies of serotonin metabolites have not shown any difference between hyperactive subjects and controls [Wender et al., 1971; Shetty and Chase, 1976; Shaywitz et al., 1977].

Pharmacological Studies

Pharmacological probes have been studied to address the serotoninergic hypothesis by using L-Tryptophan, which is the amino acid precursor of serotonin, and fenfluramine, a medication that depletes brain serotonin when used chronically. These drugs have been shown in some studies to cause minor improvement in ADHD behaviors but on most occasions the response is minimal or doubtful.

Serotonin and Associated Disorders

There is at least one area where the importance of serotonin in ADHD associated disorders may be important. Using adults with diagnosed conduct disorders associated with aggressiveness and impulsivity (all of whom had been conduct disordered children), Brown et al. [1982] showed decreased levels in the cerebrospinal fluid of the 5-HIAA metabolite of serotonin.

There appear to be definite sub-types of ADHD such as hyperactivity manifesting in childhood associated with some elements of aggression. Although it is probably only a small subset in terms of frequency, some children with ADHD may be exhibiting problems due to dysfunctional serotoninergic pathways and these children may have aggressiveness as a major component of their problematic behaviors.

DOPAMINE-NOREPINEPHRINE INTERACTION HYPOTHESIS

Recent studies by most investigators have focused on the possible interactions between the norepinephrine and dopamine systems within the CNS as being responsible for the symptoms seen in ADHD. Previously it was hoped that ADHD would be like some metabolid disorders or Parkinson's disease for which there is evidence for a single selective neurotransmitter defect being involved. However, the biochemistry of the CNS is such that the synthesis of dopamine can be regulated by the amount of norepinephrine present [Cooper et al., 1982]. This observation makes it unlikely that either dopamine or norepinephrine metabolism could be altered without affecting the activity of the other neurotransmitter. Using somewhat simplistic logic, the fact that there are so many effective medications for the treatment of ADHD, with each medication having a multitude of different biochemical effects, adds further proof that more than one neurotransmitter system is involved.

Subtypes of ADHD

Since research into defining possible sub-types of ADHD is still in its infancy, studies of small groups of children may well dilute the information available regarding those children who have a *single* neurotransmitter problem that accounts for their difficulties. It is still possible that Wender's hypothesis [1971] could be at least partially true; that is, there may be some children with hyperactivity who have a single biochemical lesion in either the norepinephrine or the dopamine system. The remainder of this chapter, however, will examine the evidence for the interaction or combined-effect theories.

Metabolic Interactions

A number of studies have been done which show that there probably is a different ratio of urinary HVA (dopamine metabolites) to MHPG (norepinephrine metabolites) in children with ADHD compared to control children.

In other cases, this difference in correlation between HVA and MHPG did not appear until the children were treated with stimulant medications. A study done by Shekim et al. [1982] showed a lower ratio of urinary HVA to MHPG in ADHD subjects and a larger positive ratio in the normal control children. Changes in this ratio occur in children who have been shown to respond behaviorally to stimulant medications such as dextroamphetamine.

The effect of stimulants on urinary excretion of HVA seemed to depend on the pre-treatment levels of both the urinary HVA and MHPG. In all of the stimulant responders dextroamphetamine decreased the urinary MHPG. However, for those responders who had low baseline HVA and normal MHPG the stimulant increased the urinary HVA levels. In those responders who had normal HVA and low MHPG the stimulant medication seemed to decrease the urinary HVA. In both situations, the HVA/MHPG ratio was increased.

A later study [Shekim et al., 1983] showed that giving amphetamine *increased* urinary HVA in those subjects who clinically improved (all of whom had significantly lower baseline HVA levels than controls) to levels similar to the normal children. Shekim et al. [1982] suggested that, at least for dextroamphetamine, stimulant effects as seen by changes in HVA levels "may depend on relative sensitivity of pre-synaptic autoreceptors of dopamine as well as norepinephrine, in comparison to post-synaptic receptors" (see Fig. 3). Another groups of researchers, led by Zametkin [1987, 1988], have re-analyzed some of the research studies on which these conclusions were based and have indicated some serious "methodological difficulties."

A carefully designed study by Shaywitz et al. [1987], however, supports the conclusions of Shekim. More important, that study demonstrates that amphetamine and methylphenidate have greatly different CNS effects as indicated by changes in plasma HVA levels: plasma HVA increased 54.4% in those children who were given amphetamine, however, with methylphenidate, no HVA increase was found. It was thus concluded that, despite the similarities in clinical effectiveness between the methylphenidate and amphetamine, there is an important difference in biochemical actions with D-amphetamine probably affecting dopaminergic mechanisms as well.

Arnold et al. [1977] used either the D or L isomer of amphetamine to study behavioral effects on children with hyperactivity. The D isomer of amphetamine has both noradrenergic and dopaminergic functioning; however, the L isomer only has noradrenergic functioning. There was no difference in behavioral changes between the children receiving the two isomers except on an attentional scale with those having received the D isomer doing somewhat better.

Interaction Theory—"Tuning and Switching"

Theories have been developed as to how dopamine and norepinephrine systems may act in consort, and investigators have orchestrated a type of choreography for possible interactions. An example of this work is based on the research of Robert Oades [1987]; but it was earlier [1985] that Oades proposed that norepinephrine activity "tunes" the relationship between the incoming signal and the "noise" from other sources. It is then the dopaminergic system that assists the switching between "channels" to supply input to different regions of the brain.

As primary supporting evidence for the norepinephrine tuning theory, Oades cites many studies dealing with visual and auditory perception. Facilitation of noradrenaline pathways by stimulation increases the responses to visual input. In a similar fashion, increased norepinephrine discharges have been shown to improve electrical responses to auditory tones using animal models.

As secondary evidence, Oades describes the multitude of animal studies evaluating inforamtion processing, learning, and behavior following either increase of norepinephrine into certain brain regions and various brain lesioning studies. Essentially this research demonstrates that attention and learning is decreased when there is less norepinephrine activity present in the brain, especially in the midbrain areas.

Although there appears to be enough experimental evidence to justify the role of norepinephrine as a "tuning mechanism" for attentional and activational brain systems, the evidence of dopamine systems acting as a "switching mechanism" is less compelling. Oades admits that three methodological problems make this part of the theory difficult to substantiate: (1) sectioning or lesioning parts of the brain often affect more than just the target area (such as the nerve cells of the norepinephrenergic system); (2), specific neurotransmitter blockers and antimetabolites often are not completely specific to one system; (3) finally, the actual tissue levels of pharmacological probes, such as has been pointed out with the use of D-amphetamine, can make a difference on what system is primarily affected. It should also be obvious that plasma levels do not reflect completely what is occurring at a cellular level.

One action of the dopaminergic system, as hypothesized by Oades, is to promote switching between alternative sources of information. The primary evidence that has been gathered in support of this theory relates to behavioral changes occurring after lesioning studies or after treatment with D-amphetamine. An example of this latter type of evidence is the study by Evenden and Robbins [1983]. In order to accept this particular research as evidence for the dopaminergic switching mechanism, one must first assent to the pharmacological evidence that amphetamines at low doses affect the dopamine system rather than the norepinephrine system.

In the research by Evenden and Robbins, rats were trained using a paradigm designed to measure response switching. The rats were trained to respond to two locations in a Y-type maze with a random schedule of reinforcement for each of the two locations. At low doses the amphetamine treated animals had an increased amount of switching of responses. At high doses, however, this tendency was reversed so that a decrease in switching occurred.

Interaction Theory—"Stress Related"

There are alternative hypotheses that entertain the theory of an interaction of norepinephrine and dopamine systems responsible for the attentional and activity symptomatology seen with ADHD. Work done by Antelman and Caggiulia has led to the development of several hypotheses dealing with stress-related interactions between brain norepinephrine and dopamine systems. Although their work does not specifically address ADHD, they do suggest a relationship to Tourette's syndrome, a disorder shown to be frequently associated with ADHD.

In their model, it is theorized that under conditions of stress, decreased dopamine activity occurs initially, which may or may not then be counterbalanced by a similar decrease in norepinephrine activity. One important piece of evidence that supports their theory is the ability of amphetamine to cause hyperactivity in laboratory animals following depletion of norepinephrine or dopamine in the brain. Equal depletion of norepinephrine and dopamine has been shown to cause a decrease in spontaneous motor activity but did not reverse the overactivity caused by amphetamine [Evetts et al., 1970]. Depleting only norepinephrine not only did not change spontaneous motor activity but actually enhanced the overactivity produced by amphetamine. Similar trends are seen when a norepinephrine receptor blocking agent such as phentolamine is given and the effect on feeding (before and after amphetamine treatment) is observed in animal models.

In apparent contradiction to the theories of Oades, however, Antelman and Caggiula [1977] point to evidence that there is a "regulatory influence of norepinephrine on dopamine." There appears to be a "deregulation" process that can create a number of abnormal behavioral situations. In their synthesis, based on a number of research studies (human subjects with Parkinson's disease, schizophrenia, or manic depressive disorders as well as several animal models) that involve the depletion or destruction of dopamine pathways, they hypothesize a counterbalancing to the decreased dopamine by a similar decrease occurring in norepinephrine activity. In some situations decreased dopamine activity may occur under conditions of stress or excitement. Interestingly it has been noted that ADHD children can have fewer problems with distractibility during periods of extreme excitement or increased stress.

Neuroanatomical Evidence for Interactions

In a recent review by Zametkin and Rapoport [1987] they present further evidence to support a view that both norepinephrine and dopamine may be interlinked in a pathological model for ADHD. A possible explanation for the findings in ADHD could be explained by norepinephrine inhibition of frontal cortex that would, in turn, act on lower striatal pathways that are being driven by dopamine agonists. The ultimate answers to these theories may well depend on what one is looking for, such as with the story of the blind men and the elephant. If you just look at one feature of ADHD, such as behavior, one theory (take your choice—norepinephrine, dopamine, or serotonin) may fit the results of one particular research study. If you look at another outcome measure, such as vigilance or attention or possibly even academic improvement, then another neurochemical theory may seem more plausible.

Further animal as well as human behavioral studies are needed to add power to the hypothesis of dopamine-norepinephrine interactions. It is unlikely, however, that other neurotransmitter systems will be considered appropriate candidates to explain the essential features of attentional and learning behaviors.

NEUROANATOMICAL AND NEUROPHYSIOLOGICAL ASPECTS

Before the possible interactions between neurotransmitter systems in children with ADHD can be more adequately studied, it is important for additional basic research to be done to further our understanding of the complicated behaviors found in both ADHD as well as normal attentional processes. In all probability, attention is composed of, or inter-related to, a number of subprocesses and components such as arousal, selectivity, vigilance, and motivation. It is very likely that each of these areas has its own neuroanatomic and neurochemical aspects. In the following section possible neuroanatomical correlates to the neurochemical processes of ADHD will be briefly addressed. Major brain areas that have been linked to attentional processes—the cortical, striatal, and limbic areas of the brain—will be the ones primarily addressed in this review.

Neuroanatomical Theories

A number of neuroanatomical theories regarding the etiology for ADHD have been described. The organicity of the problems seen in ADHD was primarily responsible for the early descriptions of it being part of the symptom complex of "minimal brain dysfunction." Laufer and colleagues [1957] proposed the etiology of "diencephalic dysfunction." The diencephalon includes the hypothalamus, thalamus, subthalamus, and epithalamus. The thalamus and subthalamus serve as pathways between the basal ganglia and motor cortex. This suggests a possible explanation for the hyperactivity often seen in children with ADHD. The theory of diencephalic dysfunction cannot be totally ruled out based on the current evidence.

The reticular-activating system (RAS) is also in this area, and it was suggested by Satterfield and Dawson [1971] that ADHD reflected a problem of underarousal of the RAS. Subsequent research, however, has not lent much credence to this "underarousal theory." Early neuroanatomical theories have been disproved as certain neurophysiological techniques have improved. Rosenthal and Allen [1978] demonstrated that autonomic arousal did not necessarily decrease in children with ADHD, as was called for by the underarousal or low reticular-activating system excitation model. They based their findings on the fact that skin conductance does not increase as would be expected with stimulant therapy, but rather decreased.

Other studies have focused on the ability of the frontal lobe of the cortex to provide mediation of other cortical as well as striatal and basal ganglia structures [Mattes, 1980; Gualtieri and Hicks, 1985]. In addition to the frontal lobes' influence, there is that of the reticular-activating system, which appears to be related somewhat reciprocally to frontal lobe functioning. The other midbrain structures besides the reticular-activating system that are probably involved include the thalamus. caudate, and hippocampus.

Major Neural Pathways

Figure 4 is a schematic diagram that depicts most of the known pathways by which catecholamines and other neurotransmitters could effect control of overall motor activity. There appear to be direct pathways from the norepinephrine containing areas in the brain stem through the basal ganglia, particularly the substantia nigra, to the cortical areas. Norepinephrine has also been proven to affect the biosynthesis of dopamine both in the cortical and basal ganglia regions [Cooper et al., 1982].

A second direct pathway probably is also involved with projections from the locus coeruleus to the cortex. Researchers have also shown that there is an extensive laminar and regional distribution of noradrenergic fibers in the innervation of the cortex [Morrison et al., 1982]. Aston-Jones and Bloom [1981] have demonstrated that environmental stimulation can alter these norepinephrine discharges, and they suggest that such discharges improve "transmission flow" on CNS pathways, important for appropriate response to unexpected external events.

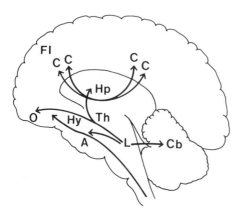

Figure 4 Diagramatic representation of major catecholamine Pathways within the brain. (A = amygdala, C = cortex, Cb = cerebellum, Fl = frontal lobe, Hp = hippocampus, Hy = hypothalamus, L = locus coeruleus, O = olfactory nucleus, Th = thalamus).

Norepinephrine Pathways

There are a number of norepinephrine systems in the brain that probably play a role in the etiology of the problems seen in ADHD. The most important of these is a system originating in the locus coeruleus in the brain stem reticular formation area that sends fibers through the dorsal bundle and the median forebrain bundle to the cortex. This system may play a role in arousal, affect, and attention [Iversen, 1980]. This is a complex system that functions by sending out influences throughout the cortex and even subcortical areas. Evidence of clonidine having a positive effect in ADHD has added further preliminary evidence to support a role for this system. Clonidine influences the locus coeruleus by its effect as an α-II stimulator.

In addition to the locus coeruleus system, there are two other important norepinephrine systems. The first is the lateral tegmental system, in which cell bodies located in the medulla and pons send axons to subcortical areas, especially the diencephalon and hypothalamus. The second is a system of systems—numerous norepinephrine systems in the medulla and spinal cord, primarily bilateral sympathetic nerves to the spinal cord. It is obvious that some side effects of stimulant medications, such as increases in blood pressure, probably are mediated by such pathways. These side effects occur especially if stimulants are given in high doses. What remains uncertain, however, is the importance of these pathways under the usual circumstances of low-dose treatment. However, it remains evident that most medications useful in the treatment of ADHD appear to have important effects on these noradrenergic pathways.

Dopamine Pathways

There is a known distribution of dopamine functioning neurons in both the brain stem and diencephalon. The four main dopaminergic pathways or tracts from these areas are to relatively distant brain regions.

1. There is the nigrostriatal tract, which begins in the substantia nigra and functions primarily as an inhibitor of cholinergic neurons in the basal ganglia. These dopaminergic neurons coordinate movements. The well-known and well described disorders that occur when these neurons are dysfunctional include Parkinson's disease, chorea, and tardive dyskinesia.
2. The next projection is the tuberoinfundibular tract. This tract begins in the arcuate nucleus of the hypothalamus and suppresses prolactin and the release of growth hormone.
3. The third projection is the mesolimbic mesocortical tract. This cortical pathway probably modulates emotion and sensory input into the cortex.
4. The last is a chemoreceptor trigger zone, which is sensitive to dopaminergic stimulation and is related to the CNS vomiting mechanism.

Of these four tracts the first and the second probably fit best with the symptoms seen with ADHD. Although children with ADHD do not have severe motor problems, such as seen in Parkinson's disease, they usually do have significant motor-control problems.

The Nigrostriatal Tract

In first dopamine pathway, the nigrostriatal-tract structures, there is a dependency of interactions between cholinergic and dopaminergic activity that is essential for proper motor coordination. Recent neurophysiological studies on children with learning disabilities [Rolandson and Stephens, 1985; Desch, 1988] address the possible relationships of a transcortical sensorimotor feedback loop that may involve basal ganglia and dopaminergic systems. Children with learning disabilities had abnormal, seemingly primitive or immature, electromyographic responses of an extremity when response was induced by electrical or mechanical stimulation of sensory afferents leading to the electromyographic (EMG) activity (similar to tendon tap except induced by electrical stimulation or movement). Although these studies are very limited and do not involve or do not directly mention whether these children had ADHD, the motor-control problems clinically seen with learning disabled and ADHD children appear to be similar.

The Tubuloinfundibular Tract

In regard to the second dopaminergic pathway, the tubuloinfundibular tract, most studies have indicated that stimulant therapy for ADHD does effect growth hormone secretion and hypothalamic functioning. Since stimulant therapy is well known to have an anorectic effect on appetite, a number of researchers have implicated the hypothalamus as an area that may relate to the etiology for ADHD; Wender [1971] was the first to hypothesize a deficit in hypothalamic function.

A number of studies have looked at growth hormone secretion. Aarskog et al. [1977] found growth hormone levels elevated above pretherapeutic levels after chronic methylphenidate treatment. Shaywitz et al. [1982] reported growth hormone and prolactin levels that increased in relation to peak methylphenidate levels. However, Greenhill et al. [1980] did not document any change in nighttime secretion of growth hormone in children on chronic methylphenidate treatment. Further studies of hypothalamic function may be able to lend more support to this theoretical association.

The Mesolimbic Tract

There is only one study reported at the present time that has addressed the role of the third pathway, the mesolimbic system, in relation to ADHD. Porino and colleagues [1984] gave low doses of amphetamine to laboratory animals. There was a more selective stimulation of certain areas of the brain rather than the large effects that occur when higher doses are used (the typical situation in most animal studies). Since it has been demonstrated by a number of studies that children with ADHD also have mood changes and excitability, both limbic symptoms, it is reasonable to continue examining the possible implications of mesolimbic system effects.

Some animal models demonstrate increased motor activity after damage of certain midbrain and higher brain areas. Destruction of nerve endings in the mesolimbic pathway of laboratory rats has been shown to generate a permanent syndrome of increased motor activity and failure to respond appropriately to sensory stimuli. In this animal model, the symptoms are usually remedied by treatment with D-amphetamine [Solanto, 1984].

Serotonin Pathways

As with the neurochemical studies, there is very little neuroanatomical evidence to support a serotonin hypothesis, at least as a major contributing factor for the etiology of ADHD. Research has failed to identify any distinct pathways for serotonin activity in the brain. There are however, two major anatomic areas that are related to serotonin distribution. The first is in the frontal lobe, which plays a role in arousal and possibly in motor activity. In addition, in parts of the hypothalamus, serotonin may be related to regulating temperature, eating, and other metabolic activities. A possible relationship of serotoninergic brain lesions to ADHD symptoms is based on a single study by Brown et al. [1982] that correlated aggression in adults with low spinal fluid serotonin metabolites. There was also evidence of limbic dysfunction in these aggressive adults. There do exist studies of animal models which indicate that problems with serotonin metabolism causing subsequent aggressive activity may be secondary to hypothalamic dysfunction.

Midbrain and Neocortical Influences

The human animal is, however, more complex in terms of brain structure in a phylogenetic sense compared to the common laboratory animals used in basic research. It is therefore reasonable to assume that higher brain levels are involved in the attentional and motor problems seen with ADHD. Any thalamic and hypothalamic dysfunctions that exist may well be secondary to brain dysfunction at these higher levels.

Further up the brain function control ladder come the hippocampus and related structures. These are older parts of the forebrain that in man are actually enclosed by the highest level of cortical development, the neocortex. Milner et al. [1966, 1971] described a patient with a lesion of the hippocampus that severely impaired both long-term memory and attention span. Luria and colleagues [1973] demonstrated increased distractibility and problems with association and memory in patients with hippocampal lesions.

A number of preliminary studies, such as that by Mason and Iverson, correlate the importance of norepinephrine projections to the hippocampus in the process of selective attention. Lesions in the dorsal bundle of the hippocampus severely inhibit both attentional learning and processes. This "dorsal bundle extinction effect" appears to cause rats to be "unable to ignore a relevant stimuli" [Mason and Iverson, 1979].

Limbic System Theories

In the theories of Vinogradova [1975] there are two inter-related attentional circuits at work: one is a "limbic circuit" referred to as the "informational circuit," which receives and processes information from a multitude of sensory areas; and the other is the "regulatory circuit" in which emotional systems and hypothalamic areas are related. The link between these two systems is the hippocampal nucleus, which serves as an "evaluator" of the stimulus to determine the degree of input to the reticular formation and ascending reticular fibers to the higher levels of the brain. Thus, this nucleus is thought both to be an arousal system as well as a recognition system. Although these are only hypothetical at the present time, these theories help to explain the findings in animal models in which selective attention for new stimuli decreased when the hippocampus is directly or indirectly interfered with.

Sensorimotor System Theories

Recently research in ADHD has begun to focus on the importance of sensorimotor cortical areas, especially that part of the frontal lobe most closely interlinked with the precentral motor cortex. Mattes [1980] has focused on the importance of the dopaminergic pathways of the frontal lobe. Recent support for this frontal lobe hypotheses has come from imaging studies and studies of cerebral blood flow. Lou et al. [1984] used a xenon 133 inhalation technique to document a central hypoperfusion in the frontal lobes in ADHD children compared to sibling controls. Methylphenidate increased perfusion in the mesencephalon and basal ganglia but decreased perfusion in motor and primary sensory cortical areas. More recently, these same researchers, using a similar technique, found hypoperfusion also evident in lateral striatal and posterior periventricular areas but increased perfusion in occipital areas [Lou et al., 1989, 1990]. Recent clinical neuropsychological studies further support the idea of frontal lobe dysfunction in children and adults with ADHD and hyperactivity [Chelune et al., 1986].

Adults with ADHD have described their hyperkinesis as similar to that seen with patients who have akathisia as a side effect of neuroleptics that block dopamine receptors. [Bloomingdale et al., 1983]. Children and adults with ADHD also complain of the same sleep disturbances due to motoric neuronal discharge causing sudden jerky movements, as do patients with akathisia. Sydenham's chorea, which has been attributed to dopamine deficiency in the corpus striatum structures, also presents frequently with restless, fidgety behavior similar to the clumsiness and restlessness seen in children with ADHD. Obviously akathisia and Sydenham's chorea are not considered to be primarily attentional problems, so the pathology in children and adults with ADHD mostly likely involves other dopamine-sensitive systems or other neurotransmitter systems.

CURRENT OPINIONS ON
ADHD NEUROPATHOLOGY

Zametkin and Rapoport [1986] have presented an extensive review of both neurochemical and neuroanatomical studies in ADHD. It is their conclusion that the weight of evidence currently favors dysfunction in the frontal areas where dopaminergic neurons enter the central frontal lobe to reach the prefrontal cortex from subcortical areas. These are considered to be the primary sites that play the central role in the etiology of symptoms in ADHD. Damage or dysfunction of this important brain area leads to "deficits in impulse control" (frontal functions), attentional problems (brain stem function), and learning problems (higher cortical function). The blood flow studies of Lou et al. [1984, 1989, 1990] showing hypoperfusion in frontal areas lend further support for this hypothesis. Obviously, other systems that are more difficult to test, such as the various noradrenergic systems and the dopaminergic meso-limbic pathways, may also have important roles. Ultimately the pathology may be found to be the result of a combination of multiple areas of dysfunction.

DIRECTIONS FOR FUTURE RESEARCH AND POSSIBLE TREATMENTS
Deficit versus Lag

There are a number of seemingly unrelated areas of research that may eventually lead to better understanding of the neurophysiology of children with ADHD. Only recently have such neurophysiological testing methods as somatosensory and visual evoked potential responses been applied to children with ADHD. There has always been the difficulty in assigning the etiology of ADHD to actual damage to the brain (the deficit approach) as opposed to a neuromaturational dysfunction (the lag approach). Some of the newer neurophysiological procedures, if done in a longitudinal fashion, may help to decide between these hypotheses. In addition to neurophysiological testing, neurochemical correlates related to attentional problems may also be applied in a longitudinal approach to delineate changes occuring over months, years, or perhaps decades.

It has been shown by repeated studies that while some children with attentional difficulties seem to "outgrow" their problems, others continue having problems into adulthood. Permanent neurological damage with its related neurochemical abnormalities would help to explain this outcome difference between these two groups of patients, both of whom had ADHD as younger children.

Etiology of ADHD

Increasing evidence has also been accumulating on deficiencies or toxins that can damage or alter the developing fetal brain. Much of this research, such as the studies related to the fetal alcohol syndrome, may be found to relate to possible etiologies for ADHD. Researchers such as Johnston [1988] have demonstrated a number of toxins that can alter the proper development of neurotransmitters and receptors. Deficiencies in such nutrients as essential fatty acids or some vitamins at critical stages in fetal development has also been shown by animal studies to lead to similar neuropathology. Although ADHD is unlikely to be the result of a single toxin or deficiency, this type of research will likely lead to a clearer understanding of what may cause ADHD, at least in some individuals.

Subgroups of ADHD

Despite the overwhelming attention paid to addressing abnormalities in neuro-anatomy or neurochemical dysfunctions in the etiology of ADHD, there still remains only a handful of studies that agree sufficiently to allow one to say that some progress has been made in understanding this syndrome complex. In the future, rather than attempting to group all children with ADHD as a totality, sub-groups of ADHD will be uncovered as clinicians and researchers continue to investigate responders and nonresponders to stimulant medications as well as those children whose hyperactivity actually gets worse with stimlant medication. It may well be that these "anomalous" subjects may have the most clearly defined neurochemical or neuroanatomical abnormalities.

REFERENCES

Aarskog, D., Fevang, F. O., Klove, H. (1977). The effect of stimulants and metylphenidate on secretion of growth hormone in hyperactive children. *J. Pediatr.* *90*:136.

Abel, J. J. (1901). Further observations on epinephrine. *Johns Hopkins Hosp. Bull.* *12*:80.

Antelman, S. M., Caggiula, A. R. (1977). Norepinephrine-dopamine interactions and behavior. *Science 195*:646.

Arnold, E., Molinoff, P. B., Rutledge, C. O. (1977). The release of endogenous norepinephrine and dopamine from cerebral cortex by amphetamine. *J. Pharmacol. Exp. Ther. 202*:544.

Aston-Jones, G., Bloom, F. E. (1981). Activity of norepinephrine containing locus coeruleus neurons in behaving rats anticipates fluctuations in the sleep-waking cycle. *J. Neurosci. 1*:887.

Bhagauan, H. N., Coleman, M., Coursina, D. B. (1975). The effect of pyridoxine hydrochloride on blood serotonin and pyridoxal phosphate contents in hyperactive children. *Pediatrics 55*:437.

Bloomingdale, L. M., Gold, M. S., Davies, R. (1983). Some possible neurological substrates in attention deficit disorders. *Acta Paedopsychiatry (Basel) 49*:47.

Bradley, C. (1937). The behavior of children receiving benzadrine. *Am. J. Psychiatry 94*:577.

Brown, G. L., Ebert, M. H., Goyer, P. F. (1982). Aggression, suicide and serotonin: Relationships to CSF amine metabolites. *Am. J. Psychiatry 139*:741.

Brown, G. L., Ebert, M. H., Hunt, R. D., Rapoport, J. L. (1981). Urinary 3-methyoxy-4-hydroxyphenylglycol and homovanillic acid response to d-amphetamine in hyperactive children. *Biol. Psychiatry 16(8)*:779-87.

Chelune, G. J., Ferguson, W., Koon, R., Dickey, T. O. (1986). Frontal lobe disinhibition in attention deficit disorder. *Child Psychiatry Hum. Dev. 16*:221.

Coleman, M. (1971). Serotonin concentrations in whole blood of hyperactive children. *J. Pediatr. 78*:985.

Cooper, J. R., Bloom, F. E., Roth, R. H. (1982). *The Biochemical Basis of Neuropharmacology.* (*4th ed.*) New York: Oxford University Press, p. 173.

Desch, L. W. (1989). Assessing neurodevelopmental aspects of motor control by use of a non-invasive EMG technique. *Ped. Res. 24*:355A.

Donnelly, M., Zametkin, A. J., Rapoport, J. L., Ismond, D. R., Weingartner, H., Lane, E., Oliver, J., Linnoila, M., Potter, W. Z. (1986). Treatment of childhood hyperactivity with desipramine: Plasma drug concentration, cardiovascular effects, plasma and urinary catecholamine levels, and clinical response. *Clin. Pharmacol. Ther. 39*:72.

Elliot, T. R. (1904). On the action of adrenaline. *Proc. Physiol. Soc. London*, p. 8.

Evetts, K. D., Uretsky, N. J., Iversen, L. L., Iversen, S. D. (1970). Effects of 6-hydroxydopamine on CNS catecholamines, spontaneous motor activity and amphetamine induced hyperactivity in rats. *Nature 225*:961.

Evenden, J. L., Robbins, T. W. (1983). Increased response switching, perseveration, and perseverative switching following d-amphetamine in the rat. *Psychopharmacology (Berlin) 80*:67.

Ferguson, H. B., Pappas, B. A., Trites, R. L., Peters, D. A., Taub, H. (1981). Plasma free and total tryptophan, blood serotonin, and the hyperactivity syndrome: No evidence for the serotonin deficiency hypothesis. *Biol. Psychiatry 16*:231.

Gittelman-Klein, R., Klein, D. F., Katz, F., Kesore, F., Pollack, E. (1976). Comparative effects of methylphenidate and thioridazine in hyperkinetic children. *Arch. Gen. Psychiatry 33*:1217.

Greenhill, L. L., Puig-Antich, J., Halpern, F., Sachar, E. J., Rubenstein, B., Chambers, W., Fiscina, B., Florea, J. (1980). Growth disturbances in hyperkinetic children. *Pediatrics 66*:152.

Gualtieri, C. T., Hicks, R. E. (1985). Neuropharmacology of methylphenidate and a neural substitute for childhood hyperactivity. *Psychiatr. Clin. North Am. 8*:875.

Irwin, M., Belendink, K., McCloskay, K., Freedman, D. X. (1981). Tryptophan metabolism in children with attention deficit disorder. *Am. J. Psychiatry 138(8)*: 1082.

Iverson, S. D. (1980). Brain chemistry and behavior. *Psych. Med. 10*:527.

Johnston, M. V., Barks, J., Greenamyre, T., Silverstein, F. (1988). Use of toxins to disrupt neurotransmitter circuitry in the developing brain. *Prog. Brain Res. 73*:425.

Khan, A. U., DeKirmenjian, H. (1981). Urinary excretion of catecholamine metabolites in hyperkinetic child syndrome. *Am. J. Psychiatr. 138*:108.

Kornetsky, C. (1970). Psychoactive drugs in the immature organism. *Psychopharmacologia 17*:105.

Laufer, M. W., Denhoff, E., Solomons, G. (1957). Hyperkinetic impulsive disorder in children's behavior problems. *Psychosom. Med. 19*:38.

Levy, F., Hobbes, G. (1988). The action of stimulant medication in attention deficit disorder with hyperactivity: Dopaminergic, noradrenergic, or both? *J. Am. Acad. Child Adolesc. Psychiatry 27*:802.

Lou, H. C., Henriksen, L., Bruhn, P. (1984). Focal cerebral hypoperfusion in children with dysphasia and/or attention deficit disorder. *Arch. Neurol. 41*:825.

Lou, H. C., Henriksen, L., Bruhn, P., (1990). Focal cerebral dysfunction in developmental learning disabilities. *Lancet 335*:8.

Lou, H. C., Henriksen, L., Bruhn, P., Brnër, H., Nielsen, J. B. (1989). Striatal dysfunction in attention deficit and hyperkinetic disorder. *Arch. Neurol. 46*:48.

Luria, A. R. (1973). The frontal lobes and the regulation of behavior. *Psychophysiology of the Frontal Lobes*. (K. H. Pribham, A. R. Luria, eds.), Academic Press, Orlando, pp. 3-26.

Mason, S. T., Iversen, S. D. (1979). Theories of the dorsal bundle extinction effects. *Brain Res. Rev. 1*:107.

Mattes, J. A. (1980). The role of frontal lobe dysfunction in childhood hyperkinesis. *Comprehen. Psychiatry 21*:358.

Milner, B. (1966). Amnesia following operation on the frontal lobes. In: *Amnesia*. Whitty, C. W., and Zangwill, O. L., eds. London, Butterworths, p. 109.

Milner, B. (1971). Interhemispheric differences in the localization of psychological processes in man. *Br. Med. Bull. 27(3)*:272.

Morrison, J. H., Foote, S. L., O'Connor, D., Bloom, F. E. (1982). Laminer, tangential and regional organization of the noradrenergic innervation of monkey cortex; dopamine-B-hydroxylase immunochemistry. *Brain Res. Bull. 9*:309.

Murphy, D. L. (1989). Fenfluramine and dextroamphetamine treatment of childhood hyperactivity. *Arch. Gen. Psychiat. 46*:205.

Oades, R. D. (1985). The role of noradrenaline in tuning and dopamine in switching between signals in the CNS. *Neurosci. Biobehav. Rev. 9*:261.

Oades, R. D. (1987). Attention deficit disorder with hyperactivity (ADDH): The contribution of catecholaminergic activity. *Prog. Neurobiol. 29*:365.

Porrino, L. J., Lucignani, G., Dow-Edwards, D., Sokoloff, L. (1984). Dose dependent effects and acute amphetamine administration on functional brain metabolism in rats. *Brain Res. 307*:311.

Rapoport, J. L., Quinn, P. O., Bradbard, G., Riddle, K. D., Brooks, E. (1974a). Imipramine and methylphenidate treatments of hyperactive boys. *Arch. Gen. Psychiatry 30*:789.

Rapoport, J. L., Quinn, P. O., Scribanic, N., Murphy, D. L. (1974b). Platelet serotonin of hyperactive school age boys. *Br. J. Psychiatry 125*:138.

Rapoport, J. L., Mikkelsen, M. D., Ebert, M. D., Brown, G. L., Weise, B. S., Kopin, I. J. (1978). Urinary catecholamines and amphetamine excretion in hyperactive and normal boys. *J. Nerv. Ment. Dis. 166*:731.

Rapoport, J. L., Zametkin, A., Donnelly, M., Ismond, D. (1985). New drug trials in attention deficit disorder. *Psychopharm. Bull. 21*:232.

Robbins, T. W., Sahakian, B. J. (1979). Paradoxical effects of psychomotor stimulant drugs in hyperactive children from the standpoint of behavioral pharmacology. *Neuropharm. 18*:931.

Rowlandson, P. H., Stephens, J. A. (1985). Cutaneous reflex responses recorded in children with various neurological disorders. *Dev. Med. Child. Neurol. 27(4)*:434.

Rosenthal, R. H., Allen, T. W. (1978). An examination of attention, arousal, and learning dysfunctions of hyperkinetic children. *Psych. Bull. 85*:689.

Satterfield, J. H., Dawson, M. E. (1971). Electrodermal correlates of hyperactivity in children. *Psychophysiology 8*:191.

Shaywitz, B. A., Cohen, D. J., Bowers, M. B. J. (1977). CSF monoamine metabolites in children with minimal brain dysfunction: Evidence for alteration of brain dopamine. *J. Pediatr. 90*:67.

Shaywitz, S. E., Hunt, R. D., Jatlow, P., Cohen, D. J., Young, J. G., Pierce, R. N., Anderson, G. M., Shaywitz, B. A. (1982). Psychopharmacology of attention deficit disorder: Pharmacokinetic, neuroendocrine, and behavioral measures following acute and chronic treatment with methylphenidate. *Pediatrics 696*:688.

Shaywitz, B. A., Klopper, J. H., Yager, R. D., Gordon, J. W. (1976). Paradoxical responses to amphetamine in developing rats treated with 6-hydroxydopamine. *Nature 261*:153.

Shaywitz, B. A., Gillespie, S. M., Shaywitz, S. E. (1987). Neurochemical influences of stimulants in children with attention deficit disorder: d-amphetamine versus methylphenidate effects on plasma urinary monoamines and metabolites. *Ann. Neurol. 22*:409.

Shekim, W. O., DeKirmenjian, H., Chapel, J. L. (1977). Urinary catecholamine metabolites in hyperkinetic boys treated with d-amphetamine. *Am. J. Psychiatry 134*:1276.

Shekim, W. O., DeKirmenjian, H., Chapel, J. L. (1979). Urinary MHPG excretion in minimal brain dysfunction and its modification by d-amphetamine. *Am. J. Psychiatry 136*:667.

Shekim, W. O., Javaid, J., Davis, J. M., Bylund, D. B. (1983). Urinary MHPG and HVA excretion in boys with attention deficit disorder and hyperactivity treated with d-amphetamine. *Biol. Psychiatry 18*:707.

Shekim, W. O., Javaid, J., Dekirmenjian, H., Chapel, J. L., Davis, J. M. (1982). Effects of d-amphetamine on urinary metabolites of dopamine and norepinephrine in hyperactive boys. *Am. J. Psychiatry 139*:485.

Shen, Y. C., Wang, Y. F. (1984). Urinary 3-methoxyhydroxy-phenylglycol sulphate excretion in seventy-three school children with minimal brain dysfunction syndrome. *Biol. Psychiatry 19*:861.

Shetty, T., Chase, T. N. (1976). Central monoamines and hyperactivity of childhood. *Neurology 26*:1000.

Solanto, M. V. (1984). Neuropharmacological basis of stimulant drug action in attention deficit disorder with hyperactivity: A review and synthesis. *Psychol. Bull. 95*:387.

Vinogradova, O. S. (1975). Functional organization of the limbic system in the process of registration of information: Facts and hypotheses. In: *The Hippocampus, Vol. 2: Neurophysiology and behavior.* Isaacson, R. L., and Pribham, K. H., eds. New York, Plenum Press, p. 3.

Von Euler, U. S. (1948). Assay of noradrenalin and adrenalin is extracts of nerves and tissues. *Nature (London) 162*:570.

Wender, P. (1971). *Minimal Brain Dysfunction Syndrome in Children.* New York, Wiley, p. 163.

Wender, P. H. (1984). Remarks on the neurotransmitter hypothesis. In: *Attention Deficit Disorder: Diagnostic, Cognitive and Therapeutic Understanding*. Bloomingdale, L. M., ed. New York: SP Medical & Scientific Books, pp. 67-72.

Wender, P. H., Wood, D. R., Reimherr, F. W., Ward, M. A. (1983). An open trial of pargyline in the treatment of attention deficit disorder, residual type. *Psychiat. Res. 9*:329.

Wender, P., Epstein, R. S., Kopin, I. J., Gordon, E. K. (1971). Urinary monoamine metabolites in children with minimal brain dysfunction. *Am. J. Psychiatry 127*: 1411.

Werry, J., Aman, M. (1975). Methylphenidate and haloperidol in children: Effects on memory and activity. *Arch. Gen. Psychiatry 32*:790.

Winsberg, B. G., Yepes, L. E. (1978). Antipsychotics (major tranquilizers, neuroleptics). In: *Pediatric Psychopharmacology: The Use of Behavior Modifying Drugs in Children*. Werry, J. S., ed. New York: Brunner/Mazel, p. 234.

Yu-cun, A., Yu-feng, W. (1984). Urinary 3-methoxy-4-hydroxyphenyglycol sulfate secretion in seventy-three school children with minimal brain dysfunction syndrome. *Biol. Psychiatry 19*:861.

Zametkin, A. J., Karoum, F., Linnoila, M., Rapoport, J. L., Brown, G. L., Chuang, L. W., Wyatt, R. J. (1985). Stimulants, urinary catecholamines, and indoleamines in hyperactivity: A comparison of methylphenidate and dextroamphetamine. *Arch. Gen. Psychiatry 42*:251.

Zametkin, A. J., Karoum, F., Rapoport, J. L., Brown, G. L., Wyatt, R. J. (1984). Phenylethylamine excretion in attention deficit disorder. *J. Am. Acad. Child Adolesc. Psychiatry 23*:310.

Zametkin, A. J., Rapoport, J. L. (1986). The pathophysiology of attention deficit disorder with hyperactivity. In: *Advances in Clinical Child Psychology*. Lahey, B. B., and Kazdin, A. E., eds. New York, Plenum Press, p. 86.

Zametkin, A. J., Rapoport, J. L. (1987). Neurobiology of attention deficit disorder with hyperactivity: Where have we come in 50 years? *J. Am. Acad. Child Adolesc. Psychiatry 26*:676.

Zametkin, A. J., Rapoport, J. L. (1988). Pathophysiology of ADHD (letter) *J. Am. Acad. Child Psychiatry 27*:389.

Diagnosis

5

Appropriate Use of Measures of Attention and Activity for the Diagnosis and Management of Attention Deficit Hyperactivity Disorder

Thomas A. Blondis

University of Chicago Pritzker School of Medicine, Chicago, Illinois

Jeffrey H. Snow

University of Arkansas for Medical Sciences, Little Rock, Arkansas

Mark Stein and Nancy J. Roizen

University of Chicago Pritzker School of Medicine, Chicago, Illinois

> *"We are interested in learning more about what the distributions of normal and hyperactive children look like on the various tests that define this factor. At the moment, I can only say that the distributions of scores of the normal sample on several of the tests seem to reveal considerable skewness on the "bad" end. It is as if something is responsible for producing more children who do badly on these tests than one would expect by chance."*
>
> [Douglas, 1972]

Minimal developmental handicaps continue to be split, subgrouped, and recategorized by predominant features, contrasting test performances, and associated problems. The construct of an attentional disorder has been redefined twice within seven years and will no doubt be changed again by the American Psychiatry Association (APA) when it publishes the revision of its *Diagnostic and Statistical Manual*. Currently, North America uses the broadly defined DSM-III-R [1987] criteria, while the World Health Organization's International Classification of Diseases (ICD-9) definition of "Hyperkinetic Syndrome of Childhood" is used in Great Britan and Europe (Table 1) [Prendergast et al., 1988].

The diagnosis of the "lumping" disorder ADHD can be only the starting point for the clinician. If significant subgroupings of attentional disorders do exist, then there should be corresponding differences in the cognitive processes, behaviors, and performances in children who have one subtype or dysfunction when contrasted with another. These differences should be distinct and not merely indicative of severity (i.e., interval on a scale of severity), as some investigations [Gilberg et al., 1989] have suggested. Such differences should not only be demonstrable by test measures alone, but ideally should also correlate with observable clinical differences between one subtype and another. It remains to be determined whether or not ADHD

Table 1 Differing Diagnostic Criteria for Low-Severity Developmental Disorders

Disorder	Symptoms	Origin
ADHD	8/14 behaviors[a] Impulsivity Hyperactivity Inattentiveness	American Psychiatric Association, DSM-III-R, [1987]
Hyperkinetic Syndrome of Childhood	Essential features[b] Distractibility Short attention span Extreme overactivity[c] Disinhibition[c] Poor organization[c] Occasional underactivity[d] Other symptoms Impulsivity Marked mood fluctuation Aggression	World Health Organization, US Dept. of Health and Human Service, International Classification of Diseases, [1980]

[a]Onset before age seven excludes pervasive developmental disorder.
[b]Exclusions are symptomatic of another disorder.
[c]Symptoms occur during early childhood.
[d]Symptom occurs during adolescence.

is secondary to an underlying psychological processing deficit or some other form of psychopathology. If it is determined that a child has a primary attentional disorder, it is important that the measures define the specific cognitive and behavioral problems in order that a successful plan of habilitation can be formulated [Blondis et al., 1989 a,b].

The diagnosis of an ADHD child should not be based on how a child behaves on a given day for one developmental professional. Sleator and Ullmann [1981] demonstrated that observation by the physician in the office setting could not adequately differentiate a child with an attentional disorder. Children with the disorder characteristically present with a variable pattern of attentional behavior, and also generally do much better in a one-to-one structured setting. The ecological context of the child's behavior is essential for the evaluation and habilitation practice (Figure 1). In order to evaluate the "whole" child, it is important to get an accurate account of how he or she functions in the classroom during the learning process, on the playground while interacting with peers, at home and in the neighborhood relating to adults, peers, and siblings. Without the use of well-standardized instruments that account for the child's behavior in his various relationships and environments, too much of the diagnostic decision making for the inconsistently manifested behaviors basic to this disorder will be left up to the personal bias of the professional. Objective measures can offer only a quantitative framework within which team members work, but the importance of such a framework should not be underplayed. Once such a quantitative score is introduced as a factor, it will never be completely discounted.

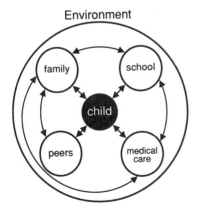

Figure 1 Ecology of the school-aged child. The school-aged child relates to family, school, peers, and health-care providers. For the welfare of the child with ADHD, it is imperative that the caretakers from the school, home, and health-care center take time to communicate with one another.

One must keep in mind that each measure is a vehicle to help the clinical examiner determine the child's developmental level, "thinking," and behavior. Most tests measure a variety of processes: "the score" doesn't define "the process." For this reason, it is important that each evaluation include a clinical assessment and that qualitative findings be encompassed within the professional report. A good example is a child who does poorly on a continuous performance task that is a test of visual recognition. Rather than equate poor performance with poor attention, the clinician needs to rule out other possibilities. The child may have done badly because of a visual impairment, central visual processing deficit, or because of an affective disorder.

The appropriate use of quantitative measures of attention, activity, behavior, and other developmental parameters aids accurate diagnoses and improves the therapeutic program by accurately delineating the difficulties that need to be addressed before the child can achieve more efficient learning, adaptive maturation, personal and social success. For this reason it is important that the professional make some use of valuable cognitive and behavioral measures that have been developed. It is equally important to construct a critical system to evaluate both the instrument or test and the way it is used. The focus of this chapter is to outline measures that are commonly used and define their content, problems, limitations, and biases. These measures will be placed in the context of their use by the interdisciplinary team for diagnosis and habilitative purposes.

Worthwhile instruments will have been thoroughly researched before they are made available for clinical use. It is necessary that the clinician review the sensitivity, selectivity, reliability, and validity of the instrument before he decides to use it. Likewise, it is detrimental if an instrument too often identifies the child to have a score indicative of a problem that is later ruled out by the assessment (poor selectivity). A questionnaire or test that is marketed prior to undergoing tests of interexaminer or test-retest reliability should be avoided. Various tests of validity are also necessary, and in the case of questionnaires it is most important that the ratings be tested in relation to a more objective and refined measure such as the use of direct observation scales that are scored by professionals [Barkley, 1988]. An instrument that fails to demonstrate co-positivity when compared to a better instrument or a clinical team diagnosis (sensitivity) should be avoided. For this reason the authors have excluded questionnaires and tests that are available but have not reported adequate reliability or validity investigations of the instrument. This chapter was not written to critique poorly constructed instruments, and the authors include only instruments that may in the present or the future have some value to the clinician working with children who have attentional aberrations.

The idea of an "interdisciplinary team" often evokes images of cost in-effectiveness. However, to address the diagnosis and habilitation of a com-plex and diversified disorder such as ADHD, it is essential that an efficient communication process be developed for those professionals who are caring for the multiple aspects associated with the disorder. It is difficult to imagine that a comprehensive assessment can occur without a "core" of professionals that include a child psychologist, a special educator, a developmental pedia-trician, and a social worker or family therapist. Depending on the complica-tions that the ADHD child presents with, it is sometimes necessary to bring in other consultants who also must be able to effectively communicate with the "core team." Each professional will utilize measures unique to his or her discipline. Currently, there is no single measure that can define ADHD. In the absence of a "gold standard" to guide diagnosis, collective problem solving by a group of professionals who have used accurate measures coupled with qualitative observations is most desirable.

Because this is a *developmental* disorder, it is extremely important that the professionals involved in examining and assessing the patient know the developmental fundamentals of attention and its relationship to active work-ing memory and cognitive operations. This requires a background in the knowledge of the normal and abnormal development of attentional pro-cesses.

DEVELOPMENTAL ASPECTS OF ATTENTION

In order to evaluate the child with ADHD, it is essential that the clinician know when and how the average child develops central processing abilities and how the failure to develop cognitive and motor control affects the ADHD child [Fletcher and Taylor, 1984]. This section provides an overview of attentional processes and the potential consequences of their delayed or dys-functional development.

Normal Development of Attentional Processes

The *neonate's attention* is primitive. Posner and Rothbart [1981] differen-tiate between alertness and attention. It is well known that the neonate can habituate, but is this a function of the loss of the alert state or "attention"? Posner and Rothbart postulate that recognition can be confused with habit-uation. According to this view the neonate habituates when there is a reduc-tion of the flow of information from the recognition pathway into the alert-ing system; the alerting system then fails to activate. Such a lowered level of alerting often leads to sleep. Infant attention then appears to be linked primarily to visual stimuli. Hence a visual-external bound attention is dominated by the salient dimensions of the stimulus, which include contrast, contour, and movement.

During the first year of life the infant becomes less bound to exogenous stimuli and develops more internal control over eye, hand, and body movements. Attention starts to become less "stimulus bound" at 3 months when the infant develops "decision rules" [Olson, 1976]. These rules are nontransferable strategies that are stored in the infant's long-term memory. In Olson's visual information processing system, short-term memory directs prehabituation inhibition, while long-term memory rules characterize true habituation. Thus, beginning at about 3 months of age the infant is developing recognition of stimuli.

An infant develolping at a normal rate will exhibit accomodative imitation beginning at 9 months. With this transition attentional processes become increasingly inseperable from memory processes. The infant is now the "actor" and decides what he or she will perceive, although the actor's repertoire remains obviously quite limited at this stage [Flavell, 1963]. Moving into the exploratory stages of attentional processes, the toddler (and later the pre-schooler) operates on an overt level and is very much guided by the external environment [Wright and Vlietstra, 1975] Although logical search skills have been shown to develop beginning as early as 18 months of age [Haake and Somerville, 1985], this method does not become the dominant attentional strategy until school age. Children by the age of 5 years will usually approach a perceived stimulus systematically [Abravanel, 1968].

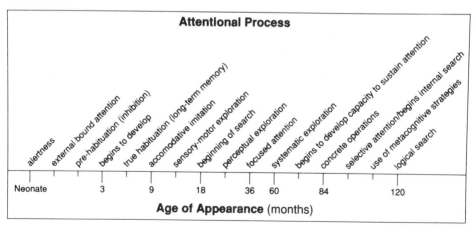

Figure 2 Developmental scale of attentional processes. Early development of attention is primarily exploratory, while later development includes goal direction, logical search, and organization.

The concept of *focused* attention involves directing one's thought process to a specific target; clearly this requires the ability to inhibit internal distractions. At age 3 years children begin to be able to focus attention. However, few researchers have investigated when normal children develop the ability to focus attention on a specific target.

Young children show more eye movements when visually inspecting objects both the first time the object is presented and also upon subsequent viewings. [Zinchenko et al., 1963] This is most likely related to the child's limited ability to sustain active focus (e.g., maintain concentration on one idea for more than 5 minutes). When a child is presented with age-attractive themes, he can passively focus for far longer periods of time. Preschool children are attracted by the salience of fast moving, colorful, and exciting stories. The active maintenance of attention on a target idea or task (*sustained attention*) requires directed effort. This capability requires such self-regulation elements as stimulus selection, learning, and the inhibition of irrelevant response. Some investigators have proposed that sustained attention requires that the individual exert effort, but no studies have isolated this element. The self-regulation elements imply that the child is no longer exploratory in his approach toward stimuli.

How selective is the exploratory preschool child's attention? Luria [1959] designed a study in which children were asked to press a button when a light appeared. The accurate response was present at age 3 years. A second task added the condition that the button be pushed only with the presentation of a specific color. Children at age 5 could successfully respond to this task.

Wright and Vlietstra [1975] summarize four levels at which mature attention (search) can be differentiated from immature attention (exploration). At the *behavioral* level, the exploring child is an impulsive and rapid responder. The more mature search is goal directed and task oriented. As viewed in relation to *cause*, the exploration stage is dominated by salient, reinforcement-correlated features; whereas, the search stage is controlled by informational needs and logical restraints. Although exploration versus search can be viewed from the standpoint of maturation of attention, the individual never completely outgrows exploratory attention. If the *task* consists of a novel stimulus and there are no active demands or constraints, an exploratory approach may be appropriate. Also, tasks requiring divergent or imaginative thinking may best be met with the use of a more open-ended form of perceptual/thought process. When the correct solution to a logical problem is the goal, the search process is the better mode of information processing. From the standpoint of *time*, exploration precedes search, and logical search is an elaboration of perceptual search. Although the exploration process is never obsolete, as the child matures the search mode should represent more of his thought process. A problem develops when the child is not consciously increasing his use of the search mode.

Within the realm of perceptual and logical search, the child develops the ability to focus on central features of a stimulus and "filter" that material which does not meet his informational needs. The more mature mind is capable of ignoring stimuli of no use in order to facilitate problem solving or the development of an idea [Hagen and Hale, 1973]. Generally, most children are able to successfully *selectively attend* by middle childhood.

Abnormal Development of Attention and Activity

The hyperactive or attention disordered child has frequently been described as "always on the go" and "acting without thinking." It is clear that such a child has not developed adequate control over motor activity, thought, or emotion. Some ADHD children experience a driven restlessness that is not channeled effectively toward a particular goal. In a longitudinal study of children diagnosed as hyperactive in elementary school the "always on the go" symptom resolved in adolescence; however, the adolescents continued to have difficulty with control over impulsive responses [Weiss et al. 1971]. Other investigators have disputed this finding [Cantwell, 1985]. In either case, one can agree that these behaviors are caused either by nonreflective responses and failure to "inhibit" motor movement or by impulsiveness and a failure to "control" movement.

The descriptor *inhibit* is more accurate for the ADHD child. *Control* implies that it is within the child's capabilities to slow down and reflect. For the ADHD child it may be possible to develop better control, but the cause is biologic; it is the child's *failure to develop neural inhibition* [Accardo, 1980; Shulman et al., 1965]. Instead of a nervous system that modulates activity and allows the child to use attention to meet cognitive demands, the child needs to use cognitive strategies to control a nervous system that doesn't automatically modulate itself or successfully process new information without strenuous concentration. The fact is, this motor driven behavior is much like that sometimes displayed by the brain damaged or mentally retarded child [Strauss and Werner, 1942]. We have not yet been able to determine why inhibition of movement or impulse doesn't develop normally or to identify what part of the brain is responsible for this inhibition.

Several investigators have studied the impact that delayed development of sustained attention has on the development of higher cognitive processes [Hamlett et al., 1987; Tant and Douglas, 1982; Weingartner et al., 1980]. These higher processes relate to the ability to guide cognition. This might mean selecting a useful strategy to solve a problem or monitoring the efficacy of a particular approach to problem solving. Weingartner et al. [1980] demonstrated that normal controls did better than ADHD children under free-recall conditions and attributed this to the ADHD group's poor organizational skills and poor processing of memory items. Both Hamlett et al. and Tant and Douglas found that ADHD children verbalize less strategy information when asked to explain how they solved a problem. Whether this deficit is secondary to interference with verbal processing stemming from deficient attention and inhibition to a high incidence of associated language disabilities among ADHD children remains unclear at this time. It is important that ADHD children be taught metacognitive skills such as mnemonics, both problem solving and memory techniques may be very useful in helping the child learn to set goals, organize, and cluster memory items for better retention.

Perseveration is an abnormal pattern of fixed attention to one idea or stimuli. Frequently noted among brain injured and autistic children, it has not been a focus for study among ADHD children. Although it is not a characteristic finding in this population, poorly developed attentional processes make the ADHD child at risk for engaging in such repetitive and regressive behavior. Clinical experience suggests that perseveration is not uncommon among ADHD children with associated learning disabilities. It is important to recognize that attentional deficits may variably exhibit either too short or too long an attention span.

This sketch of attentional development is essential to understanding measures that are reviewed in this chapter. These include questionnaire(s), direct observation procedures, cognitive tasks associated with attentional processes, and neuropsychological tests. Processes mentioned here are discussed in relation to each of the cognitive tasks, and the importance of a developmental understanding of the ADHD child is expanded during the discussion of neuropsychological tests.

CHOOSING A QUESTIONNAIRE SYSTEM

During the past two decades, clinical researchers in the fields of psychology, psychiatry, education, and pediatrics have developed some relatively reliable and valid rating scales that deal with children's problems. A valid quantitative scale can help the clinician review various opinions of what the central behavioral difficulties of the child are.

The questionnaire is an instrument that the clinician can use to evaluate the whole child in the context of his relationships to self, family, peer, and school. Every developmental team has its own unique personnel, perspective, and approach. The choice of a questionnaire system will depend upon these team characteristics.

Before choosing a questionnaire, team members should evaluate the strengths, weaknesses, and utility of the questionnaires under consideration. The parameters to examine include:

1. *Reliability*:   Will the series of questions and their resulting ratings elicit accurate and consistent responses? This is reflected in both inter-observer (each parent answers the same questionnaire) and test-retest (the same parent answers the questionnaire two or more times) reliabilities.

2. *Aggregation Principle*:   Reliability and validity can be strengthened when the different raters (self, teacher, and parents) choose like responses to the same questions (Table 2).

3. *Standardization*:   A cogent normed and standardized test rating scale assists the clinician in relating the index of the child's performance to the standardization sample.

4. *Rating*:   The quantitative questionnaire determines that the score is a given number of standard deviations from the mean. In some instances, a patient profile that includes areas significantly [greater than 2 standard deviations (>2 SD)] below the mean can aid the clinician in differential diagnosis.

5. *Range*:   To be aware of any potential cognitive and behavioral problem, it is important that the instrument include questions that pertain to rare thinking patterns and behaviors. A broad range can help the clinician assess additional symptoms. For example, if a child scores >2 SD above the mean on the Child Behavioral Checklist (CBCL) for inattention and also scores >2 SD above the mean for delinquent, the clinician must consider the possibility of a co-occuring conduct disorder. If a great number of behavioral symptoms are of concern, the clinician may decide that the child could also benefit from a behavioral psychology or a child psychiatry evaluation.

6. *Effects*:   The clinician needs to consider effects that influence the reliability and validity of questionnaire results. The *practice effect* only applies when the instrument is used on a number of occasions. The *halo effect* causes the rater's overly negative or positive opinions about the child to influence the way he responds to specific questions. This is a universal phenomenon that in some ways is the opposite of regression toward the mean. The halo effect bolsters the argument that raters from different environments should be used and that the aggregation principle be utilized. The *negative response bias* (e.g., angry reactionary parent) adds further support for the use of several respondents.

7. *Follow-up*:   Some questionnaires are suited for use on a day-to-day basis for the purpose of determining changes in academic productivity or rates of undesirable behaviors. Obviously, a less time consuming questionnaire is more suitable for this purpose; but the clinician would need to adjust for loss of range and completeness.

8. *Level of Difficulty*:   The clinician needs to consider the reading level and comprehension of the parents and the child asked to complete the questionnaires. Obviously if an instrument takes a parent several hours to complete, compliance is going to be poor.

Table 2 Questionnaires: Level of Difficulty and Aggregation Principle

Questionnaire/Questionnaire System	Aggregation Principle	Number of Items	Reading Level (i.e., grade equivalent)
Child Behavior Checklist (CBCl)		138	5
CBCl Teacher Report Form (TRF)		126	6
CBP	+ + + +		
Yale Children's Inventory (YCI)	+	63	9.5
Conners Parent Reading Scale (CPRS)		93	11
Conners Parent Rating Scale-Revised (CPRS-R)		48	4
Conners Teacher Rating Scale (CTRS)		39	8
Conners Teaching Rating Scale-Revised (CTRS-R)		28	4
Conners Rating Scale	+ + + +		
The Pupil Rating Scale Revised (PRS-R)	+	24	14
Behavior Rating Profile (BRP)	* + + + +	124	4
ADD-H: Comprehensive Teacher Rating Scale (ACTeRS)	+	28	6

The reading level assessment took into consideration the instructions on the questionnaire and the behavioral questions themselves, but did not consider medical history related questions (questions which did not figure in the scoring) or the instructional manual.

*, system.

+, one questionnaire only.

+ +, parent and teacher questionnaire.

+ + +, parent, teacher, and student questionnaire.

+ + + +, parent, teacher, student, and other type of questionnaire.

9. *Utility*:   Finally, cost is a factor that needs to be considered. There are costs for the questionnaire materials, time spent grading and recording results of the scale, and discussing the results with family. Many questionnaire systems now offer computer programs to cut down on the time spent grading results, this can be a further benefit if the clinician is interested in storing the data for research purposes.

Behavioral Questionnaires

The number of quantitative behavioral questionnaires has greatly increased over the past twenty years. We have chosen to include only those that are most applicable to children with ADHD, have undergone adequate investigation, and include questionnaires for the parent, teacher, and child.

Child Behavioral Profile (CBP)

The CBP is a system of questionnaires that includes the *Child Behavioral Checklist* (CBCl), the *Teacher's Report Form* (TRF), *Youth Self-Report Form* (YSRF), and a *Direct Observation Form* (DOF) [Achenbach and Edelbrock, 1979; Edelbrock and Achenbach, 1984; Edelbrock et al., 1986; Freeman, 1985; Reed and Edelbrock, 1983]. In addition to statistically analyzing a wide range of behavioral data, the system also provides quantitative ratings of academic performance and social competence.

The CBP has undergone and continues to undergo scrupulous standardization. The populations used for the various components have been large and included children from all areas of the United States; and there have been several cross cultural studies. Each questionnaire includes a comprehensive manual, scoring templates, and an optional computer program. With the exception of research trials to establish halo effects and practive effects, the CBP satisfactorily addresses all of the essential characteristics that a questionnaire system should contain.

Conners Questionnaires

This is the first hyperactivity scale to have been designed for use by both parent and teachers. A point of confusion has existed with these scales because both the original and revised versions have been in use over the past decade. The revised versions by Goyette are shorter, more easily read by both parents and teachers, and better validated. Specifically, inter-rater reliability scoring method (e.g., comparing mother's score to father's score) is better in the revised versions [Goyette et al., 1978]. Both original and revised versions have undergone adequate factor analysis and standardization [Conners, 1973; Edelbrock et al., 1984; Goyette et al., 1978; Trites et al., 1982]. Trites et al. [1982] also equated the factors of sex and age norms. In addition, Conners [1985a) subsequently piloted the *ADD-H Adolescent Self-Report*, but data testing the reliability and validity of the Self-Report has been insufficient to date. The absence of a clear manual that contains norms and an explanation of the administration, scoring, and grading of each of the scales remains a major impediment to ease of use as well as assurance of quality [Martin et al., 1986]. Also, the range of the Conners Self-Report is limited and may be somewhat dated. Conners, in collaboration with other creators of behavioral questionnaires, has recently investigated to try to determine which questions resulted in responses that point to the core symptoms of ADHD [Achenbach et al., 1989].

Behavior Rating Profile (BRP)

Both the design and the scoring of this scale attempts to improve accuracy and understanding of the child across appropriate environments and individual perceptions. The authors of this scale designed it this way because of their belief that other behavioral scales have only poor to fair reliability and validity. The scale has a built in aggregation factor. Each part of the scale (home, school, peer, self) yields an overall behavioral competence score. The scoring form is designed to demonstrate the magnitude of difference between each rater's perception [Brown and Hammill, 1981, 1986; Hammill and Bartel, 1986].

In addition to the Parent Rating Scale (PRS), Teacher Rating Scale (TRS), and Student Rating Scale (SRS), the BRP contains a Sociogram. This instrument has sixteen items for the child's classmates to answer, such as, "Which of the students in your class would you most like to sit with at lunch?" and "Which of the students in your class would you least like to sit with at lunch?" While it is a time-consuming instrument to use, this optional scale will yield a ranking of the most and least popular children in the class. It is not essential to include this part of the BRP. If one is trying to determine the popularity of the child as well as his own perception of how he is viewed by his peers, the patient, a neighborhood child, and a fellow student can complete a sociogram form.

The BRP drew its normative data from an unselected sample of 1,326 students, 847 parents, and 645 teachers from eleven states. The manual contains tables of selected reliability data; the published validity data is based on only 27 children. The CBP manual is more comprehensive and detailed. The major drawback of the BRP is that it does not yield a specific quantitative score related to attentional behavior or, for that matter, any other specific behavioral area. One would have to scan the questions on each scale to determine whether or not attention was the primary problem [Witt, 1985].

Behavioral Follow-Up Questionnaire Systems

These are quite useful for monitoring the efficacy of medication but inadequate for the initial assessment of a child with an attentional or behavioral problem. Such instruments need to be abbreviated. It is preferable that ratings be done at the same time *daily* to prevent a concluding image the teacher may have at the end of the week and also to control for the behavior during a particular segment of the curriculum. If it is done only once a week or at different times each day, significant halo effects may influence the results.

The first such questionnaire was the *Conners Abbreviated Teachers Rating Scale* (CATRS). Conners selected from his original teacher version ten questions that loaded most heavily for hyperactivity. This scale has also come to be called the "hyperkinetic index." Conners has declared that this is inaccurate, since it really represents a "psychopathology index" [Conners and Barkley, 1985]. Because of the admixture of aggressive behavior items, it is possible for a child to have significant attentional problems and not score

2 SD above the mean. A group of investigators found that scores on the CATRS correlated with the aggression, school performance, and adaptive functioning externalizing scales of Achenbach's Child Behavioral Profile (CBP). The ten questions are very easy for an elementary school teacher to complete daily, and investigations have shown that achievement of lower scores on the index correlate with improved classroom performance.

Another scale used to evaluate treatment is the *ADD-H: Comprehensive Teacher Rating Scale* (ACTeRS). This instrument was specifically designed for monitoring behavioral changes over time. The normative sample was sufficiently large, but the standardization was done in one university town [Ullmann et al., 1984]. The scale is somewhat more cumbersome for teachers to manage on a daily basis because it includes twenty-eight questions. Nevertheless, it is an effective method for monitoring interventions and progress toward improved attentional and inhibitory behavior [McBride, 1988].

Other Behavioral Questionnaires

Other well standardized and potentially valuable quantitative questionnaires for the assessment of ADHD children are available. The Revised Behavior Problem Checklist [Quay, 1983] is a well-standardized multi-informant scale. The same questionnaire is completed by parent and teacher or other professional. The revised edition is promising, but currently has limited published normative data for parent ratings. Most other scales are for use exclusively by the teacher or by the parent. This makes the use of the aggregation principle more difficult. The Children's Behavior Rating Scale (CBRS) [Neeper and Lahey, 1986] and the Personality Inventory for Children (PIC) [Wirt et al., 1981] are two worthwhile behavioral instruments that fall into this last category; the CBRS is a teacher questionnaire and the PIC is specifically for parents.

Developmental Questionnaires

Several questionnaires have been developed that stress aspects of development other than behavior. These questionnaires can be used by different professionals from the interdisciplinary team, depending on which professional focuses on the area of development that the particular questionnaire stresses. This information should be obtained before the professional evaluates the child so that the assessor is better able to evaluate suspected areas of developmental delay as measured by the questionnaire. Just as in the case of the behavioral questionnaires, the quantitative results obtained on the basis of the developmental questionnaires represents only a crude screen. We have included several adequately standardized questionnaires. In addition to screening behavior problems, the Yale Children's Inventory (YCI) also assesses several developmental parameters including communication and cognition. The scale is comprised of eleven subscales, each of which contains between four and seven items and is broken down into a cognitive and a broad-band grouping of behavior.

YCI is designed to be completed by the parent. This scale has several advantages for pediatricians interested in obtaining information about genetic factors and medical history. Standardization, however, is currently lacking; the subject population is small and exclusively from the state of Connecticut. A manual and a more cross-cultural standardization base would be valuable, and at present, the questionnaire is available only through the author. Nevertheless, this scale shows great potential for more in-depth screening and assessment [Shaywitz et al., 1986, 1988].

The *Pupil Rating Scale Revised* (PRSR) was developed to more effectively identify children who were at such sufficient risk for a specific learning disability that they warranted a complete psychoeducational work-up. Administration of this teacher's questionnaire is straightforward: the instrument includes questions related to auditory comprehension, spoken language, orientation (i.e., judging time, judging relationships), motor coordination, and personal/social behavior. It contains twenty-four items rated on a five-point scale with the average score being three. The questionnaire yields verbal, nonverbal, and total scores. Scores falling 1 SD below the mean indicate the need for more in-depth assessment. The scale can be qualitatively probed to determine which questions or subscales contributed to the child's failure. Current reliability and validity data are adequate for screening children with learning difficulties. Correlations with intelligence are low, but the scale is meant to measure *failure to learn* rather than *cognitive ability*. The manual is complete, and clearly written [Myklebust, 1981].

The *Carey Temperament Scales* are parent-completion questionnaires that attempt to describe the development of their child's *behavioral style*. Infant todder, behavioral, and middle-childhood questionnaires are available. Temperament scales are particularly helpful for assessing preschool children. Results can help the team determine how the child best learns and what facilitates better behavioral responses. This in turn is useful for parent counseling and behavior-management training. Validity and reliability are acceptable for parents who have completed secondary school [Carey, 1980, 1982; Hegvik et al., 1980; Thomas and Chess, 1977].

Interpretation of questionnaires must be approached with caution [Barkley, 1988]. Reliability of all questionnaire systems should be considered less than optimal, and halo and practice effects must be taken into account. Furthermore, biases require that parent, teacher, and student (if the child has reached middle-school age) versions all be used, and the aggregation principle applied. Questionnaires offer the cautious evaluation team of professionals a poten-

108042

tial vehicle from which significant patient and environmental information can be gathered.

DIRECT OBSERVATION PROCEDURES

Until recently, naturalistic and analogue assessment procedures have been used with ADHD children primarily in research settings. These behavioral observation procedures allow for the tabulation of operationally defined behaviors in different situations. Investigators utilizing direct observation procedures often sample target behaviors that are characteristic of the referral problem, such as "off-task" or "activity level." In addition, information regarding other behaviors (e.g., tantrums) as well as related antecedent, consequent, and nonproblem behaviors can also be obtained [Haynes, 1978]. Observations can be made of the child, siblings, classmates, mothers, fathers, and peers [Haynes and Wilson, 1979].

Naturalistic and structured laboratory observations of parent-child interaction have consistently detected differences in the rates and sequences of child/parent behaviors. For example, Cunningham and Barkley [1979] utilized a variation of the response class matrix developed by Mash et al. [1973]. Mother and child interactions were observed in a clinic playroom during two consecutive 15-minute periods, one of free play and one of parental commands (e.g., putting toys away, standing up). Mothers of hyperactive children issued more commands and attempted to redirect the child's independent play, while control mothers provided more praise. During the command segment, mothers of hyperactive children issued more commands, directives, and praise following child off-task and negative behavior. The hyperactive children were less cooperative and compliant than the control children.

One of the first coding systems developed for classroom use was the Stony Brook Code [Abikoff and Gittelman, 1985]. This coding system has shown adequate reliability and sensitivity to treatment effects. In addition, hyperactive and nonhyperactive children can be discriminated. [Abikoff et al., 1980]. This ten-item system includes interference, off-task, noncompliance, minor motor movement, gross motor movement, out-of-chair, physical aggression, threat, solicitation, and absence of behavior. Unfortunately, this system is complex and probably not practical for most clinical settings.

One of the most promising direct observation procedures that can be used for either clinic or classroom observation is the restricted academic task developed by Millich et al. [1980]. For the clinic procedure, children are given a set of math problems one year below thier grade placement and instructed to complete them when they are left alone in a clinic playroom. As Barkley et al. [1988] points out, one of the most difficult problems for children with

ADHD to complete is a relatively mundane task independent of adult supervision.

The sum of occurrences of off-tasks, fidgets, vocalizations, talking to mother, playing with the object, and out-of-seat results in the aggregate behaviors score. This system is relatively easy to learn and can also be used in the classroom setting where a classmate can be coded for comparison purposes. Prior research has demonstrated adequate reliability, stability over a 2-year period, and evidence of discrimination of ADHD children from both non-ADHD and non-ADHD conduct disordered children [Millich et al., 1983]. In addition, the restricted academic task is very sensitive to stimulant medication effects [Barkley et al., 1988].

A major advantage of these procedures is that they allow for the direct measurement of several high-rate behaviors or symptoms of ADHD that otherwise would only be assessed through indirect means. Moreover, qualitative information is also generated that may differ in important facets from parental and teacher reports. It may lead to a specific intervention or to a distinct tailoring of an intervention. Issues of reliability and validity must always be weighed when selecting a method of direct observation. Utility remains a drawback because of the time investment of trained personnel.

In summary, direct observation procedures can yield reliable and valid data that can be useful in the diagnosis, treatment planning, and evaluation of medication. Although this is a more direct measure of external behavior than the questionnaire, direct observation remains an indirect method of evaluating internal behavior. The next three sections evaluate attempts to use more direct methods of measuring the child's attentional processes.

SPECIFIC COGNITIVE TASKS

Numerous attentional and memory tasks are now available to the clinician. Most are still in the investigative stage of development and lack adequate standardization. Some are linked to neurophysiologic measures such as *event related potentials* or *brain electrical activity mapping,* and almost all are marketed as computer software. Some claim to accurately distinguish the child with ADHD from children without attentional dysfunctions. Others have been used to study the difference between "hyperactive" children and those without hyperactivity [Douglas and Peters, 1979; Swanson, 1985; Taylor, 1986]. Some of these tasks do not require the use of higher order cognitive processes, while others necessitate the use of meta-cognitive memory strategies [Weiss and Laties, 1962]. Some researchers tend to focus on tasks interrelated with attention according to which component of attention is their primary concern [Swanson, 1985]. Table 3 categorizes the tests to be

Table 3 Cognitive Tasks and the Processes They Require: Measures of Components of Attention

Instrument	Parameters Task Assesses			
	Inhibition	Sustained Attention	Search	Executive Processes
Continuous performance task (CPT)	+	+		
Go-no-go paradigm	+	+		
Delayed reaction time task (DRTT)	+	+		
Choice reaction time task (CRTT)	+	+		
Matching-to-sample task (MST)	+	+	+	
Paired-associative learning (PAL)	+	+	+	+

discussed according to the four attentional parameters discussed earlier. We have chosen to discuss those types of tasks that have proven to be most successful at discriminating children with attentional problems, showing major group differences when these children are compared to children who have no attentional difficulties. Although many of these tests are commercially available, few include a sufficiently large standardized population and still fewer publish a comprehensive and clearly written manual.

Continuous-Performance Test (CPT), a sustained attention task that was pioneered by Rosvold et al. [1956], has been used in numerous research studies involving attention, management of ADHD with stimulant medication, and diagnosis of children who are hyperactive or have attentional problems [Conners, 1985; Douglas and Peters, 1979; Gordon, 1986; Klee and Garfinkel, 1983]. Among attentional tasks, the CPT has the most well-established norms [Conners, 1986] and represents a single operational definition of attentional problems [Klee and Garfinkel, 1983; Klorman et al., 1984]. During CPT the child is instructed to press either a button or a space bar if a specific sequence of numbers or letters appears on the monitor when it has been preceded by a previously specified sequence of numbers or letters. Errors are either of omission (poor focus or sustained focus on stimulus) or of commission (response to the wrong stimulus because of a presumed poor inhibition of impulse). Vigilance decrements occur in children without attentional dysfunctions, but the CPT has consistently differentiated children with significant attentional problems from controls. Variable parameters include total number of stimuli presented, test duration, stimulus duration, and interstimulus interval (ISI) [Conners, 1986]. Although no uniformly standard version of the CPT exists, a number of versions of the CPT are readily available to the researcher.

The *go–no-go* paradigm [Trommer et al., 1988] has demonstrated promising results as a measure of inattention and impulsivity. The child is asked to respond to five "go" signals (one tap), five "no-go" signals (two taps), and a trial identical to the first is repeated. The stimulus is presented at 25-second intervals. The subject moves the index finger in response to a "go" signal, while he makes no response to a "no-go" signal. A visual or auditory stimulus can be used. The child should use his dominant hand for signaling. In the Trommer et al. study, the investigators evaluated the paradigm as a diagnostic procedure and did not evaluate performance under stimulant medication conditions. Children who had attentional deficits without hyperactivity made the most errors of omission and commission initially, but also showed the greatest improvement over time. Children with hyperactivity made less progress when compared to the nonhyperactive attention deficit disordered children and to a control group.

Reaction time tasks have been used as measures of attention [Douglas and Peters, 1979]. The *delayed reaction time task* (DRTT) has been specifically used to study the sustained attention and poor inhibitory control of ADHD children and non-ADHD children [Cohen et al., 1971; Douglas and Parry, 1983; Douglas, 1985]. The DRTT consists of a warning signal, an interval, a reaction signal, and a response. The child receives the warning signal, a delay period follows, and then a reaction signal. The child is expected to make some response to the reaction signal. In the Douglas test, for example, the child is depressing a key during the delay period and then is expected to release the key in response to the reaction signal. Thus the child is asked to establish readiness when the warning signal is introduced, maintain readiness over time, delay (inhibit) response over time, and inhibit responses to inappropriate stimuli as well. Using the DRTT, differences between ADHD and non-ADHD children have been demonstrated relating to specificity of warning signal and response to noncontingent partial reward.

Choice reaction time tasks (CRTT) are modified versions of the DRTT [Sargeant and Scholten, 1983]. The subject is first presented with the target, then instructed to make the quickest response possible. The task then begins with the presentation of stimuli followed by a warning signal (usually a loud tone). Following a 2000 msec delay period, an imperative signal is given. The child is asked to respond "yes" or "no" by a pair of microswitches, and to not respond if the answer is neither yes nor no (catch). A recorder links into a computer for calculations of response latency and response scoring. The load of the target stimuli is increased (e.g., from two-digit sequence to three-digit sequence), and in the Sergeant and Scholten task the child undergoes 96 trials that include 40 "yes" responses, 40 "no" responses, and 16 catch responses. Memory load and display load are the independent variables; dependent variables include reaction time and error rate. The test significantly differentiated ADHD children from non-ADHD children.

Matching-to-sample (MTS) tasks are especially helpful for defining inhibitory control [Kagan et al., 1966]. The child is shown a target and then asked to identify matching figures that are presented either clustered together or on a computer screen. The child is able to review the target. Some investigators record the "time-to-first-response" [Swanson, 1985]. Investigations of this method have yielded conflicting results, especially with regard to what dependent variables change when ADHD children take stimulant medication. One study recorded eye movements of ADHD children with an MTS task, and found that stimulant medication increased the number of comparisons between the target picture and the response to a series of pictures (perceptual search vs. inhibition vs. both) [Flintoff et al., 1982]. Another study used a stimulus window and demonstrated that inspection ratio (number of times each stimulus window is opened) varies according to what dosage of stimulant medication is used [Sprague, 1984]. In addition to measuring focus, inhibition, sustained attention, and search, this task can measure selective attention. The problem is being able to select which component is causing the child's failure. This cannot be improved with the use of the current quantitative system, which counts the number of omissions and commissions [Rapoport et al., 1974]. During this task some children with major attentional dysfunction become perseverative and begin circling every figure.

Paired associate learning (PAL) tasks have proven useful for discriminating children with attentional problems from normal children. This is a novel "learning" task that requires executive operations. The child is typically presented with pairs of words, of letters, or a pairing of a particular symbol with a word. For example, the child listens while a list of word pairs is presented. Next the stimulus word is presented and the child attempts to respond with the word that had originally been paired with it. Numbers of lists and lengths of lists vary in different versions of the test [Douglas et al., 1986; Stephens et al., 1984]. Some investigators continue the task until the child's recall of pairs is perfect. Douglas varied the number of word pairs depending upon how well the child did with the first fifteen word pairs.

If the child can apply a metamemory strategy like a mnemonic, he will excell on a PAL test. Results of investigations of ADHD children with and without stimulant medication on this test have varied, although they *at the least* support that stimulants are indirectly responsible for improved performance [Stephens et al., 1984; Swanson and Kinsbourne, 1979]. Swanson et al. [1983] hypothesized that the PAL may be sensitive to whether or not a child is experiencing a decrease in learning because of stimulant overdosage. Several versions of the PAL are available in both computerized and noncomputerized forms [Swanson, 1985]. This test is quite useful for the older child, but because it demands the use of executive operations, it is of little use for a child under 8 years of age.

Many other cognitive tasks have been used to determine both sustained attention and inhibition, and investigators have reported that ADHD children treated with stimulant medication demonstrated improved performance on these measures: Wisconsin Card Sorting Task, Porteous Mazes, analogue classroom tasks, Embedded Figures Test, Field Dependence. The clinician and researcher should beware of tests that have not consistently demonstrated a major differential between the ADHD children and non-ADHD children. Those tests are digit span, coding, and information sub-tests of the WISC-R, the Stroop Color-Word Test, and the Santostefano-Paley Color Distraction Test.

None of these instruments used alone is diagnostic. The misuse of these tests will only increase misdiagnosis and incomplete diagnosis, failure to identify accompanying learning disabilities, and other psychopathology. Every one of these tasks involves central processes other than attention (visual and auditory input, sequential input and output, and memory), which also impact on the child's performance. Taylor [1986] argued that the failure of ADHD children to do well on the CPT may be due to something other than lack of sustained attention and that these measures do not define the child's deficit at all. This approach is misleading also. Their utilization by competent professionals in an interdisciplinary team setting will only strengthen diagnosis and habilitative recommendations.

NEUROPSYCHOLOGICAL MEASURES

The neuropsychological assessment of children is a complex procedure that demands the inclusion of more factors than traditional neuropsychology. As outlined by Fletcher and Taylor [1984], basic assumptions about neuropsychological functioning that are derived from research and clinical work with adults should not be blindly generalized to child-patient populations. Children are developing organisms, and brain dysfunction/damage can have differing effects, depending on when it occurs in the developmental process. "Developmental neuropsychology" then accounts for the time of the childhood lesion, sequence and rate of development, and the transition from one stage of development to another. The age at which time the damage occurred and the severity and extent of the damage is as critical to the developmental neuropsychologist as lateralization and localization of the lesion. Findings in research studies of brain-damaged children support the concept of accounting for the time at which the damage occurred and the intensity of damage. Aram et al. [1985] showed that children who experienced unilateral damage to either hemisphere early in development had generalized depression of verbal and nonverbal intellectual scores. These authors also discovered that both right- and left-hemisphere damage sustained during early childhood depressed language functions. The pattern of language deficit was somewhat different for left-hemisphere damaged children as opposed to those who suffered right-hemisphere lesions. Both groups (i.e., left-hemisphere lesions and right-hemisphere lesions) had low word fluency abilities. In addition, the left-hemisphere damage group showed syntactic production deficits, and the right-hemisphere damage group showed deficits in lexical comprehension. Snow and Desch [in press] found that children with early onset conditions (e.g., congenital anomalies and generalized developmental delays) tended to have more dysfunctional cognitive patterns than children at risk for later onset disorders (e.g., s/p central nervous system infections and s/p head trauma). The results of these and other investigations emphasize the importance of a pediatric neuropsychological analysis that integrates developmental concepts.

A developmental neuropsychological assessment with ADHD children can shed light on the cognitive profile of the child. If not carefully handled, though, even an experienced child psychologist can also make mistaken conclusions. Given the pattern of poor inhibition (i.e., impulsivity) and poor focus, the neuropsychologist must determine whether the results of specific tests are attributable to true dysfunction or are the consequence of poor attentional processes and/or neural control. Take for example the fingertip number writing task from the Halstead-Reitan Neuropsychological Battery for Children [Reitan, 1969], a commonly used neuropsychological battery. The administration of this subtest involves having the child identify numbers written on their finger tips. The task is obviously sensitive to tactile skills, but also requires some degree of sustained focus. Therefore, if an ADHD child performs poorly on this task, is it because of difficulties with integration of tactile information, difficulty sustaining attention, or a combination of both? The ultimate decision as to the underlying etiology of the dysfunction has important diagnostic and habilitation implications.

Given the complexity of completing neuropsychological assessments with the ADHD child, there are several factors that are critical to a useful evaluation. First, the neuropsychological assessment should be a component of a more comprehensive evaluation procedure. It is risky at best to view neuropsychological findings in the absence of other important information. More enlightened decisions concerning neuropsychological functioning are inevitably gleaned when the patterns found are viewed in relation to and integrated with medical factors, social/emotional status, educational history/psychoeducational functioning, and speech/language skills. The neuropsychologist is most effective as a member of an interdisciplinary team. The importance of observing the child during the testing situation cannot be stressed enough. Such qualitative observations (i.e., not so much merely focusing on whether or not the child makes an error, but analyzing how the child commits the error) are just as important as the quantitative test score patterns yielded by the evaluation. The final consideration always involves accounting for developmental factors. This includes, but is not limited to, interpreting the results in relation to age and developmental status of the child, developmental history, medical history, familial history, and overall intelligence of the child.

Neuropsychological Testing Procedures

At this point, we would like to provide a brief overview of neuropsychological assessment procedures used with children. This review is by no means comprehensive and readers who wish to further investigate should consult Nussbaum and Bigler [1989], Golden [1989], Telzrow [1989], and Teeter [1986] for more indepth discussions of various techniques.

Probably the most widely used procedures are the Halstead-Reitan Neuropsychological Test Battery for Children and the Reitan-Indiana Neuropsychological Test Battery [Reitan, 1969]. Both of these batteries contain subtests sensitive to sensory-perceptual abilities as well as motor skills (see Tables 4 and 5). In addition, there are tests within the batteries that provide indices of abstraction abilities and skill at shifting response mode. A major criticism of these batteries centers around the notion that each merely represents a downward extension of the original adult version, with little consideration for developmental factors. Another weakness of these assessment procedures is their limited assessment of memory abilities.

Another battery designed for children is the Luria-Nebraska Neuropsychological Battery-Children's Revision [Golden, 1986]. This assessment procedure consists of eleven primary scales and yields a number of different types of scores (Table 6). The subtests do tap a number of different skills and the test does appear useful for discriminating normal from brain-damaged children [e.g., see Wilkening et al., 1981]. Other research has indicated rather limited clinical utility with learning disabled populations [Snow et al., 1984]. This is particularly important in relation to ADHD children since so many have associated learning disabilities.

There are several other measures that can provide important neuropsychological information. Tests used in a traditional psychoeducational evaluation (such as intellectual measures, academic achievement tests, and tests of visual-motor integration) are usually an integral part of a comprehensive developmental neuropsychological evaluation. Measures that focus on the assessment of memory, such as the Benton Visual Retention Test [Benton, 1974] or the Selective Reminding Task [Bushke and Fuld, 1974] supplement

Table 4 Subtests from the Halstead-Reitan
Neuropsychological Test Battery for Children

Subtest	Skill Assessed
Category test	Concept formation
Tactile performance test	Kinesthetic/spatial
Finger tapping	Motor speed
Speech-sound perception	Auditory Discrimination
Seashore rhythm	Auditory Discrimination
Trail-making test	Visual Scanning/sequencing
Grip strength	Hand strength
Sensory perceptual exams	Basic sensory Functions
Tactile form recognition	Tactile integration
Tactile finger localization	Finger agnosia
Finger-tip number writing	Tactile integration
Aphasia screening	Basic language Functions

Table 5 Subtests of the Reitan-Indiana
Neuropsychological Test Battery

Subtest	Skill Assessed
Category test	Concept formation
Tactual performance test	Kinesthetic/spatial
Grip strength	Hand strength
Finger tapping	Motor speed
Finger symbol writing	Tactile integration
Tactile finger localization	Finger Agnosia
Tactile form recognition	Tactile integration
Sensory perceptual exams	Basic sensory Functions
Matching test	Motor coordination
Color form test	Visual sequencing
Progressive figures test	Visual sequencing
Matching pictures test	Visual Discrimination and categorization
Target test	Visual sequencing and memory
Individual performance tests	Visual discrimination and motor skills

Table 6 Subtests from the Luria-Nebraska
Neuropsychological Battery-Children's Revision

Subtest	Skill Assessed
Motor skills	Motor speed/coordination and constructional abilities
Rhythm	Auditory perceptual
Tactile	Tactile integration
Visual	Visual discrimination and integration
Receptive speech	Auditory discrimination and integration
Expressive speech	Expressive output
Writing	Basic copying and spelling
Reading	Letter and word identification
Arithmetic	Number concepts and calculation
Memory	Auditory and visual memory
Intellectual processes	Basic cognitive abilities

most traditional batteries and provide information that is particularly useful in relation to the ADHD child. The Wisconsin Card Sorting Test [Heaton, 1981] provides a measure of abstraction abilities and is sensitive to perseverance of responses. In general, the neuropsychologist needs to dictate the assessment and determine what measures are needed and most appropriate. It is not enough to merely administer the same standard battery to all ADHD children, but there should be flexibility and clinical judgment employed during the assessment procedure. This type of approach toward neuropsychological evaluations will provide information of more value to the child, parents, and professionals who work with the child. Nevertheless, current neuropsychological measures generally add little to the more traditional psychoeducational assessment of ADHD children. Its use should be reserved for cases involving associated psychological processing problems that remain unclear after traditional testing has been completed.

FUTURE HORIZONS: RESEARCH MEASURES

Technological instrumentation does not yet play a role in the ADHD patient's clinical evaluation. However, clinical research has demonstrated that several technologies may be useful diagnostic methods of clinical examination in the future.

Regional cerebral blood flow (rCBF) studies could be a way of defining the neuroanatomical locus of an ADHD child's deficit. One study compared the differences in rCBF following xenon 133 inhalation between groups of academically normal siblings, ADHD siblings, and verbal dyspraxic siblings [Lou et al., 1984]. ADHD children were tested both with and without administration of methylphenidate (MPH). A reaction time task was used on the ADHD group during rCBF measurement. The 11 children with ADHD showed an extreme variability of reaction time latency. In all 11 ADHD children hypoperfusion was seen centrally over the frontal lobes, and 7 of the ADHD group also had hypoperfusion of the caudate nuclei area. After MPH administration (6 ADHD patients), all ADHD-MPH patients showed increased flow in the central regions.

One wonders what areas of the normal child's brain become hyperperfused during a reaction time task. It might be that a low metabolic activity of attentional areas is a corollary of abnormal working of the brain in ADHD children but is not the actual cause. Again, as with all methods, a standardization would have to be developed that would account for the differences that are seen in the cognitive processing of the child at different developmental ages and stages. In this study the number of controls was too small, and the study lumped all ages together. Further studies using this technology may elucidate the neural structures that account for attentional processing in children and may be one way of recognizing neural changes that occur as the child develops selective attention and the ability to modulate attention to meet task demands. Exposure to radioactive xenon is another limiting factor.

Studies of event-related potentials (ERP) in the areas of attention and cognition are frequently found in the neuroscience literature. Progress has been hampered by an imprecise understanding of the functional significance and neurological substates of ERPs by those clinicians researching them [Kurtzberg et al., 1984]. The studies with regard to children present even more hurdles. Since neither the neural substrates of ERPs nor their psychological correlates have been well defined for adults, defining ERPs in the maturing brain presents a problem of defining developmental substrates without a foundation of known anatomical, chemical, or physiological ERP substrates [Otto et al., 1984].

Klorman has undertaken studies that record the ERPs of normal children and children with attentional aberrations [Klorman et al., 1984]. His standardization group is homogenous, and he has aimed at very specific diagnoses for the group under investigation. He advocates developing more stringent ERP standards that would yield fewer false positives and negatives than reliance and base rates would normally allow. Hyperactive children display improved CPT performance as well as a significant increase in the amplitude of the late positive component (LPC) of their evoked responses after the administration of precise doses of stimulant drugs. It was only during the most difficult form of the CPT (when the memory load was greatest) that LPC amplitude was significantly greater for the stimulant group than it was for the placebo group. In a similar study the same investigators administered both the CPT, and the PAL to 22 normal male undergraduates during double blind placebo and MPH states [Strauss et al., 1984]. Under placebo conditions accuracy and speed decreased over the course of the CPT. In the MPH state the decrease in performance was significantly reduced. Under placebo conditions the late positive wave, P464, showed significantly decreased amplitude and increased latency; whereas in the MPH state P464 amplitudes decreased less and latencies increased less. The PAL performance showed significant improvement per trial block, but data for placebo and MPH sessions were nearly the same. Careful not to over-generalize, this group of investigators concluded that at the present time late ERP components lack the specificity that is necessary for the clinician to obtain significant diagnostic information from their use.

Neurochemistry is another potential diagnostic test of the future. There is a very large body of research in this area. The results overall have been disappointing, and lab testing as a viable clinical measure of ADHD remains years away.

The early use of neurophysiologic and neuroradiographic methods for the neural assessment of mildly handicapping central nervous system conditions appears promising. Potentially this area contains the key to unlock the door to man's true understanding of these disorders. Without a definitive neuroanatomical and neurophysiological definition, ADHD remains a medical mystery.

INTERDISCIPLINARY TEAM: THE GOLD STANDARD

Minor neurodevelopmental disorders were recognized a quarter century ago, and a disorder focusing on attention deficits was defined a decade ago by the American Psychiatric Association. The neurocognitive complexity of the disorder and the ecological factors working on the patient make a definition made up of behavioral questions an inadequate measure of this (these) disorder(s). To make accurate decisions and avoid duplication of care, communication between developmental and behavioral professionals is imperative for any child who has significant school, social, or behavioral problems. The interdisciplinary team is the ideal method of professional interchange. Whatever the forum, it is necessary for all professionals to obtain an ecological perspective of the child's behaviors through quantitative questionnaires. In most cases it will be possible to couple this with the team assessment to determine whether or not the patient has ADHD. The interdisciplinary forum works through a problem-solving process covering cognitive, communicative, motor, medical, psychosocial, and behavioral areas of patient function. Through this process team deductions will comprehensively address the individual's problems and habilitative needs, and most associated diagnoses or problems will be established. The team interplay often clarifies parts that may be unclear because questions for each assessment are framed within the perspective of the particular discipline (i.e., doctor must focus interview toward medical diagnosis; whereas, family therapist's questions may focus on interactions of patient within the family and at school). If a "team meeting" is not possible, a conference call is a second option.

Which professionals should be included in a core evaluation of a child who presents with chief complaints of inattention or hyperactivity? Figure 3 depicts the developmental pediatric scheme that includes both a core group of professionals and also a secondary group the composition of which depends on the suspected associated dysfunctions of the patient. "Other therapists" refers to pediatric occupational therapists and physical therapists, recreational therapists, and adaptive physical educators in specific cases. Whenever possible the child's school personnel should be present for the clinical staffing conference. This will facilitate the integration of team diagnoses and recommendations into the child's school curriculum.

There is no easy formula, nor definitive use of tests that will assure an accurate diagnosis and effective team prescription [Blondis, 1991]. A component team that understands how to use available measures will make informed and correct decisions, diagnoses, and recommendations.

CONCLUSIONS

This chapter has reviewed several of the measures used in the assessment of the pediatric patient who presents to the clinic with inattention and/or hyperactivity. Psychoeducational measures, medical examination, and family therapy measures are discussed in other chapters. The developmental principles and test evaluation principles discussed in this chapter should be applied to any instrument that is used by a professional. Qualitative notations that reflect test behavior should be a major part of the evaluation measure whenever possible. Quantitative questionnaires are a mainstay of the evaluation of children with school problems. The professional must always match the level of difficulty of the questionnaires used to the reading and comprehension level of the caregiver. Halo effects can be analyzed by comparing results of the parent, teacher, and self questionnaires. The self questionnaire is useful in that the middle school and adolescent patient must reflect upon his or her behavior and will have a much clearer idea of what the clinical assessment represents and will be better prepared for counseling. In trying to help each patient to become goal-directed, the self questionnaire may stimulate this process by requiring self-reflection. Because of the broad range of psychopathology associated with ADHD child [Accardo et

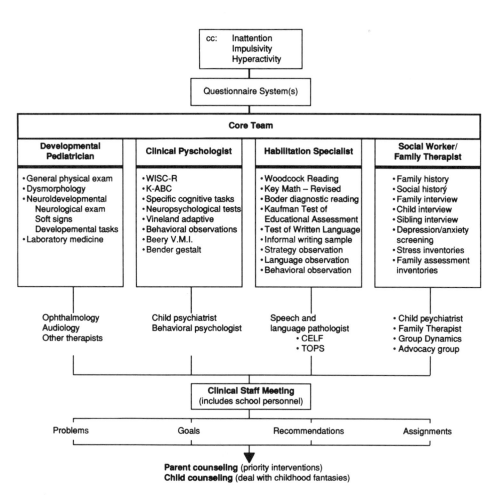

Figure 3 Developmental pediatric interdisciplinary process. The core team develops close communication and is able to avoid duplication of specific testing, but at the same time makes qualitative notations of the child's thought processes and behavior at different times. The figure shows which member of the team is responsible for evaluating the need for particular specialty involvement beyond the scope of the core team expertise.

al., 1990], it is important to include questionnaires that cover a wide range of behaviors.

The Child Behavioral Profile is a well-standardized questionnaire series that includes a broad range of behavioral questions. The parent, teacher, and self questionnaires were designed in such a way that responses to the same questions can be compared on all three scales. This facilitates the use of the aggregation principle as well as an analysis of halo effects. The questionnaires are not difficult to answer, requiring a fourth-grade reading level. These questionnaires stand up to scrutiny across parameters of analysis and, therefore, can be endorsed when used by qualified developmental professionals. However, other questionnaires should be considered depending on geographic region, parent education, focus of the case, and other factors. The Carey Temperament Questionnaires are particularly useful for preschool children who are having problems with social and emotional growth and development. Some direct observation procedures are well standardized and offer more specific behavioral data than one can obtain from the use of questionnaires. The utility of direct behavioral observation measures remains a problem.

Other measures covered within the context of this chapter are optional but can be useful if administered and interpreted by well-qualified clinicians. It is not good practice to have a psychology intern administer and evaluate a child's performance on a specific cognitive task or a neuropsychological battery. In general, the level of complexity of the case will determine the intensity of evaluation. Complexity and severity are not to be confused, sometimes the most complex child is the child with a mild disorder.

REFERENCES

Abikoff, H., Gittelman, R. (1985). Classroom observation code: a modification of the Stony Brook code. *Psychopharmacol. Bull. 21*:901.

Abikoff, H., Gittelman-Klein, R., Klein, D. (1980). Classroom observation code for hyperactive children: a replication of validity. *J. Consult. Clin. Psychol., 48*:555.

Abravanel, E. (1968). The development of intersensory patterning with regard to selected spatial dimensions. *Monogr. Soc. Res. Child Dev. 33*:527.

Accardo, P. J., Blondis, T. A., Whitman, B. (1990). Disorders of attention and activity in a referral population. *Pediatrics. 85*:426.

Accardo, P. J. (1980). *A Neurodevelopmental Perspective on Specific Learning Disabilities.* Baltimore: University Park Press.

Achenbach, T. M., Conners, C. K., Quay, H. C., Verhylst, F. C., Howell, C. T. (1989). Replication of empirically derived syndromes as a basis for taxonomy of child/adolescent psychopathology. *J. Abnorm. Child Psychol., 17*:299.

Achenbach, T. M., Edelbrock, C. S. (1983). *Manual for the Child Behavior Checklist and Revised Child Behavior Profile.* Burlington, VT: University of Vermont Department of Psychiatry.

Achenbach, T. M., Edelbrock, C. S. (1979). The Child Behavior Profile II. boys aged 12-16, girls aged 6-11 and 12-16. *J. Consult. Clin. Psychol. 47*:223.

American Psychiatric Association (1987). *Diagnostic and Statistical Manual.* 3rd Ed. Revised. Washington, D.C.: American Psychiatric Association, p. 50.

Aram, D. M., Ekelman, B. L., Rose, D. F., Whitaker, H. A. (1985). Verbal and cognitive sequelae following unilateral lesions acquired in early childhood. *J. Clin. Exp. Neuropsychol., 7*:55.

Barkley, R. A., Fischer, M., Newby, R. F., Breen, M. J. (1988). Development of a multimethod clinical protocol for assessing stimulant drug response in children with attention deficit disorder. *J. Clin. Child Psychol., 17*:14.

Barkley, R. A. (1988). Child behavior rating scales and checklists. In: *Assessment and Diagnosis in Child Psychopathology.* Rutter, M., Tuma, A. H., Lann, I. S., eds. New York: The Guilford Press, pp. 113-155.

Benton, A. L. (1974). *Revised Visual Retention Test.* 4th Ed., New York, The Psychological Corporation.

Blondis, T. A. (1991). Attention deficit hyperactivity disorder. In: *Developmental Disabilities in Infancy and Childhood.* Capute, A. J., Accardo, P. J., eds. Baltimore. Paul H. Brookes Publishing.

Blondis, T. A., Accardo, P. J., Snow, J. H. (1989a). Measures of attention deficit, Part I: Questionnaires. *Clin. Pediatr. 28*:222.

Blondis, T. A., Accardo, P. J., Snow, J. H. (1989b). Measures of attention deficit, Part II: Clinical perspectives and test interpretation, *Clin. Pediatr., 28*:268.

Brown, L. L., Hammill, D. C. (1981). The reliability of four measures of children's behavior with deviant populations. *Behav. Dis., 6*:180.

Brown, L. L., Hammill, D. D. (1986). *Behavior Rating Profile.* Austin, TX: Pro-Ed.

Buschke, H., Fuld, P. A. (1974). Evaluating storage, retention, and retrieval in disordered memory and learning. *Neurology 24*:1019.

Cantwell, D. P. (1985). Hyperactive children have grown up. *Arch. Gen. Psychi. 42*: 1026.

Carey, W. B. (1982). Validity of parental assessments of development and behavior. *Am. J. Dis. Child., 136*:97.

Cohen, N. J., Douglas, V. I., Morgenstern, G. (1971). The effect of methylphenidate on attentive behavior and autonomic activity in hyperactive children. *Psychopharmacol. Bull., 22*:282.

Conners, C. K. (1973). Rating scales for use in drug studies with children. *Psychopharmacol. Bull., Special Issue*:24.

Conners, C. K. (1985a). Issues in the study of adolescent ADD-H. *Psychopharmacol. Bull., 21*:243.

Conners, C. K. (1985b). The computerized continuous performance test. *Psychopharmacol. Bull., 21*:891.

Conners, C. K., Barkley, R. A. (1985). Rating scales and checklists for child psychopharmacology. *Psychopharmacol. Bull., 21*:809.

Cunningham, C. E. & Barkley, R. A. (1979). A comparison of the interaction of hyperactive & normal children with their mothers in tree play and structured tasks. *Child Dev. 50*:217.

Douglas, V. I. (1985). The response of ADD-H children to reinforcement: theoretical and clinical implications. In: *Attention Deficit Disorder.* Bloomingdale, L. M., ed., New York: Spectrum Publications.

Douglas, V. I. (1972). Stop, look, listen: the problem of sustained attention and impulse control in hyperactive and normal children. *Can. J. Behav. Sci., 4:*259.

Douglas, V. I., Parry, P. A. (1983). Effects of reward on delayed reaction time task performance of hyperactive children. *J. Abnorm. Child Psychol. 11:*313.

Douglas, V. I., Peters, K. G. (1980). Toward a clearer definition of the attentional deficit of hyperactive children. In: *Attention and Cognitive Development.* Hale, G. H., Lewis, M., eds. New York: Plenum Press, p. 173.

Edelbrock, C., Costello, A. J., Dulcan, M. K., Conover, N. C., Kala, R. (1986). Parent-child agreement on child psychiatric symptoms assessed via structured interview. *J. Child Psychol. Psychi., 27:*181.

Edelbrock, C., Greenbaum, R., Conover, N. C. (1984). Reliability and concurrent relations between the teacher version of the Child Behavior Profile and the Conners Revised Teacher Rating Scale. *J. Abnorm. Child Psychol., 13:*295.

Edelbrock, C., Achenbach, T. M. (1984). The teacher version of the Child Behavioral Profile: I, boys aged 6-11 and 12-16. *J. Consult. Clin. Psychol., 47:*223.

Flavell, J. H. (1963). *The Developmental Psychology of Jean Piaget.* New York: Van Nostrand, p. 152.

Fletcher, J. M., Taylor, H. G. (1984). Neuropsychological approaches to children: towards a developmental neuropsychology. *J. Clin. Neuropsychol., 6:*39.

Flintoff, N. M., Barron, R. W., Swanson, J. M. (1982). Methylphenidate increases selectivity of visual scanning in children referred for hyperactivity. *J. Abnorm. Child Psychol., 10:*145.

Freeman, B. J. (1985). Review of the Child Behavior Checklist. *The Ninth Mental Measurement Yearbook.* Mitchell, J. V., ed. Lincoln: University of Nebraska Press.

Gilberg, I. C., Gilberg, C., Groth, J. (1989). Children with preschool minor neuro-developmental disorders, V: neurodevelopmental profiles at age 13. *Dev. Med. Child Neurol., 31:*14.

Golden, C. J. (1989). The Nebraska Neuropsychological Children's Battery. In: *Handbook of Clinical Child Neuropsychology.* Reynolds, C. R., Fletcher-Janzen, E., eds. New York: Plenum Press.

Golden, C. J. (1986). *Manual for the Luria-Nebraska Neuropsychological Battery: Children's Revision.* Los Angeles: W. P. S.

Gordon, M. (1986). Microprocessor-based assessment of attention deficit disorders (ADD). *Psychopharmacol. Bull., 22:*288.

Goyette, C. H., Conners, C. K., Ulrich, R. F. (1978). Normative data on the revised Conners Parent and Teacher Rating Scales. *J. Abnorm. Child Psychol., 6:*221.

Haake, R. J., Somerville, S. C. (1985). Development of logical search skills in infancy. *Dev. Psychol. 21:*176.

Hagen, J. W., Hale, G. H. (1973). The development of attention in children. *Child Psychol., Vol. 7.* Minneapolis: University of Minnesota Press, p. 117.

Hamlet, K. W., Pellegrini, D. S., Conners, C. K. (1987). An investigation of executive processes in the problem-solving of attention deficit disorder-hyperactive children. *J. Pediatric Psychol., 12:*227.

Hammill, D. D., Bartel, N. R. (1986). *Teaching Students with Learning and Behavioral Problems.* Boston: Allyn and Bacon, p. 234.

Haynes, S. N., Wilson, C. C. (1979). *Behavioral Assessment: Recent Advances in Methods, Concepts, and Applications.* Jossey-Buss.

Haynes, S. N. (1978). *Principles of Behavioral Assessment.* New York: Gardner Press.

Heaton, R. K. (1981). *Wisconsin Card Sorting Test.* Odessa, FL: Psychological Assessment Resources.

Hegvik, R. L., McDevitt, S. C., Carey, W. B. (1982). The Middle Childhood Temperament Questionnaire. *J. Dev. Behav. Pediatrics, 3*:197.

Kagan, J., Pearson, L., Welch, L. (1966). Modifiability of impulsive tempo. *Educ. Psychol., 57*:359.

Klee, S. H., Garfinkel, B. D. (1983). The computerized continuous performance task: A new measure of inattention. *J. Abnorm. Child Psychol., 11*:487.

Klorman, R., Bauer, I. O., Coons, H. W., Lewis, J. L., Peloquin, L. J., Perlmutter, R. A., Ryan, R. M., Salzman, L. F., Strauss, J. (1984). Enhancing effects of methylphenidate on normal young adults' cognitive processes. *Psychopharmacol. Bull., 20*:3.

Kurtzberg, D., Vaughan, H. G., Courchesne, E., Friedman, D., Harter, M. R., Putnam, L. E. (1984). Developmental aspects of event-related potentials. *Ann. N.Y. Acad. Sci., 425*:300.

Lahey, B. B., Pelham, W. E., Schaughensy, E. A., Atkins, M. S., Murphy, H. A., Hynd, G., Russo, M., Hartdagen, S., Lorys-Vernon, A. (1988). Dimensions and types of attention deficit disorder. *J. Am. Acad. Child Adolesc. Psychi., 27*:330.

Levy, F. (1980). The development of sustained attention (vigilance) and inhibition in children: some normative data. *J. Child Psychol. Psychi., 21*:77.

Lou, H. C., Henriksen, L., Bruhn, P. (1984). Focal cerebral hypoperfusion in children with dysphasia and/or attention deficit disorder. *Arch. Neurol., 41*:825.

Luria, A. R. (1959). Experimental study of the higher nervous activity of the abnormal child. *J. Mental Defic. Res., 3*:1.

Martin, R. P., Hooper, S. R., Snow, J. H. (1986). Behavior rating scale approaches to personality assessment in children and adolescents. In: *The Psychological Assessment of Child And Adolescent Personality.* Knoff, H. M., ed. New York: Guilford Press.

Mash, E. J., Terdal, L. G., Anderson, K. (1973). The response class matrix: A procedure for coding parent-child interactions. *J. Consult. Clin. Psychol., 40*:163.

McBride, M. C. (1988). An individual double-blind crossover trial for assessing methylphenidate response in children with attention deficit disorder. *J. Pediatrics 113*:137.

Milich, R., Loney, J. Landau, S. (1980). Independent dimensions of hyperactivity and aggression: A validation with playroom observation data. *J. Abnorm. Psychol., 91*:183.

Milich, R., Loney, J., Whitten, P. (1983, August). Two-year stability and validity of playroom observation of hyperactivity. Paper presented at the annual meeting of the American Psychological Association, Anaheim, CA.

Myklebust, H. R. (1981). *The Pupil Rating Scale Revised.* San Antonio, TX: The Psychological Corporation.

Neeper, R., Lahey, B. B. (1986). The Children's Behavior Rating Scale: a factor analytic development study. *School Psychol. Rev., 15*:277.

Nussbaum, N. L., Bigler, E. D. (1989). Halstead-Reitan neuropsychological test batteries for children. In: *Handbook of Clinical Child Neuropsychology.* Reynolds, C. R., Fletcher-Janzen, E., eds., New York: Plenum Press.

Olson, G. M. (1976). An information-processing analysis of visual memory and habituation in infants. In: *Habituation: Perspectives from Child Development. Animal Behavior, and Neurophysiology.* Tighe, R. J., Leaton, R. N., eds., Hillsdale, N.J.: Lawrence Erlbaum.

Otto, D., Karrar, R., Halliday, R., Horst, R. L., Klorman, R., Squires, N., Thatcher, R. W., Fenelon, B., Lelord, G. (1984). Developmental aspects of event-related postentials aberrant development. *Ann. N.Y. Acad. Sci., 425*:319.

Posner, M. I., Rothbart, M. K. (1981). The development of attentional mechanisms. *Nebraska Symposium on Motivation Cognitive Processes,* Vol. 28. Howe, H. E., ed., University of Nebraska Press, Lincoln/London.

Prendergast, M., Taylor, E., Rapoport, J. L., Bartko, J., Donnelly, M., Zametkin, A., Ahearn, M. B., Dunn, G., Wieselberg, H. M. (1988). The diagnosis of childhood hyperactivity. A U.S.-U.K. crossnational study of DSM-III and ICD-9. *J. Child Psychol. Psychi. 29*:289.

Quay, H. C. (1983). A dimensional approach to behavior disorder: the Revised Behavior Problem Checklist. *School Psychol., 12*:244.

Rapoport, J. L., Quinn, P. O., Bradbard, G., Riddle, K. D., Brooks, E. (1974). Imipramine and methylphenidate treatments of hyperactive boys. *Arch. Gen. Psychi., 30*:789.

Reed, M. L., and Edelbrock, C. (1983). Reliability and validity of the Direct Observation Form of the Child Behavior Checklist. *J. Abn. Child Psychol., 11*:521.

Reitan, R. M. (1969). *Manual for Administration of Neuropsychological Test Batteries for Adults and Children.* Indianapolis, IN.

Rosvold, H. E., Mirsky, A. F., Saranson, I., (1956). A continuous performance test of brain damage. *J. Consult. Clin. Psychol., 20*:343.

Sergeant, J. A., Scholten, C. A. (1983). A stages-of-information approach to hyperactivity. *J. Child Psychol. Psychi., 24*:49.

Shaywitz, S. E., Schnell, C., Shaywitz, B. A., Towle, V. R. (1986). Yale Children's Inventory (YCI): an instrument to assess children with attentional deficits and learning disabilities 1. scale development and psychometric properties. *J. Abnorm. Child Psychol., 14*:347.

Shaywitz, S. E., Shaywitz, B. A., Schnell, C., Towle, V. R. (1988). Concurrent and predictive validity of the Yale Children's Inventory: an instrument to assess children with attentional deficits and learning disabilities. *Pediatrics, 81*:562.

Shulman, J., Kasper, J., Trone, F. (1965). *Brain Damage and Behavior: A Clinical-Experimental Study.* Springfield, IL: Charles C. Thomas.

Sleator, E. K., Ullmann, R. K. (1981). Can the physician diagnose hyperactivity in the office? *Pediatrics, 67*:13.

Snow, J. H., Desch, L. W. (In press). Subgroups based on medical developmental, and growth variables using a sample of children and adolescents referred for learning difficulties. *Int. J. Clin. Neuropsychol.*

Snow, J. H., Hynd, G. W., Hartlage, L. W. (1984). Differences between mildly and more severely learning disabled children on the Luria-Nebraska Neuropsychological Battery-Children's Revision. *J. Psychol. Assess.* 2:23.

Sprague, R. L. (1984). Preliminary report of cross-cultural study and cognitive strategies of ADD children. *Attention Deficit Disorder. Vol. 1* Bloomingdale, L. M., ed., New York: Spectram Publications, p. 211.

Stephens, R. S., Pelham, W. E., Skinner, R. (1984). State-dependent and main effects of methylphenidate and pemoline on paired-associate learning and spelling in hyperactive children. *J. Consult. Clin. Psychol., 52*:104.

Strauss, A. A., Werner, H. (1942). Disorders of conceptual thinking in the brain-injured child. *J. Nerv. Ment. Dis., 96*:153.

Strauss, J., Lewis, J. L., Klorman, R., Peloquin, L. J., Perlmutter, R. A., Salzman, L. F. (1984). Effects of methylphenidate on young adults' performance and event-related potentials in vigilance and a paired-associates learning test. *Psychophysiology 21*:609.

Swanson, J. M. (1985). Measures of cognitive functioning appropriate for use in pediatric psychopharmacological research studies. *Psychopharmacol. Bull., 21*:887.

Swanson, J. M., Sandman, C. A., Deutsch, C., Baren, M. (1983). Methylphenidate hydrochloride given with or before breakfast: I. behavioral, cognitive, and electrophysiological effects. *Pediatrics, 72*:49.

Swanson, J. M., Kinsbourne, M. (1979). The cognitive effects of stimulant drugs on hyperactive children. In: *Attention and Cognitive Development* Hale, G. A., Lewis, M., New York: Plenum Press.

Tant, J. L., Douglas, V. I. (1982). Problem solving in hyperactive, normal, and reading disabled boys. *J. Abnorm. Child Psychol., 10*:285.

Taylor, E. A. (1986). Attention deficit. In: *The Overactive Child* Taylor, E. A., ed., London, MacKeith Press, p. 73.

Teeter, P. A. (1986). Standard neuropsychological test batteries for children. In: *Child Neuropsychology: Clinical Practice.* San Diego: Academic Press.

Telzrow, C. F. (1989). Neuropsychological applications of common educational and psychological tests. In: *Handbook of Clinical Child Neuropsychology.* New York: Plenum Press.

Thomas, A., Chess, S. (1977). *Temperament And Development.* New York: Brunner/Mazel Publishers.

Trites, R. L., Blouin, A. G. A., Laprade, K. (1982). Factor analysis of the Conners Teacher Rating Scale based on a large normative sample. *J. Consult. Clin. Psychol., 50*:615.

Trommer, B. L., Hoeppner, J-A. B., Lorber, R., Armstrong, K. J. (1988). The go-no-go paradigm in attention deficit disorder. *Ann. Neurol., 24*:610.

Ullman, R. K., Sleator, E. K., Sprague, R. L. (1985). A new rating scale for the diagnosis and monitoring of ADD children. *Psychopharmacol. Bull., 21*:915.

Weingartner, H., Rapoport, J. L., Buchsbaum, M. S., Bunney, W., Mikkelson, E. J., Caine, D. (1980). Cognitive processes in normal and hyperactive children and their response to amphetamine treatment. *J. Abnorm. Psychol., 89*:25.

Weiss, G., Minde, K., Werry, J. S., Douglas, V. I., Nemeth, E. (1971). Studies on the hyperactive child: a five-year follow-up. *Arch. Gen. Psychi., 24*:409.

Weiss, B., Laties, V. G. (1962). Enhancement of human performance by caffeine and the amphetamines. *Pharmacol. Rev. 14*:1.

Wilkening, G. N., Golden, C. S., MacInnes, W. D., Plaisted, S. R., and Hermen, B. P. (1981). The Luria Nebraska Neuropsychologic Battery Children's Revision: a preliminary report. Paper presented at the annual meeting of the American Psychologic Association, Los Angeles.

Wirt, R. D., Seat, P. D., Broen, W. E., Lachar, D. (1981). *Personality Inventory for Children-Revised*. Los Angeles: Western Psychological Services.

Witt, J. C. (1985). Review of the behavior rating profile. In: *The Ninth Mental Measurement Yearbook*. Mitchell, J. V., ed., Lincoln University of Nebraska Press.

Wright, J. C., Vlietstra, A. G. (1975). The development of selective attention: from perceptual exploration to logical search. In: *Advances In Child Development And Behavior*. Reese, H. W., ed. New York: Academic Press, p. 196.

Zinchenko, V. P., Van Chzhi-tsin, Tarakanov, V. V. (1963). The formation and development of perceptual activity. *Soviet Psychol. Psychiatry, 2*:3.

6

The Physical Examination of the Child with Attention Deficit Hyperactivity Disorder

Pasquale J. Accardo

St. Louis University School of Medicine, St. Louis, Missouri

Thomas A. Blondis and Nancy J. Roizen

University of Chicago Pritzker School of Medicine, Chicago, Illinois

Barbara Y. Whitman

St. Louis University, St. Louis, Missouri

> Watson: *How did you deduce that this man was intellectual?*
>
> Holmes: *It is a question of cubic capacity; a man with so large a brain must have something in it.*
>
> [Doyle "The Adventure of the Blue Carbuncle"]

Many physical correlates of attention deficit hyperactivity disorder (ADHD) and learning disabilities have been reported: (a) physiological markers such as skin conductance, blood pressure, and heart rate responsiveness; (b) electroencephalographic markers such as evoked response technology; and (c) biochemical markers including various attempts to associate peripheral chemical substances with complex and highly localized central nervous system neurotransmitter dysfunction. The level of refinement of such measures and their interpretations are most severely hampered by the lack of specificity of the diagnostic entities to which they are matched. Most of the research literature in the field describes the experimental technology with the utmost refinement of detail, while the subject population remains poorly differentiated clinically.

This chapter focuses on two sets of physical markers useful to the clinician in the office setting—soft neurological signs and minor dysmorphic features. Although their role is still in need of clarification, they have remained active research topics for more than a quarter of a century. Much of this research work has attempted but failed to document a unique diagnostic function. Such an unrealistic goal suggests unfamiliarity with the basic principles of static encephalopathy and dysmorphology.

MINOR NEUROLOGICAL DYSFUNCTION

A soft neurological sign describes a finding that is normal at an earlier age but remains beyond the age at which the child normally develops the motor, sensory, or inhibitory capacity that eliminates or replaces it [Wright, 1982]. The word "soft" is thus somewhat misleading: such signs are undoubtedly more difficult to appreciate and require a developmental framework for the clinician to utilize them in interpreting the child's problems. For this reason Touwen and Prechtl [1970] referred to them as "minor" neurological signs, and Denckla [1985] labeled them "subtle" signs.

The very concept of a neurological sign that changes (usually in the direction of normality) with age, is only sometimes (and variably) present, and is state dependent seems paradoxical if not contradictory. It is as if a child at one examination were to exhibit hypertonicity, increased deep tendon reflexes, upgoing Babinskis, dysarthria, and agitation, but then several hours later presented with floppiness, decreased to absent deep tendon reflexes, downgoing Babinskis, and a more normal speech pattern in a state of calm. These latter findings are not soft neurological signs but rather hard ones; their variability is not atypical but classic for extrapyramidal cerebral palsy. Unlike most neurological disorders, cerebral palsy represents a complex group of syndromes whose diagnosis rests on a functional disability (motor delay) accompanied by an often bewildering array of changing neurological signs [Capute and Accardo, 1991]. The older concept of minimal brain dysfunction interpreted the signs and symptoms of ADHD and various learning disability profiles as reflections of a mild cerebral palsy and recommended the inclusion of tests of minor neurological dysfunction in their assessment [Clemens, 1966]. The modern insistence on trying to reduce this complex clinical picture to a single marker—whether finger tapping, dermatoglyphics, or a behavioral checklist score—ignores several generations of clinical experience and, if applied to a diagnosis such as cerebral palsy, would almost force one to conclude: (a) that there is more than reasonable doubt that cerebral palsy, or at least specific subtypes thereof, exists; (b) that the individual items of the classical neurological examination in isolation and sometimes together contribute little to the diagnosis; and (c) that on the basis of the neurological examination, the implication of brain damage or brain dysfunction as an etiology or correlate of such confusing clinical pictures is unwarranted in the majority of cases.

While some care and consistency need to attend the eliciting of signs of minor neurological dysfunction, much greater attention needs to be given to the spectrum of associated neurodevelopmental disabilities. In an elegant study, Cohen et al. [1967] investigated developmental changes in performance on a standardized battery of soft neurological signs. The study was elegant not because of the research methodology utilized to quantify the overflow movements, but because it attempted to distinguish the contribution of a number of diagnostic variables to the evolving pattern. They demonstrated independent effects for age, IQ, and the presence of motor diagnoses; in addition, these effects were found to be cumulative. Given these complex interactions, the most needed refinements in the study of "soft" neurological signs pertain to the correlated diagnoses.

SOFT NEUROLOGICAL SIGNS

The reliability of soft or subtle neurological signs (SNS) remains controversial, and if a sign is unreliable it would obviously be of little value as a neurological marker during childhood. In general, sensory related signs have proven the most unreliable and have confirmed Touwen and Prechtl's [1970] earlier clinical impressions [Denckla, 1985; Stokman et al., 1986]. Signs associated with motor performance and the inhibition of associated movements have generally been determined to be reliable [Mikkelsen et al., 1982; Rutter et al., 1970; Stokman et al., 1986], although these conclusions have been contested [Vitiello et al., 1989].

Several investigators have demonstrated that SNS represent a viable way of differentiating groups of children with learning delays or attentional deficits from those without any such delays [Snow et al., 1988; Whitmore and Bax, 1986; Wolff et al., 1985]. These signs disappear earlier among girls than boys, but it remains unclear whether this renders them less useful in the assessment of girls with school problems [Shafer et al., 1986; Younes et al., 1983]. Whether SNS differ among races and with regard to lateralization has been poorly studied to date. Signs that depict associated movements of "neurological overflow" may continue on into adulthood among individuals who have experienced no academic difficulty [Blondis et al., 1990; Fog and Fog, 1963]. These same signs have proved to be useful as markers for children with ADHD [Denckla and Rudel, 1978; Fog and Fog, 1963]. It is important for the examiner to measure both the intensity and frequency of associated movements, if one intends to consider them indices of neurological dysfunction [Blondis et al., 1990].

How valid are SNS as markers of ADHD or psychological processing disorders? Reliable SNS may be of considerable use, especially among boys. Shafer et al. [1986] demonstrated that boys from the National Collaborative Perinatal Project who exhibited significant SNS at age 7 continued to manifest SNS in the form of dysdiadochokinesis, mirror movements, dysgraphesthesia, and motor slowness at age 17. In the largest longitudinal study ever undertaken, Hertzig [1982] showed significant decreases in the intensity of SNS in addition to catch-up as the children advanced in age. The overall conclusion at this time would be that SNS findings support ADHD and specific learning disability diagnoses in middle childhood, but their absence in older children does not indicate the absence of such a disorder.

The two SNS batteries with published norms are the *Neurological Examination of Subtle Signs* (NESS) and the *Quick Neurological Screening Test* (QNST) [Denckla, 1985; Mutti et al., 1978; Vitiello et al., 1989]. These two tests provide useful levels of comparison for children at different ages. However, the skilled physician should be able to recognize the child who has significant subtle signs, especially if he knows the age at which each sign usually diminishes (Table 1).

The NESS (originally the PANESS) has been clinically researched by the National Institutes of Health (NIH) and the National Institute of Mental Health (NIMH) but is not yet commercially available. The normative data provide only a rough guideline; investigators are encouraged to obtain their own local socioeconomic and demographic norms. Vitiello et al. [1989] recently showed that some of the NESS signs were much more reliable than others. Those signs that demonstrated a high degree of both interrater and test-retest reliability included hand and eye preference by pantomine, walking on a line, walking heel-to-toe forward, hand overflow in walking on outside of feet. Those signs with very poor reliability included mirror overflow in finger tapping and mirror overflow in pronation-supination. It should be noted that the NESS does not assess each sign for intensity and frequency of overflow movement.

The QNST was designed to test neurointegration as it relates to learning. The test was also developed so that it could be used by nonmedical disciplines. The authors base the QNST on studies of an undifferentiated group of 1,231 subjects. The manual includes pictures that compare normal and abnormal body posture and performance. The individual test items are less quantitative than the NESS, and it is unlikely that the reliability of these items is as good as the items in the NESS. As reported in the manual, standardization of this instrument is poor to fair at best [Mutti et al., 1978]. Children are classified based on an overall tabulated score on 15 subtests:

Table 1 Soft (Subtle) Neurological Signs Related Affected Function and Age

Name of Sign	Function Affected				Age at Disappearance,[b] Years
	Sensory	Motor B and C[a]	Neural Inhibitory	Praxis	
Poor touch localization	+				5
Unable to stand on one foot (20 seconds)		+			6
Finger agnosia	+				6
Left-right confusion				+	6
Motor slowness during single motor movement[c]		+			7
Unable to hop on one foot (20 times)		+			7
Dystonic finger-to-finger (successive, 5 cycles)		+			7
Poor recognition of double simultaneous touch of hand and cheek (extinction test)	+				7
Dysdiadochokinesis		+		+	8
Dysrhythmic skipping		+		+	8
Mirror finger movements (synkinesias-intense, frequent)			+		9
Impersistent motor stance (eyes closed, 30 seconds)	+	+			9
Asterognosis	+				10
Absence of choreiform movement during motor stance			+		10
Impersistent tandam balance (eyes closed, 20 seconds)	+	+			10
Dysrhythmic sequential hops		+		+	10
Arm overflow during gait on inside and outside of feet (fog sign)			+		11

[a]Motor Balance and Coordination function.

[b]Age at disappearance represents approximation of age at which 75% of children no longer evidence this sign.

[c]An example of a single motor movement would be simple hand patting or foot tapping.

High score: the subject is likely to have trouble learning

Suspicious moderate score: because some items are scored high, this child is at-risk for a learning problem

Normal score: achieved by persons unlikely to have learning difficulties

Lateralized SNS findings sufficient to be noticed but not sufficient to lead to a focal neurological diagnosis are uncommon and of little practical importance. Their theoretical interest, however, remains high despite the fact that asymmetry is rarely recorded on clinical or research protocols. Shapiro and Dotan [1986] were unable to relate the direction of the sequential-simultaneous discrepancy on the Kaufman Assessment Battery for Children to focal neurologic signs. That all 14 of their cases with hemisphere localization had such discrepancies suggests that a more comprehensive learning profile might succeed in correlating lateralized neurodysfunction with learning deficits and processing style.

A STUDY OF SOFT NEUROLOGICAL SIGNS

We reviewed the neurological findings on all children presenting to a developmental disabilities clinic over a period of 6 years [Accardo et al., 1990]. This study included children between the ages of 6.5 and 13.5 years. Children with IQs below 70 were excluded; the presence of a motor diagnosis that might interfere with, or confuse, the interpretation of neurological signs (such conditions as cerebral palsy, arthrogryposis, and hydrocephalus) was also grounds for exclusion. The only neuromotor diagnoses allowed were clumsy child syndrome or apraxia. For the 454 children who met these criteria, the mean age was 9.3 years (standard deviation 1.9 years); there were 323 boys (71.1%) and 131 girls (28.9%). Educational level of parents was used as a descriptor for social class and is detailed in Table 2: 359 (79.1%) were Caucasian and 92 (20.3%) were black. The mean IQ was 94.3 (standard deviation 14.1). Learning disability was diagnosed in 398 (87.7%) children, attention deficit disorder without hyperactivity in 92 (20.3%), and attention deficit disorder with hyperactivity in 135 (29.7%). There were 56 (12.3%) children without any learning problems and 227 (50%) children without any attentional problems.

All children were administered an expanded neurological examination, which included 25 items, that supplemented the classic assessment of cranial nerves, tone, and deep tendon reflexes with a detailed evaluation of minor neurological dysfunction of gait and sensory motor abilities (Table 3). Mild deviations on the classical neurological examination were counted as contributors to this expanded pediatric neurodevelopmental assessment when they did not lead to a diagnosis of more severe neurological impairment. (As noted above, such cases had been excluded from this study.)

Table 2 Social Class Distribution for Soft Neurological Sign Study

Level	Descriptor	No.	%
5	Professional	12	2.6
4	College	57	12.6
3	High School	276	60.8
2	Grade school	66	14.5
1	Less than grade school	15	3.3
0	Mental retardation	15	3.3
Unknown		13	2.9
Total		454	100.0

Social class was based on parental educational level; the grade achievement of the parent with the higher educational level was used when the parents were discrepant with the exception of those families where one parent was mentally retarded. In some cases of adoption or foster placement, the educational level of the biological parents remained unknown.

Table 3 Soft Neurological Signs (SNS)

1. Cranial nerves: III, IV, V		13. Motor overflow
2. VII		14. Rapid alternating
3. IX, X		movements
4. XII		15. Fine finger movements
5. Tone		16. Stereognosis
6. Deep tendon reflexes, upper extremity		17. Graphesthesia
		18. Bender face-hand test
7. Deep tendon reflexes, lower extremity		19. Gaits: Walking
		20. Running
8. Babinski response		21. Toe
9. Finger-to-nose test		22. Heel
10. Choreiform movements		23. Hop
11. Spooning		24. Direct Fog
12. Motor impersistence		25. Indirect Fog

Each of the 25 items was scored as normal or deviant for age. In addition each was scored as symmetrical or asymmetrical, but that data is not being reported here. Scored minor deviations on the first eight items (the classical neurological examination) were never sufficient to qualify for a neurological diagnosis other than ADHD, learning disability, clumsy child syndrome, and apraxia. For children under age 10 years, the Fog tests were scored only for asymmetry.

With 25 the highest possible score, the soft neurological sign (SNS) indices ranged from 0 to 18 with a mean of 5.64 and a standard deviation of 3.57. The children were divided into two diagnostic subgroups: attention deficit disorder with hyperactivity and attention deficit disorder without hyperactivity. Between the SNS scores of the 92 children with attention deficit disorder but without hyperactivity (mean 5.67, standard deviation 3.43) and those of the 135 children with attention deficit disorder with hyperactivity (mean 5.98, standard deviation 3.69), an analysis of variance revealed no significant difference. Hyperactivity did not appear to act as a neurological finding. A Pearson r yielded no correlation between SNS scores and IQ. However, the presence of a learning disability, an attentional problem, or both yielded significantly higher SNS scores than the absence of both but did not discriminate one from the other [Table 4; Figure 1]. Using a cutoff of one standard deviation above the mean to create extreme groups yielded rates for the absence of learning disability of 7.6% for the higher scoring SNS group (SNS 10) and 13.1% for the lower scoring SNS group (SNS 10). Learning disability and attention deficits did appear to behave like neurological variables.

DYSMORPHOLOGY

The second half of the twentieth century has seen the flowering of syndromology with the identification of numerous chromosomal, genetic, and teratogenic syndromes, many of which have associated neurodevelopmental findings such as mental retardation and specific learning disability patterns. Some of the most common patterns were among the last to be identified— fetal alcohol effect and fragile X chromosome. And while the initial reports focused on the more severe developmental outcomes, later studies identify a much wider spectrum of developmental disability even extending into the nonhandicapped range.

Table 4 Soft Neurological Sign SNS Scores in Attention Deficit Hyperactivity Disorder and Learning Disability

Patients, no.		Pooled Variance Estimate		
Group 1	Group 2	T Value	Degrees of Freedom	2-Tail Probability
34	22	−2.80	54	0.007[a]
193	205	0.01	396	0.993
34	193	−2.49	225	0.014[a]
22	205	1.09	225	0.277
34	205	−2.50	237	0.013[a]
22	193	1.08	213	0.282

See Figure 1 for the diagnostic identification of the groups compared.
[a]Significant ($p < 0.05$) difference between group 1 and group 2.

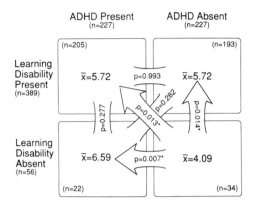

Figure 1 Soft neurological sign (SNS) scores in attention deficit hyperactivity disorder and learning disability.

Although an increasing percentage of developmental disorders exhibit a positive genetic or familial pattern, the number of diagnosable medical etiologies remains small. Clinicians have noted the high incidence of nonspecific dysmorphic features in a variety of developmental disabilities while waiting for the confirmation that is emerging from molecular genetics and high resolution chromosomal localization studies.

Associations have been reported both for individual stigmata as well as for clusters of minor malformations. Extreme microcephaly, for example, has long been recognized as a marker for mental retardation [Avery et al., 1972; Pryor and Thelander, 1968]. As the degree of microcephaly increases, the probability and severity of the associated cognitive limitation increases [Martin, 1970; O'Connell et al., 1965]. Clinically, however, microcephaly is more appropriately considered a nonspecific marker for the entire spectrum of developmental disorders. Even profound microcephaly does not guarantee retardation but may indicate instead a severe language disability [Accardo and Whitman, 1988]. Mild degrees of microcephaly have been associated with specific learning disabilities. [Smith, 1981]. Microcephaly, in turn, has been related to abnormal scalp-hair patterning [Smith and Gong, 1974], which can also correlate with ocular hypertelorism [Smith and Cohen, 1973] and serious underlying brain malformations [Smith and Greely, 1978]. The Simian crease is a common finding in Down syndrome and the Sydney line in congenital rubella [Purvis-Smith, 1972]. While these and other unusual palmar crease patterns (Figure 2) are not specific for either a given syndrome or even the presence of developmental abnormality, they do significantly correlate with hyperactivity [Lerer, 1977] and a variety of neurodevelopmental and other disorders [Johnson and Opitz, 1971, 1973].

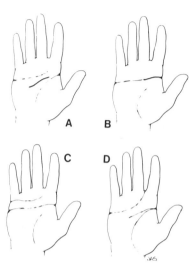

Figure 2   Palmar crease patterns: (A) normal palmar crease pattern; (B) simian crease or single transverse palmar crease; (C) Sydney line or lengthened proximal transverse palmar crease; and (D) extended distal transverse palmar crease, a normal variant labeled A_1, a_4 according to the schema of Dar et al. [1977].

MINOR DYSMORPHIC FEATURES

Aristotle's *Physignomica* was the earliest attempt to systematize observations on national and familial characteristics. In 1775 the *Physignomische Fragmente* of Johann Caspar Lavater (1741-1801) inaugurated the modern interest in physiognomy. In contrast to the splinter pseudosciences of palmistry and phrenology, physiognomy analyzed human traits from the consideration of a wide variety of observations including head size, head shape, facial features, the hands and palms, the gait and other gestures [Tytler, 1982; Wechsler, 1982]. It is this comprehensiveness rather than its uneven mixture of truth and error that entitle it to be considered a forerunner of modern syndromology. This is especially true as genetic research continues to uncover syndromic associations with patterns of learning and behavior in nondisabled individuals.

The currently accepted grouping of minor malformations derives from the *petits signes mongoliens* or microstigmata of Down syndrome [Daryn, 1961;

Keizer, 1957]. This standardized checklist of dysmorphic features (Table 5) has been correlated with the entire spectrum of neurodevelopmental disorders, associated disabilities and risk factors (Table 6). Dysmorphology indices (DYS) of 4 or less are considered within the normal range; scores of 5 and above are suspect. High DYS scores are associated not only with the presence of hyperactivity and ADHD but also with the predictability of ADHD in infancy. But this positive correlation holds for only a fraction of ADHD children. If DYS indices do not accurately differentiate normal from ADHD children, then what do high or low DYS scores tell us about

Table 5   Minor Dysmorphic Features

Electric hair
Hairwhorl abnormality
  Absent
  Multiple
  Poorly defined
  Clockwise
  Frontal
Head circumference greater than 1.5 standard deviations
  above or below the mean for age
Epicanthal folds
Hypertelorism (increased inner canthal distance)
Low-set ears
Absent ear lobules (adherent lobes)
Other pinnae abnormalities
  Malformed
  Protuberant
  Flattened
  Rotated
Palate, high arched or steepled
Geographic tongue
Clinodactyly of fifth finger
Palmar crease abnormality
  Simian
  Sydney
  Other
Sandal gap deformity of the toes
Syndactyly of toes, partial
Long middle toe

Adapted from Waldrop [mimeograph] and Waldrop and Halverson [1971].

Table 6 Minor Dysmorphic Features as Biological Markers for
Neurodevelopmental Disorders and Their Risk Factors

Association	Researchers
Mental retardation	Ireland [1877]
	Tredgold [1908]
	Burke [1931]
	Penrose [1949]
	Smith and Bostian [1964]
Cerebral palsy	Miller [1989]
Autism	Campbell et al. [1978]
	Links et al. [1980]
	Links [1980]
	Walker [1977]
Schizophrenia	Green et al. [1987]
	Gualtieri et al. [1982]
	Guy et al. [1983]
Prematurity	Drillien [1972]
	Largo et al. [1986]
Pre and perinatal complications	Firestone and Prabhu [1983]
	Quinn and Rapoport [1974]
	Steg and Rapoport [1975]
	Rapoport et al. [1977]
Familial occurrence	Firestone and Prabhu [1983]
	Firestone et al. [1978]
Hyperactivity cluster in boys	Firestone et al. [1976]
	Fogel et al. [1985]
	Gillberg [1983]
	Gillberg et al. [1983]
	Halverson and Victor [1976]
	Quinn and Rapoport [1974]
	Waldrop and Goering [1971]
	Waldrop and Halverson [1971]
	Waldrop et al. [1968]
Hyperactivity cluster in girls	Fogel et al. [1985]
	Halverson and Victor [1976]
	Waldrop et al. [1976]
	Waldrop and Halverson [1971]
Clumsiness	Waldrop and Halverson [1971]
	O'Donnell et al. [1979]
Paternal hyperactivity	Quinn and Rapoport [1974]
	Quinn et al. [1977]
Infant irritability	Burg et al. [1978a]
	Burg et al. [1978b]
	Burg et al. [1980]
	Quinn et al. [1977]
	Rapoport et al. [1977]

Table 6

Association	Researchers
Learning Disability	Steg and Rapoport [1975]
	Rosenberg and Weller [1973]
Plasma dopamine beta	Rapoport et al. [1974]
hydroxylase	Rapoport et al. [1977]
Hyperactivity, aggressiveness/	Jacklin et al. [1980]
assertiveness in girls	

Updated from Accardo (1980). Almost all the above studies used the scoring system derived by Waldrop (Table 5).

ADHD children? High DYS scores have been traditionally interpreted as supportive of morphogenetic disturbances involving ectodermal derivatives and occurring in the first trimester. While this etiologic contribution is important from the standpoint of parent counseling as well as from the perspective of new syndrome identification, it is hypothesized that DYS scores may correlate with specific neurodevelopmental behavioral clusters. Steg and Rapoport [1975] and Rosenberg and Weller [1973] reported a possible association with learning disabilities. The fact that most correlations between ADHD and DYS focus on preschool children or utilize only screening measures for learning disorders allows that the primary association may be with learning and cognition rather than with attention and hyperactivity. A cursory review of diagnostic categories for groups of children with high and low DYS scores provides preliminary support for this hypothesis (Table 7). In their study of 80 children with lateralized upper limb reduction defects, Dlugosz et al., [1988] noted that although left-sided involvement was more common, learning disabilities and reading disorders were significantly correlated with right-sided involvement. Such work would seem to recommend further research into the relation between the lateralization of minor malformations and specific learning disability patterns.

CONCLUSION

Soft neurological signs (SNS) and minor dysmorphic features (DYS) are both nonspecific and nondiagnostic markers for problems of learning and behavior in children [Krouse and Kauffman, 1982; Pomeroy et al., 1988; Tupper, 1987]. They have low sensitivity and high specificity, and the marked overlap in the scores for these signs of organicity between normal and developmentally disordered children does not make these indices useful to diagnose the presence of a developmental disability. In the presence of a developmental disorder, however, a high SNS score supports a brain involvement

Table 7 Dysmorphology Indices in Attention Deficit
Hyperactivity Disorder, Learning Disability, and Mental
Retardation

	Dysmorphology Index			
	Low (DYS = 0)		High (DYS ≥ 6)	
	No.	%	No.	%
	168	100	132	100
ADHD				
present	56	33.3	44	33.3
absent	112	66.7	88	66.7
Learning Disability				
present	71	42.3	74	56.1
absent	97	57.7	58	48.9
Mental Retardation				
present	59	35.1	40	30.3
absent	109	64.9	92	69.7

The scoring system used unweighted sums and differed from
the more typical gradings in two particulars. First, since head
circumference was recorded to the nearest half standard deviation, the true cut off is 1.75 standard deviations; that would
make this item more restrictive. Second, a larger variety of
palmer crease patterns was scored as abnormal (Figure 2);
this item would therefore be less restrictive in this scoring
system. The population was the same as that reported in
Table 3 and Figure 1 except that exclusions were on the basis
of previously identified genetic and dysmorphic syndromes,
and mental retardation was not excluded.

pattern, and a high DYS index supports a prenatal if not genetic etiology.
Low SNS and DYS scores do not rule out organic involvement. High scores
are sufficient but not necessary conditions for organicity in the presence of
neurodevelopmental syndromes. For the undiagnosed middle-school age
child who presents with problems in learning or behavior, the SNS examination should grade the intensity and frequency of associated movements.
Current SNS and DYS batteries remain weak with regard to cross-cultural
standardization of reliability and validity.

A more careful delineation of cognitive processing styles offers the greatest promise for clarifying the contribution of these biological markers to
ADHD. Lateralization and assymmetry of both SNS and DYS should contribute to the future subtyping of ADHD and learning disabilities. The refinement needed for accurate SYS and DYS does not recommend their use as
screening instruments, but their ease of administration and noninvasiveness
support their inclusion as part of the routine pediatric neurodevelopmental
assessment of children with ADHD and learning disabilities.

REFERENCES

Accardo, P. J. (1980). Minor physical anomalies. In *A Neurodevelopmental Perspective on Specific Learning Disabilities.* Baltimore: University Park Press, pp. 104-107.

Accardo, P. J., Blondis, T. A., Whitman, B. Y. (1990). Disorders of attention and activity level in a referral population. *Pediatrics 85*:426-431.

Accardo, P. J., Whitman, B. Y., (1988). Severe microcephaly with normal nonverbal intelligence. *Pediatric Rev. Commun. 3*:61-65.

Avery, G. B., Meneses, L., Lodge, A. (1972). The clinical significance of "measurement microcephaly." *Am. J. Dis. Child. 123*:214-217.

Blondis, T. A., Snow, J. H., Accardo, P. J. (1990). The integration of soft signs in formal and academically at-risk children. *Pediatrics 85*:421-425.

Burg, C., Hart, D., Quinn, P., Rapoport, J., (1978a). Newborn minor physical anomalies and prediction of infant behavior. *J. Autism Child. Schiz. 8*:427-439.

Burg, C., Quinn, P. Q., Rapoport, J. (1978b). Clinical evaluation of one-year old infants: Possible predictors of risk for the "hyperactivity syndrome." *J. Pediatric Psychol. 3*:164-167.

Burg, C., Rapoport, J., Bartley, L., Quinn, P. O., Timmins, P. (1980). Newborn minor physical anomalies and problem behavior at age 3. *Am. J. Psychiatry 137*:791-796.

Burke, N. H. M. (1931). Stigmata of degeneration in relation to mental deficiency. *Proc. Roy. Soc. Med. 24*:413-428.

Campbell, M., Geller, B., Small, A. M., Petti, T. A., Ferris, S. H. (1978). Minor physical anomalies in young psychotic children. *Am. J. Psychiatry 135*:573-575.

Capute, A. J., Accardo, P. J., Eds. (1991). *Developmental Disorders in Infancy and Childhood.* Baltimore: Paul H. Brookes.

Clemens, S. D. (1966). *Minimal Brain Dysfunction in Children—Terminology and Identification.* Washington, D.C.: U.S. Public Health Services.

Cohen, H. J., Taft, L. T., Mahadeviah, M. S., Birch, H. G. (1967). Developmental changes in overflow in normal and aberrantly functioning children. *J. Pediatrics 71*:39-47.

Dar, H., Schmidt, R., Nitowsky, H. M. (1977). Palmar crease variants and their clinical significance: A study of newborns at risk. *Pediatric Res. 11*:103-108.

Daryn, E. (1961). Problems of children with "diffuse brain damage." *Arch. Gen. Psychiatry 4*:299-306.

Denckla, M. B. (1985). Revised neurologic examination of subtle signs. *Psychopharmacol. Bull. 21*:773.

Denckla, M. B., Rudel, R. G. (1978). Anomalies of motor development in hyperactive boys. *Ann. Neurol. 3*:231.

Dlugosz, L. J., Byers, T., Msall, M. E., Marshall, J., Lesswing, A., Cooke, R. E. (1988). Relationships between laterality of congenital upper limb reduction defects and school performance. *Clin. Pediatrics 27*:319-324.

Drillien, C. M. (1972). Aetiology and outcome in low-birthweight infants. *Dev. Med. Child Neurol. 14*:563-574.

Firestone, P., Lewy, F., Douglas, V. I. (1976). Hyperactivity and physical anomalies. *Can. Psychiatric Assoc. J. 21*:23-26.

Firestone, P., Peters, S., Rivier, M., Knights, R. M. (1978). Minor physical anomalies in hyperactive, retarded and normal children and their families. *J. Child Psychol. Psychiatry 19*:155-160.

Firestone, P., Prabhu, A. N. (1983). Minor physical anomalies and obstetrical complications: Their relationship to hyperactive, psychoneurotic and normal children and their families. *J. Abnorm. Child Psychol. 11*:207-216.

Fog, E., Fog, M. (1963). Cerebral inhibition examined by associated movements. In *Minimal Cerebral Dysfunction: Clinics in Developmental Medicine, No. 10.* Bax, M., MacKeith, R. C., eds. London: Spastics Society with Heinemann Medical, pp. 52-57.

Fogel, C. A., Mednick, S. A., Michelsen, N. (1985). Hyperactive behavior and minor physical anomalies. *Acta Psychiatry Scand. 72*:551-556.

Gillberg, C. (1983). Perceptual, motor and attentional deficits in Swedish primary school children: Some child psychiatric aspects. *J. Child Psychol. Psychiatry 24*: 377-403.

Gillberg, C., Carlstrom, G., Rasmussen, P. (1983). Hyperkinetic disorder in seven-year-old children with perceptual, motor and attentional disorder deficits. *J. Child Psychol. Psychiatry 24*:233-246.

Green, M. F., Satz, P., Soper, H. V., Kharaki, F. (1987). Relationship between physical anomalies and age at onset of schizophrenia. *Am. J. Psychiatry 144*:666-667.

Gualtieri, C. T., Adams, A., Shen, C. D., Loiselle, D. (1982). Minor physical anomalies in alcoholic and schizophrenic adults and hyperactive and autistic children. *Am. J. Psychiatry 139*:640-643.

Guy, J. D., Majorski, L. V., Wallace, C. J., Guy, M. P. (1983). The incidence of minor physical anomalies in adult male schizophrenics. *Schizophrenia Bull. 9*: 571-582.

Halverson, C. F. Jr., Victor, J. B. (1976). Minor physical anomalies and problem behavior in elementary school children. *Child Dev. 47*:281-285.

Hertzig, M. E. (1982). Stability and change in nonfocal neurological signs in learning-disabled children and controls. *J. Am. Acad. Child Psychiatry 21*:231.

Ireland, W. W. (1877). *On Idiocy and Imbecility.* London: J. and A. Churchill.

Jacklin, C., Maccoby, E. E., Halverson, C. F. (1980). Minor physical anomalies and preschool behavior. *J. Pediatr. Psychol. 5*:199-205.

Johnson, C. F., Opitz, E. (1971). The single palmar crease and its clinical significance in a child development clinic: Observations and correlations. *Clin. Pediatrics 10*: 392-403.

Johnson, C. F., Opitz, E. (1973). Unusual palmar creases and unusual children: The Sydney line and "type C" palmar lines and their clinical significance in a child development clinic. *Clin. Pediatrics 12*:101-112.

Keizer, D. P. R. (1957). Mongolism and other congenital abnormalities. *Lancet 2*: 344-345.

Krouse, J. P., Kauffman, J. M. (1982). Minor physical anomalies in exceptional children: A review and critique of research. *J. Abnorm. Child Psychol. 10*:247-264.

Largo, R. H., Molinari, L., Comenale Pinto, L., Weber, M., Duc, G. (1986). Language development of term and preterm children during the first five years of life. *Dev. Med. Child Neurol. 28*:333-350.

Lerer, R. J. (1977). Do hyperactive children tend to have abnormal palmar creases? Report of a suggestive association. *Clin. Pediatrics 16*:645-647.

Links, P. S. (1980). Minor physical anomalies in childhood autism. Part II: Their relationship to maternal age. *J. Autism Dev. Disorders 10*:287-292.

Links, P. S., Stockwell, M., Abichandani, F., Simeon, J. (1980). Minor physical anomalies in childhood autism. Part I: Their relationship to pre- and perinatal complications. *J. Autism Dev. Disorders 10*:273-285.

Martin, H. P. (1970). Microcephaly and mental retardation. *Am. J. Dis. Child. 119*: 128-131.

Mikkelsen, E. J., Brown, G. L., Minichiello, M. D., Millican, F. R., Rapoport, J. L. (1982). Neurologic status in hyperactive, eneuretic, encopretic and normal boys. *J. Am. Acad. Child Psychiatry 21*:75.

Miller, G. (1989). Minor congenital anomalies and ataxic cerebral palsy. *Arch. Dis. Childhood 64*:557-562.

Mutti, M., Sterling, H. M., Spalding, N. V. (1978). *Quick Neurological Screening Test,* Rev. Ed. Novato, CA: Academic Therapy Publications.

O'Connell, E. J., Feldt, R. H., Stickler, G. B. (1965). Head circumference, mental retardation, and growth failure. *Pediatrics 36*:62-66.

O'Donnell, J. P., O'Neill, S., Staley, A. (1979). Congenital correlates of distractibility. *J. Abnorm. Child Psychol. 7*:465-470.

Pomeroy, J. C., Sprafkin, J., Gadow, K. D. (1988). Minor physical anomalies as a biologic marker for behavior disorders. *J. Am. Acad. Child Adolescent Psychiatry 27*:466-473.

Penrose, L. S. (1949). *The Biology of Mental Defect.* London: Sidgwick and Jackson.

Pryor, H. B., Thelander, H. (1968). Abnormally small head size and intellect in children. *J. Pediatrics 73*:593-598.

Purvis-Smith, S. G. (1972). The Sydney Line: A significant sign in Down's Syndrome. *Austral. Pediatric J. 8*:198-200.

Quinn, P. O., Rapoport, J. L. (1974). Minor physical anomalies and neurologic status in hyperactive boys. *Pediatrics 53*:742-747.

Quinn, P. O., Renfield, M., Burg, C., Rapoport, J. L. (1977). Minor physical anomalies: A newborn screening and one-year follow-up. *J. Am. Acad. Child Psychiatry 16*:662-669.

Rapoport, J. L., Pandoni, C., Renfield, M., Lake, C. R., Ziegler, M. G. (1977). Newborn dopamine-β-hydroxylase, minor physical anomalies, and infant temperament. *Am. J. Psychiatry 134*:676-679.

Rapoport, J. L., Quinn, P. O., Lamprecht, F. (1974). Minor physical anomalies and plasma dopamine-beta-hydroxylase in hyperactive boys. *Am. J. Psychiatry 131*: 386-390.

Rosenberg, J. B., Weller, G. M. (1973). Minor physical anomalies and academic performance in young school children. *Dev. Med. Child Neurol. 15*:131-135.

Rutter, M., Graham, P., Yule, W. (1970). *A Neuropsychiatric Study in Childhood. Clinics in Developmental Medicine. Nos. 35/36.* London: S. I. M. P. with Heinemann Medical; Philadelphia: Lippincott.

Shafer, S. Q., Stokman, C. J., Shaffer, D., Ng, S. K. C., O'Connor, P. A., Schonfeld, I. S. (1986). Ten-year consistency in neurological test performance of children without focal neurological deficit. *Dev. Med. Child Neurol. 28*:417.

Shapiro, E. G., Dotan, N. (1986). Neurological findings and the Kaufman Assessment Battery for Children. *Dev. Neuropsychol. 2*:51-64.

Smith, R. D. (1981). Abnormal head circumference in learning-disabled children. *Dev. Med. Child Neurol. 23*:626-632.

Smith, D. W., Bostian, K. E. (1964). Congenital anomalies associated with idiopathic mental retardation: Frequency in contrast to frequency in controls in children with cleft lip and palate, and in those with ventricular septal defect. *J. Pediatrics 65*: 189-196.

Smith, D. W., Cohen, M. M. (1973). Widow's peak scalp-hair anomaly and its relation to ocular hypertelorism. *Lancet 2*:1127-1128.

Smith, D. W., Gong, B. T. (1974). Scalp-hair patterning: Its origin and significance relative to early brain and upper facial development. *Teratology 9*:17-34.

Smith, D. W., Greely, M. J. (1978). Unruly scalp hair in infancy: Its nature and relevance to problems of brain morphogenesis. *Pediatrics 61*:783-785.

Snow, J. H., Blondis, T. A., Brady, L. (1988). Motor and sensory abilities with normal and academically at-risk children. *Arch. Clin. Neuropsychol. 3*:227.

Steg, J. P., Rapoport, J. L. (1975). Minor physical anomalies in normal, neurotic, learning disabled, and severely disturbed children. *J. Autism Childhood Schizophrenia 5*:299-307.

Stokman, C. J., Shafer, S. Q., Shaffer, D., Ng, S. K.-C., O'Connor, P. A., Wolff, R. R. (1986). Assessment of neurological "soft signs" in adolescents: Reliability studies. *Dev. Med. Child Neurol. 28*:428.

Touwen, B. C. L., Prechtl, H. F. R. (1970). *The Neurologic Examination of the Child with Minor Nervous System Dysfunction: Clinics in Developmental Medicine. No. 38.* London: S. I. M. P. with Heinemann Medical.

Tredgold, A. F. (1908). *A Text-Book of Mental Deficiency (Amentia).* Baltimore: William Wood and Company.

Tupper, D. E., Ed. (1987). *Soft Neurological Signs.* Orlando, FL: Grune and Stratton.

Tytler, G. (1982). *Physiognomy in the European Novel.* Princeton, NJ: Princeton University Press.

Vitiello, B., Ricciuti, A. J., Stoff, D. M., Behav, D., Denclka, M. B. (1989). Reliability of subtle (soft) neurological signs in children. *J. Am. Acad. Child Adolesc. Psychiatry 28*:749.

Waldrop, M. F. (no date). Manual for assessing minor physical anomalies. Laboratory of Developmental Psychology. (Mimeographed) 15 pp.

Waldrop, M. F., Bell, R. Q., Goering, J. D. (1976). Minor physical anomalies and inhibited behavior in elementary school girls. *J. Child Psychol. Psychiatry 17*:113-122.

Waldrop, M. F., Goering, J. D. (1971). Hyperactivity and minor physical anomalies in elementary school children. *Am. J. Orthopsychi. 41*:602-607.

Waldrop, M. F., Halverson, C. F., Jr. (1971). Minor physical anomalies and hyperactive behavior in young children. In *Exceptional Infant* Vol. 2. Hellmuth, J., Ed. New York: Brunner/Mazel, pp. 343-380.

Waldrop, M., Pedersen, F., Bell, R. (1968). Minor physical anomalies and behavior in preschool children. *Child Dev. 39*:391-400.

Walker, H. A. (1977). Incidence of minor physical anomalies in autism. *J. Autism Childhood Schizophrenia* 7:165-176.

Wechsler, J. (1982). *A Human Comedy: Physiognomy and Caricature in 19th Century Paris.* Chicago: University of Chicago Press.

Whitmore, K., Bax, M. (1986). The school entry medical examination. *Arch. Dis. Child.* 61:807.

Wolff, P. H., Gunnoe, C., Cohen, C. (1985). Neuromotor maturation and psychological performance: A developmental study. *Dev. Med. Child Neurol.* 27:344.

Wright, F. S. (1982). General considerations and approach to learning disabilities. In *The practice of Pediatric Neurology,* Swaiman, K. F., Wright, F. S., eds. St. Louis, MO C. V. Mosby, pp. 1083-1089.

Younes, R. P., Rosner, B., Webb, G. (1983). Neuroimmaturity of learning-disabled children: A controlled study. *Dev. Med. Child Neurol.* 25:574.

7

Psychoeducational Data

Jeffrey H. Snow

University of Arkansas for Medical Sciences, Little Rock, Arkansas

Karen J. Cunningham

Eastern Illinois University, Charleston, Illinois

"Children are not simply micro-adults, but have their own specific problems."

[Bela Schick]

Psychoeducational assessment with the attention deficit hyperactive disorder (ADHD) child is an integral part of the overall evaluation-treatment plan. Most ADHD children experience some type of learning difficulty [Barkley, 1981, 1987; Pelham & Bender, 1982]. This may range from mild classroom disruption to severe learning disabilities. Because of this, the ADHD child is likely to be referred for some type of psychoeducational assessment. This assessment should focus on providing information that will facilitate adjustment to the educational setting for the ADHD child. In this sense, the evaluation is critical for the success or failure of academic intervention conceived and implemented in the school environment. This chapter is designed to provide an overview of critical issues concerning the psychoeducational assessment of ADHD children. Basic considerations as well as reviews of specific testing procedures will be presented. Conclusions concerning the assessment of ADHD children will also be discussed.

GENERAL CONSIDERATIONS

Barkley [1987] outlined major factors that need to be considered when completing an evaluation with an ADHD child.

1. Assessments must focus on the primary symptoms of the disorder such as sustained attention, impulse control, and overactivity.
2. The assessment needs to incorporate a number of professionals since ADHD has so many associated difficulties such as learning problems.
3. Testing methods that have adequate normative data should be selected.
4. Multiple informants should be utilized, since the disorder generally presents itself in a number of different settings.
5. Because the disorder often persists well into adolescence, assessment procedures should be selected that span a wide age range.
6. Social exchange between the child and the parent should be evaluated.

Considering these factors, it does seem imperative that a comprehensive psychoeducational assessment be completed with the ADHD child.

In conducting an assessment with any child, it is important that the evaluation be comprehensive and provide specific information beyond merely reporting test scores or giving broad-based diagnostic categories. Psychoeducational assessment with the ADHD child needs to provide information that not only facilitates the diagnostic process, but also yields data useful for academic intervention planning. Since many of these children have associated learning disabilities (LD), programming that focuses beyond merely facilitating attention processes is often necessary. Academic strategies that address the needs of the child are also needed. These strategies are tailored to the individual child, and the psychoeducational evaluation should play a major role in the formulation of these strategies.

In examining recent literature, it is quite apparent that the LD population is not a homogeneous group, but rather consists of a number of distinct subgroups [Doehring et al., 1979; Fisk and Rourke, 1979; Lyon et al., 1982; Mattis et al., 1975; Rourke and Finlayson, 1978; Snow et al., 1985; Snow and Hynd, 1985; Snow et al., 1987; Watson et al., 1983]. It should be remembered that ADHD is considered a separate disorder from LD. However, because such a high percentage of ADHD children also meet eligibility for diagnosis of LD, it is likely that ADHD-LD children are not homogeneous in the type of learning difficulty evidenced but approximate the general LD population. Given this consideration, the psychoeducational assessment of these children should focus on providing very specifc and useful information.

When completing a psychoeducational assessment with an ADHD child, it is not enough to provide overview and general diagnostic information. The psychologist needs to integrate all available information and provide a comprehensive cognitive-academic profile of the child. For example, it is not sufficient to merely label a child, then support the label with standard test results. How helpful is it to other professionals and parents to simply report that the child is ADHD with an associated reading disability? In all likelihood, everyone involved with the case is very much aware of the child's attention and reading difficulties. What the psychoeducational evaluation should provide is very specific information about the child's cognitive processes as well as his/her strategies for dealing with academically based material. This demands that the psychologist not only pay attention and utilize standard scores but also focus on qualitative aspects of the assessment process.

QUANTITATIVE AND QUALITATIVE TESTING PROCEDURES

Both quantitative and qualitative analyses should play an integral role in the psychoeducational evaluation process. Most psychologists will utilize standardized instruments (some of which will be reviewed in following sections) that provide standard scores of some type. Standardized instruments that yield normative based scores are necessary for providing important data about the ADHD child. Among other types of information, standard scores will provide the psychologist with the level of the child's overall intellectual ability, relative standing in academic areas such as reading and arithmetic, social/adaptive skills, etc. In addition, in most states standardized test results are usually required to qualify an ADHD child for any special education services. This, however, is only one level of interpretation. Qualitative analysis of the child's strategies and behavior is another level that enhances the psychoeducational assessment. Qualitative assessment involves the analysis of how the child goes about the task and how certain errors are committed.

Qualitative analysis is particularly important when completing evaluations with ADHD children. Standardized test scores can sometimes be misleading with the ADHD child because of attention and impulsivity factors. For example, is the child truly deficient in the areas of reading or arithmetic simply because he/she scores low on standardized academic batteries? Were these low scores attributable to a true learning disability, or merely a consequence of the child's difficulties in maintaining attention during the testing procedure? Skilled psychologists should be able to make such decisions by focusing on the qualitative aspects of the child's behavior during the testing situation. What this suggests is that it is critical that the psychologist do at least some if not all of the testing with the child. Qualitative observations can also provide information about different strategies that can be utilized for academic programing. For example, it may be observed that the child engages in a number of verbal mediation strategies during the assessment procedure. This could have a direct consequence for recommendations about what may be useful with that particular child. The psychologist may also gain insight as to what may not work with the particular child. The psychologist may observe that the child has weaknesses in dealing with certain types of material or that certain processes are deficit. Strategies can then be formulated that attempt to either remediate these deficiencies (if this is possible) or work around these difficulties. In general, qualitative analysis provides insight into how the child goes about a task and how errors were committed. This type of information nicely supplements quantitative tests scores and enhances the utility of the psychoeducational evaluation.

Qualitative analysis also involves observing behaviors during the testing situation. This is particularly important with the younger ADHD children since standardized tests at younger ages may provide only limited types of data. One type of behavior that should be closely observed and charted (if possible) is the degree of impulsivity in terms of responding. A measure of this can include response latencies to different levels of questions. A pattern that may emerge with younger ADHD children is that of relatively short response latencies that do not often correspond to item difficulty (i.e., they respond as quickly to more difficult items as to easier items). Another behavior to pay attention to is the activity level of the child. Is the activity level fairly constant during the session, or does it fluctuate with increasing time of the evaluation? It may also be important to note changes in activity based on the type of task administered. In other words, a child may be relatively calm during administration of cognitive-type tests but may become extremely active during more academically based measures. This type of information not only provides insight as to the individual differences of the ADHD child but also aids in the differential diagnosis of ADHD as opposed to other cognitively/emotionally based disorders. Finally, observation of behavior during the testing session can provide valuable information as to what types of reinforcement may be most appropriate for the particular child. The child may function nicely with simple verbal praise or may require more tangible reinforcers to obtain optimal performance. This type of data can be directly translated to a more effective behavior management program to be utilized with the child in the school and/or home environment.

Selecting the Test Instrument

Selecting appropriate testing instruments to use with the ADHD child depends on a number of factors. Obviously, the age of the child is an important consideration. Extensive batteries may not be feasible with younger ADHD children, at least not feasible to attempt in one sitting. In these instances it is important to conduct the assessment over a number of sessions to obtain optimal results.

Barkley's [1987] comment about selecting instruments that span a wide age range should also be considered. Research evidence suggests that associated academic difficulties with ADHD children often persist well into adolescence and even adulthood [Lambert, 1988; Satterfield et al., 1982]. Because of this, it is likely that these children and adolescents will be subjected to a number of reevaluations throughout their academic careers. Selecting the same or similar instruments will allow the psychologist to assess progress made by the child. This is not to say that the psychologist should get locked into a set battery that is routinely administered. Each psychoeducational evaluation should provide new and useful information. This calls for flexibility in the selection of testing instruments and the manner in which the assessment is conducted.

Yet another important consideration in choosing measures is the language functioning of the ADHD child. Language disorders are frequently associated with ADHD [Chess and Rosenberg, 1974; Gualtieri et al., 1983]. Cantwell and associates observed that ADHD was the most common psychiatric diagnosis in their investigations with language-disordered children [Baker and Cantwell, 1982; Cantwell and Baker, 1980; Cantwell et al., 1980]. A recent investigation by Love and Thompson further indicated the potential language difficulties associated with ADHD [Love and Thompson, 1988]. They utilized a large sample of children referred to a metropolitan clinic. A high percentage of these chilren (48.3%) had a dual diagnosis of language disorder and ADHD. The language pattern most frequently observed was combined expressive and receptive skill deficits.

The potential language dysfunction of the ADHD child has two major implications for the psychoeducational assessment. The first involves the need for the psychologist to maintain close communication with the speech/language clinician because these professionals provide information concerning the presence or absence of a language disorder and, if present, the exact nature of the dysfunction. The second involves the selection and interpretation of testing instruments. Many of the measures used with standardized psychoeducational assessments load very heavily on language abilities because language is such a major factor with most cognitive and academic tasks. But not all measured skills are completely contingent on language functioning. Take for example neuropsychological abilities. Basic sensory and motor assessments are critical to adequate neuropsychological assessments; yet there is a potential problem if such tests become too contingent on language skills and rely too heavily on the comprehension of complex directions. In this instance, a lower score may indicate either the child's inability to integrate motor or sensory skills or difficulty in comprehending complex directions. In other words, the psychologist needs to focus on the way in which children are having difficulty with certain tasks and realize that this may be the result of a pervasive language disorder rather than more specific skill deficits.

Medication Considerations

Whether or not the child is on medication at the time of the assessment is an important consideration. The most commonly prescribed and widely researched medication administered to ADHD children is methylphenidate (Ritalin); the literature indicates varied results. Schowalter [1979] found difficulties associated with the use of stimulant medication. Detrimental effects were noted in the areas of academic achievement and also parent-child interactions. Other studies report more positive results [Ballinger et al., 1984; Rapport et al., 1985; Reid and Borkowski, 1984; Sprague and Sleator, 1977]. Ballinger et al. and Sprague and Sleator found increased performance on various learning tasks with various doses of stimulant medication. Rapport et al. reported increased academic performance as well as significantly better ratings of behavior for children on stimulant medication as opposed to those on placebo. Reid and Barton investigated the effects of stimulant medication on sustained attention as well as cognitive processing. These authors found significant improvement in not only attention skills, but also increased efficiency in cognitive processes. As several authors have pointed out, the effects of using stimulant medication depend on a number of factors including the child, the task or tasks examined, and the dosage [Volkmar et al., 1985; Gadow, 1985]. In any event, psychologists completing psychoeducational assessments of ADHD children will certainly assess some who are taking stimulant medication.

There are potential side effects associated with methylphenidate that can affect performance on cognitive based tests. Nervousness, anxiety, insomnia, and drowsiness can be associated with use of stimulant medication [Scarnati, 1986]. Murray [1987] reported that the use of methylphenidate can suppress REM sleep. Depression is another symptom associated with use of this medication. The psychologist needs to be aware that these as well as other side effects may be present with ADHD children. Again, it is important to closely monitor the performance of the child during the assessment procedure. Obviously, factors such as anxiety, fatigue, or depression can directly impact on test performance. If possible, it may be advantageous to delay testing until the child has stabilized on the medication. If testing cannot be delayed, these factors should be thoroughly discussed in the written report. In this regard, it is important for the psychologist to maintain close contact with the pediatrician.

One final point to consider in relation to medication issues is whether the child should be on or off the medication during the testing. In general, it is probably advantageous for the child to remain on medication during the assessment procedure. The goal of the psychoeducational assessment is to provide information useful for educational programming. It is, therefore, to the psychologist's advantage to obtain results that truly reflect the child's cognitive and academic functioning. The literature does suggest that for the majority of ADHD children, the properly administered and monitored dose of stimulant medication is likely to enhance testing performance.

Assessing the Validity of the Test Results

Once the psychologist has completed the psychoeducational evaluation, the all important task of interpretation begins. A major consideration with this process is to assess the validity of the results obtained. This can only be achieved by reflecting on factors in the testing situation as well as the child's behavior during the testing session(s). There are the obvious factors such as room temperature, level of noise, interruptions, etc., that would be considered with any evaluation. More unique and important to assessments with ADHD children are the within subject variables, for example, the child's activity level during the assessment and the degree to which attention difficulties and impulsivity may have affected the test results, and how easily distracted the child was by external stimuli. Previous assessments or medication side-effects are also important factors. All of these variables and their effects on the testing performance need to be evaluated by the psychologist in arriving at overall conclusions as to whether the psychoeducational assessment is a valid estimate of the child's true cognitive and academic abilities.

Given the need to assess the validity of test results, as well as the advantage of focusing on qualitative as well as quantitative aspects of performance, it is absolutely necessary that the psychologist conduct at least a major portion of the psychoeducational evaluation. Assessment models that focus on technicians administering tests with the psychologist then interpreting the results are limited by the types of information they can provide. Technician reports of behavior during the evaluation are no substitute for direct observation. This is not to argue that only the psychologist should have direct contact with the ADHD child. It is advantageous to have the child work with as many different people as possible to cross-validate observations or note significant behavior changes from one examiner to another. The psychologist is the person, however, who is ultimately responsible for bringing all the information together into a meaningful assessment. Having direct contact with the child enhances the psychologist's ability to do this and provides the psychologist with valuable observational information.

REVIEW OF SPECIFIC TESTING INSTRUMENTS

This section focuses on reviews of specific testing instruments that may be used in psychoeducational evaluation. Due to space limitations, the reviews may seem somewhat limited, but the intent is to provide an introduction and overview of the material.

Intelligence Tests

An integral component of most psychoeducational assessments is the administration and interpretation of the individual intelligence test. There are a number of good general cognitive measures available that can provide useful information. This section will review several of the more commonly used measures (e.g., the Wechsler scales) as well as more specialized tests (e.g., the Lieter International Performance Scale).

Wechsler Scales

The most commonly administered tests of intellectual ability are the scales developed by Wechsler [1967, 1974, 1981]. They are the Wechsler Preschool and Primary Scale of Intelligence, the Wechsler Intelligence Scale for Children —Revised, and the Wechsler Adult Intelligence Scale—Revised. The Wechsler scales are divided into two major scales (verbal and performance) with a number of subtests comprising each scale. The measures yield an overall score (full scale IQ), scores for each of the major scales (verbal and performance IQ scores), and scaled scores for each subtest. Interpretation involves, at the very least, analysis of the three IQ scores and perhaps more indepth analysis of subtest score patterns or even item score patterns within a subtest. It should be noted that from a psychometric sense, the most reliable measures are the IQ scores (due primarily to the fact that these are the longest indices on the test). As the psychologist moves to more specific analysis of subtests or even specific items, the reliability decreases and the measurement error increases. It is, therefore, usually best to supplement such interpretations with additional psychometric and/or observational data.

   Another level of interpretation advocated with the Wechsler scales is analysis of factor scores. Factor analytic studies with both the WISC-R and WAIS-R indicate the presence of three factors commonly described as verbal comprehension, perceptual organization, and freedom from distractibility [DeHorn and Klinge, 1978; Johnston and Bolen, 1984; O'Grady, 1983; Ryan et al., 1983]. (Interested readers should consult Kaufman [1979] for detailed descriptions of each factor.) In brief, the verbal comprehension factor closely approximates the Verbal Scale; the perceptual organization factor has loadings from most of the Performance Scale subtests; while the freedom-from-distractibility factor cuts across both scales.

Logically, it would appear as if the freedom-from-distractibility factor would be a highly useful index for the identification of ADHD children, since it is felt by many that this third factor is a direct reflection of concentration and attentional processes [Silverstein, 1977]. This may not be the case. Not all experts agree that this third factor necessarily reflects mere attentional processes. Other interpretations of skills reflected by this construct include short-term memory, numerical ability, and sequencing skills [Bannatyne, 1974; Baumeister and Bartlett, 1962]. Research investigations have yielded mixed results in terms of the relationship of the freedom-from-distractibility factor with external ratings of attention and activity level [Nalven and Puleo, 1968; Reschly and Reschly, 1979]. Zarski et al. [1987] did not find significant differences among normal, special education, and ADHD children on the freedom-from-distractibility factor. What this suggests is that from a clinical standpoint, the psychologist should exercise caution when interpreting this factor. Indeed, a depressed score may reflect poor attentional processes, deficit short-term memory, poor numerical facility skills, difficulties with sequencing, or any combination of these. It is likely that most ADHD children may evidence problems in any or all of these areas. The ultimate interpretation of the freedom-from-distractibility factor calls for integration of information from a number of sources including other test scores, observations of behavior, and information provided by significant others.

While there are potential limitations to the interpretation of the freedom-from-distractibility factor, it still should be examined with each potential ADHD child evaluated. The examination of the factor is relatively simple. The mean for the three subtests (arithmetic, coding, and digit span) comprising the factor should be calculated and compared with the mean scores of the other two major factors (verbal comprehension and perceptual organization). Kaufman [1979] recommends that for a meaningful interpretation, the freedom-from-distractibility factor should be at least three points below the other two factors. Kaufman also suggests that the scoring pattern within the factor be examined. He felt that the three subtests should all be within three points of each other in order to interpret the factor as reflecting a more unitary attentional difficulty as opposed to a more specific skill deficit (e.g., difficulties with short-term auditory memory that significantly affect digit span and arithmetic but is not a factor with coding).

Another pattern of subtests that can be examined is known as the ACID (Arithmetic, Coding, Information, and Digit Span) profile. These subtests have been identified as being particularly difficult for children with specific learning disabilities [Sattler, 1989]. The psychologist may want to examine this profile with an ADHD child if an associated learning disability is suspected.

In summary, the Wechsler Scales are a very valuable tool in the assessment of ADHD children. Given valid results, they provide the psychologist with an idea as to the child's overall intellectual skills. Various other levels of interpretation can shed light on strengths and weaknesses of different cognitive skills. All this information can contribute significantly to the diagnosis of ADHD children as well as remedial intervention strategy planning.

Woodcock-Johnson Psychoeducational Battery: Tests of Cognitive Ability (WJPB)

The Woodcock-Johnson Psychoeducational Battery [Woodcock, 1977] is comprised of two major sections. The section of concern here is the Tests of Cognitive Ability. The WJPB is an individually administered measure that takes anywhere from 50 to 120 minutes. There are a number of scores that can be obtained with this test. The major scores yielded are the Broad Cognitive index, which is based on the entire test, and what are called "cluster scores." Cluster scores can be obtained in the areas of verbal ability, reasoning, perceptual speed, and memory. The measure also yields aptitude scores in the areas of reading, mathematics, written language, and knowledge.

While much of the available empirical literature supports the reliability and validity of the WJPB as a general cognitive measure, there are several factors that psychologists who use this test with ADHD children should be aware of [Breen, 1984; McGrew, 1986]. Factor analytic studies using the WJPB do not tend to support the differentiation of the different cluster or aptitude areas [McGrew, 1985]. McGrew found that a two-factor solution was most appropriate. The primary factor was verbal ability with the second factor appearing to reflect nonverbal/visual-spatial skills. This would suggest that the psychologist exercise some caution in interpreting the different cluster areas as distinct and unique indices. Another concern with the WJPB focuses on the use of the test with LD children. Much of the evidence in this area indicates that the WJPB yields significantly lower scores with these children than other intelligence tests [Reeve et al., 1979; Ysseldyke et al., 1981]. This can pose a problem since such a high percentage of ADHD children have associated learning difficulties. Cummings and Moscato [1984] indicated yet another problem associated with the use of the WJPB with language-disordered children. These authors point out that available literature suggests the battery has a very strong language component. The net result is potential underestimation of overall cognitive functions with language-disordered children. Again, this is a major concern in relation to ADHD since so many of these children evidence some type of language deficit.

A final caution about WJPB centers around the memory cluster. Psychologists should be aware that the subtests that comprise this cluster are merely relying on short-term auditory memory. Since a comprehensive assessment of memory functions is so important with ADHD, it is recommended that psychologists supplement this test with additional measures that are sensitive to areas such as short-term visual and tactile memory as well as delayed memory and memory with interference.

While the overall tenor of this review may seem negative, this should not be interpreted as a firm condemnaiton of the WJPB. The psychometric properties of the test are basically sound. The battery also has some rather unique subtests not common to other intelligence tests. The WJPB can be a useful test with the ADHD population when supplemented with other assessment techniques.

It should also be noted that the WJPB has recently been revised. The Woodcock-Johnson Psychoeducational Battery—Revised (WJPB-R) [Woodcock, 1988] is similar in structure to the WJPB but has been revised to assess a broader array of cognitive factors. Of particular interest for the assessment of ADHD children are two memory factors (long-term retrieval and short-term retrieval) and a factor that reflects speed of cognitive processing (processing speed). Research investigations will shed light on the utility of this revised test with ADHD children.

Kaufman Assessment Battery for Children (K-ABC)

The K-ABC [Kaufman and Kaufman, 1983] is a measure designed to assess specific cognitive processes. It includes four scales: (a) sequential processing, (b) simultaneous processing, (c) achievement scale, and (d) nonverbal scale. There are a number of specific subtests on the scale, although the number of subtests administered depends on the age of the child. The test was designed based on a strong theoretical standpoint (the Luria-Das Simultaneous, Successive Processing model), which the Kaufman's felt was a strength of their measure in relation to many other available intelligence tests [Kamphaus and Reynolds, 1987]. Another distinguishing feature of the K-ABC was an attempt to minimize the need for verbal skills with the cognitive processing scales.

The K-ABC should be used as a supplemental measure when assessing ADHD children. Focusing on simultaneous and successive processing can provide a psychologist with another dimension of cognitive skills. The Kaufman's are to be commended for incorporating this theoretical model in the construction of this test, although there is the potential for oversimplification of rather complex processes. Psychologists interpreting these scales should be aware of the interactive nature of cognitive-neuropsychological processes. To assume that the Simultaneous Scale is merely reflecting simultaneous skills and the Sequential Scale is merely reflecting sequential skills is somewhat naive. Obviously, a number of other factors can affect performance on either or both of these scales. In this sense it is perhaps wise for the psychologist to interpret these scales from an "asymmetry" standpoint. In other words, assume that the Sequential Scale is asymmetrically assessing sequential skills, but that other skills (including simultaneous processing) are contributing to the variance. Another strength of the K-ABC in relation to ADHD children is the low verbal demands involved with the cognitive processing scales. This implies that the battery may be particularly useful with the ADHD language-disorder child. A major shortcoming of the test, however, is the heavy reliance on short-term memory skills. What advantages are gained by the lack of emphasis on verbal comprehension involved, may be more than offset by this factor. In summary, these authors are in agreement with Sattler [1988] in suggesting that the K-ABC not be used as the primary measure of intelligence with clinical assessments.

McCarthy Scales of Children's Abilities (MSCA)

The MSCA [McCarthy, 1972] is a cognitive measure designed for younger children (ages 2.6 to 6.5). The MSCA contains three primary scales (verbal, perceptual-performance, and quantitative) and two supplementary scales (memory and motor). The test also yields a general cognitive index, which is based on the total scores of the three primary scales. The psychometric properties of the test are very good. Studies have also generally supported the validity of the instrument [e.g., Bickett et al., 1984; Goh and Youngquist, 1979; Harrison, 1981]. Some concern has been raised regarding the factor structure of the measure, since several studies have not replicated the original structure reported [Keith and Bolen, 1980; Purvis and Bolen, 1984]. This may suggest some caution in interpreting the different scales.

Overall, the MSCA is good measure of cognitive ability, which can be useful in the assessment of ADHD children. The measure contains a number of different types of tasks that assess a wide array of behaviors. The motor scale is particularly useful in providing information beyond most traditional intelligence tests and nicely supplements the behavioral-developmental profile of the child. The fact that the memory scale does not figure into the calculation of the general cognitive index is another advantage that makes the test particularly useful with ADHD children. Two minor shortcomings of the measure are considerable dependence on verbal skills with several of the subtests and the fact that the test is standardized with such a limited age range. The latter point has implications for follow-up assessments as the ADHD child gets older.

Other Intelligence Measures

Two other intelligence measures that may be useful with the ADHD child are the Leiter International Performance Scale (LIPS) [Leiter, 1948] and the Columbia Mental Maturity Scale (CMMS) [Burgemeister et al., 1972]. The LIPS is a nonverbal test of intelligence originally designed to be used with children with severe motor or sensory deficits or who evidence difficulty with expressive language. Problems have been noted in terms of the standardization and outdated norms of the LIPS [Sattler, 1988]. The CMMS is also a nonverbal measure of intellectual ability. The standardization and norms provided for this test are superior to that for the LIPS. Adequate psychometric properties are also reported for the CMMS. The potential limitations of this measure include limited age range (3 to 9 years) and items that focus almost exclusively on reasoning ability.

Either the LIPS or the CMMS may be the test of choice when dealing with a severly language impaired ADHD child. The scores yielded by these measures will give the psychologist a good measure of the child's nonverbal intellectual abilities. Psychologists using these measures should be aware of their rather narrow scope and realize that they are not interchangeable with more comprehensive measures of intelligence. The tests can provide good supplemental information.

This concludes the section on intelligence tests. Again due to space limitations, not all of the available measures useful with ADHD children were reviewed. Readers interested in a more extensive review should consult Sattler [1988]. See Table 1 for a summary of the major strengths and weaknesses of the tests reviewed.

Academic Achievement Tests

The individual assessment of academic skills is an important part of any psychoeducational evaluation. The assessment of a child's academic achievement is often necessary for classification purposes. Psychometric achievement measures provide norms with which the psychologist can determine whether a child's academic skills are commensurate with age or grade level expectations. Several tests that measure academic achievement are available and can be used appropriately in assessing ADHD children.

Peabody Individual Achievement Test (PIAT)

The PIAT [Dunn and Markwardt, 1970] is designed for screening students from kindergarten through grade 12. The measure takes approximately 30 to 40 minutes to administer. The PIAT has five subtests that assess mathematics, reading recognition, reading comprehension, spelling, and general

Table 1 Strengths and Weaknesses of Cognitive Testing Measures

Instrument	Strengths	Weaknesses

Wechsler Scales	Available research
	Verbal and
	  performance scales
	Factor scores
	  (freedom-from-
	  distractibility)
	Appropriate scales for
	  ages preschool
	  through adult
		Freedom-from-
		  distractibility factor
		  reflects multiple
		  skills; caution in
		  interpretation is
		  needed

Woodcock-Johnson
Battery
	Variety of test items
	Up-dated norms
	  (particularly with
	  revised edition)
		Differentiation of cluster
		  scores unsupported
		Memory cluster limited
		  to strictly auditory
		  memory
		Test relies significantly
		  on language functions

K-ABC	Different measures of
	  processing style
	Theoretical foundation
	Minimization of
	  verbal skills
		Caution needed in
		  interpretation of
		  scales representing
		  processing styles
		Loads heavily on
		  short-term memory

McCarthy Scales	Good variety of subtests
	Scores yielded for a
	  number of different
	  scales
	Memory scale taps both
	  auditory and
	  visual memory
	Motor scale is a
	  good supplement and
	  can provide important
	  developmental
	  information
		Considerable verbal
		  skills needed
		Limited age range
		Need for
		  up-dated norms

information. A multiple choice format requiring either a verbal or motor (i.e., pointing) response is used for the mathematics, reading comprehension, and spelling subtests. The reading recognition subtest uses a combination of multiple choice items and letters or words the child must read aloud to the examiner. The general information subtest requires the child to respond orally.

Reported psychometric properties of the PIAT are fairly strong. The test was well standardized and has adequate reliability [Dean, 1977; Lamanna and Ysseldyke, 1973; Wilson and Spangler, 1974]. The test has also demonstrated a strong relationship with other achievement tests as well as measures of intellectual ability [Baum, 1975; Bray and Estes, 1975; Sattler, 1988].

The PIAT is a well-standardized general achievement test for grades K-12 that is useful as a screening device in identifying a student's general level of achievement in areas in which more in-depth assessment is needed. While the PIAT has been found to have satisfactory validity with special populations, a factor to consider when using the test with an ADHD child is the multiple choice format. Appropriate response to visual multiple choice stimuli requires the ability to focus, sustain attention, and inhibit impulsive responding, all of which are very difficult for the ADHD child. Since attentional factors are involved in correctly responding to multiple choice items, the psychologist needs to closely monitor the assessment and evaluate the validity of the results.

Wide Range Achievement Test—Revised (WRAT-R)

The WRAT-R [Jastak and Wilkinson, 1984] is a quick and easily administered achievement test. It takes approximately 20 to 30 minutes to administer and is divided into two levels: level I is for children ages 5 to 12 and level II is for individuals 12 to adulthood. The WRAT-R has three subtests, measuring reading (word recognition and pronunciation, not comprehension), spelling, and arithmetic. Raw scores from the WRAT-R can be transformed into grade equivalents, percentile ranks, stanines, standard scores, scaled scores, and T-scores. It should be noted that grade equivalents do not take into consideration instructional differences, socioeconomic level, or age of the person taking the test.

The WRAT-R is a widely used achievement test because it is short and easily administered, provides standard scores, and measures academic skills in three different areas. The test does not have a reading comprehension component, nor does it measure understanding of complex mathematical problems. Socioeconomic factors were not considered with the standardization of the test and reliability data are scant. In general, the WRAT-R should be used only as a quick screening device to identify individuals who may need further academic assessment.

Kaufman Test of Educational Achievement (KTEA)

The KTEA [Kaufman and Kaufman, 1985] was introduced as an alternative for such tests as the PIAT and the WRAT-R. The KTEA assesses reading, mathematics, and spelling skills for grades 1 through 12. There is a brief form and a comprehensive form of the test. The brief form assesses reading, mathematics, and spelling with three separate subtests and takes about 15 to 30 minutes to administer. The comprehensive form assesses the same skills with five subtests and takes about 30 to 60 minutes for grades 1 to 3 and 60 to 75 minutes for grades 4 to 12.

While the KTEA is a fairly new instrument and considerable research needs to be completed, early findings suggest the potential utility of the measure. The test was well standardized and has more than adequate reliability. Validity information indicates that subtests from the KTEA have considerable shared variance with more established measures of academic achievement. The test does appear to be a useful instrument for the assessment of academic skills and is a more comprehensive alternative to other measures. The KTEA also provides a method for evaluating student errors. This should be particularly beneficial when assessing ADHD children in that error analysis helps in determining whether incorrect responses indicate a true lack of skills or a deficit of attention and impulsivity in responding.

Woodcock-Johnson Psychoeducational Battery: Tests of Achievement (WJPB)

The WJPB cognitive measure was discussed previously. The other major component of this battery is the tests of academic achievement. The WJPB is a wide range comparison set of tests that is designed to be used with individuals from 3 to 80 years of age. The tests of achievement cover 10 areas including reading, spelling, capitalization, punctuation, mathematics, and knowledge of science, humanities, and social studies. The achievement subtests are grouped into the following five major clusters: (a) reading, (b) math, (c) written language, (d) knowledge, and (e) skills.

The WJPB is basically, a psychometrically sound instrument. The standardization of the test was quite comprehensive. Advantages of the battery include the diversity of skills assessed and the relative ease of administration. The test does appear to be a good measure of academic achievement constructs, although further research as to the utility of the instrument with special populations such as ADHD children is certainly needed.

Woodcock Reading Mastery Test (WRMT)

The WRMT [Woodcock, 1973] is a diagnostic reading measure designed for students from kindergarten through grade 12. The test has five subtests and two forms. Either form can be administered in 30 to 50 minutes. The subtests of the measure are as follows: (a) letter identification, (b) word identification, (c) word attack, (d) word comprehension, and (e) passage comprehension. The raw scores of each subtest can be converted to age equivalents, grade equivalents, percentile ranks, or standard scores. Separate gender and socioeconomic status norms are provided. Additionally, mastery scores can be obtained that provide an indication of an individual's reading proficiency at 75%, 90%, and 95% percent accuracy. These mastery scores can then be interpreted in terms of failure reading level, reading grade score, and easy reading level.

The WRMT is one of the most widely used reading tests available, probably because it is easy to administer and covers a number of areas. Another advantage of the measure is that it is diagnostic in nature, which affords the opportunity for more indepth analysis and interpretation of the individual subtests. There are limitations, however, that should be considered. First, the letter identification subtest may artificially inflate scores for older students. Second, the analogy format of the word comprehension subtest has been questioned. Impulsive responding on this subtest by ADHD children could skew their scores.

The WRMT has recently been revised. The Woodcock Reading Mastery Test—Revised (WRMT-R) [Woodcock, 1987] is quite similar to the WRMT with a few additions including a readiness section, expanded subtests, and diagnostic aids such as error analysis. In general, the test should retain it's basic value as a diagnostic inventory with ADHD children. The diagnostic aids may facilitate a more indepth qualitative analysis of reading skills, which should lead to more comprehensive and useful recommendations.

Key Math Diagnostic Test (KMDT)

The KMDT [Connolly et al., 1971] is an untimed test that measures arithmetic skills. It is designed for use primarily with children from grades 1 through 6; however, there is no upper limit for informal clinical or remedial use. The KMDT consists of 14 subtests in three major areas: (a) content, (b) operations, and (c) applications. Most of the items are presented orally by the examiner using color plates in an easel kit. The student is required to respond verbally to the items. Administration time is approximately 30 minutes. The raw scores for each subtest are added and the total test raw score is converted to a grade equivalent. The authors suggest the test results be examined in four ways: (a) total test performance, (b) area performance, (c) subtest performance, and (d) item performance.

The KMDT is a useful assessment instrument with children in the elementary school grades. The fact that it is a diagnostic test suggests that very specific information about mathematical skills can be obtained. Available research does indicate that it is a useful instrument with LD children [Greenstein and Strain, 1977; Kratochwill and Demuth, 1976]. Certainly, the broad range and diversity of item content, the colorful format, and the absence of reading and writing requirements make the KMDT appealing for use with exceptional children. Psychologists should be aware that there is a good deal of language comprehension and verbal response required by this test. This is an important consideration when assessing the ADHD-language disordered child.

The KMDT has also been recently revised. The Key Math Revised: A Diagnostic Inventory of Essential Mathematics [Connolly, 1988] is very similar to the original test. Up-dated norms and methods of interpretation are the primary enhancements of this assessment battery. Research investigations will shed light as to the utility of the test with ADHD children.

This concludes the brief section on academic achievement measures. Table 2 provides an overview summary of the strengths and weaknesses for each of the tests reviewed. It should be noted again that only the more widely used measures were reviewed. We also restricted our review to norm-referenced tests. Psychologists and others working with ADHD children should utilize a number of different procedures when assessing academic skills including informal assessments and criterion-referenced tests.

Tests of Visual-Motor Integration

The tests reviewed in this section are concerned with assessing visual-motor perception and integration. These receptive and expressive skills are important in the processing of information and their measurement is especially useful in evaluating children with possible learning difficulties or neurological deficits [Sattler, 1988]. Tests of visual-motor integration are helpful in assessing a child's sensory and motor modalities and for planning remedial strategies. It is valuable to keep in mind that ADHD children do tend to perform well below normal children on tests of visual-motor functioning. ADHD children tend to respond more quickly and make more errors than non-ADHD children. It is important for the psychologist to closely observe the ADHD child completing the task and try to determine if there is a true visual-motor processing deficit or if lowered performance is merely due to impulsive responding.

Bender Visual Motor Gestalt Test (Bender-Gestalt)

The Bender-Gestalt [Bender, 1938] is the most popular test of visual-motor integration. This popularity is due in part to the ease of administration and

Table 2 Strengths and Weaknesses of Academic Achievement Testing Measures

Instrument	Strengths	Weaknesses
PIAT	Provides good screening measure for basic academic skills	Need for up-dated norms Multiple choice format is susceptible to impulsive type responding
WRAT-R	Up-dated norms Short and easy to administer	Reading section only measures reading recognition Caution in interpretation of arithmetic section
KTEA	Up-dated norms Provides good overall measure of achievement Error analysis component	Need for more research with ADHD children
Woodcock-Johnson Battery	Wide variety of academic skills assessed Up-dated norms	Need for more research with ADHD children
Woodcock Reading Mastery Test	Up-dated norms (particularly with revised edition) Diagnostic test allows for advantages with interpretation Assesses distinct skill areas of reading	Letter identification subtest may inflate scores for older children Format of word comprehension subtest susceptible to impulsive responding
Key-Math	Diagnostic test Wide variety of skills assessed Up-dated norms (revised edition)	Requires a good deal of language comprehension and verbal responses

the purported use of the test as a psychological and personality test as well as a visual-motor measure. The Bender-Gestalt consists of nine geometric figures drawn on 4 × 6 inch white cards. The figures are presented one at a time and the child simply copies the figures on a blank sheet of paper.

The most commonly used scoring system for the Bender-Gestalt is the Koppitz Developmental Scoring System [Koppitz, 1975]. This system is based on the presence or absence of errors in drawings. A four-category system is used to classify errors: (a) distortion of shape, (b) perseveration, (c) integration, and (d) rotation. The total number of errors is compared to norms for the child's age and can be transformed into standard scores, percentiles, or age equivalents.

The clinical utility of the Bender-Gestalt and the Koppitz scoring system has been the focus of considerable research. The interrater reliability for the Koppitz system is reportedly high [Neale and McKay, 1985]. Previous studies have found differential rates for types of errors committed. In general, this literature suggests that integration errors are the most common, followed by distortion errors, with the least common being perseveration and rotation errors [Neale and McKay, 1985]. A recent study, however, indicated that the Koppitz error scores had limited utility in differentiating clinical subtypes [Snow and Desch, 1988]. These authors found that multivariate analysis of Bender-Gestalt error scores yielded two subgroups, one with relatively normal functioning and the other with numerous errors. These results suggest that psychologists should exercise some caution in interpreting error scores.

The Bender-Gestalt is a useful instrument for assessing visual-motor integration ability and can add important information to the overall psychoeducational assessment of the ADHD child. Although the test has been used as a measure of nonverbal intelligence, brain injury, emotional status, and academic readiness, it should not be used as the sole diagnostic instrument for any of these purposes. The Bender-Gestalt's strongest psychometric asset is its use as a measure of visual-motor integration with children, particularly those between 5 and 8 years of age.

Developmental Test of Visual-Motor Integration (VMI)

The VMI [Beery, 1982] is a visual-motor test designed for use with children 4 to 13 years of age. The test consists of 24 geometric figures arranged in a sequence of increasing complexity (figures range from a vertical line to a three-dimensional star). The figures are presented in a standard test booklet in which the child copies the designs. The examiner may discontinue testing after the child fails three consecutive figures. The figures are scored on a pass-fail basis and the raw score (total correct) can be converted to a standard score, percentile rank, or age equivalent.

The VMI is a very easy test to administer and appears to be a useful measure of visual-motor skills. However, some degree of subjectivity is required to score responses and significant scoring differences among examiners have been found [Snyder et al., 1981]. Scores on the VMI have been found to discriminate LD from normal children, although the educational significance of this is questionable. Research also indicates that the VMI and the Bender-Gestalt should not be used interchangeably, as they yield different scores and have been found to measure different constructs [Lehman and Breen, 1982; Porter and Binder, 1981].

Table 3 lists the major strengths and weaknesses for the visual-motor measures discussed.

Adaptive Behavior Scales

Adaptive behavior scales measure a child's ability to function independently and to satisfactorily meet social and environmental demands. Adaptive behavior skills are frequently incorporated into assessment with children at most age levels, and adaptive behavior scales have a number of uses including: (a) identifying areas of behavioral strength and weakness of an individual, (b) providing an objective basis for comparison of an individual's progress over time, (c) comparing ratings of an individual in different settings (e.g., home, school, institution), (d) comparing the ratings of different raters, and (e) stimulating new intervention or treatment programs [Sattler, 1988]. Adaptive behavior scales, when combined with other assessment results, provide useful and important information about a child. One of the potential problems associated with the scales is that they depend on a third person or persons for data that makes them subject to distortion and/or bias. Raters may differ in their familiarity with the child, their tolerance for behavior

Table 3 Strengths and Weaknesses of Visual-Motor Testing Measures

Instrument	Strengths	Weaknesses
Bender-Gestalt	Easy to administer System of error analysis	Several scoring systems with questionable validity
	Particularly useful with children 5 to 8 years	Format is susceptible to impulsive responding
VMI	Well-structured measure Easy to administer	Format is susceptible to impulsive responding

problems, their personality, their expectations for the child, and their willingness or tendency to use certain ratings on the scale. Raters reveal their own attitudes toward the child and the child's behavior in completing the scale. These attitudes should be considered when evaluating the results of an ADHD child's adaptive behavior measure.

Vineland Adaptive Behavior Scales (VABS)

VABS [Sparrow et al., 1984] is a revision of one of the oldest and most popular adaptive behavior scales, the Vineland Social Maturity Scale [Doll, 1965]. VABS is designed to measure the adaptive skills of handicapped and nonhandicapped individuals from birth through age 18. The instrument has an interview format and requires an informant who is familiar with the behavior of the individual being tested. There are three editions of the VABS: (a) the Survey Form, (b) the Expanded Form, and (c) the Classroom Edition. Each edition measures adaptive behavior in four domains: (a) communication, (b) daily living skills, (c) socialization, and (d) motor skills. These four domains form the Adaptive Behavior Composite. The Survey and Expanded Forms also include a maladaptive behavior domain that deals with negative behaviors that may interfere with adaptive functioning. Standard scores and percentiles can be calculated for each of the domains.

VABS appears to be a good overall measure of adaptive behavior, although further research on the utility of the measure with ADHD children is needed. There has also been some concern expressed about the interview format and the difficulty of eliciting and scoring responses appropriately [Oakland and Houchins, 1985]. Because the instrument is conducted with a significant other and not the child directly, the ADHD condition should not have a direct bearing on the validity of the test results. This is a major advantage of using this instrument with this special population.

AAMD Adaptive Behavior Scale—School Edition (ABS-SE)

The ABS-SE [Lambert et al., 1981] is designed to measure a child's adaptive behavior within a school setting. The ABS-SE is similar to the original AAMD Adaptive Behavior Scale [Nihira et al., 1974], which was designed for and normed with the institutionalized mentally retarded. However, the ABS-SE does not measure domains that are not relevant to a classroom setting. The test can be used with children from 3 through 16 years of age and can be useful in diagnosis, placement, and program planning. It takes approximately 30 minutes to administer and the information is collected by one of three methods: (a) first-person assessment, (b) third-party assessment, or (c) interview. First-person assessment involves having a person familiar with the child complete the evaluation form. Third-party assessment involves the input of multiple informants with the evaluation process. The interview format involves the psychologist conducting comprehensive interviews with significant others and then completing the form based on the information obtained.

The ABS-SE consists of two parts. Part One measures personal independence in daily living skills and includes the following nine domains:

1. independent functioning
2. physical development
3. economic activity
4. language development
5. number and time
6. vocational activity
7. self-direction
8. responsibility
9. socialization

Part Two is concerned with the assessment of maladaptive behavior and consists of the following 12 domains:

1. violent and destructive behavior
2. antisocial behavior
3. rebellious behavior
4. untrustworthy behavior
5. withdrawal
6. stereotyped behavior and odd mannerisms
7. inappropriate interpersonal mannerisms
8. unacceptable vocal habits
9. unacceptable or eccentric habits
10. hyperactive tendencies
11. psychological disturbance
12. use of medications.

Five factors have been identified for the ABS-SE and are used in scoring.

1. personal self-sufficiency
2. community self-sufficiency
3. personal-social responsibility
4. social adjustment
5. personal adjustment

Standard scores and percentile can be derived with this measure.

The ABS-SE appears to be another strong instrument for the assessment of adaptive skills with the ADHD child. The fact that it is concerned with behavior in the school environment is a definite asset. Psychometric data is

Table 4   Strengths and Weaknesses of Adaptive
Behavior Testing Measures

Instrument	Strengths	Weaknesses
Vineland	Up-dated norms Comprehensive format that assesses a number of behavioral domains Measure involves the interview of a significant other	
AAMD	Focuses on behavior in the school environment	Further research needed with ADHD children
	Provides assessment of wide array of behaviors	Further research needed with ADHD children

lacking with the instrument, and psychologists should interpret the result with some caution.

Summarized results for the adaptive behavior scales can be seen in Table 4.

FINAL CONSIDERATIONS

The key to an adequate psychoeducational evaluation with the ADHD child is that the assessment is broad based. Because of space limits, we have specifically focused our review to a limited number of standardized instruments. There are numerous other assessment instruments available to the psychologist that can provide useful psychoeducational information. In addition to formal standardized testing, it may also be useful to incorporate informal assessments during the evaluation procedure. This can include structured activities designed to see how the child responds to certain teaching techniques (e.g., whole-language approach toward reading). Another useful technique is follow-up with standardized tasks. This involves readministration of particular subtests in order to observe certain strategies that the child is utilizing. The informal or readministration procedures can often have more direct generalization to the classroom.

Behavioral observations should also be incorporated into the psychoeducational evaluation. The importance of incorporating behavioral observations obtained during the testing session(s) itself was discussed earlier. The observational data should not only include observations completed during the testing situation, but also classroom observations as well as standard behavior checklists completed by parents/guardians and/or teachers. These behavioral observations add another dimension to the evaluation beyond the mere reporting of test scores. Direct observations as well as synthesis of behavioral observation data with test results will further enhance the opportunity to formulate more meaningful recommendations.

It is very important that information from significant others be obtained and utilized in the psychoeducational evaluation process. Input from parents and teachers can provide insight into observations yielded from the evaluation itself. The more sources of data that are incorporated into the assessment procedure, the more reliable and valid the evaluation becomes. This enhances the opportunity to provide truly meaningful psychoeducational data with the ADHD child.

The psychoeducational assessment is an integral part of the multidisciplinary evaluation of the ADHD child. It provides some insights as to the cognitive/behavioral correlates of the associated physiological condition. In this regard, it nicely supplements information provided by the developmental pediatrician and other physicians (e.g., pediatric neurologists). The measures of cognitive and academic abilities provided by the psychologist should give other professionals a broader perspective from which to interpret their results. And finally, the psychoeducational assessment yields data that allows the multidisciplinary team to more effectively communicate results and recommendations to parents and school personnel.

REFERENCES

Baker, L., Cantwell, D. P. (1982). Psychiatric disorder in children with different types of communication disorders. *J. Commun. Dis. 15*:113.

Ballinger, C. T., Varley, C. K., Nolen, P. A. (1984). Effects of methylphenidate on reading in children with attention deficit disorder. *Am. J. Psychiatry 141*:1590.

Bannatyne, A. (1974). Diagnosis: A note on recategorization of the WISC scaled scores. *J. Learn. Disab. 7*:272.

Barkley, R. A. (1981) *Hyperactive Children: A Handbook for Diagnosis and Treatment.* New York: Guilford.

Barkley, R. A. (1987) The assessment of attention deficit-hyperactivity disorder. *Behav. Assess. 9*:207.

Baum, D. D. (1975). A comparison of the WRAT and the PIAT with learning disability children. *Ed. Psychol. Meas. 35*:487.

Baumeister, A. A., Bartlett, C. J. (1962) A comparison of the factor structure of normals and retardates on the WISC. *Am. J. Mental Defic. 66*:641.

Beery, K. E. (1982). *Revised Administration: Scoring and Teaching Manual for the Developmental Test of Visual-Motor Integration.* Cleveland: Modern Curriculum Press.

Bender, L. (1938). A visual motor gestalt test and its clinical use. *Am. Orthopsychi. Assoc. Res. Mono.* no. 3.

Bickett, L., Reuter, J., Stancin, T., (1984). The use of the McCarthy Scales of Children's Abilities to assess moderately retarded children. *Psychol. Schools 21*:305.

Bray, N. M., Estes, R. E. (1975). A comparison of the PIAT, CAT, and WRAT scores and teacher ratings with learning disabled children. *J. Learn. Disab. 8*:519.

Breen, M. J. (1984). The temporal stability of the Woodcock-Johnson Tests of Cognitive Ability for elementary-aged learning disabled children. *J. Psychoeduc. Assess. 2*:257.

Burgemeister, B. B., Blum, L. H., Lorge, I. (1972). *Columbia Mental Maturity Scale*, 3rd Ed. San Antonio, TX, The Psychological Corporation.

Cantwell, D. P., Baker, L. (1980). Psychiatric and behavioral characteristics of children with communication disorders. *J. Pediatric Psychol. 5*:161.

Cantwell, D. P., Baker, L., Mattison, R. E. (1980). Factors associated with the development of psychiatric disorder in children with speech and language retardation. *Arch. Gen. Psychiatry 37*:423.

Chess, S., Rosenberg, M. (1974). Clinical differentiation among children with initial language complaints. *J. Autism. Child. Schiz. 4*:99.

Connolly, A. J. (1988). *KeyMath Revised: A Diagnostic Inventory of Essential Mathematics*. Circle Pines, MN: American Guidance Service.

Connolly, A. J., Nachtman, W., Pritchett, E. M. (1971). *The KeyMath Diagnostic Arithmetic Test*. Circle Pines, MN: American Guidance Service.

Cummings, J. A., Moscato, E. M. (1984). Research on the Woodcock-Johnson Psycho-Educational Battery: Implications for practice and future investigations. *School Psychol. Rev. 13*:33.

Dean, R. S. (1977). Analysis of the PIAT with Anglo and Mexican-American children. *J. School Psychol. 15*:329.

DeHorn, A., Klinge, V. (1978). Correlations and factor analysis of the WISC-R and the Peabody Picture Vocabulary Test for and adolescent psychiatric sample. *J. Consult. Clin. Psychol. 46*:1160.

Doehring, D. G., Hoshko, I. M., Bryans, B. N. (1979). Statistical classification of children with reading problems. *J. Clin. Neuropsychol. 1*:5.

Doll, E. A. (1965). *Vineland Social Maturity Scale*. Circle Pines, MN: American Guidance Service.

Dunn, L. M., Markwardt, F. C., Jr. (1970). *Peabody Individual Achievement Test*. Circle Pines, MN: American Guidance Service.

Fisk, J. L., Rourke, B. P. (1979). Identification of subtypes of learning-disabled children at three age levels: A neuropsychological, multivariate approach. *J. Clin. Neuropsychol. 1*:289.

Gadow, K. D. (1985). Relative efficacy of pharmacological, behavioral, and combination treatments for enhancing academic performance. *Clin. Psychol. Rev. 5*:513.

Goh, D. S., Youngquist, J. A. (1979). A comparison of the McCarthy Scales of Children's Abilities and the WISC-R. *J. Learn. Disab. 12*:344.

Greenstein, J., Strain, P. S. (1977). The utility of the KeyMath Diagnostic Arithmetic Test for adolescent learning disabled students. *Psychol. Schools 14*:275.

Gualtieri, C. T., Koriath, U., Van Bourgondien, M., Saleeby, N. (1983). Language disorders in children referred for psychiatric services. *J. Am. Acad. Child Psychiatry 22*:165.

Harrison, P. L. (1981). Mercer's Adaptive Behavior Inventory, the McCarthy Scales, and dental development as predictors of first-grade achievement. *J. Educ. Psychiatry 73*:78.

Jastak, S., Wilkenson G. S. (1984). *Wide Range Achievement Test-Revised.* Wilmington, DE: Jastak Associates.

Johnston, W. T., Bolen, L. M. (1984). A comparison of the factor structure of the WISC-R for blacks and whites. *Psychol. Schools 21*:42.

Kamphaus, R. W., Reynolds, C. R. (1987). *Clinical and Research Applications of the K-ABC.* Circle Pines, MN. American Guidance Service.

Kaufman, A. S. (1979). *Intelligent Testing with the WISC-R.* New York: John Wiley and Sons.

Kaufman, A. S., Kaufman, N. L. (1983). *K-ABC: Kaufman Assessment Battery for Children.* Circle Pines, MN: American Guidance Service.

Kaufman, A. S., Kaufman, N. L. (1985). *Kaufman Test of Educational Achievement.* Circle Pines, MN: American Guidance Service.

Keith, T. Z., Bolen, L. M. (1980). Factor structure of the McCarthy Scales for children experiencing problems in school. *Psychol. Schools 17*:320.

Koppitz, E. M. (1975). *The Bender Gestalt Test for Young Children,* (Vol. 2): *Research and Application.* New York: Grune and Stratton.

Kratochwill, T. R., Demuth, D. M. (1976). An examination of the predictive validity of the KeyMath Diagnostic Arithmetic Test and the Wide Range Achievement Test in exceptional children. *Psychol. Schools 13*:404.

Lamanna, J. A., Ysseldyke, J. E. (1973). Reliability of the peabody Individual Achievement Test with first-grade children. *Psychol. Schools 10*:437.

Lambert, N. M. (1988). Adolescent outcomes for hyperactive children: Perspectives on general and specific patterns of childhood risk for adolescent educational, social, and mental health problems. *Am. Psychol. 43*:786.

Lambert, N. M., Windmiller, M., Tharinger, D., Cole, L. J. (1981). *AAMD Adaptive Behavior Scale-School Edition.* Monteray, CA: CTB/McGraw-Hill.

Lehman, J., Breen, M. J. (1982). A comparative analysis of the Bender-Gestalt and Beery-Buktenica Tests of Visual-Motor Integration as a function of grade level for regular education students. *Psychol. Schools 19*:52.

Leiter, R. G. (1948). *Leiter International Performance Scale.* Chicago: Stoelting Co.

Love, A. J., Thompson, M. G. G. (1988). Language disorders and attention deficit disorders in young children referred for psychiatric services: Analysis of prevalence and a conceptual synthesis. *Am. J. Orthopsychi. 58*:52.

Lyon, R., Stewart, N., Freedman, D. (1982). Neuropsychological characteristics of empirically derived subgroups of learning-disabled readers. *J. Clin. Neuropsychol. 4*:343.

Mattis, S., French, J. H., Rapin, I. (1975). Dyslexia in children and young adults: Three independent neuropsychological syndromes. *Dev. Med. Child Neur. 17*:150.

McCarthy, D. A. (1972). *Manual for the McCarthy Scales of Children's Abilities.* San Antonio, TX: The Psychological Corporation.

McGrew, K. S. (1985). Investigation of the Verbal/Nonverbal structure of the Woodcock-Johnson: Implications for subtest interpretation and comparisons with the Wechsler Scales. *J. Psychoed. Assess. 3*:65.

McGrew, K. S. (1986). *Clinical Interpretation of the Woodcock-Johnson Tests of Cognitive Ability*. Orlando, FL: Grune & Stratton.

Murray, J. B. (1987). Psychophysiological effects of methylphenidate (ritalin). *Psychiatry Rep. 61*:315.

Nalven, F. B., Puleo, V. T. (1968). Relationship between Digit Span and classroom distractibility in elementary school children. *J. Clin. Psychol. 24*:85.

Neale, M. D., McKay, M. F. (1985). Scoring the Bender-Gestalt test using the Koppitz developmental system: Interrater reliability, item difficulty, and scoring implications. *Pers. Motor Skills 60*:627.

Nihira, K., Foster, R., Shellhaas, M., Leland, H. (1974). *AAMD Adaptive Behavior Scale* (Rev. Ed.). Washington, D.C.: American Association on Mental Deficiency.

Oakland, T. D., Houchins, S. (1985). Testing the test: A review of the Vineland Adaptive Behavior Scales, Survey Form. *J. Counsul Dev. 63*:585.

O'Grady, K. E. (1983). A confirmatory maximum likelihood factor analysis of the WAIS-R. *J. Consul. Clin. Psychol. 51*:826.

Pelham, W. E., Bender, M. E. (1982). Peer relationships in hyperactive children: Description and treatment. In: *Advances in Learning and Behavioral Disabilities*. Gadow, K., Bialer, E., eds. Greenwich, CT: JAI, p. 365.

Porter, G. L., Binder, D. M. (1981). A pilot study of visual-motor development intertest reliability: The Beery Developmental Test of Visual-Motor Integration and the Bender Visual Motor Gestalt Test. *J. Learn. Disab. 14*:124.

Purvis, M. A., Bolen, L. M. (1984). Factor structure of the McCarthy Scales for males and females. *J. Clin. Psychol. 40*:108.

Rapport, M. D., Stoner, G., DuPaul, G. J., Birmingham, B. K., Tucker, S. (1985). Methylphenidate in hyperactive children: Differential effects of dose on academic, learning, and social behavior. *J. Abnorm. Child Psychol. 13*:227.

Reeve, R. E., Hall, R. J., Zakreski, R. S. (1979). The Woodcock-Johnson Tests of Cognitive Ability: Concurrent validity with the WISC-R. *Learn. Disab. Quart. 2*: 63.

Reid, M. K., Borkowski, J. G. (1984). Effects of methylphenidate (ritalin) on information processing in hyperactive children. *J. Abnorm. Child Psychol. 12*:169.

Reschly, D. J., Reschly, J. E. (1979). Validity of WISC-R factor scores in predicting achievement and attention for four sociocultural groups. *J. School Psychol. 17*: 355.

Rourke, B. P., Finlayson, M. A. J. (1978). Neuropsychological significance of variations in patterns of academic performance: Verbal and visual-spatial abilities. *J. Abnorm. Child Psychol. 6*:121.

Ryan, J. J., Prifitera, A., and Larsen, J. (1983). Reliability of the WAIS-R with a mixed patient sample. *J. Consul. Clin. Psychol. 51*:460.

Satterfield, J. H., Hoppe, C. M., Schell, A. M. (1982). A prospective study of delinquency in 110 adolescent boys with attention deficit disorder and 99 normal adolescent boys. *Am. J. Psychiatry 139*:795.

Sattler, J. M. (1988). *Assessment of Children* (3rd Ed.). San Diego: Jerome M. Sattler.

Scarnati, R. (1986). An outline of hazardous side effects of ritalin (methylphenidate). *Inter. J. Addic. 21*:837.

Schowalter, J. E. (1979). Paying attention to attention deficit disorder. *Pediatrics* *64*:546.

Silverstein, A. B. (1977). Alternative factor-analytic solutions for the WISC-R. *Educ. Psychol. Meas. 37*:121.

Snow, J. H., Cohen, M., Holliman, W. B. (1985). Learning disability subgroups using cluster analysis of the WISC-R, *J. Psychoeduc. Assess. 4*:391.

Snow, J. H., Desch, L. W. (1988). Subgroups based on Bender-Gestalt error scores. *J. Psychoeduc. Assess. 6*:261.

Snow, J. H., Hynd, G. W. (1985). A multivariate investigation of the Luria-Nebraska Neuropsychological Battery-Children's Revision with learning-disabled children. *J. Psychoeduc. Asses. 3*:101.

Snow, J. H., Koller, J. R., Roberts, C. D. (1987). Adolescent and adult learning disability subgroups based on WAIS-R performance. *J. Psychoeduc. Asses. 5*:7.

Snyder, P. P., Snyder, R. T., Massong, S. F. (1981). The Visual-Motor Integration Test: High interjudge reliability, high potential for diagnostic error. *Psychol. Schools 18*:55.

Sparrow, S. S., Balla, D. A., Cicchetti, D. V. (1984). *Vineland Adaptive Behavior Scales.* Circle Pines, MN: American Guidance Service.

Sprauge, R. L., Sleator, E. K. (1977). Methylphenidate in hyperkinetic children: Differences in dose effects on learning and social behavior. *Science 198*:1274.

Volkmar, F. R., Hoder, L., Cohen, D. J. (1985). Inappropriate use of stimulant medications. *Clin. Pediatrics 24*:127.

Watson, B. U., Goldgar, D. E., Ryschon, K. L. (1983). Subtypes of reading disability. *J. Clin. Neuropsychol. 5*:377.

Wechsler, D. (1967). *Manual for the Wechsler Preschool and Primary Scale of Intelligence.* San Antonio, TX: The Psychological Corporation.

Wechsler, D. (1974). *Manual for the Wechsler Intelligence Scale for Children-Revised.* San Antonio, TX: The Psychological Corporation.

Wechsler, D. (1981). *Manual for the Wechsler Adult Intelligence Scale-Revised.* San Antonio, TX: The Psychological Corporation.

Wilson, J. D., Spangler, P. F. (1974). The Peabody Individual Achievement Test as a clinical tool. *J. Learn. Disab. 7*:384.

Woodcock, R. W. (1973). *Woodcock Reading Mastery Tests.* Circle Pines, MN: American Guidance Service.

Woodcock, R. W. (1977). *Woodcock-Johnson Psycho-Educational Battery: Technical Report.* Allen, TX: DLM Teaching Resources.

Woodcock, R. W. (1987). *Woodcock Reading Mastery Tests-Revised.* Circle Pines, MN: American Guidance Service.

Woodcock, R. W. (1988). *The Woodcock-Johnson Psycho-Educational Battery Revised.* Allen, TX: DLM Teaching Resources.

Ysseldyke, J., Shinn, M., Epps, S. A. (1981). A comparison of the WISC-R and the Woodcock-Johnson Tests of Cognitive Ability. *Psychol. Schools 18*:15.

Zarski, J. J., Cook, R., West, J., O'Keefe, S. (1987). Attention deficit disorder: Identification and assessment issues. *Am. Mental Health Coun. Assoc. J. 4*:5.

8

Attention Deficits in Children with Hearing or Visual Impairments

Monica H. Ultmann

St. Louis University School of Medicine, St. Louis, Missouri

Desmond P. Kelly

Southern Illinois University School of Medicine, Springfield, Illinois

> *"Eye hath not seen, nor ear heard."*
>
> [Corinthians 2:9]

Efficient sensory input is a basic prerequisite in the hierarchy of cognitive processes necessary for learning and performing. Attentional deficits in children who are already struggling with either visual or hearing impairments place them at double jeopardy for learning or functional impairment. It is therefore vital that attentional difficulties in this population be diagnosed early and treated aggressively.

While it is reasonable to assume that children with sensory impairments are at least as likely as others to manifest attentional deficits, there are additional risk factors to be considered. Impairment of memory and inattention are sensitive indicators of neurologic dysfunction, and those individuals whose sensory deficits are secondary to some form of central nervous system insult would then be expected to be at an even higher risk for associated attentional deficits. There is, however, a paucity of literature regarding the prevalence and impact of attentional deficits in children with sensory impairments. Based on the existing literature and our own clinical observations, this chapter will present approaches to the diagnosis and treatment of attention deficit hyperactivity disorder (ADHD) in hearing and visually impaired pediatric populations.

HEARING IMPAIRMENT

Hearing impairment, in its varying forms, affects the lives of many children. It is sometimes referred to as a hidden problem because of difficulties with early diagnosis and because of the absence, frequently, of outward manifestations of the dysfunction. There are two broad categories of hearing loss—sensorineural and conductive (Table 1); these differ significantly in etiology

Table 1 Spectrum of Causes of Hearing Loss

I. Genetic
  A. Sensorineural
    1. Genetic deafness without associated anomalies
      a. Autosomal dominant
      b. Autosomal recessive
      c. Sex-linked
    2. Genetic deafness with associated anomalies
      a. Waardenburg syndrome
      b. Pendred syndrome
      c. Usher syndrome
      d. Refsum syndrome
  B. Conductive
    Ossicular anomalies
    Treacher collins
    Osteopetrosis
II. Nongenetic
  A. Sensorineural
    1. Prenatal
      a. Infections
        i. Rubella
        ii. CMV
        iii. Toxoplasmosis
      b. Maternal disease
        i. Diabetes
        ii. Hypothyroidism
    2. Perinatal
      a. Prematurity
      b. Asphyxia
    3. Postnatal
      a. Meningitis
      b. Encephalitis
      c. Trauma
  B. Conductive
    1. Chronic otitis media

and in management approaches. Varying degrees of impairment occur and different classification systems are used based on the level of hearing loss. These can be described as follows:

1. mild hearing loss, 27-40 decibel (dB) loss
2. moderate hearing loss (hard of hearing), 40-70 dB loss
3. severe hearing loss (partial hearing), 70-90 dB loss
4. profound hearing loss (deaf), greater than 90 dB loss

Individuals with mild hearing loss would have difficulty hearing faint speech and would benefit from, for example, preferential seating in a classroom. Those with moderate hearing loss would benefit from the use of hearing aids. Partial hearing usually necessitates special educational placement and communication skills training, and the profoundly deaf are dependent on visual sources for learning language and communication skills.

Given the wide spectrum of hearing loss, it is not surprising that estimates of the prevalence of deafness vary widely. The reported incidence of congenital deafness ranges from 1 in 1500 to 1 in 4000 [Gerber, 1977]. According to a recent national survey [Wolff and Harkins, 1986], there are an estimated 78,000 hearing-impaired children receiving special educational services in the United States. This estimate does not include children with milder degrees of hearing loss who are mainstreamed at school or the more severely developmentally disabled individuals (a relatively high percentage of whom are deaf) who are in residential institutions.

While the incidence of severe conductive hearing loss has decreased with the advent of antibiotics and improved surgical techniques, the increasing numbers of extremely premature infants who survive the newborn period, coupled with survivors of serious illnesses that were previously fatal, has resulted in a large new population of children at risk for hearing loss. The issues and controversies surrounding intermittent conductive hearing loss secondary to otitis media also bear further discussion and will be addressed later in this chapter.

Etiological Heterogeneity

Any discussion of cognitive dysfunction in deaf children must take into consideration the marked etiological heterogeneity within this population. While the cause of deafness is usually unknown in up to 40% of deaf children, identified etiologies range from a bewildering array of genetic syndromes to a wide variety of pre- and postnatal neurologic insults [Jaffe and Kongismark, 1977]. Individuals whose deafness results from genetic factors affecting peripheral hearing pathways are likely to have a different functional profile from those whose deafness constitutes part of a genetic syndrome with multisystem involvement. In turn, genetically deaf children are likely to differ functionally from those whose deafness is secondary to central nervous system injury or infection. Vernon [1969] addressed the influence of etiology on behavior in a study of 1468 deaf students in California. He found a higher incidence of behavioral problems in general in children whose deafness was secondary to Rh incompatibility, prematurity, or rubella. Likewise, in their classic studies of rubella embryopathy, Chess and Fernandez [1980 a,b] noted a higher incidence of impulsivity in those children whose deafness was accompanied by other physical handicaps. Using brain electrical activity mapping techniques (BEAM), Wolff and Thatcher [1990] demonstrated differences in cortical organization between deaf and hearing children, particularly in the left frontal-temporal and bilateral frontal regions. Further discrepancies were noted between children with hereditary deafness and those deaf children with noninherited physical causes who were neurologically at risk. In general the latter group showed fewer compensatory changes than their genetically deaf counterparts. In our own pilot studies, we have seen that while the overall incidence of ADHD among a group of students at a residential school for the deaf, as rated by their classroom teachers and dormitory supervisors, was not significantly higher than the general population, those students whose deafness was due to a noninherited physical cause were more than twice as likely to have attention problems than those with inherited deafness [Kelly et al., 1990].

Another group of children with hearing loss who have been the subject of more intensive study are those who experience intermittent conductive hearing loss secondary to recurrent or persistent otitis media during the critical early years of language development [Wright, 1988]. We are also learning that children with unilateral sensorineural hearing loss are more vulnerable to learning problems than was previously thought to be the case [Culbertson and Gilbert, 1986]. In addition to the functional heterogeneity related to varying etiologies, the timing of onset of deafness is another important factor. Hearing impairment sustained after 3 to 5 years of age, when speech and language have already been acquired, will have a diminished effect relative to comparable losses in the prelinguistic period [Nober and Nober, 1977].

Aggravating Factors

Language Disabilities, which have a high incidence in the hearing-impaired population, have a considerable impact on their overall cognitive functioning [Davis et al., 1986]. So many vital cognitive functions (such as aspects of memory and the expression of ideas and feelings) are largely mediated by language that disabilities in these areas lead to serious perturbations. It has been postulated that deficits in verbal mediation of self-control contribute to increased levels of impulsivity and that aggressive behavior in the deaf might reflect frustrated attempts to verbally express emotions [Cohen, 1980].

It has been reported that up to 28-30% of deaf children have *associated handicaps* including visual impairment, mental retardation, or cerebral palsy [Mencher, 1983]. These multiply handicapped, hearing-impaired children warrant unique consideration in diagnostic and therapeutic planning. Children with deafness secondary to maternal rubella ("rubella-deaf") have been the subject of extensive research [Chess and Fernandez, 1980 a,b] and provide a model for the challenges posed by the multiply handicapped child. However, researchers in this area have tended to focus on children with overt evidence of neurologic dysfunction such as cerebral palsy. As alluded to in our discussion of etiological factors, the nongenetic causes of deafness are likely to place affected children at risk for subtle neuropsychologic dysfunction in addition to more obvious neurological deficits. In this regard the multiply handicapped hearing-impaired child might represent only the tip of the iceberg. In their review of the *1982-1983 Annual Survey of Hearing Impaired Children and Youth,* Wolff and Harkins [1986] noted that specific learning disabilities and emotional/behavioral problems ranked second and third behind mental retardation among the additional handicaps manifested by deaf students.

The *Familial environment* surrounding the hearing-impaired child would seem to contribute to his outcome, as it has been demonstrated that deaf children of deaf parents generally function better than those born to parents without hearing impairment. The argument presented to support these findings is that deaf parents (or other relatives) are able to communicate more fully with their children from birth. In contrast, deaf children born to hearing parents are apt to be diagnosed late, and to that is coupled the attendant guilt and confusion [Harris, 1978]. While there are compelling reasons why optimal language stimulation and support from early infancy would presage improved functioning, this argument does not give sufficient credit to etiology. Deaf children of hearing parents are more likely to fall into the group with noninherited physical causes who are already at risk for other neuropsychologic dysfunction.

ADHD in Hearing-Impaired Children

Using current diagnostic criteria, there has been little research into the actual prevalence of ADHD in the hearing impaired. However, there have been studies of emotional and behavioral dysfunction as well as specific ADHD traits such as impulsivity in the deaf population. The earlier literature has in general suggested higher rates of impulsivity and social problems in the hearing impaired [Freeman et al., 1975]. As with other research in this population, many of the studies have been beset by a number of methodological problems including population bias, disregard of etiological factors, and the use of instruments that are poorly normed for deaf students [Liptak and Siple, 1981].

Personality or behavioral traits frequently cited as characteristic of deaf children include rigidity, suspiciousness, lack of empathy, and deficits in internal controls or impulsivity [Chess and Fernandez, 1980a]. Chess and Fernandez [1980b] noted that 58.8% of those rubella-deaf children with associated physical handicaps manifested features of impulsivity in contrast to rates of 21% for those who were "deaf only" and 3% for normal hearing controls. Most of the impulsive behaviors were characterized as aggressive. Using psychological test markers for impulsivity (such as the Porteus Maze Test and Draw a Line Test), Altshuler's group [1976] studied children in Yugoslavia as well as the United States and noted a higher incidence of impulsivity in the deaf students. These reports raise the question of whether audition is necessary for impulse control. In contrast, in his study of a group of maladjusted deaf children in England, Williams [1970] reported a broad range of psychiatric classifications, with the group labeled "hyperkinetic disorder" accounting for only 10% of the diagnoses.

Recently those deaf children categorized as multihandicapped hearing-impaired have been more closely evaluated. Epidemiologic studies indicate these children are at increased risk for behavioral disorders including the Strauss syndrome (hyperactivity, restlessness, and distractibility) [Vernon, 1982]. Wolff and Harkins [1986] note that of 53,899 deaf school children in special education, 30% had additional handicapping conditions including learning disabilities (8.1%) and emotional or behavioral problems (5.6%). While actual figures for the prevalence of ADHD were not included in the survey, it was noted that many of the children were likely to have attentional deficits. In a study of 100 deaf Maryland school children, Wolff et al. [1990] reported that 20% of the children scored more than one standard deviation above the mean on the hyperactivity index of the Conner's Teacher Rating Scale.

In our residential school study, we made use of a standardized questionnaires such as the Conner's Parent Questionnaire [Conners, 1969], the ADD-H Comprehensive Teacher Rating Scale (ACTeRS) [Ullman et al., 1986] and the Attention-Activity sections of the ANSER Questionnaires [Levine, 1985]. Utilizing a clinical cutoff on the ACTeRS of scores below the 20th percentile as evidence of attentional problems, 23% of the deaf students met this criterion in contrast to 20% for the normative population. However, more striking differences became evident when students were grouped by cause of deafness. Only 14% of the students with hereditary deafness were rated as having attention problems in contrast to 38% of those with noninherited physical causes [Kelly et al., 1990].

Diagnosis of ADHD in Hearing-Impaired Children

As with the general population, there is no diagnostic gold standard for ADHD in the hearing impaired. Reliance has to be placed on rating scales and reports of behavior inside and outside of the classroom as well as direct observation of patterns of attention and performance during the clinical evaluation. In addition, the use of objective measures of concentration, vigilance, distractibility, and impulsivity are especially applicable to this population. It is, of course, important to ensure that any such test instruments have been standardized for use with the deaf population, which is not the case in most instances. If we are to consider the impact of the attention deficit as a criterion for decisions regarding diagnostic labeling and intervention, more generous cutoffs might be indicated, given that visual inattention or distractibility will have a more profound effect on the performance of a deaf student. Another potential pitfall in diagnosis is the concept of attentional deficits secondary to processing disorders. It is recognized that in students with learning disabilities, particularly language and auditory processing weaknesses, lack of reinforcement for maintaining attention (that is, inability to understand what is being said or taught to them in spite of paying attention) can result in secondary inattention as well as other behavioral problems in the classroom. The classroom inattentiveness of deaf children could be a reflection of associated language and learning disabilities leading to frustration, inattention, and acting out. Thus their ADHD profile could indicate a specific cognitive dysfunction or be the outward behavioral manifestation of a combination of neuropsychologic dysfunctions. Evaluation for underlying or associated problems is, therefore, even more important in the diagnostic workup of a deaf child with attentional difficulties. In addition, consideration needs to be given to the fact that auditory distractibility may be variable. In those children with residual hearing, environmental auditory stimuli could prove more distracting than for children with either normal hearing or profound deafness.

Our pilot studies [Kelly et al., 1990] indicate that the commonly used rating scales for ADHD are applicable to the hearing-impaired population and demonstrate acceptable validity and reliability. The usefulness of questionnaires that measure a child's performance over time and in varying circumstances reaffirms the importance of questionnaires in the routine diagnostic process. During physical examination and psychologic or educational testing, the professional will need to keep in mind that the child may not be able to clearly comprehend instructions. The inclusion of measures of memory and other cognitive processes can add richness to the description of the neuropsychologic functioning of the hearing-impaired child. Objective clinical measures including computerized assessment (continuous performance tasks) to measure sustained and divided attention, impulsivity, and distractibility hold promise in this special population provided that norms are established and testing conditions standardized. Electrophysiologic measures such as visual-evoked potentials and BEAM offer promise as research techniques but are not yet reliable for clinical decision making.

Intermittent Conductive Hearing Loss

There is continuing controversy regarding the long-term effects of recurrent and persistent otitis media with effusion (OME) with associated mild conductive hearing loss. OME presents in early childhood and continues to have an impact on later development, particularly the acquisition of language during sensitive developmental periods. There is also concern regarding the overall effect of early hearing loss and language delay on later academic achievement. While recent research indicates little evidence for overall academic underachievement in children with OME, findings do suggest a link with subsequent attention deficits. Roberts et al. [1989] prospectively studied a group of children identified at birth to be environmentally at risk. These children attended a developmental day care center, and their middle ear status was closely monitored during the first few years of life. Subsequent evaluation of this cohort in the third grade revealed less task orientation and decreased ability to work independently in those children who had frequent episodes of OME. Other studies [Adesman et al., 1990; Bennett and Furukawa, 1984; Oberklaid et al., 1989; Wright et al., 1988; Zinkus and Gottlieb, 1980] have indicated a link between intermittent conductive hearing loss, attentional deficits, and learning disabilities. Hagerman and Falkenstein [1987] have found in their clinic population of children with ADHD that there was a strong correlation between the frequency of episodes of OME and the degree of severity of ADHD.

There is no doubt that a variable degree of conductive hearing impairment—from negligible to 50 dB—accompanies OME. The challenge to the primary care physician is to decide how aggressively to pursue OME. The question remains as to whether early otitis media and ADHD are causally related or simply have predisposing determinants in common. While the majority of children with recurrent otitis will not manifest later attentional deficits, these children as a group do warrant close monitoring as they progress through school. Paradise and Rogers [1986] have reviewed the controversy surrounding a unified approach to treatment in this population.

Unilateral Sensorineural Hearing Loss

In spite of previous assumptions that children with unilateral hearing loss were not at risk for academic difficulties, Culbertson and Gilbert [1986] have shown that monaural deafness, especially when severe or profound, may be associated with secondary behavioral adjustment difficulties (including inattention to tasks) as well as academic dysfunction. Bess and Tharpe [1984] report that almost 50% of their population of monaurally deaf students had either failed a grade or required resource assistance in school.

VISUAL IMPAIRMENT

As in hearing-impaired individuals, there is marked etiological heterogeneity in the visually impaired population. The degree of functional visual loss present in individuals varies from mild loss through light perception to total blindness. Thus individuals identified as being "blind" carry with them a wide range of abilities and impairments. Currently the U.S. Public Health Service defines blindness as:

> Visual acuity, in the better eye with correction, of not more than 20/200 or a defect in the visual field so that the widest diameter of vision subtends an angle no greater than 20°. [Schloss, 1963]

In order to facilitate a uniform definition of visual impairment for epidemiological and research purposes, the World Health Organization adopted the following classification system in 1970 (with reference to the better of the two eyes):

1. Visual impairment: Snellen acuity no better than 6/18 meter (m) (corrected) or a visual field no better than 20 degrees.
2. Social blindness: Snellen acuity no better than 6/60 m (corrected) or a visual field no better than 20 degrees.
3. Virtual blindness: Snellen acuity no better than 1/60 m or a visual field of less than 10 degrees.
4. Total blindness: no light perception. [Davidson, 1983]

It is important to remember that the ophthalmologic evaluation and determination of *functional* residual vision in infants and young children is difficult to perform. The strict definition of "blindness" in this population is thus less accurate for both epidemiological classification and for qualifying for financial benefits and special education services. In the United States, approximately 64 infants and children per 100,000 population are blind or significantly visually impaired, while another 100 children per 100,000 have less serious visual impairment [Davidson, 1983].

A discussion of the cognitive and behavioral development in the visually impaired pediatric population must take into account the age at which the visual loss occurred (neonatal versus childhood period), the etiology of the visual loss and whether or not other coexisting disabilities are present. In infants and children with presumed congenital visual impairment the leading causes appear to be prenatal influences such as genetic, anatomic malformations, infectious, and toxic. In perinatal cases, low birthweight, oxygen supplementation, and complicated neonatal medical courses may contribute to the development of retinopathy of prematurity. The etiologies of acquired visual loss include injuries, infection and neoplasms (Table 2).

ADHD in Visually Impaired Children

As with the hearing-impaired population, there has been little research into the actual prevalence of attentional deficits in the visually impaired population. Studies that have examined personality and social development, psychopathology, and the attainment of locus of control in visually impaired children have suffered from a number of methodologic problems including small sample size, etiologic heterogeneity, the use of rating scales that have not been adequately normed on the visually impaired population, and the absence of matched control groups.

Visually impaired children have been variably described in the literature as hypoactive and passive and, in the case of those children who have received inconsistent handling, hyperactive with tantrums [Jan et al., 1977]. Internal locus of control, which reflects independence and self-sufficiency, is less established in younger, visually impaired children than in age-matched sighted children [Land and Vineberg, 1965; Parsons, 1987].

Behavioral and emotional disturbances have been described in the visually impaired [Warren, 1984]. The data suggest that children with varying degrees of visual impairment do exhibit difficulties with social and emotional adjustment. Using the Behavior Problem Checklist, Schnittjer and Hirschoren [1981] identified three aspects of behavior present among 104 visually impaired residential school students: (a) conduct problems characterized by overt aggression, (b) personality problems involving anxious-withdrawn behavior, and (c) inadequacy—immaturity involving attentional efficiency and attentional problems such as distractibility, restlessness, and short attention span. The attentional findings were thought to be secondary to other behavioral difficulties. They concluded that the observed behavioral patterns did not differ from those occurring in other populations, including a group of hearing-impaired students studied previously [Hirschoren and Schnittjer, 1979] and were therefore probably largely independent of the visual handicap. Using the Child Behavior Checklist [Achenbach, 1978; Achenbach and Edelbrock, 1979; Edelbrock and Achenbach, 1980], School Behavior Checklist [Miller, 1972], and the Behavioral Problem Checklist (original and revised)

Edelbrock, C., Achenbach, T. M. (1980). A typology of child behavior profile patterns: Distribute and correlates for disturbed children aged 6-16. *J. Abnorm. Child Psychol. 8*:440.

Freeman, R. D., Malkin, S. F., Hastings, J. O. (1975). Psychological problems of deaf children and their families: A comprehensive study. *Am. Ann. Deaf 120*: 391.

Gerber, S. E. (1977). High risk registry for congenital deafness. In: *Hearing Loss in Children*. Jaffe, B. F., ed. Baltimore: University Park Press, p. 73.

Hagerman, R. J., Falkenstein, A. R. (1987). An association between recurrent otitis media in infancy and later hyperactivity. *Clin. Pediatrics 26*:253.

Harris, R. I. (1978). The relationship of impulse control to parent hearing status, manual communication and academic achievement in deaf children. *Am. Ann. Deaf 123*:52.

Heinze, A., Helsel, W. J., Matson, J. L., Kapperman, G. (1987). Assessing general psychopathology in children and youth with visual handicaps. *Australia New Zealand J. Dev. Disabil. 13*:219.

Hirshoren, A., Schnittjer, C. J. (1979).

Jaffe, B. F., Konigsmark, B. (1977). Types of hearing loss in children. In: *Hearing Loss in Children*. Jaffe, B. F., ed. Baltimore: University Park Press, p. 283.

Jan, J. J., Freeman, R. D., Scott, E. P. (1977). *Visual Impairment in Children and Adolescents*. New York: Grune and Stratton.

Kelly, C. (1981). Reliability of the Behavior Problem Checklist with institutionalized male delinquents. *J. Abnorm. Child Psychol. 9*:243.

Kelly, D. P., Kelly, S. J., Jones, M., Moulton, N., Verhulst, S. J., Bell, S. (1990). Hearing loss and attention deficits: Etiological considerations. *Am. J. Dis. Child. 144*(4):439 (abstr.).

Land, S. L., Vineberg, S. E. (1965). Locus of control in blind children. *Exceptional Children. January*:257.

Levine, M. D. (1985). *The ANSER System Questionnaires*. Cambridge, Massachusetts: Educators Publishing Service.

Liptak, G. S., Siple, P. A. (1981). Behavioral problems in deaf children: Methodologic and theoretical considerations. *J. Dev. Behav. Pediatrics 2*(1):9.

Mencher, G. T. (1983). Hearing loss and multiple handicaps: Occurence and effects. In: *The Multiply Handicapped Hearing Impaired*. Mencher, G. T., Gerber, S. E., eds. New York: Grune and Stratton, p. 5.

Miller, L. C. (1972). School Behavior Checklist: An inventory of deviant behavior for elementary school children. *J. Consult. Clin. Psychol. 38*:134.

Morrow, L. W. (1985). Teaching self-control to dually diagnosed deaf students: Promising procedures. *Am. Ann. Deaf 130*:502.

Nober, E. H., Nober, L. W. (1977). Effects of hearing loss on speech and language in the post babbling stage. In: *Hearing Loss in Children*. Jaffe, B. F., ed. Baltimore: University Park Press, p. 630.

Oberklaid, F., Harris, C., Keir, E. (1989). Auditory dysfunction in school children. *Clin. Pediatrics 28*:397.

O'Brien, D. H. (1987). Reflection-impulsivity in total communication and oral deaf and hearing children: A developmental study. *Am. Ann. Deaf 132*:213.

Paradise, J. L., Rogers, K. D. (1986). On otitis media, child development and tympanostomy tubes: New answers or old questions? *Pediatrics 77*:88.

Parsons, S. (1987). Locus of control and adaptive behavior in visually impaired children. *J. Visual Impairment Blindness November*:429.

Quay, H. C. (1977). Measuring dimensions of deviant behavior: The Behavior Problem Checklist. *J. Abnorm. Child Psychol. 5*:278.

Quay, H. C. (1983). A dimensional approach to behavior disorder: The Revised Behavior Problem Checklist. *School Psychol. Rev. 12*:244.

Quay, H. C., Peterson, D. R. (1975). *Manual for the Behavior Problem Checklist.* (Privately printed.)

Quay, H. C., Peterson, D. R. (1983). *Interim Manual for the Revised Behavior Problem Checklist.* (Privately printed.)

Roberts, J. E., Burchinal, M. R., Collier, A. M., Ramey, C. T., Koch, M. A., Henderson, F. W. (1989). Otitis media in early childhood and cognitive, academic and classroom performance of the school-aged child. *Pediatrics 83*:477.

Schloss, J. P. (1963). Implications of altering the definition of blindness. *Research Bulletin No. 3.* New York: American Foundation for the Blind, p. 111.

Schnittjer, C. J., Hirshoren, A. (1981). Factors of problem behavior in visually impaired children. *J. Abnorm. Child Psychol. 9*:517.

Ullmann, R. K., Sleator, E. K., Sprague, R. L. (1986). *ADD-H Comprehensive Teacher Rating Scale.* Champaign, Illinois: Metri Tech, Inc.

Vernon, M. (1969). Multiply handicapped deaf children: Medical, educational and psychological considerations. Washington, D.C.: The Council for Exceptional Children, Inc.

Vernon, M. (1982). Multihandicapped deaf children: Types and causes. In: *The Multihandicapped Hearing Impaired.* Tweedie, D., Shroyer, E. H., eds. Washington, D.C.: Gallaudet College Press.

Warren, D. H. (1984). *Blindness and Early Childhood Development,* 2nd ed. Rev. New York: American Foundation for the Blind.

Williams, C. E. (1970). Some psychiatric observations on a group of maladjusted deaf children. *J. Child Psychol. Psychiatry 11*:1.

Wolff, A. B., Harkins, J. E. (1986). Multihandicapped students. In: *Deaf Children in America.* Schildroth, A. N., Karchmer, M. A., eds. Boston: College Hill Press, p. 55.

Wolff, A. B., Thatcher, R. W. (1990). Cortical reorganization in deaf children. *J. Clin. Exp. Neuropsychol. 12*:2.

Wolff, A. B., Kammerer, B. L., Gardner, J. K., Thatcher, R. W. (1990). The Gallaudet neurobehavioral project: Brain behavior relationships in deaf children. *J. Am. Deafness Found.* (in Press).

Wright, P. F., Sell, S. H., McConnell K. B., Sitton, A. B., Thompson, J., Vaughn, W. K., Bess, F. H. (1988). Impact of recurrent otitis media on middle ear function, hearing and language. *J. Pediatrics 113*:581.

Zinkus, P. W., Gottlieb, M. I. (1986). Patterns of perceptual and academic deficits related to early chronic otitis media. *Pediatrics 66*:246.

Treatment

9

Living with a Hyperactive Child: Principles of Families, Family Therapy, and Behavior Management

Barbara Y. Whitman

St. Louis University, St. Louis, Missouri

Carla Smith

Cardinal Glennon Children's Hospital, St. Louis, Missouri

> *"Nobody who has not been in the interior of a family can say what the difficulties of any individual of that family may be."*
>
> [Jane Austen, *Pride and Prejudice*]

The child with attention deficit hyperactivity disorder (ADHD) presents a special challenge to parents. Usual modes of parenting are ineffective. If this is a first or only child, this ineffectiveness can get translated over time to the notion that the parents themselves are ineffective. If this child is one of a sibling group, this translation may result in the conclusion that the child is defective—usually in personality and character—a conclusion that the child himself may come to believe. Thus a whole layer of negative emotions and inappropriate judgements comes to surround an already difficult situation. Family therapy and behavior management with such children and their caretakers requires an understanding of the special nature of families, an understanding of family systems theory, an understanding of the impact of ADHD on a child and his family and a very critical and selective use of current family therapy and behavior management strategies—because few of these therapies accomodate themselves to the presence of neurologically driven behaviors in any family member, especially children. Failure to understand the limits of these theories and techniques when applied to families with ADHD children is to place these families in a situation that "blames the victim" and worsens the situation for all concerned. A brief look at the components of the usual parenting interaction will illustrate our meaning.

At the most fundamental level of analysis, usual parenting techniques consist of three steps:

1. a statement of expectations (e.g., "In our family we do . . .", "You may not do . . .", or at the younger ages "No! No!" perhaps paired with "Here play with . . .; *this* isn't for little folks")
2. a statement of consequences for failure to comply either by comission or omission (e.g., "If you do . . . then . . . will occur" or "You knew you weren't supposed to do . . . and you did; therefore, . . . will occur"), or a statement of positive consequences for compliance with an expectation (e.g., "If you keep your room clean all week, you can go swimming")
3. an application of consequences for the behavior chains completed in steps 1 and 2

The "normal" (translate non-ADHD) child usually learns within one to three applications of steps 1 through 3 that parents mean business. Over time, step 1, when clearly stated, becomes sufficient by itself to effect wanted behavioral outcomes. At the simplest conceptual level, most parenting is a basic, uncomplicated stimulus/response model that over time is shortened to a stimulus/latent-threat-of-response/model.

Not so with the ADHD child. Stimulus-response modes of parenting, if unmodified, fail. Not because the child hasn't learned the rules and information contained in the stimulus-response chain. Quite the contrary, if asked about the rules relating to any specific situation, most of the children can tell you both the rule and their infraction of it. These parenting modes fail because of these children's organic drivenness and their attentional deficits, impulsivity, and distractability. When questioned, most parents say they can live with the high activity level, if present; it is the consequences of the impulsivity and the attentional deficits that wreak havoc in these families. Too frequently, parents respond to this organic drivenness by (a) escalating punitive modes to the point of aggression and harmfulness and/or (b) completely giving up any positive parent interventions and an avoiding parent-child interaction until a crisis demands a response. In either of these response sets, if ~~WOW~~ n is requested, it is usually for the distraught parent, not for the ~~WOW~~ his disorder.

Par ~~WOW~~ g programs suffer the same "normal" bias. The assumptions of programs advocating "logical consequence" mechanisms include the assumption that the child has the ability to stop and think, weigh the outcomes, and purposefully choose. Programs training for "parent effectiveness" base their models on the outcomes of clear, concise empathic communication processes alone or combined with behavioral contracting. These models also implicitly assume a capacity for clear logical goal-directed choice unimpeded by organic driveness of behavior and thought. Thus parents, with all good intentions (often colored by desperation), systematically apply their newly acquired tools—and fail, leaving both parent and child more frustrated, more short-tempered, and feeling more defeated.

Normalcy assumptions are the substrate of most traditional behavior management programs as well. Thus, time out removes the child from the current situation thereby alleviating further difficulty at that moment. But the unwritten agenda of time out (a time "to contemplate one's sins") is lost on the ADHD child as a means of shaping behavior, for frequently the child has forgotten the infraction and missed the lesson taught by pairing the infraction with the timeout.

Unfortunately, parents of ADHD children can take little comfort in the current research and intervention literature. Research focusing on the parent-ADHD child dyad is decidedly negative in tone, takes a reactive rather than a pro-active view of behavior, focuses predominantly on mothers, uses a interaction coding scale heavily weighted toward describing negative behaviors, places negative interpretation on parental directive—a parental behavior that may be, in fact, a most appropriate pro-active behavior—and perpetuates a tone of maternal inadequacy or hostility as the predominant stimulus for behavior difficulties in most ADHD children.

Similarly, family therapy intervention efforts, by nature of built-in theoretic bias, suffer from the same "normalcy" assumption inherent in more narrowly focused parent-training programs. Continuation of the child's intense behavior levels, unremitting attentional problems, and persistant impulsivity and distractability are seen as evidence that the parents are failing at their "executive subsystem" functions. Some extend this theoretical logic to the view that the child serves a symptomatic deflecting function for a dysfunctional marital relationship, moving the focus of the intervention efforts from qualities and behaviors in the parent-child interaction to that of the marital dyad. The assumption in this instance is that if the marital difficulties are resolved, the child will be cured. While it is true that marriages under the onslaught of such an ADHD child often become strained, the reciprocal direction of effects does not hold when the child is organically driven.

This chapter departs from most of this current literature in the following ways. (a) It recognizes those families with ADHD children as a special population of families for whom intervention strategies must incorporate both the special nature of the family system containing an ADHD child; and (b) it takes a pro-active structural/preventive approach to the management of these families and children rather than a reactive, discipline-based approach. In order to fully understand this strategy, we must first develop a common understanding of families and the unique properties in that social system that we call a family that make parenting ADHD children both a challenge and a stress. We will first develop a primer of family concepts, look at some of the subtleties of the diagnostic process that impact on parental acceptance of the special needs of this child, briefly review current empirical findings, then move to the special nature of the interventive process with these families.

A PRIMER OF FAMILY CONCEPTS

Conceptually, a family is a social system that includes individuals related to each other by way of mutual and reciprocal affections and loyalties and is comprised of a household or households that persist over years and decades. Entry occurs through birth, marriage, or adoption, and members exit only by death, if then [Terkleson, 1980]. This definition highlights the centrality of family dynamics and allows for family structures beyond the traditional two-parent family (e.g., single-parent families, extended family caretakers, homosexual couples raising children). This definitional focus is supported by current child development research that documents the greater impact of family "process" over family "composition" in determining developmental outcomes.

A family, while clearly a definable social organization, differs from other social organizations in three fundamental ways: (a) a shared and predictable life cycle, (b) membership that is virtually permanent, and (c) a dynamic primacy of affectional relationships rather than task fulfillment. Each individual in a family transverses a continuous and (relatively) predictable life cycle. However, unlike an individual, a family life cycle is not bracketed at either end by birth or death [Combrinch-Graham, 1985]. The family's life cycle can be conceptualized as a series of stages with transitional points that occur repeatedly in each generation and that include both an awareness of the past and an anticipation of the future. Commonly defined stages in this life cycle include: leaving home, single young adults; the joining of families through marriage; the new couple; families with young children; families with adolescents: launching children and moving on; and families later in life [Carter and McGoldrick, 1988] (Figure 1). The passage of members from one stage to the next is neither a cataclysmic nor a quiescent process but

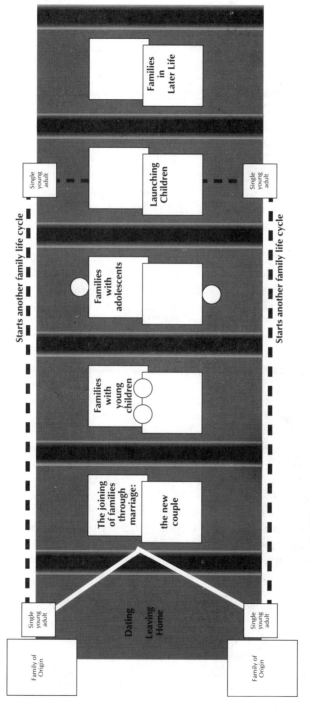

Figure 1 Stages of the family life cycle.

rather a dynamic one that occurs continuously and in the context of the family as a whole.

Membership in a family is virtually permanent. Unlike most organizations, a family offers no routine method of departure. The emotional basis of familial relationships is such that, even when physically absent, inclusion as part of the group endures. Family membership is simply not subject to resignation, firing, or expiration. Like the family life cycle itself, membership in a family acknowledges a past and suggests a future. For example, a child may "lose" a parent through death or divorce, and whether or not that parental role is filled by someone else, the child remains emotionally influenced by the "absent" biological parent, and family dynamics recognize the paradox of the "presence" of the "absent" parent. Similarly, when a young adult woman marries, membership in her family of origin is not terminated; she remains, to varying degrees, "daddy's little girl."

Family relationships are primarily affectional. In a family the emotional bonds of attachment, loyalty, and positive regard are paramount; the successful performance of roles and duties, though welcomed, is secondary. That is, family members are valued for "being" not "doing." Stereotypically, father is the primary breadwinner, while mother, who also may work outside the home, is in charge of housework; the children's "job" is school. If father gets fired or earns less than mother, he is still loved and remains father. Mother is still highly valued and maintains her nurturing, emotional role even when the house is a mess; children are not disowned if they bring a bad report card home. While success is welcomed, a higher value is placed on the affectional bond. A sense of belonging is what is most important.

The very characteristics that set a family system apart from other social systems also serve to illustrate the difficulty for those families with an ADHD child. With the birth of a child the family life cycle and predictable family dynamics shift. However, the ADHD infant can dominate the family at this point and skew these shifts in uncomfortable ways. Often restless and colicky, this child overtaxes the new parents' resources and abilities, thus raising doubts in the parents' minds concerning their ability to parent. Since ADHD is chronic and unremitting, the condition asserts an impact on the child and family indefinitely, affecting their interactions with, and expectations for, that child even into adulthood. Family members' emotional ties are tempered, if not distorted, by the presence of the attention deficit and its accompanying characteristics: impulsivity, distractability, and hyperactivity. Parents' ability to attach and identify with the child is often adversely affected by the ADHD condition.

In addition to the impact of ADHD on the total family system, the ADHD condition is an inherent part of the child; it affects how he thinks, feels, perceives the environment, and behaves. Because the disorder is both insidious and pervasive, it is difficult to realize that the ADHD is not easily mastered by the child. ADHD represents a variable that must be considered along with the child's personality, temperament, and cognitive ability. As the disorder is part and parcel of the child, family considerations of, and interactions with, the child are mediated by the ADHD. In effect, the presence of the disorder is like an additional member of the family, an entity with weighted impact on nonsummativity outcomes.

Circular Causality

Clearly children do not exist autonomously and independently. They impact on and are impacted on by their surroundings, with their families playing the most significant role in their lives. This idea is formalized in the concept of circular causality, which recognizes that any action by a family member results in a reaction from the family system as a whole and conversely any action at the family level results in a reaction from each individual. This concept takes on an added significance when discussing parents' interactions with an ADHD child. In daily living with an ADHD child, it is difficult, if not impossible, to isolate the "causes" of specific behaviors since much of this child's behavior is impulsively driven. Thus intervention strategies must account for this driveness as deterministic and view the "routine" concept of circular causality through a different lens. When this more distant view is missing, too often the family is held directly accountable for the difficulty such a child presents both within the family itself and in other social contexts. This topic will be discussed later in further detail.

STRESSORS

Just as the families' internal interactions are mutually determined, families do not exist devoid of external influences. There are two such categories of influences on families: horizontal and vertical stressors (Figure 2).

In all families, the fact that their relationships are virtually permanent, involuntary, and irreplaceable can be a source of both relative security and considerable stress. Which feeling predominates will depend on two further characteristics of family systems: nonsummativity and circular causality.

Nonsummativity

The principle of nonsummativity recognizes the family as an entity of its own; it is greater than, and different from, the sum of its parts. Nonsummativity, which is derived from general systems theory, dictates that the rela-

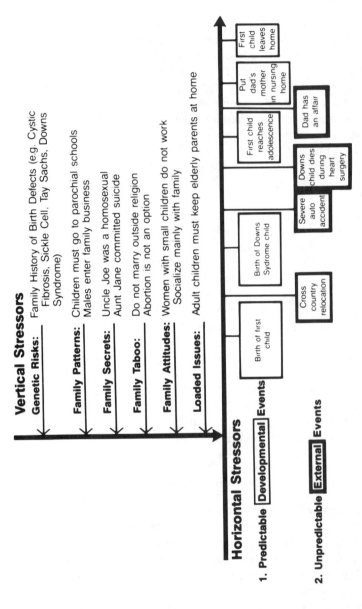

Figure 2   Conceptual sources of stress—horizontal and vertical. [Adapted from Carter, B. and McGoldrick, M. 1988.]

tionships among the components, rather than the components themselves, are the most important descriptors of the system.

When looking at the relationship between any two people in a family, one must consider the impact of the other members on that particular dyadic relationship. For example, if parents are arguing, the subject of the argument is pertinent; more important is the outcome of that argument on the mother-child relationship, the father-child relationship, and the relationship of the parental unit vis-à-vis the child. Families with ADHD children often have points of contention regarding childrearing, discipline, and other family issues. These matters may be discussed directly with the child or just between the parents; at the same time the issues also enter the marital relationship. Siblings impact and are impacted on in a similar way. Nonsummativity then, is an operational principle in all families, helping to shape family relationships, interactions, and patterns.

Horizontal Stressors

Horizontal stressors are events that impact on a family as it moves forward in time. These include both predictable developmental events (the birth of a child or the eventual death of a family member) and those unpredictable external events that may disrupt a family or society (job layoff, catastrophic illness, or war). Meeting such challenges is a fundamental and ongoing task of a family. Families differ markedly in their ability to handle such stresses. Family dysfunction may result if horizontal stressors overwhelm the family's ability to adapt and adjust.

Vertical Stressors

Vertical stressors are specific familial characteristics and patterns of relating that are transmitted through several generations to the current one. They compose the framework within which a given family operates. Included is the family biologic/genetic makeup as well as family attitudes, taboos, labels, and expectations. Examples of these stressors are: "Do not marry outside of your race/religion/social class" or "Our family always excels academically." Messages with a more toxic impact ("family secrets" like "Uncle Joe was an alcoholic" or "Aunt Mary is a psychiatric patient") also fashion the family response to its members and to the external environment. Vertical stressors are also present in more routine contexts; for example, how one makes purchases or responds to authority is effectively influenced by previous familial patterns.

When horizontal stressors intersect with vertical stressors, the resulting anxiety is multiplied. For example, the birth of a cognitively limited child into a family that expects (and has produced) only gifted children can severely tax the family's coping ability. Recognizing how horizontal and verti-

Table 1 Family Characteristics and Constructs

	Definition	Normative Example	ADHD Example
Characteristics Shared and Predictable life	Family members pass through generally expected and identifiable stages. There is an inherent awareness of the past and an anticipation of the future.	Two young adults leave their families of origin to marry. Soon, they have a child and happily begin their "new" family.	A young couple has their first child who is irritable, colicky, and difficult to comfort. They begin to question their parenting abilities and wonder if they were truly ready to start a family.
Membership permanence	A member of a family remains a part of that group as he/she passes through life's stages. Even if physically absent, the member's emotional connection to the family remains.	At her wedding, the bride is given away by her father who tells her, "You'll always be my little girl."	Because of his extreme behavior, Brian is sent to live at a residential treatment center. His family calls and visits often, maintaining their relationship.
Primacy of Affectional Ties	The emotional bonds of positive regard and loyalty are more highly valued than successful role performance. Members are loved for who they are, not what they do.	A mother offered to make a costume for her daughter's school play, even though she couldn't sew. When the mother admitted her failure, the little girl said, "That's ok, Mommy. I love you and just want you to watch me in the play."	Cindy received poor marks in effort, conduct, and peer relations on her report card. Her father discussed the situation with her, commenting on how the ADHD can make being in school difficult and that he and her mother knew that even when she tries hard, things can go wrong. He stressed they loved her no matter what kind of marks she got.

Constructs		
Nonsummativity	A family as a social group is greater than and different from the sum of its members. The relationships among the members actively serve to define the system.	In the Smith family, Billy's ADHD is viewed as an additional family "member." Billy and the ADHD affect the entire family. Activities are planned and interactions are tempered by the ADHD.
	Nancy and Tod get married. Their mutual friends now must deal with this new social unit. Nancy and Tod haven't necessarily changed as individuals, but they are now members of a larger system and their behavior will reflect that.	
Circular causality	Family interactions do not have a distinct "beginning" or "end." Any external factor or action by a member results in a reaction from the family system. Because these interactions are continuous, a causal or linear relationship cannot be made for any given event.	Whenever Mrs. Williams asks her son Kevin to do something, she has to repeat herself several times. The louder her voice gets, the less he seems to listen. He gradually gets more and more active and impulsive, and Mrs. Williams usually ends up sending him to his room.
	Carol complains her sister Sue is mean to her and never shares her clothes and makeup. Sue says Carol always takes her things without asking and gets her in trouble with their parents.	
Horizontal stressors	Events a family must cope with and address over time. These include developmental changes, like a child going away to college, as well as unexpected external changes, like a job layoff or a recession.	When Mrs. Jones gets home from work, she learns her son Tommy has been suspended from school and the bus for not following directions and disturbing others. Mrs. Jones will have to take a day off to meet with the principal before Tommy can go back to school or ride the bus.
	Sally, a recently divorced mother, is adjusting to her new social and economic situation while continuing to care for her teenage children who are starting to date and learning to drive.	

197

Table 1 (continued)

	Definition	Normative Example	ADHD Example
Vertical stressors	Patterns that compose the framework within which a family functions. Included are attitudes, expectations and "family secrets" that are transmitted through several generations. They help fashion how a family responds to its members and its external environment.	Julie was met with unexpected resistance and displeasure when she told her mother she would like to attend the local state university. The women in her mother's family have always attended a certain small liberal arts college in the east.	Susan has an uncontrollable child. She must not discipline him at all. What a shame, all the children in our family are usually so well behaved.

cal stressors interact is essential in helping families manage their ADHD child. Any given horizontal stressor can exacerbate an already difficult situation or take on unexpected significance within a particular family's vertical stressor history (Table 1).

RESOURCE SUPPLY AND DEMAND
Toward Homeostasis

The ADHD child exacts demands on the family in addition to the stressors just described. Too often, however, the focus of behavioral interventions for an ADHD child is restricted to school behaviors; considerably less attention is given to the parents' comfort and ability in managing the child at home. The principles of nonsummativity and circular causality remind us that the child, while exhibiting difficulty on an individual level, also influences life at the family level. This is especially noticeable as the family attempts to maintain homeostasis. Homeostasis is the equilibrium a system maintains internally and the balance it keeps with the external environment. ADHD families have difficulty establishing a working homeostasis due to the particular characteristics of their child's behavioral symptoms. The never-ending, neurologically driven impulsiveness of the ADHD child provides direct opposition to the family's attempts to reach a comfortable homeostatic level. Thus unless carefully managed and structured, life becomes reactive and chaotic rather than proactive and stable.

An ADHD child requires extraordinary family resources. By definition, this child is biologically different, requiring an increased expenditure of time, effort, money, and emotion. The equation of parental input and child output is skewed, for this child responds to words and actions differently than other children. Let us briefly look at the increased physical, financial, temporal, and emotional demands of these parents.

Physical Demands

Hyperactive ADHD children are described as "always on the go" or "powered by a motor." Excessive activity coupled with impulsivity demand closer supervision and increased mobility from parents. Keeping up with, and protecting, such a child is physically taxing, if not exhausting. Anticipatory planning to stay ahead of a child who is hard to focus, easily distracted, and profoundly eager to explore can wear down/out the most creative parent. Nor does the child's growth and development bring relief; the restless infant becomes the toddler in perpetual motion, and then the extremely active school-age child. Many parents are constantly exhausted from the sheer physical demands, and since these children have abnormal and lessened sleep patterns, the healing of sleep is also denied these parents. Besides managing their ADHD child, parents must also meet the routine tasks of daily living. Rearing other children, performing household duties, and the demands of work outside the home further intensify the physical demands on these parents.

Financial Demands

The ADHD child exacts financial costs as well. Diagnosis, evaluation, routine monitoring of medication, the medicine itself, and often the expense of counseling for the child and the family are costs beyond those incurred for the normal child. Long-term follow-up and treatment render the cumulative costs staggering. Frequently today's insurance reimbursement excludes the care of these children on a psychiatric, rather than a neurological basis, thus compounding the financial burdens.

Temporal Demands

The ADHD child requires an additional time commitment. Much time is spent supervising behavior, continually refocusing to tasks demanding completion, and attempting to understand how the ADHD manifests itself with this particular child. Routine parenting often takes longer by virtue of the child's need to have directions repeated, progress monitored, and compliance or completion immediately reinforced. Thus the daily process of parenting and disciplining becomes increasingly complicated and time consuming. The necessary behavior management requires greater parental involvement. Also, because ADHD children have difficulty in school and in other social settings, they will require more "special attention" and parental assurance that they are in fact "okay."

Emotional Demands

Emotional interaction with an ADHD child is one of the most difficult and confusing aspects of the disorder for parents. ADHD infants often are hard to comfort or satisfy, leading parents to feel inadequate. As the child grows, and the behaviors associated with the disorder are unending, parents begin to feel guilty, believing they have done something wrong to make their child "this way." They also feel angry at the child who is chronically difficult to handle and who continually misbehaves. These emotions are compounded by guilt and embarrassment at having such feelings toward one's own child. Though such feelings are legitimate and understandable, parents often believe they are not "supposed to" be upset in this way by their own child [Wender, 1987].

Partially in response to these feelings, and partially in response to how the child behaves, parental discipline may be ambiguous and inconsistent, rather than firm and consistent. Further, discipline itself often becomes an emotion-laden issue since the ADHD child's response to discipline is inconsistent as well. When asked about discipline, parents often report "nothing works" or "there isn't anything we haven't tried." The task of child management and of helping the child to develop appropriate behavior is frustrating and at times overwhelming. Parents then become depressed and increasingly angry at their perceived "failure." Often they conclude, and the conclusion is often reinforced by others, that their child's problems are merely a reflection of their own. Resulting miscommunication and ill feelings regarding the child and the ADHD, and between the family and involved professionals, can hamper therapeutic efforts and further perpetuate the child's and family's frustration. While emotional difficulties do not occur in every family with an ADHD child, it is important to recognize that many difficult feelings may exist and temper how the family will respond to diagnosis and treatment. Early diagnosis and early family intervention can often prevent a buildup of inappropriate family interaction patterns and a buildup of negative emotions attached to these patterns. ADHD is a unique disorder in that diagnosis is often delayed several years after the onset of symptoms. Three pathways to diagnosis have been identified [Whitman, 1986].

PATHWAYS TO DIAGNOSIS

The "lightning bolt" path to diagnosis (Figure 3) has no identifiable preparatory course. Most often, this diagnostic process occurs as a result of an insult to a previously normal child or as a result of the birth of a genetically damaged child. However, sometimes the ADHD diagnosis has a similar impact in parents who have never viewed their child's behavior as extraordinary. Initially these parents may deny the diagnosis because the possibility of a difficulty never crossed their minds. Often this is true when the child is a first child and the parents have had no experience with other children or when parents notice some difficulty with their child but ascribe it to their own deficiencies. In other instances the parents' latitude of allowable behavior is so broad that they simply have never seen this child as different—and are annoyed that someone else does.

The "house divided" pathway (Figure 4) occurs when one parent has considered or suspected the presence of a problem, while the other parent did not recognize such a possibility. In addition to the child's problems, there is tension and emotional conflict between the parents as a result of their lack of consensus. With the confirmation of the ADHD diagnosis comes the

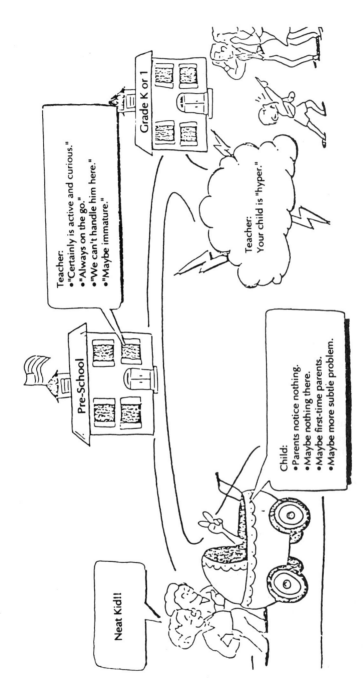

Figure 3   Pathways to diagnosis: Lightning Bolt.

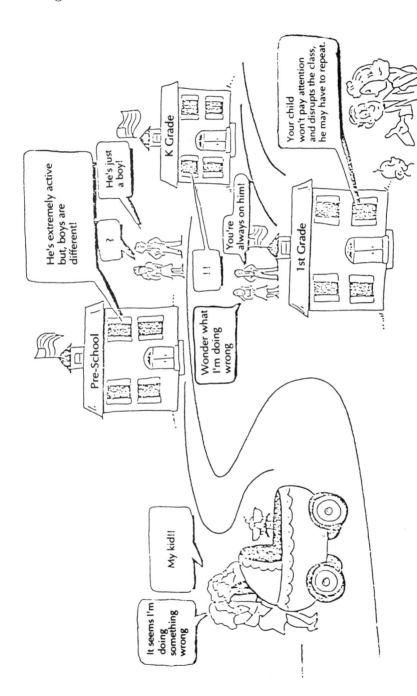

Figure 4 Pathways to diagnosis: House Divided.

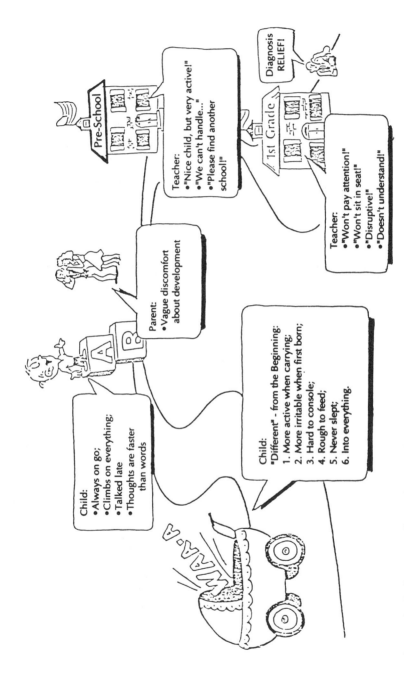

Figure 5 Pathways to diagnosis: Dawning Awareness.

realization that the parents will have to address the marital issues resulting from their disagreement in addition to seeking remediation for the child. Up until this point, the family has been experiencing and tolerating to some degree a conflictive and uncertain existence.

"Dawning awareness" (Figure 5) closely resembles the general category of acceptance of the diagnosis; from early on, their child seemed "different." As the child develops, the extended family looks at the child and the child's parents disapprovingly; their social life is limited, and tension mounts as repeated attempts at discipline are ineffective. When the child reaches school age, the teacher senses difficulty as well, and the child is referred for evaluation. When the diagnosis of ADHD is made, the parents feel vindicated at last. They're not "crazy"; there is something wrong. It's not them and it's not their child. It's a condition that is manageable. That explanation is much more acceptable (and true) than "He's a bad child" or "They're bad parents."

Regardless of the pathway by which parents receive a diagnosis, a diagnosis almost always precipitates a crisis for the family system. Inwardly, the parents experience a number of sometimes conflicting emotions. Outwardly, family life may be disrupted by increased parental irritability, an increased level and intensity of intrafamilial conflict, an inability to maintain a routine schedule, and a general sense of disorganization. This crisis state can last 6 to 12 weeks, after which family life restabilizes. Depending on a number of factors, the family can reorganize into a healthier system

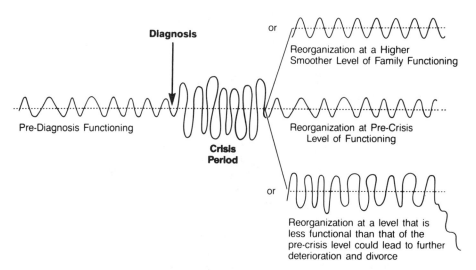

Figure 6   Impact of diagnostic crisis and possible outcomes.

than before or can return to a precrisis (prediagnostic) level; some, unfortunately, decay to an organizational level that is less functional than before (Figure 6).

FAMILY RESPONSE TO DIAGNOSIS

ADHD is not a condition the child can manage alone; thus the family's need to be involved must be recognized, legitimized, and supported. As noted, it is often several years after onset before the actual diagnosis is made. Thus, while the child has been living in the family and perceived as "hyperactive," "stubborn," or "difficult," the origin of these traits has not been officially recognized as a neurological, rather than a merely behavioral description. As a result, the family has evolved ways of responding to the stresses of the ADHD child. At the time of diagnosis, parental perceptions of the child, of themselves, and of their adaptive modes often come up for review. Three distinct categories of parental response to the diagnosis are seen: denial, tolerance, or acceptance [Parker 1988]. Often this initial attitude predicts a family's subsequent functioning.

Denial

Denial can manifest itself in one of two ways: (a) with a complete malabsorption of what the diagnosis implies and a resultant failure to respond in any way to the child's needs or (b) with anger and defensiveness. Those who respond with anger and defensiveness do not yet accept their child's neurological difference as causative and often assert that the child really can control his/her behavior but willfully and malevolently refuses to do so. Family frustration with the behavior is downplayed and dismissed ("He'll grow out of it," "She usually isn't like this") or is attributed to external causes ("The teacher doesn't like him" or "Being around his friend next door makes him act like this"). If parents do not grow to accept the diagnosis, they usually continue trying to prove there is nothing wrong with their child. Attempts to change the child's behavior and to present themselves as a "normal" family eventually fail. Parents become increasingly frustrated and angry that the child continues the behaviors and fails to meet their unrealistic expectations. At the same time the child's behavior may worsen, reflecting his own sense of failure, frustration, disappointment, and anxiety at the lack of acceptance and understanding. Increased defiance can be the child's way of communicating his need for help to the parents.

Those who respond with apparent obliviousness to the diagnostic implications externally appear similar to those who present anger and defensiveness. In this pattern the child's behavior is ignored rather than responded to, demands for a response by schools or other authorities elicit accusations of external causation, and attempts to require the family to respond can lead to the removal of the child to alternative living arrangements.

Tolerance

Parents who simply tolerate the diagnosis acknowledge the words but not the meaning. Often relieved that the diagnosis means "It's him and not us," the translation of that awareness to day-to-day living is lacking. Like the denying parents, these parents continue to feel that their child really can control his/her behavior, and they question the existence of a chronic underlying problem. There seems to be an occult assumption that now that they know what to call the condition and have cooperated with the provision of school services, "it" should go away or be "cured." They recognize that their child's behavior and attention remain variable but note that since it is better sometimes in school, it must be that the child simply gets lax in his newly learned ability to control these difficulties. Since they see some improvement, yet fail to recognize the chronicity of the disorder, they voice feelings that they are being taken advantage of ("Who's he trying to kid? I've seen him do that before with no problem."). As a result, discipline and acceptance of the child varies. Parents are not sure what to expect from the child, and as a result of their inconsistency, the child is unclear as to what parents expect as well.

Acceptance

Parents who accept the diagnosis of ADHD usually do so with a sense of relief. These parents have felt all along that their child is different, and while being somewhat reluctant to hear that they are correct, they welcome the possibility of effective treatment. When the condition is described, parents often nod their heads while listed symptoms are recognized, and they offer examples of their own experiences with the child. Accepting parents understand that the condition is a permanent part of their child and that this diagnosis is only the first step in the treatment process. These parents view the ADHD as the problem or target of intervention, rather than the child. Because of their understanding of the condition, accepting parents join forces with their child to deal with the ADHD. They advocate for their child and, in doing so, enhance their positive regard for the child, as well as the child's self-esteem.

Parents' level of acceptance of the ADHD diagnosis impacts their feelings toward their child's behaviors and the impact of these behaviors on the family. Failure to initially reach full diagnostic "acceptance," however, does not preclude eventually achieving a constructive approach to ADHD. Similarly, even the most accepting family will most certainly experience some difficulties with their child. Though acceptance of the diagnosis is a prerequisite to effective treatment, the time frame of this acceptance and the functional level of the families may vary. Regardless of where a family starts, they can adjust to the diagnosis and treatment of the disorder. Accepting the diagnosis is a recognition that management of ADHD is a life-long process. Treatment regimens can assist the family in achieving a functional level that is appropriate for them. It is important to note that this level will not remain constant; some periods and events are weathered easily, while others will present more formidable challenges to the child and family.

CLINICAL RESEARCH

Clinical approaches to these families have been supplemented by research to empirically define the characteristics of ADHD families. Research in this area represents an important first step in understanding the interactional effects of ADHD, child temperament, and parenting style. Studies suggest the disruption of family circumstances and negative parent-child relations are associated with the identification of the child's behavior as deviant [Hartsough and Lambert, 1982]. ADHD children have been described as less compliant and more oppositional than non-ADHD children [Barkley, 1985]. As a result, their mothers give more directives and are more reprimanding than mothers of non-ADHD children [Befera and Barkley, 1985]. This pattern is replicated in the differing interactions observed between mothers and their ADHD and non-ADHD sons [Tarver-Behring et al., 1985].

It has been noted that stressful mother-child interactions and other significant family life events may hinder the parents' ability to develop appropriate means of addressing a pre-schooler's hyperactivity and inattentiveness, resulting in a persistence of behavioral problems [Campbell et al., 1986, 1987]. Others suggest that, conversely, "the more deviant, hyperactive, aggressive 3-year old elicits greater conflict in their mother-child interactions and, directly or indirectly, thereby contributes to greater family stress" [Barkley 1988]. These explanations are consolidated in Bell and Harper's [1977] model of reciprocal effects in parent-child interactions. In this model, parent behavior is viewed as contingent on and elicited by child behaviors in the continuous flow of parent-child exchanges. Subsequent child behaviors are considered to be largely determined by the parental antecedent behavior. However, child behaviors may play an even larger role in controlling interactions than parent behaviors, depending on the context of the situation, task demands, and the characteristics of the child.

In an attempt to evaluate the direction of effects in parent-child interactions, Humphries et al. [1978], Barkley and Cunningham [1979], and Barkley et al. [1984] altered the characteristics of a sample of ADHD children via medication to note the reactions of their mothers in subsequent task-focused situations. Ritalin decreased the amount of noncompliant behavior in the children and increased their initiation and maintenance of compliance to the assigned tasks. As a result, the mothers' number of commands decreased, and in some cases their rate of praise for their children in the medicated state increased as well. These studies lend support to the position that the larger part of the difficulty in mother-ADHD child interactions originates from the severity of the child's symptomatology rather than from the inadequate or punitive childrearing practices of their mothers. Parental personality and care giving abilities no doubt affect the mother-child relationship, but they cannot be identified as predominant causes for extreme difficulty in that relationship. In each individual case, a unique combination of the child's symptoms and abilities, coupled with environmental factors, helps to determine both symptom presentation and eventual outcome [McGee et al., 1989]. While emanating from a different theoretical and research tradition, these findings add empirical substance to the concept of circular causality and point out the skewed nature of family interaction patterns in families who must contend with an ADHD child.

INTERVENTION

In general, the task of parenting is greatly underestimated. Even non-ADHD children present formidable challenges to parents. While parents do not cause a child's ADHD, parental views of, and responses to, this child impact on treatment efficacy and outcomes. Just as parents need to come to accept the ADHD diagnosis, they need also to accept the fact that the core symptoms of inattention, impulsivity, distractability, and overactivity will tend to persist despite any intervention. Rather than view the child's behavior as a personal affront, parents must remember that most of the behaviors are symptoms of a treatable disorder; the behaviors are neither malevolent nor purposeful but rather the reflection of a neurological deficit. Achieving a level of diagnostic acceptance along with the facts of ADHD presentation provides the substrate enabling parents to effectively meet the behavioral challenges.

The ultimate goal of all child discipline is the achievement of internal self-controls (Table 3). This goal holds for ADHD children, but the methods are different and the process is hampered by the ADHD symptoms. A child with ADHD often requires alternative educational and parenting methods. Parenting skills are typically developed through instinctual responses and the continuous incorporation of previous experience. This leaves the parents of an ADHD child at a distinct disadvantage. Their child is organically different, and unlikely to respond to traditional discipline. Knowing how to

Table 2 Family Therapy Emphasis for LD and ADHD Children

Step in Process	Goals		
	1	2	3
Therapeutic objective	Increase ability to control behavior and internalize controls. Enhance decision-making and problem-solving abilities.	Identify realistic behavioral and educational goals toward the achievement of progress	Frustration tolerance while developing responsibility for tasks and discovering methods of compensation
Task for child	Use behavior charts and recognize and accept areas of difficulty. Strive to improve and recognize improvements are possible and influenced by trying: "I can listen . . . stop and think . . . talk about mistakes."	Accurate but positive self-appraisal. Recognition that disability is something he/she *has* not all he/she *is*. "I'm good at ____." . . . "____ is hard for me." Understand everyone has to balance strengths and weaknesses to varying degrees.	Acknowledge anger, disappointment, and frustration. Learn the feelings are acceptable and can be expressed in appropriate ways. Try to learn things in ways that work for the child: "It's OK to ask for help."

Task for parent	Learn and utilize behavior management techniques. Apply them in a firm and consistent manner within particular family structure. Separate feelings about the child from feelings about misbehavior so problems can be handled and discussed productively.	Appreciation and positive regard for child "as is." Accept disability, manage grief, and support self-esteem efforts. Remind child of his/her strengths and provide opportunities for them to be demonstrated.	Tolerate bouts with frustration. Encourage expression of negative feelings in an acceptable way. Support attempts to find alternative solutions.
Desired outcome	Self-control. Recognition of increased cooperation and communication is valued by both parent and child. Enhanced parent-child relationships. Decrease in family stress	Enhanced self-esteem. Decreased anxiety and pressure to be "normal." Increased tolerance of difference.	Healthy recognition and management of frustration. Ability to compensate and achieve success in different ways.

Adapted from Ziegler, R. and Holden, L. [1988].

effectively parent such a child is never an innate ability. Parents must consciously learn the skills that will enable them to provide that structure for their child. Eisenberg [1966] identifies two fundamental dimensions of managing ADHD: (a) reordering the environment to facilitate external behavioral control with gradual internalization of these limits and (b) altering the physiologic characteristics of the disorder through the use of medication.

Behavior Management

Behavior management rather than responsive discipline is the process of choice for managing ADHD children. While appropriately used adjunctively with drug therapy, studies indicate that drug therapy in the absence of behavior management precludes positive outcomes [O'Leary et al., 1976; Satterfield et al., 1979]. Schachar et al. [1987] postulate that parents of drug responders will be even more receptive to child management training programs. Since ADHD presents differently in each child, treatment plans should be individualized for each child and family.

A behavior "management" approach connotes the ability to plan ahead and prevent the need for responsive discipline; it does not suggest an ability to erase a difficult situation. Behavior management, like personnel management implies planning and structure that frame the overall operation of the "family" company, while allowing the growth and development of individual talents and expression.

Behavior management is not a "cure" or a "quick fix" for ADHD, nor is it the "answer" to every situation. It is a framework within which specific techniques are employed to establish and maintain structure and consistency in the home.

Behavior management training is best facilitated in a one-to-one therapeutic relationship with adjunctive group sessions. Because parents are learning new skills, it is important for them to realize that it is all right (and expected) that things will go wrong from time to time and to occasionally feel overwhelmed [Caul, 1986]. Just as a child learning to develop self-control must adjust to a growth process and learn from mistakes, learning to parent with behavior management is a growth process as well.

The foundational concepts of behavior management are structure, routine, consistency, communication, clarity, and constructive consequences. We will look briefly at each of these components.

Structure

Structure embraces both organization of decision-making family "personnel" and temporal and procedural predictability. Like a company's organization chart, an ADHD family must have clearly defined and responsive lines of authority, decision making and enforcement coupled with a defined set of operating procedures. This clear and functional structure and set of procedures serves to make life safe, predictable, and minimizes the number of overwhelming and confusing stimulus situations impacting on this stimulus sensitive child. Thus, many reactive behavior situations are avoided by judicious use of structure.

Routine

Within this overarching structure, temporal routines and procedural routines are essential. Breakfast at the same time each day, baths at the same time each night, defined hours of play and homework again serve to minimize the changes and stimuli with which this child must contend. Within that temporal predictability, procedural predictability further structures task accomplishment and minimizes external chaos. Clothes always placed in the same spot for dressing, the order of dressing, bath, T.V., and preparation for leaving for school such as always storing bookbags in the same spot eliminates momentary confusion and averts the responsive loss of attention, opportunity for impulsivity, or creation of tantrums. In addition, while not a diagnostic symptom, ADHD children are noted to be exquisitely sensitive to and often unable to deal with change because the management of change requires a focusing of attention, a suspension of impulsivity, and an imperviousness to distractability. Thus, the more completely daily routines of family dynamics, family life, and daily activities can be structured and routinized, the more likely it is that completion of tasks is accomplished and less time is spent on responding to ADHD driven reactions in a child.

Consistency

Consistency entails behaving the same way in a given situation every time it occurs. If an ADHD child repeatedly misbehaves in a certain way, it is likely that the parent has not consistently responded to that behavior. Consistency provides the ADHD child with the assurance and psychological safety that if he behaves in a certain way, the parent(s) will in turn respond the same way over time. Children, particularly those who have difficulty establishing self-control, need limits clearly set and consistently applied by others and go looking for these limits if they are not readily apparent. If a child is unsure of the consequences of misbehavior or if these consequences will be consistently forthcoming, then the child more frequently tests the limits. However, if a misbehavior always results in the same parental response, then the child can begin to decide if engaging in the particular behavior is worth the resulting consequence. This kind of consistency is one of the most important variables in helping a child learn to check his internal impulsivity.

Communication

In all families, the vehicle for structure, routine, and consistency is the communication process. Establishing clear and effective channels of communication is difficult, and when such channels are established, care must be taken that they are maintained. Expressing ideas and requests to a child in a direct, reasonable, and concerned way serves to provide guidance and structure for the child. Parents who communicate in this manner usually provide clearly stated rules for their child and enforce them in a clear, compassionate way. Parker [1988] calls such adults assertive parents. They manage the child by explaining themselves and allowing the child an opportunity to respond. Assertive parents use their authority to maintain an appropriate hierarchy in the home.

Ideally, assertive communication is the goal. However, two extreme forms of communication can hamper behavior management [Parker, 1988]. Overly permissive parents put their child's wishes before their own. They are easily manipulated by their children, for the parental goal is conflict avoidance and maintaining a calm home. Unfortunately, this is achieved by failing to address misbehavior. Problems are minimized to avoid antagonizing or alienating the child, thus obviating further conflict. These parents establish neither definitive rules nor clear expectations; their communication style is timid and ambiguous. The parent acquiesces if a child voices displeasure or makes a request that has been previously denied. Frequently overly permissive or passive parents ask their children if they would like to do something rather than informing them of what they are required to do [Parker, 1988].

The other extreme, the aggressive parent, utilizes threats, harsh punishments, and belittlement to make wishes known. Authority is used in a destructive way; parents demand their wishes take priority with little regard for their child's needs or desires. Sometimes these parents resort to verbal or physical abuse to achieve their ends. This communication style is more often a reflection of the parents' mood than a response to the child's behavior. Such a style can damage the child's self-esteem and promote aggressiveness tendencies and behaviors.

Assertive communication covers the wide range of possibilities between these two extremes. It requires practice, patience, and self-control. Parents remain in reasonable control of their feelings and keep in mind that conveying the message or completing the task is paramount. The child can be informed of the emotional impact of their behavior on the parent, but this emotion does not dictate parental actions. Assertive communication has identifiable characteristics that reinforce the intent and style of this approach. Parents speak in a firm voice, establish eye contact, say unambigously what they intend, and by tone convey the intent of enforcement by supervising the child's behavior and maintaining the position originally stated, despite protestations. Communicating in this fashion allows the parent to manage the child's behavior while maintaining and enhancing the child's self-esteem.

Aside from direct contact between parent and child, communication between the parents regarding discipline is critical. Parents should present a "united front," holding private discussions of disciplinary matters and disagreements. Parents who openly disagree are subject to child manipulation by way of "divide and conquer."

Clarity

Clarity of communication is as important as assertiveness. Clarity is the degree of precision of requests to the child. ADHD children benefit from directions and expectations that are explicit and specific. For example, "Clean your room" more than likely will not denote the same meaning to the child as it does to the parent. Even if parent and child have reached an understanding of what a clean room is, it is possible that the ADHD child will forget the steps that completing such a task entails. By individually delineating the requirements of a task, the parent's expectations become clearer to the child, and the child in turn has specific "steps" to follow in order to finish the job.

Constructive Consequences

Finally, consequences are responses to a child's (mis)behavior. Once clear, consistent rules are communicated to the child, consequences are the predetermined parental reaction to the child's failure to adhere to the rules. Even when known, however, consequences often don't "register" with an ADHD child until an impulsively driven act has been completed. Yet, if a child is aware of the resulting parental action and knows it will be enforced consistently, the consequence over time acquires some function as a deterrent. The old adage "the punishment should fit the crime" takes on new meaning with these children, for frequently the best consequence of a misbehavior is not punishment, but rather a constructive consequence requiring restitution or contribution. Spanking is singularly ineffective for the child to learn controls when the behavior is a consequence of neurological impulsiveness. More importantly, spanking does not identify more acceptable behavioral alternatives. Instead of labeling the behavior bad, spanking labels the child bad. Constructive consequences both allow the child to make restitution and reinforce that in spite of impulsive behavior, their personhood is worthy and they can make worthy contributions despite their disability.

Clarity and consistency both in communication and consequences are interactive foundation components of the structure necessary for living with an ADHD child. Within this structure a number of specific behavioral techniques can be employed. Several helpful general techniques will be discussed.

Management Techniques

Positive Reinforcement

Everybody (even grownups) loves a compliment. Verbal praise is a form of positive reinforcement, and social learning theory states that people generally respond better to praise than they do to punishment. A child comes to realize a particular behavior is desirable and appreciated when that behavior is met with positive reinforcement. Rewards or reinforcers can be material or social. Material rewards include gifts, stickers, and food, while social rewards include a hug, a compliment, or personal attention. Parents who "catch" their child behaving appropriately and reinforce that behavior increase the probability that the good behavior will be repeated. Positive reinforcement with an ADHD child works best when it immediately follows a behavior. The success a child feels at having a positive experience helps to provide a sense of mastery and predictability. Further, it enhances a child's self-esteem and facilitates a positive relationship between parent and child. Each time the behavior is reinforced, the likelihood of repetition increases.

To teach positive reinforcement, identify reinforcable behaviors and determine the reward(s). Praise should be genuine and specific. For example, "You really made your room look nice today. The toys are neat and your clothes are put away" will probably be more effective than "Your room looks better than usual" or "What a good boy!" Parents often initially view positive reinforcement as bribery. The explanation that positive reinforcement is a reward or a benefit for a desired behavior that has been predetermined with the child's knowledge, analogous to adults receipt of a paycheck, usually removes this onerous interpretation.

Modeling

Modeling is another technique to identify and demonstrate desired behavior. Instead of focusing on the ADHD child's misbehavior, the parent compliments another child's desired behavior. This technique can be very effective because the ADHD child sees there are alternative ways of behaving that generate success. Modeling can occur directly through positive reinforcement of other children and indirectly through imitation of parental behavior. "Do as I say, not as I do" fails more with ADHD children than with other children. Therefore, parents need to be aware of the behavioral examples they provide for their children.

Decision Making

To demonstrate decision making, children can be given choices. The ability to choose between alternatives and exercise good judgement are important skills, and the ability to accept responsibility for the decisions made are critical for achieving maturity and independence. Parents can offer ADHD children some choices over their activities and behaviors. Choices must be structured to achieve an end while still allowing a choice. For instance, "Do you want to wear a coat?" is inappropriate; however, "Do you want to wear your red or your green coat?" allows a choice within the given, if unstated, structure "You will wear a coat."

Because each ADHD child and family is unique, it is difficult to itemize the range of techniques that may serve. Instead, the rule of thumb is that parents identify behaviors they wish to target so that the techniques selected respect their personality style and family needs. Often it is helpful to have an opportunity to implement the techniques and then talk with other parents to identify alternative perspectives and solutions. Adjunctive group sessions can provide parents with the opportunity to do this as well as identify with and receive support from others in similar circumstances.

FOLLOW-UP

Follow-up studies of ADHD children produce results as varied as that of the disorder's presentation. Weiss et al. [1971] found that 25% of the hyperactive boys followed-up during a 5-year period had a history of overt antisocial behavior. While hyperactivity diminished with age, difficulties with attention and concentration persisted. Gittelman et al. [1985] reported the greatest risk factor associated with the development of antisocial behavior and drug abuse was the persistence of ADHD symptoms. In the majority of children studied, however, ADHD symptoms were ameliorated over time. Family predictors of outcome are not associated with any single initial variable, but with the additive interaction of personality characteristics, social and family parameters [Hechtman et al., 1984]. Socioeconomic status and family mental health are weighted family correlates. There is no simplistic or specific predictor for positive or negative outcomes for the ADHD child; outcomes result from a complex, interaction of family and child variables.

FAMILIES HAVE NEEDS, TOO

Siblings: The Forgotten Children

Until this point, our discussion of the family has centered on the ADHD child and parents and has left out siblings. "Left out" is how they often feel because of the attention and "special treatment" the ADHD child needs.

Siblings perceive that they are (and they often are) required to complete a greater share of chores and accept stricter consequences than the ADHD child. They come to feel guilty over their "normality" and may suspect that they need to be perfect in order to compensate for the ADHD child. Sibling reactions can vary from acting out to overachieving and "protecting" the family from its problems. Parents must remain alert to the impact of the ADHD child on other children in the family.

Family Therapy

While the family has been shown to be intrinsically involved with the ADHD child, the reaction of the family to the condition as well as their functional level varies. The problems the ADHD child poses, entirely unrelated difficulties, or a combination of such stresses can contribute to a less than optimal living situation for the family [Wender, 1987]. Family therapy is often necessary because of the puzzling organicity of ADHD and the secondary emotional, social, and behavioral effects of the disorder. The family needs support in their approach to this child. Unlike other family therapy with a child focus, the goal of family therapy with ADHD families is not the extinction of problem behavior. Rather, intervention increases in importance because the therapeutic goals relate to issues of self-control, self-esteem, and frustration tolerance.

Intermittent Contact

Ziegler and Holden [1988] describe a method of using intermittent contacts or periodic short-term counseling to meet the special needs of ADHD children and families. This approach allows for discussion of "new" family material while both therapist and family are able to maintain an optimistic view of the family and its progress. Limited contact also helps to instill competence and a sense of control in the family while allowing for long-term contact, if necessary. Further, financial resources are more efficiently used. The therapist provides constant education to the family, interpreting events and anticipating areas of possible difficulties. Therapy presents a constant challenge for the therapist and the family because of the need to discriminate the ADHD from the unique qualities and individual needs of the child and family inherent in the child's developmental period.

Supplementary Assistance

Supplementary assistance for the family can be found through nontherapeutic parent support groups and the provision of respite care. Support groups for parents of ADHD children provide an emotional outlet for parents and an informal opportunity to discuss common problems and concerns. These groups can also serve as a forum for advocacy regarding school placement and the need for and availability of other community resources. Additional behavior management techniques are often taught in these groups while facilitating social contact with others in similar circumstances and providing for an exchange of experiences among parents. Respite care provides parents with a break from the constant demands of the ADHD child while ensuring that the child is cared for by people experienced with ADHD. Parents often feel guilty about leaving their child with other caregivers, but they can be receptive to the idea when it is presented as a way that will enable them to be at their best when they are with their child.

EPILOGIA MINOR

This chapter has described the role of ADHD in the life of a child and his family. In addition, we have asserted that the family along with the pediatrician is part of a treatment team that may also include a family therapist, educator, and behavioral counselor. Like many issues facing families, ADHD is a complex, confusing, and frustrating problem. It is, however, a problem that, with the help of appropriate professionals, families can successfully understand and manage.

REFERENCES

Barkley, R. A. (1985). The social interactions of hyperactive children: Developmental changes, drug effects, and situational variation. In: *Childhood Disorders: Behavioral-Developmental Approaches*. R., McMahon, R., Peters, eds. New York: Brunner/Mazel, pp. 218-243.

Barkley, R. A. (1988). The effects of Methylphenidate on the interactions of preschool ADHD children with their mothers. *J. Am. Acad. Child Adoles. Psychiatry* 27:336-341.

Barkley, R. A., Cunningham, C. E. (1979). The effects of methylphenidate on the mother-child interactions of hyperactive children. *Arch. Gen. Psychi.* 36:201-208.

Barkley, R. A., Strzelecki, E., Murphy, J. (1984). Effects of age and Ritalin dosage on the mother-child interactions of hyperactive children. *J. Consult. Clin. Psychol.* 52:750-758.

Befera, M., Barkley, R. A. (1985). Hyperactive and normal girls and boys: Mother-child interactions, parent psychiatric status, and child psychopathology. *J. Child Psychol. Psychiatry* 26:439-452.

Bell, R., Harper, L. (1977). *Child Effects on Adults*. Hillsdale, NJ: Lawrence Erlbaum.

Biederman, J., Munir, K., Knee, D., Habelow, W., Armentano, M., Autor, S., Hoge, S. K., Waternaux, C. (1986). A family study of patients with attention deficit disorders and normal controls. *J. Psychiatry Res.* 20:263-274.

Campbell, S. B. (1987). Parent-referred problem three-year-olds: Developmental changes in symptoms. *J. Child Psychol. Psychiatry* 28:835-846.

Campbell, S. B., Breaux, A. M., Ewing, L. J., Szumowski, E. K. (1986). Correlates and predictors of hyperactivity and aggression: A longitudinal study of parent-referred problem pre-schoolers. *J. Abnorm. Child Psychol.* 14:217-234.

Cantwell, D. P. (1972). Psychiatric illness in the families of hyperactive children. *Arch. Gen. Psychiatry 27*:414-417.

Carter, E., McGoldrick, M. (1988). Overview of the changing family life cycle: A framework for family therapy. In: *The Changing Family Life Cycle: A Framework for Family Therapy,* 2nd ed. Carter, E., McGoldrick, M., eds. New York: Gardner, pp. 3-28.

Caul, J. (1986). Behavior management of the learning disordered child. In: *The Learning Disabled Child at Home and School: A Parent Training Manual.* Whitman, B., Fogarty, K., Caul, J., Adgiela, A., Accardo, P. St. Louis: Lutheran Association for Special Education, pp. 86-92.

Combrinch-Graham, L. (1985). A developmental model for family systems. *Family Process.* 24:139-150.

Eisenberg, L. (1966). The management of the hyperkinetic child. *Dev. Med. Child Neurol. 8*:593-598.

Gittelman, R., Mannuzza, S., Shenker, R., Bonagura, N. (1985). Hyperactive boys almost grown up: I. Psychiatric status. *Arch. Gen. Psychiatry 42*:937-947.

Hartsough, C. S., Lambert, N. M., (1982). Some environmental and family correlates and antecedents of hyperactivity. *Am. J. Orthopsychiatry 52*:272-287.

Hechtman, L., Weiss, G., Perlman, T., Amsel, R. (1984). Hyperactives as young adults: Initial predictors of adult outcome. *J. Am. Acad. Child Psychiatry 23*:250-260.

Humphries, T., Kinsbourne, M., Swanson, J. (1978). Stimulant effects on cooperation and social interaction between hyperactive children and their mothers. *J. Child Psychol. Psychiatry 19*:13-22.

McGee, R., Williams, S., Silva, P. A. (1989) Background characteristics of aggressive, hyperactive, and aggressive-hyperactive boys. *J. Am. Acad. Child Psychiatry 23*:280-284.

Morrison, J., Stewart, M. (1971). A family study of the hyperactive child syndrome. *Biol. Psychiatry 3*:189-195.

Morrison, J., Stewart, M. (1973). The psychiatric status of the legal families of adopted hyperactive children. *Arch. Gen. Psychiatry 28*:888-891.

O'Leary, D. K., Pelham, W. E., Rosenbaum, A., Price, G. H. (1976). Behavioral treatment of hyperkinetic children: An experimental evaluation of its usefulness. *Clin. Pediatrics 15*:510-515.

Parker, H. C. (1988). *The ADD Hyperactivity Workbook for Parents, Teachers, and Kids.* Plantation, FL: Impact Publications, p. 24.

Satterfield, J. H., Cantwell, D. P., Sutterfield, B. T. (1979). Multimodality treatment: A one-year follow-up of 84 hyperactive boys. *Arch. Gen. Psychiatry 36:* 965-974.

Schachar, R., Taylor, Z., Wieselberg, M., Thorley, G., Rutter, M. (1987). Changes in family function and relationships in children who respond to methylphenidate. *J. Am. Acad. Child Adolescent Psychiatry 26*:728-732.

Tarver-Behring, S., Barkley, R. A., Karlsson, J. (1985). The mother-child interactions of hyperactive boys and their normal siblings. *Am. J. Orthopsychiatry 55*:202-209.

Terkleson, K. (1980). Toward a theory of the family life cycle. In: *The Family Life Cycle: A Framework for Family Therapy.* Carter, E., McGoldrick, M., eds. New York: Gardner, pp. 20-52.

Weiss, G., Minde, K., Werry, J. S., Douglas, V., Nementh, E. (1971). Studies on the hyperactive child: VIII. Five year follow-up. *Arch. Gen. Psychiatry 24*:409-414.

Wender, P. (1987). *The Hyperactive Child, Adolescent, and Adult Attention Deficit Disorder through the Lifespan.* New York: Oxford University Press.

Whitman, B. (1986). The impact of a learning disorder on the child and family. In: *The Learning Disabled Child at Home and School: A Parent Training Manual.* St. Louis: Lutheran Association for Special Education, pp. 56-64.

Ziegler, R., Holden, L. (1988). Family therapy for learning disabled and attention-deficit disordered children. *Am. J. Orthopsychiatry 58*:196-210.

10

Multidisciplinary Habilitative Prescriptions for the Attention Deficit Hyperactivity Disorder Child

Thomas A. Blondis

University of Chicago Pritzker School of Medicine, Chicago, Illinois

Dana S. Clippard, Dana J. Scroggs, and Lizette Peterson

University of Missouri, Columbia, Missouri

"It does appear that self-instructional training can bring an impulsive child's overt behavior under his own verbal discriminative control. At a macroscopic level, the impulsive children, after self-instructional training, do seem to be approaching psychometric tasks differently, taking their time, talking to themselves, and improving their performance."

[Meichenbaum and Goodman, 1971]

The child with attention deficit hyperactivity disorder (ADHD) has a difficult time controlling himself/herself and must exert increased effort to maintain attention. There is no doubt that this lowers the child's learning efficiency. Some children are themselves able to compensate and strategize to overcome their difficulties, but others need interventions to progress in this domain.

This chapter offers the reader insight into strategies used by four professional disciplines—education, psychology, medicine, and speech and language therapy—that potentially can help the ADHD child expand insight and improve self-control and self-directed operations. A wide range of strategies, from simple classroom adjustments to indepth speech and language pragmatics therapy will be reviewed.

Regular classroom teachers apply strategies in their class every day for the purpose of more effectively teaching children. The choice of strategies for a child with a disability is more complex and requires more careful thought and precision. The major areas of difficulty for the ADHD child consist of dysfunctional inhibition, poorly sustained attention, delayed development of selective attention, and impaired executive processing. A multidisciplinary evaluation is needed to pinpoint the specific deficits of the individual ADHD child. During clinical staffing, various professional disciplines can prioritize the child's needs to include strategies and interventions that have the highest likelihood of building self-control, organization, and self-esteem. Their recommendations represent only the starting point, and the teachers and/or therapists will need to make adjustments to try to define those strategies that a particular child responds best to. This chapter is designed to be of use to the teacher or therapist by clearly describing different possible interventions. Regular classroom teachers will find the earlier sections to be most useful; but it is hoped that each professional caring for the ADHD child will review all sections, even those unrelated to their particular area of expertise. Each involved discipline should know what help other professionals can offer the ADHD child. It is only through such intercommunication that a multimodality approach can best impact on the ADHD child's quality of life [Satterfield et al., 1985]. While the focus is on classroom interventions, it is imperative that structure, cognitive retraining, counseling, and medication treatments be integrated into the child's life when indicated.

REGULAR CLASSROOM MODIFICATIONS
Seating and the Teacher-Feedback Zone

Where the ADHD child is seated (especially in the regular classroom) is of extreme importance to the child's success. The teacher-feedback zone is that area that the teacher views throughout the day. This does not mean that the child sits next to the teacher. If the teacher has his or her back to the child, this will be of no use for the child. If the child is seated where the teacher can see if he is paying attention to the discussion or to completing the assignment, the teacher can more easily redirect the child back to the assignment by making eye contact or by some other nonverbal tactic. It is important that the teacher consistently pay attention when the child is on task, as well as cuing the child when a change in behavior is needed. If the teacher only attends to the child when off task, this may inadvertently reward off-task behavior. Catching the ADHD child being good is central to fostering appropriate behavior.

The teacher should locate quiet and hardworking children next to the ADHD child. It is very important that pranksters not be seated next to this child. This may lead the ADHD child to try to impress the mischievious child with poorly controlled buffoonery or allow the ADHD child to be manipulated and "set up" to break class rules or be embarrassed. It is also important that the ADHD child not be seated next to bullies or arrogant children. This can contribute to the ADHD child's being physically hurt, embarrassed, or constantly teased, depending on the characteristics of the particular children.

Positive and Quiet Redirection by Teachers

Children with attentional problems may require several cues throughout the day to help refocus their attention to the task at hand or to inhibit certain self-stimulatory or internally distractible behaviors. Sometimes redirection can be as simple as saying the child's name before a comment (e.g., "John, did you know that in 1492 Columbus discovered America?"). Standing near the child or quietly placing one hand on the child are unobstrusive ways to heighten attention. If the student has a particular behavior that needs to be extinguished (e.g., pencil tapping), a discrete nonverbal cue can remind the child that the behavior being demonstrated needs to be inhibited without directing negative attention to him or her.

Use of Organizational Aids

Because students with learning disabilities often lack metacognitive skills (the awareness of one's own cognitive processes), they typically do not develop efficient organizational strategies for processing information [Mann et al., 1987]. Regular classroom teachers can employ and teach several such techniques within the days' lessons to help these students acquire habits that will enable them to compensate for their deficits. The easiest and most logical place for the teachers to begin is with the development of a definite schedule for the ADHD student. A schedule provides students with needed structure, helps them learn what behaviors are expected, and presents them with a sequence of events in advance. Times should be specified for such activities such as taking lunch count, reciting the pledge, participating in instructional activities, and preparing to go home. When changes in schedule occur (e.g., fire drill), the instructor needs to announce and explain them beforehand.

It may be beneficial for some children to have an individual schedule taped to one corner of their desk, particularly if they have additional obligations such as learning disability or speech classes. For children too young to read, pictures may be used to represent each activity (e.g., the sun for recess, sandwich for lunch, book for reading group, each with a clock face drawn to indicate the appropriate times). For children with short attention and limited persistence, the teacher needs to make a concerted effort to design a schedule that is both realistic and sensitive to the child's needs. Proceeding from short work assignments to longer ones may help. At times, it is task complexity rather than time that is problematic for ADHD students. In either case, tasks may need to be broken up into smaller, more easily managed steps. As the student learns academic and self-management skills, duration and task complexity can be increased.

Alternate highly desirable activities with less desirable activities and quiet tasks with active ones. For example, after reading group or story time, allow the student to work at an activity center completing a puzzle or making a puppet before beginning seatwork assignments. Some children benefit from short periods of physical activity between tasks in order to absorb some of their restlessness. In a large classroom, one activity center might require ten jumping jacks or toe touches. In smaller rooms, stretching or isometrics can be helpful. Also, the teacher might permit the child to walk down the hall, get a drink, or take a note to the office.

Additional strategies the teacher might use to help the student would be to seat the child next to an organized, hard-working peer model, write a list on the chalkboard of materials to be taken home, or use assignment sheets for homework. Students can be taught to use colored folders to store papers from each content area. For seatwork, a folder with pockets labeled, ''to do'' and ''done'' can be used. This keeps the work space free from clutter and distractions.

Whatever strategies are used, the teacher must explain the system carefully, demonstrate its use, make sure the student uses the system, provide positive consequences for using the system correctly, and establish a regular cleaning time for the desk or folder [Gleason, 1988].

Introduction of Variety

The average school year represents a long period of time for children. For younger students, school time seems to pass even more slowly. It can be difficult to maintain attention and motivation throughout the year, and even the most intriguing activities grow boring with repetition. However, the teacher must persevere to focus a student's attention and interest in learning tasks.

Introducing novelty, humor, and special events into the curriculum can enhance alertness and interest. Care must be taken to insure that the unique aspect of the task does not overshadow the task content (e.g., teaching the concept of gravity during science by having the children drop various objects, but the children become so excited dropping objects that they don't learn the concept). However, if the salient quality of the new stimulus is well integrated with the central task concept, attention getting techniques can be very helpful in focusing learning. It may be exciting to plan changes in the routine that expand the instructional objectives. Activities such as writing a class newspaper or producing a play are fun and offer a variety of responsibilities that can be assigned according to individual interest and ability. Additionally, such lessons provide an application and review of previously learned material.

Use Selective Attention Aids

Sustained attention and selective attention are critical variables through which a student receives information and appropriately completes academic activities. It is difficult to separate selective attention, which is based on the physical properties of the tasks, from other variables such as relevance or meaningfulness of the tasks [Gearheart, 1985]. Although much research is being produced in the area of cognitive-behavioral therapy for controlling as a method of maintaining attention, most regular classroom teachers lack the time and knowledge to use these techniques. However, there are several methods for increasing attention that the teacher can more readily incorporate into the regular classroom routine.

Advance organizers are activities the teacher performs before presenting a lesson; he or she may *introduce key vocabulary, state concepts to be learned,* and *list the behavioral expectations that will be required of the student.* Advance organizers can enhance listening skills and assist students in recognizing critical information by providing organizational cues.

Additionally, teachers may *make statements that reflect the seriousness* of the material (e.g., "Listen. The following information is very important!). When presenting critical material, the teacher may want to stand close to the ADHD student. Hughes et al. [1986] recommend using a *pause procedure during lectures* for adolescents so that they may discuss unclear information. Having students *work in pairs* during pause times (discussion and filling in gaps in their notes) has been shown to help students assimilate, clarify, and better retain the content covered [Ruhl et al., 1987].

The *use of color to highlight relevant information* is profitable for some ADHD students. In some cases, it is important to insure color is used discriminatingly to heighten awareness of isolated key concepts rather than all "important" content, in which case whole pages could be highlighted. Other visual aids such as charts, outlines, and diagrams can help children focus attention on the more important parts of the lesson.

CLASSROOM CONTINGENCIES

Classroom teachers may facilitate desirable ADHD or learning disabled student behavior by providing feedback and using more structured approaches to reinforcement and behavior management. Easy to implement techniques can be as simplistic as verbally praising a child for raising his/her hand; however, they may be formal and slightly more time consuming, such as point systems or token economies. Teachers can award points for work done correctly and handed in on time simply by marking a check on a "scorecard." The teacher can also randomly dispense a token for on-task or helpful behavior throughout the day or at the end of specific troublesome class periods. Contingency contracting is the most formal of reinforcement programs. It involves written guidelines that specify expectations and consequences (see Figure 1). Classroom teachers may need the assistance of other educational professionals (e.g., counselors, learning disability teachers) for developing and carrying out more sophisticated behavior-management systems.

Well-designed classroom contingency plans offer several benefits for the ADHD child. They can increase the frequency of appropriate classroom and social behaviors. Students can track and appreciate the progress they have made. Feedback and rewards help students become aware of the need and advantages of goal setting, which lead to establishing realistic goals independently.

Feedback

There are various forms of feedback, and the effectiveness of each type changes with the age of the student. The degree to which a form of feedback is rewarding is often the extent to which it has been paired with something the child really wants. For instance, *social feedback* (praise or criticism) is more effective with young children because they often view adults as authority figures and associate positive feedback as affiliation with a teacher they value. Primary teachers most frequently employ social reinforcement, praising children's efforts and minimizing errors. Unfortunately, it appears that the proportion of positive feedback decreases proportionately with the grade level—the older the students, the less positive feedback.

Stickers, happy faces, and high marks are examples of *symbolic feedback* that young school children equate with social approval. By the third grade, many children begin to value grades and the competitive comparison with peers that grades afford. Older students more often work for grades rather than any intrinsic motivation associated with a task. The ADHD child, however, may sometimes need pairing of symbolic feedback with more primary rewards initially (e.g., food treats for young children, privileges for older children).

Of utmost importance for the ADHD child is the opportunity to receive informative *objective feedback*, which furnishes information regarding the accuracy of a response. Objective feedback should not only focus on the rightness or wrongness of an answer, but also provide the student an explanation of the reasoning and of the process used to obtain the answer. Objective feedback can help a student recognize and correct faulty thought processes, be used as the basis for self-comparison over time, and prevent negative self-concepts. Expressed in clear, specific terms, objective feedback is especially important for ADHD children who often misinterpret information and whose performance does not always fare well relative to grade-level peers. It is preferable to provide this type of feedback as unobstrusively as possible—either privately or in small group settings. By middle to late elementary school the classroom structure has changed. The use of whole-group lessons, ability groupings, and letter grades increases and invites peer comparisons. Normative feedback becomes critically important by the junior high level [Brophy and Evertson, 1976]. For the ADHD child who has significant learning problems, the resultant frustration can contribute to a depressive mood.

Professionals who consult with classroom teachers working with ADHD children need to stress the importance of creating learning situations in which the children can perform successfully enough for positive feedback to be tendered sincerely. Feedback should occur during or immediately following a response, so that students do not continue to practice bad habits or reinforce erroneous strategies. Feedback should help the child recognize success, no matter how small, and promote motivation for continued learning efforts. Praise should be proportionate to the accomplishment; spontaneous, ideally; and descriptive.

Behavior-Modification Techniques

Several modification systems can be exercised. The ADHD child can benefit from a system used at home that emphasizes rewards and bonuses for self-care, compliance, cooperation, and outside achievements. The system at school should be targeted to the development of assignment completion, improved self-control, use of selective attention, and cognitive self-monitoring.

An effective behavioral system implies a reward for achieving a positive goal such as acquiring a new skill or withholding an offensive behavior. The reward can be as simple as *social praise* or as complicated as the use of tokens that can be traded in for money or for a reinforcer on a menu jointly developed by the parent and the child. Whatever the reward system used, the more immediate the presentation of the reward after the child has exhibited success, the greater will be its impact.

The use of social praise is essential and some ADHD children respond best to the use of *appropriate recognition* [Piontkowski and Calfee, 1979]. The regular classroom teacher cannot be too free with praise, but must seize the opportunity to use it when the ADHD child has earned acknowledgment. More liberal (but not insincere) praise can be given in a learning disability resource room, by a counselor, or at home.

The use of a simple *point system* can be an effective regular classroom technique. The ADHD child earns a point for each specified time period during which he desists from losing control or withholds a targeted harmful behavior. These points are recorded in a book and, depending on the child's age, can lead to daily or weekly rewards, such as spending a short time in the classroom doing something enjoyable [Premack, 1965].

A *token system* is more elaborate and should include a *response-cost contingency*. The child earns tokens (e.g., poker chips) that have a value attached to them (e.g., 1 = $.25). The parent develops a menu of reinforcement activities (e.g., 10 tokens = afternoon at the roller rink), along with a cost menu (e.g., hitting your brother = −2 tokens). Obviously, the system needs to be weighted so that the child maintains a positive balance in the account. The family should add the rule that a child cannot be fined beyond zero. If the child has "gone in the hole" and owes tokens, they lose their positive reinforcing value. Opportunities to earn bonus rewards should exist (e.g., 10 tokens = an "A" in a subject). The child can review his or her behavior with parents on a weekly basis with earnings for the week being based on performance for that week. Simpler token systems can be used at school.

In order for significant cognitive progress to occur within the school, a specific behavioral program is essential [Braswell and Kendall, 1988]. The ultimate goal is to phase out the external reward system and have the child's internal self-generated praise take over. However, the external system can represent the initial impetus for the child to inhibit a negative behavior or develop a helpful strategy. Although behavior-modification techniques have generally been successful, a small percentage of children have undesirable emotional reactions to response-cost contingencies [Kendall and Braswell, 1985].

Contingency Contracting

A contingency contract is an agreement between two or more parties that specifies the relationship between what one does and the consequences. For example, a student may agree to accurately and appropriately complete work at his or her desk in order to later play a computer game. Negotiating a contingency contract should be a joint effort between the student and teacher. This helps the child see the relationship between his or her behavior and its consequences, thus making the contract more meaningful. Contracts provide structure for distactible students and motivation for students resistive or seemingly disinterested in school.

The terms of the contract should be stated poseitively and clearly to both parties. It is preferable that the child have some role in constructing the contract. The demands should be reasonable and designed according to the student's ability. Once both parties have understood, agreed to, and signed the contract, the provisions should be monitored frequently to assess progress. The conditions of the contract should be followed consistently and systematically, and the reinforcement delivered as soon as the contract obligation is fulfilled. The contract should also clearly specify what will happen if the agreed upon behavior does not take place. A sample contingency contract is presented in Figure 1.

For ADHD children who attend a learning disabilities (LD) class, or for younger children who benefit from tangible rewards, it is advantageous for the LD teacher or counselor to administer the consequence. For example, if the child's goal is to complete all morning seatwork within a specified time, the child may take the completed assignments to the LD teacher or counselor to receive the reinforcement. This enables the latter professionals to monitor the child's classroom work, provides a second source of positive reinforcement, and may be a helpful time saver for the classroom teacher. Note, though, that it may be preferable, for peer relationships, to handle the contract in a more discrete manner.

INDIVIDUAL AND GROUP COUNSELING

Individual Counseling

After the diagnostic process is completed, the physician meets with the family and discusses their concerns and focuses on helping them understand their ADHD child and how they can help. Parents also harbor a great deal of guilt, and sometimes start to believe that the child is manipulating their lives and is intentionally uncaring, unhelpful, and not trying. It is essential that the physician make it clear that the child is trying to conform and that a neurological disorder is the basis for the problems. The parents will confront situa-

```
                              CONTRACT

   It is understood that _____

   a student at _____  has

   agreed to _____

   _____

   _____

   _____


   This contract will be considered to have been successfully

   completed when _____

   _____

   _____


   It is expected that the terms in this contract will be

   completed by _____day of _____, 199_.

   If the terms of this contract are successfully fulfilled, it

   is understood that _____  is

   entitled to _____

   _____


   If the terms of this contract are not successfully fulfilled,

   it is understood that_____

   _____


   Date:_____, 199_ Signatures:_____

                                 _____


   Date of Contract Completion: _____, 199_
```

Figure 1   An example of a contextual contract form. Note that consequences for both successfully completing and failing to complete the terms of the contract need to be included.

tions daily that will seem to them mistakes made because the child wasn't trying to pay attention; they must be able to subtract some of the blame to be able to respond to the child in a sensitive and productive way.

ADHD children often fantasize that their problems are insurmountable. Sometimes these children even believe that the ADHD testing they are undergoing means they are retarded or crazy. It is important that school-age ADHD children receive counseling from the professional making the diagnosis and either a social worker or family therapist. The child can initially be asked what s/he thinks were the reasons for the testing and how s/he thinks s/he did. Depending on how candid the child is and what his/her level of understanding is, the counseling session can then focus on attempting to put the child's problems in better perspective. This important process may require more than one session.

Social Skillstreaming

ADHD and LD students are often deficient in social skills and other behaviors considered important in interpersonal attraction [Bryan and Bryan, 1986]. These students are frequently rejected because of their reactions to and interactions with others. It is vital for educators to teach critical social skills to handicapped children, and it is equally important that nonhandicapped children learn to understand these children's difficulties [Subornie, 1985].

There are four general methods for teaching social skills: modeling, positive reinforcement (contingency plans), coaching, and practice. Several sequenced curriculums for teaching basic skills are commercially available. Fundamental social skills include introduction of self and others, active listening, making friends, joining in, giving and accepting criticism, getting help, asking for feedback, considering possible social consequences before acting. Some programs, such as the ACCEPTS program [Walker et al., 1983], can be taught in one-to-one, small group, or large class settings.

A typical component of social skills programs is role playing in naturally occuring situations. In role playing activities, a specific problem is identified, roles established and assigned, acted out, and then discussed. The opportunity to rehearse skills that have been didactically described and later modeled is an essential component of role playing. Also, the feedback following role playing is essential as it permits students to identify problems, choices, consequences, and solutions and gives them the opportunity to clarify feelings and practice skills. Through playing the role of someone else, the student gains some understanding of the reactions of other people and learns to cope with similar situations.

The social and emotional aberrations the ADHD population suffers is well documented. Teachers who provide social skills training not only help students acquire needed social competence, but also potentially enhance their self-confidence and self-esteem by preparing them for success in social situations. If professionals are not trained in this methodology, it may be important to refer the family to a community resource that conducts a social skills group.

MEDICATION TRIAL

ADHD children should undergo a stimulant medication trial. The short-term benefits of stimulant medication have been documented. More than 70% of ADHD children will respond positively to psychostimulants. If the student's achievment quotient is significantly below potential, if s/he has been unable to achieve behavioral control, or if the child has been unable to develop social skills and make friends, a stimulant medication trial is drastically indicated.

There are several approaches to the drug trial and management. It is essential that the physician take the time to explain the side effects of the drug. Unless s/he takes this time and makes himself/herself available to handle questions or concerns that arise, the trial may be discontinued by the parents for a trivial reason or may never be started. Some physicians assert that there is no need for a placebo versus drug trial because the change in self-control and processing among responders is so dramatic. Other physicians prefer that the child and teacher be blinded to the trial and that a follow-up behavioral scale teacher questionnaire be completed daily or weekly [Deuel, 1988; McBride, 1988]. This approach is particularly helpful if either the child or the parent has reservations about the use of medication. When the child responds positively, the behavioral questionnaire score is significantly lower during the stimulant period than during the placebo span. If the child fails to respond to one stimulant, there is good evidence to suggest that the child may significantly improve on another type of stimulant [Rapoport, 1989]. The most frequently used stimulant is methylphenidate, but some children who have not responded to this drug have responded to a dextroamphetamine preparation.

If the physician decides to use the more scientific trial, it is recommended that the teacher rate the child's behavior at noon each day. During the medication phase of the study, the child takes the short-acting medication only at home prior to leaving for school. The Conners Abbreviated Teacher Rating Scale (CATRS) is completed by the regular classroom teacher if the student is in elementary school and by several invested teachers if the student is in high school. The mean drug scores should be significantly different at the end of the study if the medication has been effective Table 1 outlines a model drug trial for a boy 7.5 years old weighing 25 kg who is administered Ritalin, dosage 0.4 mg/kg/day. This methodology is helpful only if the child's teacher is cooperative. Unfortunately there are uncooperative teachers who have reached conclusions that the child is lazy or that medication should not be used [Blondis et al., 1990].

Although the short-term benefits of stimulants are proven, research has not yet demonstrated that ADHD children experience any long-term benefits [Pelham, 1986]. The strongest evidence supports improved outcome only when stimulants are combined with other intervention modalities [Satterfield et al., 1985].

If the child is to undergo a medication trial, the physician or psychologist should discuss this also with the child. It is important that the child be able to express views and have questions answered about taking a medication. Some ADHD children dislike taking medication and become noncompliant. If it is the physician's recommendation that medication be given an adequate trial, it is important that the physician bear responsibility for making the trial a productive experience. The parents cannot explain this as effectively to the child as the physician can.

SPECIALIZED SCHOOL SERVICES

Approximately 70% of all individuals diagnosed as having ADHD will have learning disabilities [Accardo et al., 1990]. Learning disabled [LD] students

Table 1 Model Drug Trial, Using CATRS, of Placebo versus Psychostimulant

	Baseline (mean, 15.2)	Placebo (mean, 11.5)	Ritalin (mean, 3)
	16[a]	12[a]	2[a]
	22	10	4
	13	9	3
	14	18	6
	13	10	3
		8	2
		14	0
		9	8
		13	4
		11	3
TOTALS	78/5	114/10	35/10

In this model the dramatic response is indicative of an ADHD child helped by a psychostimulant medication. Ideally, this is a blind study that should take place in a regular classroom.
[a]Hyperactivity Index Score

in turn comprise the largest subgroup within the educationally handicapped population. According to the U.S. Department of Education [1985], 4.57% of persons aged 3 to 21 were receiving learning disability services. These figures suggest that the professional who diagnoses and treats ADHD must understand and be aware of all possible comorbidity and related services to ensure adequate treatment.

It should be noted that some investigators report that improvement in academic performance leads to a significant decrease in the frequency of inattentive behaviors, suggesting that inattention is incompatible with improved academic performance and such behaviors decrease when academic interventions are made [Ayllon et al., 1975; Broughton and Lahey, 1978; Marholin and Steinman, 1977].

The resource teacher must be competent, personable, able to work closely and harmoniously with other teachers and ancillary staff and assess the educational and behavioral needs of the students, and design and implement prescriptive, individualized instruction [Wiederholt, 1974]. Some of the classroom modifications that the resource teacher may recommend include reading content area tests (e.g., social studies) aloud, using tape recorders or word processors and reducing assignment length. The LD resource teacher also plans lessons to improve academic skills and enhance classroom performance. Instruction might include listening skills, reading or math skills, study strategies, or cognitive-behavioral therapy to facilitate self-control and problem solving. Perhaps the most important function of this teacher is to help students understand their limitations and gain self-confidence in their ability to cope with and prevail over their attentional dysfunction and specific learning disabilities. The resource teacher can become a trusted confidant for the student in the school setting. Individual and small discussion groups are often conducive to the expression of concerns and feelings not easily shared in large groups with nonhandicapped peers. From this interaction the resource teacher is able to modify short- and long-term goals based on knowledge of the child's social and emotional status.

For ADHD children with severe learning disabilities or behavioral problems, a self-contained classroom may represent the least restrictive environment. ADHD-LD students may receive their entire academic program within the self-contained setting or may be mainstreamed into the regular classroom for a portion of the day. (Typically, children are integrated into the regular program for art, music, and physical education.) The low teacher/ student ratio (5-15 students per teacher) permits a more individualized, carefully monitored curriculum. The very structure of these classes benefits highly inattentive, exceedingly distractible children. The realistic expectations and reduced competition better enables students to achieve at a rate commensurate with their potential, and may also enhance their self-esteem.

Some special classes are multicategorical or cross categorical, which means children with various educational handicaps are grouped together (e.g., behavioral disorders, educable mental handicap, pervasive developmental disorder, and communication disorder). Clinicians and families should inquire whether the teacher in such a classroom is trained and certified to teach children with the various disorders of such a classroom population.

Whatever placement is determined most appropriate for the ADHD child, the goal should be to help him or her acquire skills that will maximize independence in the least restrictive environment. The family must take an active and supportive role in the planning and implementation of the Individual Educational Plan (IEP) or the poorly focused child will most likely fail to develop the goal-directed processing required to maximize individual success.

OTHER INTERVENTIONS

There are numerous other interventions that have been tried with ADHD children. Some of these are promising, while others are of no use and may endanger the child. The more promising interventions include cognitive-behavioral therapy (CBT), pragmatic language therapy, and the use of microcomputers. Microcomputer use as well as therapies that have no proven efficacy for the ADHD child are discussed in separate chapters. CBT and language pragmatics will be discussed in the following two sections.

COGNITIVE-BEHAVIORAL THERAPY (CBT)

Prior to designing a CBT program for the child, it is important that diagnostic assessments be focused on the nature of the child's attentional failure. During the interdisciplinary conference the clinicians need to decide which areas of processing have been most affected and then prioritize the components of processing that have not been developed (e.g., selective attention, metacognitive memory strategies). Discussion should include what modalities can most benefit the child based on his/her individual pattern of strengths and weaknesses. If a child is very impulsive and hyperactive (but not perseverative), then the first CBT attempted should be self-talk.

Self-Guidance Through Self-Talk

Problem solving is a process that involves goal recognition, solution generation, evaluation of potential solutions, selection, and assessment of one given solution. Poor performance can result from a breakdown in any component of the process. Many training techniques exist that help impulsive children gain self-control and use problem solving to evolve solutions. Many programs use didactic, modeling, and shaping techniques to improve problem solving and ability to self-instruct. Self-instructions are self-directed comments that provide a step-by-step thinking strategy to guide the learner through the problem-solving process [Kendall and Braswell, 1985]. Modeling accompanied by explanations is more effective for teaching self-instruction skills than explanations alone [Rosenthal and Zimmerman, 1978]. Cognitive modeling combines modeled explanation and demonstration with verbalization of the model's thoughts and reasons from performing certain actions [Meichenbaum, 1977]. Meichenbaum and Goodman [1971] used modeling with verbalized self-instructions to train a group of impulsive children to reflect and respond thoughtfully on a variety of tasks. The adult models not only perform tasks, but "think aloud" as they work. One of the tasks used, matching-to-sample, is similar to the types of assignments children in the primary grades commonly receive. Models used exaggerated gestures to indicate that they were comparing each alternative to the stimulus before making a decision. Simultaneously they verbalized thoughts such as

"Let's see. I'm going to have to look at each of these to make sure that I don't choose the wrong one by mistake. How about this one here? Is this flower the same? How about the other flower? Wait a minute. That's not the same. It has too many leaves. I have to look more carefully. . . ."

In this landmark study ADHD children performed poorly on the matching-to-sample task due to the number of commissions. The cognitive modeling slowed the children's response times and increased the accuracy of their answers. The addition of the self-instructional training led to a notable decrease in errors. Other approaches such as urging the students to slow down and take their time were ineffective. A five-stage approach has been shown to be effective for teaching this method of impulse control and self-modulation (Table 2).

Table 2 Stages for Teaching Self-Regulation

Stage	Illustration
Cognitive modeling	An adult models a task while speaking aloud.
Overt, external guidance	The child performs the task under the direction of adult instruction.
Overt, self-guidance	The child performs the task while verbalizing self-instructions aloud.
Faded, overt self-guidance	The child whispers self-instructions while performing the task.
Covert self-regulation	The child performs the task while guided by inner, private speech.

Adapted from Meichenbaum and Goodman [1971].

Models demonstrate making a mistake and show how to cope with it. This is an important step for impulsive children because they tend to become frustrated and give up after committing errors. A "mastery" model implies faultless behavior from the onset, whereas, a "coping" model will portray difficulty with gradual improvement. Coping models may be more like the child who has previously encountered learning difficulties; hence, the individual adapts and improves performance. Observation of coping models may enhance self-efficacy [Schunk, 1987] and is reported to be superior to mastery models. [Meichenbaum, 1971; Sarason, 1975; Schunk, 1987].

Self-instruction typically includes five steps.

1. Defining the problem: "What is it I have to do?"
2. Stating the problem approach: "I have to look at all the choices."
3. Focusing attention: "I have to focus in, go slow, and be careful."
4. Choosing an answer: "I want this answer."
5. Self reward or coping statement: "Good. I'm doing okay so far" or "No, that isn't right. That's okay. I'll just erase. Even if I make a mistake, I can go slower and get it right next time." [Meichenbaum and Goodman, 1971; Kendall, 1977]

It is important that the language used for self-instruction be appropriate and meaningful to the child. This can be accomplished by allowing the child to help develop and select terminology.

An application of this approach is the "turtle technique" in which impulsive, aggressive children are instructed to pull in their limbs, lower their heads, and close their eyes, like a turtle, in response to an anger provoking situation [Robin and Schneider, 1974; Robin et al., 1976]. While in the turtle position, the children are taught to engage in relaxation exercises and think about a more appropriate alternative. Preliminary studies evaluating the effectiveness of this method appear encouraging.

Transfer and generalization do not occur automatically. Therefore, children need to be taught to use the strategies they acquire in different contexts. They not only need to learn what to do, but when, where, and why to do it. One way to promote generalization is to portray the behaviors modeled by different persons in different contexts. This tells the child that the new skills are useful for others and do not depend on a particular setting or model's characteristics. Therefore, not only the instructor should serve as the child's model, but parents, teachers, and other caregivers can also foster the child's emerging skills.

CBT training can take place in a one-to-one or in a small group setting. It is intended for the child to generalize the techniques to the regular classroom, home, and social settings. The leader can do his/her best to simulate events that the child would encounter in these various surroundings. This will require a great deal of practice. The ADHD child can be given homework, and return with reports of his/her attempts to apply a learned strategy to a specific situation. Without parent cooperation and involvement, accomplishing the goal of an ADHD child generalizing these strategies is doubtful.

Learning Compensatory Strategies

Once a child learns to apply CBT to simple problems, the goal should be to expand their use in more sophisticated learning and problem-solving tasks. Using self-instruction can help students learn to use imagery and elaboration, which can increase comprehension, retention, and performance. Modeling with verbalized self-instruction is not only an effective therapy and individual training technique, but may also be used in the classroom particularly to teach more complex processes. By sharing deductive schemes with the student, the instructor communicates methods to utilize those skills most meaningful to the student. If the student perceives the benefits of using CBT, s/he will be more likely to experiment with it.

Whenever the teacher introduces a new cognitive device, the steps and behaviors must be clearly outlined and modeled. For example,

> "What is it I have to do? I have to read the page. As I read, stop and ask myself what happened? What is most important? If I can answer all the questions, go to the next part . . ."

The use of key vocabulary in training sessions enables ADHD students to see the relationship and application to learning situations. The emphasis should always be on the concept or strategy to be learned rather than the specific content.

The ADHD child then needs opportunities to verbally rehearse and practice the new strategies. Practice is an important variable in learning, particularly as task complexity increases. Practice across environments promotes facility with and retention of the skill. The more automatic the skill becomes, the more cognitive resources it leaves available for focusing on other aspects of the problem-solving process.

Role in Special Education

Before a child is placed in a special education program in the public schools, an indepth psychoeducational evaluation process is completed. The assessment data helps determine the existence and nature of the disability (i.e., deficits in language, science, social studies, and visual-motor processing, poor concentration, slow writing) and the type and extent of intervention needed. These children receive a combination of formal and informal measures that rate various competencies.

Qualitative and clinical observations must be included as a major part of this assessment. Qualitative observations can be more important than quantitative scores for determining the specific intervention components of the habilitative plan. The qualitative observations can also help identify children who are good candidates for CBT. Qualitative observations should note whether the child appears to have an abnormal affect, if the child prior to attempting a task repeatedly declares that s/he will fail, whether the child will take risks, how the child reacts as the task difficulty increases, what strategies the child uses to solve problems, how the child approaches the problem, whether the child uses self-talk, whether the child has an organizational approach during the tests. It is important to determine how the child assesses his or her own performance. Does the child overrate, underrate, or accurately rate self-performance? Does the removal of time restrictions influence the child's performance? The examiner should try to perceive whether the child is aware of his or her behaviors. For instance, is the child aware of strategies that s/he is learning or is his/her application of a strategy merely a rote exercise?

Mini-lessons using cognitive-behavioral therapy can be conducted, similar to those techniques used for academic mini-lessons. If the diagnostician models a task using self-instruction, does the child respond and generalize those techniques to other items and tasks or require multiple trials and cues to approximate the behavior? Does the child recall and employ the devices if a follow-up assessment is held the next day?

The above information can be used to make inferences about the child's cognitive, metacognitive, and emotional status that test scores by themselves cannot reflect. School districts that do not have trained professionals to deliver CBT can recommend that the parents consider private therapy to facilitate the educational experience. Outside referrals must be handled cautiously by educational agencies because the district may become liable should the therapist selected be inappropriate.

Reported Efficacy of Cognitive-Behavioral Therapy

Either as an isolated modality or in combination with stimulant medication CBT does not have proven efficacy as a strategy that can be generalized or that will improve academic achievement over time. Abikoff et al. [1988] could not demonstrate significant improvement of an ADHD group that received Cognitive Therapy and Methylphenidate over groups that either received remedial tutoring and Methylphenidate or received only Methylphenidate. These investigators did not, however, include response contingencies in the training [Abikoff et al., 1988; Abikoff and Gittelman-Klein, 1987; Braswell and Kendall, 1988; Kendall and Reber, 1987], and Kendall and

Reber imply that the intervention program offered by Abikoff was not true CBT.

Several investigators have reported group differences that support the efficacy of CBT [Brown et al., 1985; Schleser et al., 1983]. However, empirical evidence for generalization remains limited, and generalization must be a central focus of any CBT program. Many of the procedures outlined by Deshler et al. [1981] to advance CBT generalization have been discussed earlier. Braswell and Kendall's [1988] summary of 10 years of CBT investigation with disordered children revealed a dismal record of controlling for subject variables, assessment of required preskills, and flexible study treatment length. It may be that such oversights are the principal reason that few studies have demonstrated long-term benefits for CBT. If a program has poor success at accomplishing CBT generalization this costly and time-consuming training could not be recommended.

PRAGMATICS OF LANGUAGE

ADHD children frequently have subtle language difficulties, and this lack of communicative competence frequently interferes with classroom success. These students are often described as disruptive, inappropriate, and lacking social etiquette. They are less often identified as deficient in language pragmatic abilities. Pragmatic incompetence can be manifested as disordered behavioral and social skills and therefore may not be identified. However, if an underlying language disorder is not diagnosed and treated, social and behavioral change may not occur, despite structured intervention targeted at these problem areas. Therefore, specific diagnosis and treatment of a pragmatic deficit is important if students are to achieve a level of communicative competence that facilitates classroom success.

What Is "Pragmatics of Language"?

Language is governed by rules. Grammar (syntax) is the most familiar and most concrete set of rules for language use. A sentence may be grammatically accurate ("Look at that"), but the situation in and intonation with which it is used will affect its interpretation and appropriateness. The study of those extra grammatical factors that govern users' choice of utterance in a particular social setting is called pragmatic [Crystal 1987; Lund and Duchan 1983; Nicolosi et al., 1978]. Such pragmatic skills include appropriate use of eye contact, turn-taking in conversation, topic maintenance and topic change, intonation and loudness of voice, as well as the use of facial expressions and gestures. More subtle areas include correct syntactical usage related to the listener's knowledge of referents and physical setting (e.g., "Can you reach the salt?") and understanding the intent of the sentence.

Identification of Pragmatic Disorders

Because pragmatics reflect the ability to use language within a context to convey, request, or exchange information (i.e. is situation dependent), standardized assessment is difficult. Several formal assessment tools have recently attempted to address the many areas dealing with rules of language usage. Among these measures are the Test of Language Competence, Evaluating Communicative Competence, and The Test of Problem Solving [Simon, 1986; Wiig and Secord, 1989; Zachmand et al., 1984].

The Test of Language Competence (TLC) evaluates a child's metalinguistic competence in such areas as ambiguities, inferences, recreating sentences, and figurative language. The manual provides instructional objectives and teaching strategies for deficit areas [Wiig and Secord, 1989]. The Evaluation of Communication Competence (ECC), however, is not a standardized measure, but rather a structured procedure to assist with systematic gathering of data about the child's communicative competence. ECC contains 21 tasks that evaluate language competence in three domains considered necessary for proficient classroom and social learning: language processing, higher order cognitive processing, and language function [Simon, 1986]. The Test of Problem Solving (TOPS) [Zachmand et al., 1984] is another nonstandardized evaluation measure that can be utilized. TOPS provides a structure in which narrative responses can be elicited from situational pictures and questions. For example, while displaying a drawing of a waitress serving two people at a restaurant, the examiner asks, "The waitress brought them hamburgers and french fries, but they ordered spaghetti. What could they do?" The TOPS pictured stimuli are designed to be relevant for elementary and middle-school aged children. The examiner can also expand on the stimuli creating additional questions or asking the student to give an example of how they would respond in a given situation (e.g., "Pretend you are talking to the waitress. What would you say?")

The identification of those students with pragmatic problems, however, probably remains best achieved through observations of their interactions in a variety of situations. Many observation formats are available that speech/language pathologists and classroom teachers may utilize to assist in the identification of deficient areas of pragmatic skills. A sample checklist is provided in Figure 2.

Approaches to Intervention

Ideally, following the identification of a pragmatic language deficit, an intervention plan should be formulated for inclusion in the student's IEP. The identified implementor(s) of a pragmatic language goal will vary depending on the student's overall academic and language skills. Students identified with deficient pragmatic language skills may or may not qualify for speech/

Child's Name:_____   Date:_____   Time:_____

Classroom:_____

Participating in classroom activity: Talking with children:
Child not involved in any activity _____   Child playing and talking to self, not aware of others _____
Child watching others in a group _____   Child talking and aware of others, but requiring only
Child engaged in own symbolic play   attentional responses from them _____
                    activity _____   Child initiating conversation and seeking responses:
Child engaged in own activity other than   (check where appropriate)
                    symbolic _____   a. Initiating about objects _____
Child engaged in own activity of any type   b. Initiating about self _____
                but aware of others _____   c. Initiating about events _____
Child engaged in group symbolic play _____   d. Initiating about others _____
Child engaged in planned group activity _____   Child directing behavior of others _____
Child engaged in non-planned non-symbolic   Child being directed by another _____
                group activity _____

Talking with Adults: (Check where appropriate)   Responds to Wh Questions: (Check where appropriate)
Initiates conversation :   a. by ignoring _____
    a. about others _____   b. by imitating _____
    b. about self _____   c. by answering when information is known to listener _____
    c. about events _____   d. by answering when information is not known to listener __
    d. about others _____
                                                  Responds to request for action: (check where appropriate)
Responds to Yes-No Questions   a. by ignoring _____
    (check where appropriate)   b. by imitating _____
    a. by ignoring _____   c. by performing request _____
    b. by imitating _____   d. by verbally refusing _____
    c. by answering when information is known
                    to listener _____   Responds to new information by: (check where appropriate)
    d. by verbally refusing _____   a. ignoring _____
                                                      b. imitating _____
                                                      c. questioning the information _____
                                                      d. adding new information which is not related _____
                                                      e. adding new information which is related _____
                                                      f. adding to new information about a related topic _____
                                                  Maintains a dialogue easily _____
                                                  Maintains a dialogue with difficulty _____

Figure 2   Pragmatics in the Classroom Observation Checklist.

language services, depending on the school district's or state education agency's guidelines. It is often true that if a student is identified with a pragmatic language deficit without documentation of other speech and/or language disorders, she may not meet the necessary educational criteria for inclusion in a special program, but the speech/language pathologist may still serve as a consultant to the classroom teacher or family providing direction and activities to implement pragmatic language intervention.

Regardless of the manner in which the service is delivered, it should be kept in mind that pragmatics is the functional use of language within a situational interaction and, therefore, intervention should be planned to address skill acquisition at this level. Individual treatment or drill activities may assist in establishing a desired behavior but will probably do little to facilitate generalization of the behavior to spontaneous interactions. Peer group activities, with the use of situational role-playing can assist the implementor in mimicking real life situations and may also elicit unplanned discourse between participants. Videotaping the activity for review and critique by the students may aid both the instructor in documenting the behaviors the students can identify as appropriate/inappropriate, and may also aid the students in the understanding and modification of their language. A variety of sources are available to provide assistance in planning activities for intervention. Among these are *A Sourcebook of Pragmatic Activities* by Johnston et al. [1984] in which "lesson plans" have been provided to "remediate the full range of pragmatic disorders." Activities are presented by targeted behavior (i.e., topicalization) and grade level of activity (prekindergarten through grade 6), and goals and instructions are delineated [Johnston et al., 1984]. Other resource books include those by Simon [1980], and Zachman et al. [1982].

CONCLUSION

Each ADHD child may have any number of accompanying diagnoses and problems, and what works for one child may not work for another with the same behavioral characteristics. All possible intervention should be considered when professionals are deciding on a treatment plan of an ADHD child but with the understanding that there is no definitive prescription for a particular child. Parents and involved professionals will need to be able to make adjustments. The educational and behavioral prescription is never a fixed prescription. Adaptability must be its chief characteristic. Validation of attempted interventions remains a difficult undertaking. For example, it is possible that a child who learns a particular strategy may not have the motivation, energy, or maturity to generalize that method at first. Study strategies learned at an early age can certainly be applied at a subsequent time. To withhold a set of strategies that have definitely benefited some ADHD patients because clinical science has not clearly shown that a majority of children will integrate these processes might be considered poor practice if the general consensus of professional opinion is that this method is indicated for this patient.

Social development can never be ignored. Social skills will have a major impact on every person's life skills. If a school district does not have the expertise to address this facet of the ADHD child's program, it is at the very least obligated to clearly communicate to the child and the family its concern. If this area of development is potentially preventing the child from achieving in school related areas, the district may also have the obligation to find and contract for outside services.

This chapter has covered several interventions that may represent a primary need of the child with an attention deficit disorder or hyperactivity. Other secondary prescriptions (e.g., adaptive physical education for a clumsy child) may also be indicated. Nothing less than such a holistic approach will begin to solve the moderately involved ADHD child's problems. The parents must be made aware of the stumbling blocks to be overcome if this is to be achieved. In many cases, family therapy will be a necessary adjunct if the ADHD child is going to have a reasonable chance to progress. Only the mildly disordered and uncomplicated ADHD child has a good chance to overcome the disorder without a multimodality, multidisciplinary prescription. The severely disordered patient may require multidisciplinary support throughout life to control such complications as antisocial personality disorder, depression, unemployment, alcoholism, and criminal behavior [Satterfield et al., 1985].

REFERENCES

Abikoff, H., Ganeles, D., Reiter, G., Blum, C., Foley, C., Klein, R. G. (1988). Cognitive training in academically deficient ADDH boys receiving stimulant medication. *J. Abnorm. Child Psychol. 16*:411.

Abikoff, H., Gittelman-Klein, R. (1987). In reply. *Arch. Gen. Psychi. 44*:296.

Accardo, P. J., Blondis, T. A., Whitman, B. (1990). Disorders of attention and activity level in a referral population. *Pediatrics 85*:426.

Ayllon, T., Layman, D., Kandel, H. J. (1975). A behavioral educational alternative to drug control of hyperactive children. *J. Appl. Behav. Anal. 8*:137.

Bandura, A. (1986). *Social Foundations of Thought and Action: A Social Cognitive Theory*. Englewood Cliffs, NJ: Prentice Hall.

Blondis, T., Desch, L., Snow, J., Clippard, D., Roizen, N. (1990). Understanding of attention deficit hyperactivity disorder by school professionals. *Dev. Med. Child Health* Supplement No. 62. *32*:33.

Braswell, L., Kendall, P. C. (1988). Cognitive-behavioral methods with children. In: *Handbook of Cognitive-Behavioral Therapies*. Dobson, K. S., ed. New York: Guilford Press.

Brophy, J., Evertson, C. (1976). *Learning from Teaching: A Developmental Perspective*. Boston: Allyn and Bacon.

Broughton, S. F., Lahey, B. B. (1978). Direct and collateral effects of positive reinforcement, response cost, and mixed contingencies for academic performance. *J. School Psychol. 16*:126.

Brown, R. T., Wynne, M. E., Medenis, R. (1985). Methylphenidate and cognitive therapy: a comparison of treatment approaches with hyperactive boys. *J. Abn. Child Psychol. 13*:69.

Bryan, T. H., Bryan, J. H. (1986). *Understanding Learning Disabilities*, 3rd Ed. Palo Alto, CA: Mayfield.

Crystal, D. (1987). Concepts of language development a realistic perspective. In: *Language Development and Disorders*. Yule, W., Rutter, M., eds. London: Mac Keith Press, pp. 48-51.

Deshler, D. D., Alley, G. R., Warner, M. M., and Shumaker, J. B. (1981). Instructional practice for promoting skill acquisition and generalization in severely learning-disabled adolescents. *Learn. Dis. Quar. 4*:415.

Deuel, R. K. (1988). Treatment of attention problems with stimulant medication. *J. Pediatrics 113*:68-70.

Friend, M, McNutt, G. (1984). Resource room programs: Where are we now? *Excep. Child. 51*:150.

Gearheart, B. R. (1985). *Learning Disabilities: Educational Strategies*, 4th Ed. St. Louis, MO: Times Mirror/Mosby.

Gleason, M. M. (1988). Study skills. *Teach. Excep. Child. Spring*:52.

Gresham, F. M. (1981). Assessment of children's social skills. *J. School Psychol. 19*: 120.

Gresham, F. M. (1981). Social skills training with handicapped children: A review. *Rev. Ed. Res. 51*:139.

Gresham, F. M. (1986). Conceptual issues in social competence assessment. In: *Children's Social Behavior: Development, Assessment, and Modification*. Strain, P. S., Guralnick, M. J., Walker, H. M., eds. Orlando, FL: Academic Press.

Hughes, A. A., Hendrickson, J. M., Hudson, P. J. (1986). The pause procedure: improving factual recall from lectures by low and middle school students. *Inter. J. Instruct. Media 13*:217.

Johnston, E., Weinrich, B., Johnson, A. (1984). *A Sourcebook of Pragmatic Activities*. Tucson, AR: Communication Skill Builders.

Kendall, P. C. (1977). On the efficaciousness of verbal self-instructional procedures with children. *Cog. Ther. Res. 1*:331.

Kendall, P. C., Braswell, L. (1985). *Cognitive-Behavioral Modification*. New York: Guilford Press.

Kendall, P. C., Reber, M. (1987). Cognitive training in treatment of hyperactivity in children. *Arch. Gen. Psychi. 44*:296.

Lund, N., Duchan, J. (1983). *Assessing Children's Language in Naturalistic Contexts*. Englewood Cliffs, NJ: Prentice-Hall.

Mann, P. H., Suiter, P. A., McClung, R. M. (1987). *Handbook in Diagnostic Prescriptive Teaching*, 3rd Ed. Boston: Allyn and Bacon.

Marholin, D., Steinman, W. M. (1977). Stimulus control in the classroom as a function of the behavior reinforced. *J. Appl. Behav. Anal. 10*:465.

McBride, M. C. (1988). An individual double-blind crossover trial for assessing methylphenidate response in children with attention deficit disorder. *J. Pediatrics 113*:137.

Meichenbaum, D. (1977). *Cognitive-Behavioral Modification*. New York: Plenum Press.

Meichenbaum, D. Goodman, J. (1971). Training impulsive children to talk to themselves: A means of developing self-control. *J. Abnorm. Psychol. 77*:115.

Nicolas, L., Harryman, L., Krescheck, J. (1978). *Terminology of Communication Disorders: Speech, Language, Hearing*. Baltimore: Williams and Wilkins.

Pelham, W. E., Jr. (1986). The effects of psychostiumlant drugs on learning and academic achievement in children with attention-deficit disorders and learning disabilities. In: *Psychological and Educational Perspectives on Learning Disabilities*. Torgensen, J. K., Wong, B. Y. L., eds. New York: Academic Press, pp. 259-295.

Piontkowski, D., Calfee, R. (1979). Attention in the classroom. In: *Attention and Cognitive Development*. Hale, G. H., Lewis, M., eds. New York: Plenum Press, pp. 297-329.

Premack, D. (1965). Reinforcement theory. In: *Nebraska Symposium On Motivation*. Levine, D., ed. Lincoln: University of Nebraska Press.

Rapoport, J. L. (1989). Conduct problems in attention deficit said to need separate therapy (quote). *Pediatric News 23*:7.

Rapoport, J. L. (1980). The "real" and "ideal" management of stimulant drug treatment for hyperactive children: Recent findings and a report from clinical practice. In: *Hyperactive Children: The Social Ecology of Identification and Treatment*. Whalen, C. K., Henker, B., eds. New York: Academic Press, pp. 247-258.

Robin, A. L., Schneider, M. (1974). The turtle-technique: an approach to self-control in the classroom. (Unpublished manuscript.) Stony Brook: State University of New York.

Robin, A. L., Schneider, M., Dolnick, M. (1976). The turtle technique: an extended case study of self-control in the classroom. *Psychol. Schools 13*:449.

Rosenthal, T. L., Zimmerman, B. J. (1978). *Social Learning and Cognition*. New York: Academic Press.

Ruhl, K. L., Hughes, C. A., Schloss, P. J. (1987). Using the pause procedure to enhance lecture recall. *Teach. Edu. Special Ed. 10*:14.

Saranson, I. G. (1975). Test anxiety and the self-disclosing model. *J. Consult. Clin. Psychol. 43*:148.

Satterfield, J. H., Satterfield, B. T., Schell, A. M. (1985). Therapeutic interventions to prevent delinquency in hyperactive boys. *J. Am. Acad. Child Adolesc. Psychi. 26*:56.

Schleser, R., Meyers, A. W., Cohen, R., Thackery, D. (1983). Self-instruction interventions with non-self controlled children: effects of discovery versus faded referral. *J. Counsel. Clin. Psychol. 51*:954.

Schultz, J., Turnbull, A. (1983). *Mainstreaming Handicapped Students: A Guide For Classroom Teachers*. Boston: Allyn and Bacon.

Schunk, D. H. (1987). Peer models and behavioral change. *Rev. Ed. Res. 57*:149.

Simon, C. (1986). *Evaluating Communicative Competence*. Tucson, AZ. Communication Skill Builders.

Simon, C. (1980). *Communicative Competence: A Functional-Pragmatic Language Program*. Tucson, AZ: Communication Skill Builders.

Stipek, D. (1984). The development of achievement motivation, *Research on Motivation in Education*. Ames, R., Ames, C., eds. Orlando, FL: Academic Press.

Stipek, D., Sanborn, M. (1983). Preschool teachers' task related interactions with handicapped and non-handicapped boys and girls. (Paper presented at the American Educational Research Association) Montreal, CA.

Walker, H. M., McConnell, S., Holmes, D., Todis, B., Walker, J., Golden, N. (1983). *The Walker Social Skills Curriculum: The ACCEPTS Program*. Austin, TX: Pro-Ed.

Wells, D., Schmid, R., Algozzine, B., Maher, M. (1983). Teaching learning disabled adolescents. *Teach. Ed. Special Ed.* 6:227.

Wiederholt, J. (1974). Historical perspectives in the education of the learning disabilities. In: *The Second Review of Special Education*. Mann, L., Sabatino, D., eds. Philadelphia: Journal of Special Education Press.

Wiig, E., Secord, W. (1989). *Test of Language Competence*. San Antonio, TX: Psychological Corporation, Harcourt, Brace, Jovanovich.

Zachman, L., Jorgensen, C., Barrett, M., Huisingh, R., Snedden, M. K. (1982). *Manual of Exercises for Expressive Reasoning*. Moline, IL: Linguisystems.

Zachman, L., Jorgensen, C., Huisingh, R., Barrett, M. (1984). *Test of Problem Solving*. Moline, IL: Linguisystems.

11

Behavioral Markers and Intervention Strategies for Regular and Special Education Teachers

Carol A. Haake

St. Louis University School of Medicine, St. Louis, Missouri

> *"The secret of education is respecting the pupil."*
>
> [Ralph Waldo Emerson]

Attentional problems in children are something like the wind. Everyone has experienced the phenomenon but it is difficult to accurately describe. Some of the difficulty results from the ongoing confusion of learning disabilities and attention deficit disorders. Attention has been suggested as the underlying deficit for learning disabilities [Dykman et al., 1971] and much research has attempted to clarify this theory [McNallis, 1987; Krupski, 1985]. This type of research, however, seldom discriminates adequately between these two distinct but often overlapping populations. Attention deficit disorder (ADD) refers to an inability to efficiently focus and sustain attention; it is often accompanied by hyperactivity. Learning disability (LD) refers to difficulty in perceiving, processing, recalling, or expressing certain types of information. Although each of these disorders may exist independently of the other, their overlap cannot be ignored. Of children with ADD, it has been estimated that from 60 to 85% will also be learning disabled [Levine 1987; Silver, 1984].

BEHAVIORAL DESCRIPTION

Although the nomenclature has been changed recently from the DSM-III [American Psychiatric Association, 1980] categories of attention deficit with or without hyperactivity to the current DMS-III-R [American Psychiatric Association, 1987] category of attention deficit hyperactivity disorder (ADHD), the essential features remain the same. A diagnosis requires that 8 of 14 listed behaviors related to inattentiveness, impulsivity, and hyperactivity be present for at least 6 months and occur with considerably more frequency than is normal for most children the same age (Table 1). An attention deficit disorder without the component of hyperactivity may now be described as "undifferentiated attention-deficit disorder."

How do these rather abstract criteria relate to the child's life in school and at home? In order to answer this question, parents of all children presenting to a developmental disabilities clinic for a multidisciplinary assessment from age 3 upward were asked to fill out an open-ended questionnaire regarding their child's behavior at home and at school. The response headings included: "Things child does or does not do in school that get him/her in trouble or cause bad grades" and "Things child does or does not do at home that are problems for him/her or other family members." A tabulation of the results reveals a descriptive profile that changes with age (Table 2).

ADHD children 3 to 6 years old were described as being out of sync with many facets of the preschool environment. At this age, peer relations were perceived as a major problem. These children were often physically aggressive or impulsive and would push and shove other children or take toys. One child got into trouble for trying to paint others. Both formal and informal group

Table 1 Summary of ADHD Diagnostic Criteria

Fidgets or squirms in seat
Difficulty remaining seated
Easily distracted
Difficulty awaiting turns
Prematurely blurts out answers
Fails to finish tasks
Difficulty sustaining attention
Shifts activities often
Difficulty playing quietly
Talks excessively
Often interrupts
Does not seem to listen
Often loses things
Engages in physically dangerous activities without thinking

Table 2 Parents' Descriptions of Problems Experienced by ADHD Children

Age		
3 to 6 years	6 to 9 years	9 to 13 years
At School		
Does not take turns	Off-task	Lack of Attention
Interrupts others' play	Daydreams	Daydreams
Hits	Rushes through work	Incomplete Assignments
Pushes	Sloppy Work	Fidgety
Takes toys	Careless errors	Does not stay seated
Does not listen	Incomplete assignments	Problems with peers
Does not heed warnings	Does not listen	"Class clown"
Rushes through work	Does not follow instructions	
	Talks inappropriately	
	Problems with peers	
	Fidgety	
	Does not stay seated	
	Disorganized	
	Loses things	
At Home		
Uncooperative or aggressive with siblings	Does not listen	Easily angered
Wants his own way	Ignores requests	Cries
Rough or careless with toys	Does not mind	Pouts
Will not take "no" for an answer	Talks back	Talks back
Forgets what he is told	Interrupts	Defiant
Into everything	Argues	Will not be quiet
Does not listen	Talks constantly	Does not mind
	Messy	Aggravates siblings
	Rough	Intimidates siblings
	Destructive	
	Does not complete tasks	
	Dawdles	
	Needs frequent reminders	
	Gets separated in crowds	
	Leaves the yard	
	Follows peers into danger	
	Does not follow rules	

activities were difficult as the children were perceived as being uncooperative, not taking turns, and interrupting others at play. Their inattention included not listening, not following directions, not heeding warnings, and not realizing when an adult was becoming upset. The scattered quality these children project was described by one parent as "thinks about more than one thing at a time." Academic problems were already apparent as complaints about "rushing through work" began to appear at this early age. A descriptive phrase given for one child was "doesn't know what's expected of him academically." These children seem to blunder through life missing all the subtle (and many not so subtle) cues to socialization and learning. This is very aptly captured by Cooper and Farran [1988] in their description of the typical kindergartner at risk for later school problems: "He is a forgetful, disorganized male. In a group, he is the one who is the most inattentive and for whom the instructions need to be repeated. He sits still for five minutes, then either blurts out something totally irrelevant or jumps up and begins to play with blocks when everyone else is listening to a story. When everyone begins working at a task or game, he wants to hear the story he missed. Finally, he begins to work appropriately, but every five minutes or so he needs to be coaxed back to his work. He never hangs his coat up in the right place."

Although these problems may be exacerbated by the school environment, they are not specific to that situation. These children also seem to be swimming upstream against the flow of family life. They aggravate and are uncooperative and rough with their siblings. They always want their own way, do not share or take turns and will not take "no" for an answer. They are rough or careless with toys and are into everything. In addition to not listening, they seem to forget what they are told. They seem irresponsible and will, without regard, undertake actions that are wrong and/or dangerous.

Within the 6- to 9-year old group, the trend begun in preschool continues. ADHD children were seen as daydreaming or not staying on task. Their rushing through their work resulted in careless errors and sloppy work. Assignments were not completed, and the children appeared to not listen and not follow instructions.

Just slightly less problematic was their inappropriate talking. It is interesting to note here that Zentall [1988] found that hyperactive children talked more than their classmates in spontaneous conversation but less than their classmates in demand situations. So these children are perceived both as talking when they are not supposed to and not answering when directly questioned. Not surprisingly, parents still reported these children to have problems getting along with their peers. This is supported by Carlson et al. [1987] who found that, compared to a normal control group, groups of ADHD elementary school children with and without hyperactivity were less often nominated as "liked most," were more often nominated as "liked least," and had lower social preference scores on sociometric measures.

ADHD children were also seen as fidgety and out of their seat more as well as disorganized. They forgot, lost, or threw away books and papers. This is obviously not a picture congruent with a happy, successful school experience. Unfortunately, the problems do not end with the school day. Two areas stand out as being seen by parents as problems at home. These children do not appear to listen. They have to be asked (or told) 3 or 4 times (or more) to do something, particularly when they are already involved in another activity. Parents often reported having to threaten the child to get a response. The second outstanding problem area was inappropriate talking. This included talking back, interrupting, arguing, and just talking constantly ("motor mouth"). It was the only category that applied slightly more to affected girls, although boys were also represented.

They were also perceived as messy ("makes *big* messes") and destructive of or rough with toys. After making the messes, of course, task completion became a problem and they "dawdled" and needed frequent reminders. At home, safety was perceived as a problem as these children would get separated in crowds, leave the yard without telling where they were going, and follow peers into dangerous situations. And, finally, they were perceived as not following rules. It is not difficult to imagine the negative interactions these children are likely to experience with many adults in their lives across many situations.

From ages 9 to 13 years, the school picture is similar. Lack of attention and daydreaming remain the major problems followed by incomplete assignments and not following directions. Although not as frequent, fidgiting, out of seat behavior, and peer problems were still reported.

It has been suggested [Landau and Milich, 1988] that the problems ADHD children have with social communication may be due to an insensitivity to changing situational demands. Such children are either unable to successfully attend to or properly decode relevant social cues, or they are unable to suppress their inappropriate behavior, so they appear more inflexible in their response style. Whatever the precise underlying cause, a new behavioral category emerges at this age level—the "class clown."

At home, however, the picture is changing. The problems most frequently reported by parents were related to the child's anger or, conversely, his over-sensitivity, crying, or pouting. Inappropriate verbalization (talking back, defiance, not being quiet when told) remained a problem even though this group included no girls. These children still do not mind and, in addition, aggravate and intimidate their siblings. Overall there seemed to be a shift from task-oriented to more emotional/behavioral concerns.

The 13-year and older sample was too small (3 boys) for generalization. Two of the 3 had school problems similar to those described earlier. And it is interesting that all 3 parents described these boys as not getting along with other family members.

These trends appear fairly consistent with the results of Brown and Bordon's [1986] review of literature regarding hyperactive/ADHD adolescents. While the activity level diminished significantly over time, these youths were still impaired with regard to attention, impulsivity, academic failure, and emotional immaturity. In addition to persistent cognitive and academic difficulties, the most pervasive complaints for the ADHD adolescents were social and conduct difficulties. Lower self-esteem and, for a large number, a tendency to develop serious psychiatric disturbances, including antisocial personality traits, severe depressive states, and even thought disorders was reported.

DIAGNOSIS

Recognizing the presence of the above typical behavior patterns in a child is the first step in considering the possibility of an ADHD diagnosis. And, indeed, the use of parent and teacher questionnaires such as the Conners Parent Questionnaire [Connors, 1978], Connors Teacher Questionnnaire [Connors, 1978], Child Behavior Checklist Report Form [Achenback and Edelbrock, 1983], and the Child Behavior Checklist [Achenback and Edelbrock, 1983], which quantify various items of behavior and attempt to differentiate the resulting behavioral patterns, have been useful in diagnosing children's attention problems. These checklists, however, describe but do not explain behavior.

Almost all children exhibit some of these behaviors at some time. There are causes other than an ADHD for disordered attention that need to be explored. It may be necessary for the classroom teacher to engage in some detective work both to suggest an initial referral and to aid in the overall evaluation. Variable attention may be related to conditions in the classroom, in the family, and within the child.

Inappropriate curriculum demands may cause frustration, acting out, or incomplete assignments.

Family transitions, such as divorce, death, or a move, may affect attention, although the significant ones will probably be of more recent onset.

A chronically understructured family may have given the child few appropriate attending behaviors.

Physical or sexual abuse will certainly impact on the child's ability to focus his attention.

The parents' mental health may also be a factor; the child of a depressed mother may have had to escalate his activity level in order to gain her attention.

Expectations for a mentally retarded child may be too high; attentional expectations should be consistent with his mental age rather than his chronological age.

A language disorder may cause the child to "tune out" due to lack of comprehension rather than lack of attention.

Emotional unrest may also significantly impair attention; for example,
both anxiety and depression may cause unfocused attention. Although
more rarely encountered, the same may be true of thought disorders.

It is beyond the scope of this chapter to discuss these conditions in depth.
Rather, the intent is to present the possible hypotheses that may need to be
explored for various children (Table 3).

An important point to consider when exploring possible underlying causes
of a child's behavior is that constitutional ADHD begins before school age,
whether or not it is diagnosed at that time [Duane, 1988]. Although it is consistently present, it is not always expressed in the same way. Over time, the
ADHD child might best be described as "consistently inconsistent." The
presence of any of these other conditions, or combination of conditions,
does not exclude ADHD as the primary cause of the student's attentional
variability. In addition, the presence of a coexisting learning disability should
always be considered. Knowledge of all the factors affecting the child's learning and behavior is vital when planning appropriate interventions.

PSYCHOMETRIC PROFILE

No clear psychometric profile has emerged that is diagnostic of ADHD.
The Wechsler Intelligence Scale for Children—Revised (WISC-R) [Wech-
sler, 1974] has been one of the instruments most frequently used to clarify
the ADHD pattern, with varying results. Thus both lower verbal IQ [Lahey
et al., 1989] and lower Performance IQ [McGee et al., 1985] have been reported to be characteristic of ADHD children. The most frequently reported
psychometric pattern characteristic of ADHD children is that of low performance on the WISC-R Freedom from Distractibility factor (FFD) [Kauf-
man, 1975]. The FFD factor is one of three identified in a factor-analytic
study of data from the WISC-R standardization sample. Deviation IQ's may
be calculated for this factor from the sum of the arithmetic, digit span, and
coding scaled scores. A depressed FFD has been reported to discriminate
children with an ADHD from children with other problems [Lufi and Cohen,
1985] and children with a pervasive ADHD from non-ADHD children [Boud-
reault et al., 1988]. Dykman et al. [1984] found this pattern among both
reading delayed and hyperactive children. Although sometimes taken for
granted by clinicians, this factor should be interpreted with caution as it may
actually be assessing short-term memory or sequencing ability. In addition,
clinical experience has identified a subgroup of ADHD children who score
relatively high on this factor while being depressed in one or both of the other
factors of verbal comprehension or perceptual organization [Kaufman, 1975].

Table 3 Alternatives To Consider When ADHD Is Suspected

ADHD-Type Behavior	Consider
Attentional problems occur only in specific classroom situations.	Performance anxiety
Given easier assignments, child attends without problems.	Curriculum demands
Attentional problems occur suddenly and were not previously apparent.	Emotional stresses stemming from crisis situation
Child is frequently absent, homework not completed, seems disorganized but responds easily to classroom structure.	Understructured family
Mother is withdrawn, lacks affect, and is unresponsive to child.	Maternal depression
Child has lacerations or abrasions unusual for age, injuries show pattern (handprint, cigarette burns, etc.), gives implausible explanation for marks, overreacts to being approached from behind, flinches when adult reaches toward him.	Physical abuse
Child acts out sexually, has sexual knowledge inappropriate for age level, fears going to the bathroom alone, shies away from physical contact, touches adults excessively or inappropriately.	Sexual abuse
Child consistently seems younger than age mates (academics, self-help, language, social interactions, as well as attention).	Mental retardation
Child attends to nonverbal but not verbal tasks, watches other children before beginning work, and/or uses simple, concrete language compared to peers.	Language disorder
Child is withdrawn, anxious, fearful, pervasively unhappy, shows a limited range of emotion, has frequent somatic complaints particularly head, stomach, and/or leg pain (may or may not be acting out).	Emotional disorders

It has also been suggested that the differentiating psychometric pattern for ADHD may change with age. Auditory tests, rather than visual, have been shown to discriminate 7-10-year-old children with an ADHD [Sutter et al., 1987]. Brown [1982], however, found that by age 14 years, hyperactive children's sustained attention had increased in efficiency with regard to auditory but not to visual stimuli. Thus, the younger ADHD child may have discrepantly low scores on auditory tasks, while the older ADHD child may show a pattern of deficient scores on visually presented subtests.

A further difficulty in diagnosing ADHD during a formal psychoeducational assessment is the fact that in a one-to-one, highly stimulating, novel situation, the child's attention may be much more focused than in daily living situations [Sleator, 1986; Levine, 1987]. However, close observation of the child's performance and behavior can often still add support to other indicators of attentional difficulty (Table 4). A review of test protocols, for example, may reveal a great deal of scatter. That is, the child may miss earlier easier items, then respond correctly to later, more difficult items. When asked to repeat a series of words or numbers, whole sets may be forgotten rather than simply omitting parts. The child may then remember all the items in the next series, suggesting her recognition of the need to focus her attention. The quality of the child's verbal responses may also provide some clues. This may be a child who associates to her own responses, rather than to the original stimuli. For example the question, "What is brown?" may result in a response such as, "A bear is brown, bears live in the woods, I have a woods by my house, I like to play there, I climb trees."

The child may appear fidgety and restless even in the one-to-one setting. He may request, or obviously need, more frequent breaks. His approach to tasks may suggest impulsivity in that he does not appear to scan all aspects of a task before responding. He may respond before the directions or the

Table 4 Observable ADHD Behaviors During Formal Assessment

Response before directions are complete
Response without considering possibilities
Tangential verbal responses
Skipping from topic to topic
Easy items incorrect, difficult ones correct
Whole stimulus forgotten, next recalled accurately
Frequent breaks requested or required
Fidgetiness or restlessness
Distracted by noise
Distracted by visual stimuli
Daydreaming during independent tasks

stimuli have been completed. Particular difficulty may be noted in his ability to wait when a delayed response is required.

Distractibility, too, can take many forms. The child may be distracted by noises or by objects around the room or may appear more internally distractible. He may work well on a direct one-to-one basis, but appear to drift or daydream when given an independent task to do. It is always important to try to determine whether it is the level of difficulty of the task that is causing the distractibility.

Despite the difficulties and limitations inherent in the assessment process, it can be diagnostically productive. These children are complex. The most obvious rationale for an extensive evaluation is to rule out the possibility of an underlying cause that mimics but is not true ADHD. Of equal importance is the need not only to determine whether or not a concomitant learning disability or language disorder exists but also to define, as far as possible, the interaction between the disorders present and to describe the impact they may be having on the child's academic, family, and social life.

These interactions can take many forms in an individual child. Levine [1987] has described nine different control systems that may be affected to varying degrees and in varying combinations in children with disordered attention (see Table 5). Thus, although there are shared attributes that justify a unified conceptual model, individual children may differ in the expression of those attributes. This results not only in differing clinical profiles but also in differing responses to therapy.

Table 5   Disordered Control Systems and How They Present

Focal	Selecting salient features from an array and allocating the optimal time to attend
Sensory	Visual, auditory, or tactile distractibility
Associative	Daydreaming when words, sights or feelings too easily elicit a protracted chain of associations
Appetite	Desperately wanting something but losing interest as soon as it is achieved
Social	An inordinate need to inspect, manipulate, or probe classmates
Motor	Lethargic or overactive with motor activity often inefficient or not goal directed
Behavioral	Not foreseeing the social consequences of actions and disclaiming any role in the illegal act because it was unplanned and happened so quickly
Communication	Being loquacious and saying the wrong thing at the wrong time
Affective	Exhibiting wide mood swings that are difficult to predict and do not always match the occasion

Adapted from Levine [1985].

In addition to the varying manifestations of attentional control deficits, a concomitant learning disability may also take various forms. Learning disability subgroup research has revealed several different subtypes [Boder, 1973; Lyon and Watson, 1981; Satz and Morris, 1981; Smith, 1970; Snow et al., 1985]. Most subtype variations fit the broad categorization of auditory, verbal, visual, visual-motor, sequential, simultaneous, or mixed. Although groups of children may have commonalities, appropriate programing requires that each child be defined by his own combination of and interaction among these variables. The more clearly both attentional and learning deficits can be defined, the better the chance of providing the most effective interventions. The negative impact of the interaction of attention and learning problems has been documented by McKinney [1989], when he subtyped LD students by behavior and followed them for 3 years. Over time, LD children with attentional and those with behavior problems displayed a declining pattern of progress relative to those in other subgroups as well as to average achievers. Although children with attention deficits and problem behavior showed the most variable subtype membership, the direction of the change was toward more maladaptive subtypes rather than toward behaviorally normal subtypes.

EDUCATIONAL PLACEMENT FOR ADHD CHILDREN

Where, then, on the spectrum of special education services, do ADHD children fit? Legally, the answer seems to be "nowhere." Although many of these children have learning problems, the definition currently used to define learning disabilities does not specifically mention attention problems.

"Specific learning disability" means a disorder in one or more of the basic psychological processes involved in understanding or in using language, spoken or written, which may manifest itself in an imperfect ability to listen, think, speak, read, write, spell, or do mathematical calculations. The term includes such conditions as perceptual handicaps, brain injury, minimal brain dysfunction, dyslexia, and developmental aphasia. The term does not include children who have learning problems which are primarily the result of visual, hearing, or motor handicaps, of mental retardation, of emotional disturbance, or of environmental, cultural, or economic disadvantage [Public Law (PL) 94-142, Sec.602(15)].

An alternative definition has been suggested by the National Joint Committee of Learning Disabilities [Hammill et al., 1981]:

Learning disabilities is a generic term that refers to a heterogeneous group of disorders manifested by significant difficulties in the acquisition and use of listening, speaking, reading, writing, reasoning, or mathematical abilities. These disorders are intrinsic to the individual and presumed to be due to central nervous system dysfunction. Even though a learning disability may occur concomitantly with other handicapping conditions (e.g. sensory impairment, mental retardation, social and emotional disturbance) or environmental influences (e.g., cultural differences, insufficient/inappropriate instruction, psychogenic factors), it is not the direct result of those conditions or influences.

Again, no mention is made of attentional problems.

Even though their behavior may be seen as deviant, ADHD children do not usually fit criteria for a behavior disorder (BD). Although "BD" is frequently used to refer to a specific handicapping condition, the term actually used in PL 94-142 is "seriously emotionally disturbed (SED)" which is defined as follows:

> The term means a condition exhibiting one or more of the following characteristics over a long period of time and to a marked degree, which adversely affects educational performance:
>
> A.   An inability to learn which cannot be explained by intellectual, sensory, or health factors;
> B.   An inability to build or maintain satisfactory interpersonal relationships with peers and teachers;
> C.   Inappropriate types of behavior or feelings under normal circumstances;
> D.   A general pervasive mood of unhappiness or depression; or
> E.   A tendency to develop physical symptoms or fears associated with personal or school problems. The term includes children who are schizophrenic. The term does not include children who are socially maladjusted, unless it is determined that they are seriously emotionally disturbed." [Federal Register, Vol. 42, No. 163, 1977, p. 42478, as amended in Federal Register, Vol. 46, 1981, p. 3866]

Slenkovich [1983] points out that PL 94-142 is an education law using educational funds and is not a social law. Thus, an inability to learn "does not refer to being behind in work, daydreaming in class, not doing homework, nor getting failing grades but requires that the student be so emotionally disturbed that he *cannot* learn." An inability to build or maintain relationships "does not refer to not having any friends, bad relationships with teachers, having socially undesirable friends nor being disliked but again requires that the student be so emotionally disturbed that he is *unable* to enter into relationships." Inappropriate types of behaviors or feelings under normal circumstances "does not refer to socially unacceptable behavior, being hyperactive and bothersome, being an impossible chore to keep in the regular classroom, shyness, 'poor self image,' anxiousness, nervousness, anger, overactive behavior, or violation of social norms. It appears to mean *pycho-tic* or *bizarre* behavior such as giggling at a funeral or running down the street pouring out gibberish.''

In comparing the characteristics listed in the SED definition to DSM-III criteria for ADHD, Slenkovich [1983, p. 28] states:

> Even though *inappropriate types of behavior or feelings under normal circumstances* may be a characteristic of this diagnosis, the characteristic does not appear to be of sufficient severity to meet the PL 94-142 requirement that it exist *to a marked degree.*

This interpretation does not include ADHD as a severe emotional disturbance under PL 94-142.

An escalation of inappropriate behaviors severe enough to warrant a diagnosis of "conduct disorder" still may not legally be considered a handicapping condition. While a DSM-III diagnosis of ADD falls under the rubric of neither emotional disturbance nor social maladjustment, a diagnosis of conduct disorder may be considered social maladjustment [Slenkovich, 1983]. But socially maladjusted children are specifically excluded from being classified as SED in the definition.

The medical nature of the diagnosis of ADHD and the efficacy of medication as an intervention combine to suggest a relationship between ADHD and the "health factor" portion of the definition. As such it could conceivably preclude a diagnosis of BD or SED. However, in reviewing a school district's placement being challenged by parents, the New York State Commission ruled that a child's placement in a class for emotionally disturbed children be upheld in that no direct evidence was presented that showed the existence of a physical condition causing an ADHD. The student had demonstrated an inability to be successful in a regular academic setting that could not be explained by intellectual, sensory, or health factors [NYSEA (1987). Case no. 11873, p. 509:129].

ADHD would thus seem to have no special education placement significance under PL 94-142 except as a condition concomitant to another disorder. *ACLD Newsbriefs* [Gruber, 1989, p. 12] published a response from Dr. G. Thomas Bellamy, Director, Office of Special Education Programs, U.S. Department of Education, reiterating this view:

> (1) ADD, in and of itself, does not meet the eligibility criteria for any recognized handicapping condition under P.L.94-142; and (2) ADD is generally considered to be a characteristic of a specific learning disability or a characteristic of a serious emotional disturbance. Although, in isolation, it would not meet the eligibility standards, in combination with other characteristics, ADD may lend supporting information for the determination of SLD or SED.

Although PL 94-142 does not address the issue of ADHD, two recent complaints filed with the Office of Civil Rights each found an ADHD child entitled to services under Section 504 of the Rehabilitation Act of 1973 [Rialto (CA) Unified School District (OCR, 1989), p. 353:201; Fairfield-Suison (CA) Unified School District (OCR, 1989), p. 353:205]. In both cases, the students were evaluated and found not to be eligible for special services based on their academic performance and were punished for their misbehaviors. Both districts involved were asked to change their policies to include the identification and provision of services to those children who are eligible for those services under Section 504 whether or not they are eligible under PL 94-142.

In a typical school setting, ADHD children may be found in a variety of classes: LD, BD, resource, self-contained and, frequently, in the regular classroom. Teachers are often unaware which of their students have or have not been diagnosed as having ADHD. The variable presentation of this disorder, particularly as it interacts with other factors, has led to much confusion as to its true impact. Some educators question its very existence. Sawyer [1989], for example, interprets the literature as reflecting the fact that ADHD may not exist as a separate syndrome and decries the use of an ADHD diagnosis as a justification to classify and place a student as LD rather than providing appropriate reading instruction. Unfortunately, the complexity of the disorder, combined with the human need to reduce complexity to a more manageable, understandable, and easily measurable form make this kind of misunderstanding all too common.

THE ADHD CHILD IN THE CLASSROOM

The classroom teacher is just one component in the constellation of persons working with the ADHD child. The disorder and its emotional overlay may require the services of physicians, family therapists, individual behavioral or psychotherapists, special education professionals, the parents and, of course, the child. In the best of all possible worlds regular communication would take place to assure consistency among all aspects in the child's program. In the real world this seldom happens. Consistent regular communication between parent and teacher should represent the bare minimum but may be the most that can be accomplished.

Within the classroom setting the most valuable asset the teacher will have is the knowledge that the ADHD child is not deliberately striving to make his own and everyone else's life difficult. ADHD is a handicap just as real as a more obvious physical deformity, and, since it is invisible, it can be more difficult to accept. This is particularly true since the child's inconsistency causes him to look as if he could do it, "if he just tried." ADHD children often make the crucial mistake of occasionally succeeding in isolated situations. This sets up the quite reasonable expectation in a logically thinking adult that if they did it once, they could do it again. Unfortunately, the children do not have the vaguest notion how to recreate the successful situation.

It is useful to know that research has shown that both mothers [Campbell, 1975; Barkley and Cunningham, 1979] and other children [Clark et al., 1988] respond reciprocally to the ADHD child. That is, the ADHD child's responses affect in turn the responses of the communication partner. Armed with this insight, the teacher can be proactive by trying to prevent difficult situations, rather than merely reacting by disciplining the child's misbehavior or noncompliance. An overview of classroom behavior patterns is needed to plan such a preventive strategy. For the regular classroom teacher, it might be necessary to begin by simply making a check mark by the names of the children in need of further observation. In the smaller special education class it may be feasible to note not only who had the problem but just when it occurred. Reid [1988] discusses the application of this observation process in detail.

This overall picture may indicate that a simple change in seating would eliminate some problems. Although the ADHD child may work better when isolated from his peers, the fact that his behavior already sets him apart from his peers makes this a strategy that should be used cautiously.

When planning to circumvent problem situations and to change inappropriate behaviors, it is important to remember that the long-term goal is not just to manage the child, but for the child to learn to manage himself. Control, and the concommitant responsibility, should gradually be turned over to the child. This is a process requiring much patience. Instead of merely structuring the environment to prevent error, this approach attempts to teach those subskills of attention and organization that come so naturally to the rest of us. This ongoing process will not be accomplished by any one teacher in any academic time frame. It is important for teachers and children alike to be satisfied with achieved progress in the right direction and not to expect perfection.

Behavior modification tactics may be a useful component in the ADHD child's program but do not always generalize to other situations. This is due, in part, to the fact that behaviors such as impulsivity and inattention are themselves a core part of the disability. Extinguishing behaviors for a short time does not provide the child with more appropriate behaviors. In addition, these children do not respond to reinforcement in the same way that other children do. In normal children, reinforcements are applied on a continuous schedule during early phases of learning and are then faded to a more intermittent schedule. ADHD children, however, do not continue to exhibit consistent behavior when rewards become intermittent. Kinsbourne [1984] has presented evidence that these children are underesponsive to reward contingencies. Either the task must be compelling in its own right or else the rewards must be concrete, frequent, and salient to keep the child involved. Unfortunately, there is also evidence [Douglas, 1984] that even positive, consistent feedback can increase impulsive responding because the ADHD child attends more to the reinforcer or person reinforcing him than to the behavior being evaluated or rewarded.

The one type of reinforcement technique that seems to be most effective with ADHD children is *response-cost*. Response-cost is a method in which the child is given a number of tokens initially and loses one each time a rule is violated. Those remaining may be used to purchase a privilege or prize. Their removal should be viewed as a feedback device rather than as a punishment and this should be made clear from the beginning. At first the feedback should be specific such as, "You were looking out the window." Later it may be more general such as, "You were being inattentive."

A method that has been successful in clinical settings is that of *cognitive behavior modification* [Meichenbaum, 1977]. This is a technique of increasing the child's use of language or inner speech as a means of improving attentiveness and reducing impulsivity. It is a structured method whereby the clinician models a strategy for problem solving that includes the steps of defining the task, generating approaches to the task, selecting and applying a strategy, self-monitoring of progress, self-evaluation and self-reward. Through modeling and practice the child is taught to use these strategies. At first the instructions are said aloud but are gradually faded to covert self-instruction with probes by the clinician to monitor the child's thinking. One reported pitfall with this process is the tendency of the child to respond in a mechanical or rote manner if active participation is not monitored. For a detailed description of this method as used in a clinical setting, see Kirby and Grimley [1986] and Chapter 10.

Cognitive behavior modification has been shown to generalize to the classroom. Manning [1988] used it to train first and third graders who were exhibiting behavior problems. Although the number of ADHD children in the group was not mentioned, many of the targeted behaviors (out of classroom; manipulating pencils, rulers, or paper; scribbling or doodling; out of seat; talking; whispering; motioning; vocal noises; body movements) were characteristic. The only difference between subject training and that of the control group was the external versus internal orientation of the instructions. For example, the experimental group practiced a modeled self-instruction such as, "I will not shout out answers." The control group read aloud externally oriented rules presented by the adult such as "You will not shout out answers." The self-instruction treatment produced for both grades a significantly better result, which was still apparent after 3 months.

Although the time involved in the training suggests its restriction to a one-on-one clinical setting where learning the strategy rather than subject matter is the goal, some aspects of this method are applicable to the classroom setting using academic content. When implementing self-instruction techniques and problem-solving strategies in the classroom, cognitive modeling has proven more effective than giving directions [Camp and Bash, 1981]. And when modeling a procedure, the coping model, which includes correcting errors, is more effective than the mastery model, which models appropriate steps to a correct answer [Kendall and Braswell, 1985]. That is, rather than doing a task right the first time, try different ways of approaching it. The coping model indirectly communicates what can be done to alleviate fear or anxiety. It does not, of course, have to be used exclusively. It should be included often enough to indicate that the problem solving is an acceptable alternative to knowing the right answer. The overall goal is for the students to spontaneously ask themselves questions such as:

1. What is the problem? or
   What am I supposed to do?
2. What is my plan?
3. Am I using my plan?
4. How did I do?

Thus, rather than simply saying "Work problems in alternate rows beginning with row 2 on page 25," a modeling method would include talking your way through the procedure.

After having written the assignment on the board the teacher might say:

"Let's see. What am I supposed to do? Wow, that's confusing! OK, first I'll find the page—there—now, what else? Alternative rows—I know that means every other one—beginning with which—Oh, yeah,—number 2. I better mark those rows before I start. Now, what's my plan? Last time I really messed up; I didn't pay attention to my +s and −s. This time I think I'll circle each one before I do it—that way, I'll *have* to look at it."

The teacher might then work a few problems, stop and say,

"Am I circling the signs? Did I do what it said? Yep—better keep going."

When finished:

"Well, let's see; looks like I did them all—didn't skip any, remembered to circle—did that help? Sure looks like it. Good job!"

A coping model would require making errors in any one of the steps and having to rethink the problem as a part of the strategy. For example, "OK, I better get started right away." After working a few problems, "Oh no— I forgot which rows to work. What can I do about that?"

It is important to keep the students involved in the process. After they are familiar with the problem-solving approach, elicit plans from them. Be careful not to judge one as being "right" or the "best." The purpose of brainstorming is to generate several plans, as different plans will be better for different students. Of course, it is always fun for students to catch their teacher in a mistake. Modeling an incorrect procedure or forgetting a part of the plan usually brings an enthusiastic response and gives the teacher a chance to reward careful thinking.

More specific self-instruction strategies can be devised for various tasks. For example, the teacher can work with the child to devise a short checklist to improve the quality of work. A writing assignment might include: (a) Did I begin each sentence with a capital letter? (b) Did I end each sentence with a punctuation mark? As initial problems are mastered, more sophisticated questions can be added, always encouraging the student to identify his own needs.

This type of individualization can sometimes become a problem in a regular classroom setting. The child who needs the intervention help does not usually want to be singled out; in addition, there will be ten other students who want one, too—the checklist, chart, or whatever is being used. One way to circumvent this problem is to initiate the intervention with those who need it and then offer it to any other student who wants it. This can be done by stating, "Antoine and Sue are trying a new way to improve their writing. They've come up with some really good ideas. If you have something you would like to work on, see me after class." This approach serves several purposes:

1. It models a problem-solving approach.
2. It focuses positive attention on the target children, making them "trend setters."
3. It promotes understanding and acceptance of individual strengths and weaknesses.
4. It may identify other student needs.
5. It relieves the teacher of the responsibility for providing the same thing for everyone.

Organizational Skills

Organizational skills represent a major area of concern for the ADHD child. This can be true of physical, temporal, and mental organization. Physical and temporal organization can be addressed using methods similar to those above. Involve the child in identifying the problem and generating solutions. A messy desk might be improved by pencil boxes, a specific place for books, and a regularly scheduled checking time with a response-cost contingency.

Assignment sheets, specific notebooks, listing of class schedules, and procedural flow charts have also been helpful.

Mental organization is somewhat trickier. Phersson and Denner (1989) present some excellent methods for teaching organization and developing study strategies through the use of the semantic organizer. A *semantic organizer* is a system for teaching organizational strategies that can help students assemble information so that it is processed into the organizing structures of the memory system in a systematic way with the intent to recall that information with relative ease. The two basic types of semantic organizers reflect the two organizing principals that underlie the representation of all knowledge: stasis, represented by a cluster organizer; and change, represented by an episodic organizer (see Figures 1, 2, and 3). These basic types may be refined into their more complex subtypes and may be adopted to a variety of uses.

Attention can also be facilitated by teaching specific attending behaviors such as "Keep your eyes on the book until you finish the page." This type of instruction is more effective than general reminders to "Pay attention" or "Stop looking around." In all instances, when training attention, the task should be one that can be readily accomplished by the child. If no progress is being made, excessive curriculum demands may be the problem rather than inattention or carelessness.

After students have reached an appropriate level of attention and accuracy or, if they have attending strategies but fail to use them, *self-monitoring* may

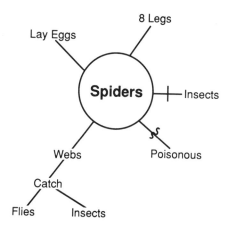

Figure 1 Semantic organizers can be used to teach organizational strategies. This is an example of a cluster organizer representing state knowledge. The straight line between "spiders" and "insects" indicates "not" while the wavy line between "spiders" and "poisonous" indicates "some." [Adapted from Pehrsson and Denner, 1989]

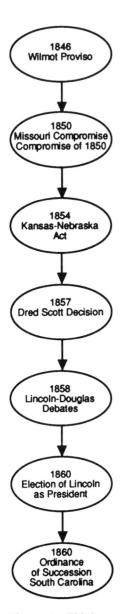

Figure 2   This is an example of an episodic organizer demonstrating a historical sequence of events. [Adapted from Pehrsson and Denner, 1989]

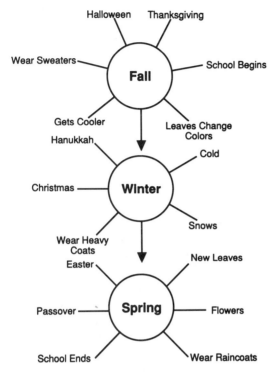

Figure 3   This episodic cluster demonstrates the relationship among three clusters representing the seasons of the school year. [Adapted from Pehrsson and Denner, 1989]

be initiated. A self-monitoring tape may be used that produces a tone at unexpected intervals. At the tone the child asks herself whether or not she was paying attention and checks her answers on a sheet or wristcounter. It is not necessary for the student to be accurate in the responses. Simply calling attention to attending seems to be adequate. Once on-task behavior has increased the student may be gradually taught to simply ask herself if she was attending [Kneedler and Hallahan, 1981].

ADHD children become less attentive when information is boring or when they are required to deal with too many details. Zentall and Gohs [1984] found that young hyperactive children responded better to global rather than detailed instructions. They suggested that when presenting new tasks, rather than provide details or a series of instructions, the teacher should indicate in general terms the relationship to other known tasks.

Whenever possible, seatwork requiring sustained attention should be alternated with more stimulating activities. The children may also be encouraged to actively interact with materials, either through a game format or the use of manipulatives. Reading aloud can also facilitate active participation. At the very least, these methods increase teachers' awareness of whether a child is involved or has drifted off. The child may also be encouraged to doodle(!), with the doodling gradually being replaced by notetaking.

In addition to responding impulsively and not maintaining attention, ADHD children often have trouble selecting the most salient features to which to attend. Vrana and Pihl [1980] found that in selective attention the meaning of the situation anticipated by the subject as based on past experience becomes important. This would suggest that Ausabel's [1968] theory that the most important predictor of learning is what a child already knows is vitally important for ADHD children. Accessing the knowledge they have will help them select that which is relevant in new information. Novak and Gowan [1984] describe a structured method for linking known to new information through concept mapping. *Concept mapping* is similar to semantic mapping [Pehrsson and Denner, 1989] but is oriented toward a visual presentation of the organization of information as related to a basic concept. It is particularly useful for the teaching and learning of content areas such as science or social studies. A basic tenet of this approach is beginning with that which is known and revising as new information is added (see Figures 4 and 5). This approach allows for the correction of previous misconceptions as well as providing an organizational structure for new information. As each category is refined further, the focus on salient information is maintained. Concept mapping also seems to be one method of incorporating Zentall and Gohs' [1984] findings regarding an initial global presentation as related to other known tasks.

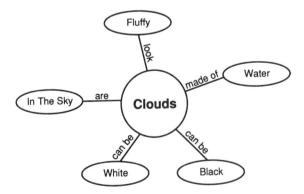

Figure 4   This is an example of a concept map representing the knowledge a child might bring to the learning situation. This initial map provides the structure into which new information can be integrated in a meaningful fashion. [Adapted from Novak and Gowan, 1984]

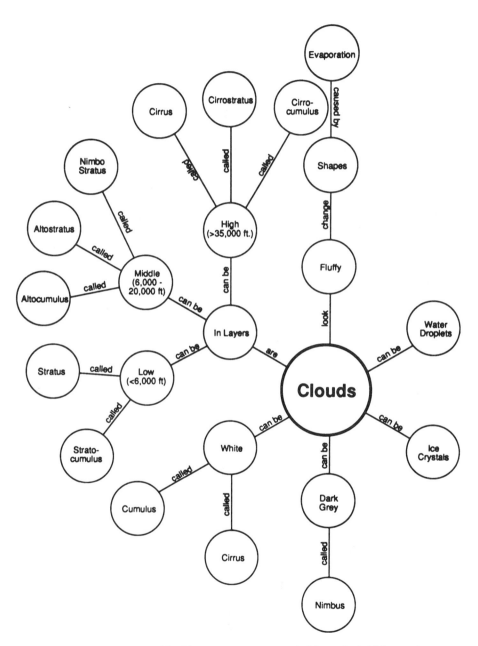

Figure 5 As demonstrated in this concept map, expanded from the initial map shown in Figure 4, new information has been added as it relates to and refines the original concept. Rather than having to select the salient features from a set of new information, the focus is on expanding that which is known. [Adapted from Novak and Gowan, 1984]

Although the classroom is the place for learning academic information and processes, social and interpersonal skills cannot be excluded. Like it or not, these skills, or more accurately the lack thereof, will certainly become apparent. Indeed, O'Brien and Obrzut [1986] suggest that it is important for the hyperactive child to be allowed to work with teachers skilled in enhancing social skills. In addition to responding impulsively, ADHD children often generate fewer problem-solving strategies than other children for given social situations. In addition, they seldom respond to punishments applied after the fact. Often the adult meting out the punishment has a totally different perception of the situation than that of the child. For example, the adult may have seen the ADHD child run up and hit another child, an obviously punishable offense. The ADHD child may have been simply trying to gain the other child's attention—with no harm meant. Therefore, the punishment related to the adult's interpretation will make no sense to the child and will probably not prevent another incident. Ultimately medication and structured social skills training in a clinical setting may be necessary for significant change to occur. However, "dialoguing" [Shure and Spivak, 1978] or "reality therapy" [Glasser, 1965] provide ways in which to gain insight into the child's perspective, actively involve the child in social problem solving, and generate alternative solutions.

Further suggestions for possible classroom modifications are listed in Table 6. In addition to working with attention deficits, it is important to remember that many of these children also have learning or language disorders. This interaction makes appropriate modifications both more difficult and more necessary. When planning for children exhibiting both disorders, it is important to identify and work through the child's strengths, circumvent weakness, and still provide successful learning experiences. For example, a disorder of written language which often a co-exists with ADHD, is pervasive and can affect all subject areas. In that case, writing deficits must be discriminated from actual knowledge. Or, in the case of an auditory-verbal deficit, visual aids should be an ongoing component of the child's program. Such complex interactions make any general statement merely a starting place in planning for the individual child whose patterns of learning and behavior are unique.

DRUGS IN THE CLASSROOM

The most controversial treatment of ADHD children is the use of psychostimulant medication. Attitudes regarding the use of medication range from the assumption that a pill is all that is required to fix the problem, to dire warnings about overmedicating children into compliance. The truth, of course, lies somewhere in between. While not a cureall, pharmacotherapy

Table 6 Further Suggestions for Possible Classroom Modifications

Present directions both auditorily and visually. Provide a demonstration of the assignment.

Give the student one-step directions to follow or present information one concept at a time.

Use concrete materials or visual aids to help keep the student focus on the task. Make assignments attractive and interesting.

Discuss an activity individually with the student to assure that he understands. Ask him to repeat information or directions to reinforce retention, or ask him to write, draw, or visualize information.

Be certain that the child looks at you when you speak to him. If he appears distracted from the task, give him cues to help him refocus his attention. For example, change the tone of your voice, state specifically that the class should listen carefully to an important point in the lecture, or write on the board while telling the class to note the information being stressed.

Periodically review and list points discussed during the course of a lecture.

Establish routines for the child's daily schedule so that he knows what happens when and what he will need to do. Make a visual flow chart with the child.

Provide periodic opportunities for purposeful movement about the room. Allow some assignments to be done at the chalkboard. Allow the child to stand so long as he is working on a task. Provide time for sitting or lying on the floor.

Shorten the length of assignments or present the student with only a few problems at one time.

Use color coding to cue the student's attention to important information.

Encourage the student to use verbal rehearsal and/or tracing strategies.

Modify the pace of the classroom. Begin the year with shorter blocks of curriculum, which may be increased as the year goes on.

Set clear, consistent limits on behavior.

Create an emotionally supportive environment where individual needs are recognized and successful experience planned.

Role play situations to help improve social behavior.

Keep the child's papers and materials at the teacher's desk to be completed and returned one at a time.

Monitor task completion.

Use preferential seating near teacher.

Develop an unobtrusive signal with the child to be used to remind him that he is off-task.

Give immediate feedback on assignments.

Use errors as learning tools.

Model and teach specific attending behavior.

can be an effective and important—and sometimes critical—component in the management of an ADHD child.

The three commonly used psychostimulants are Ritalin (generic name: methylphenidate), Cylert (generic name: pemoline), and Dexedrine (generic name: dextroamphetamine). Ritalin and Dexedrine are available in both short- and long-acting forms. Cylert is a long-acting medication that usually takes several weeks to be effective. As is true of most medications, there may be side effects. Of those reactions that may be noted by parents or teachers, the development of tic reactions, which occur in a very small percentage of children, is of sufficient concern to lead to discontinuing the medication. An earlier concern about the possibility of growth suppression has not been supported by recent research [Silver, 1984]. Other effects often subside after a few weeks of therapy or are amenable to changes in dosage, timing, or type of medication: these include decrease in appetite, difficulty falling asleep, emotional instability or sleepiness. Overall, psychostimulants have been used safely and effectively since the late 1930s [Silver, 1984]. Contrary to earlier thinking, there is a recent consensus among researchers and clinicians that adolescents, as well as adults, can sometimes benefit from stimulant drug therapy.

The optimal use of drug therapy demands a high degree of cooperation and communication between parents, teachers, and physicians. The input of the teacher is very valuable in determining a child's response to medication as she sees the child for long periods of time in a situation in which variations in attention and behavior are quite noticeable. Behavioral questionnaires are frequently used as a method of quantifying the effects of medication. A review of several commonly used questionnaires [Blondis et al., 1989] reported the Connors Abbreviated Teachers Rating Scale [Goyette et al., 1978] and the ADD-H: Comprehensive Teacher Rating Scale [Ullman et al., 1984] to be effective for medication monitoring.

In lieu of, or in addition to, behavioral checklists, it is important to note the more subtle indicators of attentional variations as well as the more overt behavioral deviations. This is particularly important when the child is not hyperactive. It is easy to report that no change occurred on cursory observation. Taking a baseline comparison with an average classmate's performance would give a better basis for future comparisons. The ADHD child might differ from the control child in time on task, playing with objects, delay in starting tasks, following directions, requests for repeated instructions, incorrect responses, not answering questions on demand, or other variables unique to the child. If the teacher has no warning that a drug trial is going to be initiated, more detailed detective work will be necessary. In observing the child, note anything that may instinctively seem unusual. It might only be possible to note the time of day with, perhaps, a few words describing the observation. At the end of the day, it would be helpful to go back and reconstruct the situation and more specifically define the change. The method of observation will vary with individual teachers. What is important is recording, in the simplest way available, these subtle variations. Although it may seem valid to see whether or not the teacher notices a change in the child without being alerted to the fact that medication is being tried, valuable information can be lost in this way. This would allow only subjective impressions in retrospect of whether or not any change occurred with no chance for objective, systematic documentation.

In addition to noting behaviors, academic performance should also be monitored. Although previous research has not shown beneficial effects on learning, these results are currently being questioned. Of particular importance is the finding that lower doses of medication facilitated performance on cognitive tasks for a majority of children but had lesser effect on teacher ratings, whereas a higher dosage had both a major effect on teacher ratings and an adverse effect on short-term memory performance [Pelham, 1986; O'Brien and Obrzut, 1986]. Famularo and Fenton [1987] report that in a group of ADHD children without accompanying hyperactivity, 8 out of 10 children showed grade improvement in at least three of the five target subjects during the methylphenidate treatment period compared with the immediately preceding academic period when no drugs were administered. Academic monitoring might include comparing handwriting samples, tabulating number of items completed, or comparing accuracy levels. No clear pattern of improvement is apparent from the literature. Therefore, a wide variety of work samples across academic subjects should be monitored. Decisions will then need to be made based on the needs of each individual child.

Psychostimulant medication, although often necessary, is rarely sufficient in itself to overcome all the problems experienced by the ADHD child. It may "open the window" or help the child control herself in order to learn but does not cause social or problem-solving strategies to emerge. Pharmacotherapy is least effective in improving peer relations. Even when teacher ratings improved, peer ratings did not. This problem needs to be addressed, particularly since peer ratings appear to be a better predictor of long-term outcome than teacher ratings [Pelham and Bender, 1981]. Evidence is growing that a multimodal treatment approach, of which medication is only one part, is probably optimal.

HOMEWORK

Homework can be a conflictual area for many children. For the ADHD child, his family, and his teacher it can become a major problem without close communication between all involved. Too often, the teacher may assume the parents are not concerned and don't work with the child. This is an easy assumption to make—too easy. Since the child occasionally will know his spelling words, he obviously must have studied. Or the assumption may be that the parent does the work for the child because the child certainly doesn't accomplish that quality and quantity of work in the class.

From their perspective, the parents may assume that their child has an inordinate amount of homework—their other children didn't have to spend hours every night at this age. Or they may assume that the teacher just is not teaching—the child hasn't the faintest idea how to do the assignments that come home.

This is assuming, of course, that the assignments get home and back to class on schedule—a major and often faulty assumption for the ADHD child. He will adamantly insist to parents that he has no homework or that the teacher didn't tell them the test was today. Or he will rush through the work beginning accurately but rapidly deteriorating as he progresses. When assignments are completed, they often never make it to the teacher, but rather end up under the bed or crumpled in the bottom of the book bag. Everyone is mad, and he is in trouble—again!

The first step toward solving the problem rather than assigning blame may be the necessary admission that the child is, indeed, handicapped. For the parents, this may mean that they can acknowledge the fact that this child will need more of their time. The question then becomes how to best use the time to the benefit of the child with the least disruption to the family. For the teacher, this may mean acknowledging that it is fair to treat this child differently. The question then becomes how to help the child learn to work up to his potential. For the child, this may mean acknowledging that sometimes he does have to work harder than others, but also that the adults around him are going to help him make it pay off.

All children benefit from a home environment and structure that assumes homework has a place in the daily schedule as surely as eating dinner and taking a bath. For the ADHD child, this structure and routine are even more important. The parents and child can work together to formulate a time schedule for accomplishing assignments based on what realistically works for them. This schedule should be written down, posted, and adhered to. It should include breaks based on the child's attention span. Generally, children need some time to unwind and perhaps have a snack when they get home from school, but homework should not wait until they are too tired to begin. There is no rule that says homework needs to be all done at one sitting. In fact, short, frequent practice sessions have been shown to increase learning better than one long session. So the schedule may be for 20 minutes before dinner and 20 after. Some children and families may prefer to set some time aside in the morning for homework. What is important is consistency not the particular schedule. On days when there is no homework, the schedule should be respected. Keep a supply of learning games and activities that may be done in that time period. Remember, learning can actually be fun. The time could also be used for reading and discussing library books. But a note of caution: reading for pleasure should be just that—pleasurable. A sure way to prevent a love of books is to insist that reading be done every day as a chore.

Long-term assignments are particularly troublesome. It is helpful to use a calendar to plan specifically how to work toward completion a little at a time and not save it all until the last minute. Studying for tests should be approached in the same manner. Study a portion, then the next day review that portion and add to it. Spelling tests may also be approached this way. Divide the list into segments; learn one segment a day and review those previously learned. The ADHD child will need a lot of help with this type of scheduling, particularly at first and probably for a longer time than you would expect. Modeling this behavior will help more than nagging. Gradually turn more responsibility over to the child as he is able to accept it.

Physical organization also needs some thought. Decide where homework is to be done. For younger children, close proximity to an adult is helpful. However, distraction should be minimized. The location decided on should be used consistently. Siblings should each have their own particular place. A sign such as "John's Office" may help define the place and set the tone. Supplies such as pencils, paper, ruler, dictionary, and whatever else becomes necessary through the year should be kept at that location. If one child's place is at the kitchen table, supplies might be kept in a labeled box nearby. Finished homework should always be placed in the same spot—either directly in the bookbag or in a specific spot to be checked routinely when leaving. The process of doing homework is an appropriate topic to be specifically included in the classroom curriculum [Canter, 1988]. Such continuity is certainly helpful to the ADHD child.

The ADHD child works best when actively interacting with the material at home as well as in class. If it is allowed, encourage underlining while studying. Older children can be encouraged to take notes; younger children might sketch pictures regarding what they've read. Parents might encourage the child to read over the chapter headings and help him formulate questions to be answered. A parent might ask the child to read a section and then tell about it. Any tactic that keeps the child actively involved will help prevent loss of attention.

These general suggestions will eliminate several areas of controversy over homework but there will be times when they are not effective. When that happens, it is important to try to pinpoint the problem. Careful documentation may show patterns of performance that can be altered. It can also facilitate a problem-solving rather than an adversarial parent-teacher relationship. Although the procedure is time consuming in the short run, it can be a very effective use of time. The parent can write down such specifics as time homework was begun, assignments attempted, amount of time child could attend without a break, length of time spent on each assignment, time when difficulty was encountered, and assignment or part of assignment that seemed to precipitate the problem. This should be done over a period of several days. Parents and teacher can then work together, using this information as a basis for generating solutions.

It may be that the difficulty is a new bit of material not thoroughly understood and some short-term help is all that is necessary. It may be a certain subject that is consistently causing trouble. It may be that the child simply cannot attend long enough to finish the amount of homework required. In the latter instance, homework will need to be prioritized or modified in length so that the child can experience success at having completed a task in a reasonable length of time. This is essential in teaching the child that consistent effort is rewarded.

In some cases teacher and parent roles will need to be specifically delineated so that they can truly work as a team and not duplicate efforts. Perhaps the teacher can monitor social studies homework during a study hall, while the parent supervises extra practice on math facts. Parents should also acknowledge their own level of frustrations and interests when planning their role. If the parent is a history buff but becomes frustrated in short order with math, this is relevant information.

Parents should not teach new material. Homework should be an opportunity to practice new skills, review skills, enrich and broaden knowledge, or complete projects or tasks too time consuming to be finished at school. It should not be a vehicle for extending school problems into the family setting. For an ADHD child to increase his attention, try to maintain consistent effort, and learn to be responsible for his work, the probability of success must be built in (Table 7).

CONCLUSION

It is important to remember that the ADHD child is first of all a child—a child whose place on the scale of individual differences places him at the more extreme end of the continuum. His particular pattern of neurological differences makes the world a confusing place. Adults tend to interact with him as if it were his fault that he does not pay attention. But, as hard as he may try, he never quite gets it together. Coupled with this, the attention deficit is often accompanied by a learning disability. The combination interacts

Table 7   Tips for Managing Homework

Use assignment sheets
Organize notebook by subjects
Plan a time schedule and stick to it
Include breaks in schedule
Provide learning activities on no-homework days
Model planning ahead for long-term assignments
Choose a specific place for studying
Keep supplies at homework location
Put completed work in specific spot
Encourage interaction with materials
Document problem areas
Engage in parent/teacher communication
Modify assignments as necessary
Delineate parent roles
Involve the child in planning
Work on gradually turning over responsibility to child
Incorporate opportunities for success

to make school, where he is required to spend many hours of his life, a difficult and frustrating place to be. Unfortunately, the problems do not end when the school bell rings. His impulsivity and lack of attention, now combined with school failure, are often a family problem.

Left untreated, this unfortunate combination often leads to an overlay of emotional problems. However, there are things we can do to help. Medication has often been found to make the biggest difference in the ability to focus attention. When a child's attention is better focused, the adults in his life have more of a chance to make a difference. That is, the opportunity to teach the strategies for organizing life that come so automatically and are taken for granted by the rest of us.

The ADHD child, like all children, needs a realistic interpretation of the world around him. For both parents and teachers, this means initially accepting the child as he really is, not as they would like him to be. To help him move closer to the way in which other people perceive the world, his perception must be taken into account. If he is upset because a friend is angry at him, it is important to respect that feeling, even though he brought it on himself. If he only meant to help but instead created a mess, then he must be given credit for trying to help before he can learn more effective and appropriate ways to do so.

Praise and encouragement must be honest and accurate to be helpful. As one parent stated: "I praise him when he's good and praise him when he's bad. When he hasn't done a good job he gets angry when he is praised. What am I supposed to do?'' Dishonest praise makes it difficult, eventually, to believe that any praise is well deserved. Encouragement should also be realistic to the situation.

Telling a struggling, frustrated child that a job is easy and fun can have only two effects: he begins to doubt either his competence or the adult's sanity. An accurate appraisal and appreciation of effort (''This is a very difficult job and you have stuck to it for 5 whole minutes'') makes it much easier to try for 6 or 7 minutes.

The forward progress is often slow and effortful and includes more steps backward than we would like to see. In this age of instant communication and quick fixes, it is difficult to deal with a problem that is complex and long term. But with patience, effort and, possibly, a little luck, the hyperactive, off-task, impulsive child may well become the energetic, creative, innovative adult.

REFERENCES

Achenbach, T. M., Edelbrock, C. (1983). *Manual for the Child Behavior Checklist and Revised Child Behavior Profile.* Burlington, VT: T. M. Achenbach.

American Psychiatric Association (1980). *Diagnostic and Statistical Manual of Mental Disorders,* 3rd Ed. Washington, D.C.: APA.

American Psychiatric Association (1987). *Diagnostic and Statistical Manual of Mental Disorders,* 3rd Ed., Rev. Washington, D.C.: APA.

Ausable, D. P. (1968) *Educational psychology: A Cognitive View.* New York: Holt, Rinehart and Winston.

Barkley, R., Cunningham, C. (1979). The effects of methylphenidate on the mother child interactions of hyperactive children. *Arch. Gen. Psychi. 36(2):*201-212.

Blondis, T. A., Accardo, P. J., Snow, J. H. (1989). Measures of attention deficit. *Clin. Pediatrics 28(5):*222-276.

Boder, E. (1973) Developmental dyslexia: A diagnostic approach based on three atypical reading-spelling patterns. *Dev. Med. Child Neurol. 15:*663-687.

Boudreault, M., Thievierge, J., Cote, R., Boutin, P., Julien, Y., Bergeron, S. (1988). Cognitive development and reading achievement in pervasive-ADD, situational-ADD and control children. *J. Child Psychol. Psychi. 29(5):*611-619.

Brown, R. T. (1982). A developmental analysis of visual and auditory sustained attention and reflection-impulsivity in hyperactive and normal children. *J. Learn. Disabil. 15(10):*614-618.

Brown, R. T. & Borden, K. A. (1986). Hyperactivity at adolescence: Some misconceptions and new directions. *J. Clin. Child Psychol. 5(3):*194-209.

Camp, B. W., Bash, M. A. (1981). *Think Aloud: Increasing Social and Cognitive Skills—A Problem-Solving Program for Children.* Champaign, IL: Research Press.

Campbell, S. B. (1975). Mother-child interaction: A comparison of hyperactive, learning disabled, and normal boys. *Am. J. Orthopsychi. 45(1):*51-57.

Canter, L. (1988). Homework without tears. *Instructor 98(2):*28-30.

Carlson, C. L., Layey, B. B., Frame, C. L., Walker, J., Hynd, G. W. (1987). Sociometric status of clinic-referred children with attention deficit disorders with and without hyperactivity. *J. Abnorm. Psychol. 15(4)*:537-547.

Clark, M. L., Cheyne, J. A., Cunningham, C. E., Siegel, L. S. (1988). Dyadic peer interaction and task orientation in attention-deficit-disordered children. *J. Abnorm. Child Psychol. 16*(1):1-15.

Connors, C. K. (1978). Normative data on revised Conners Parent and Teacher Rating Scales. *J. Abnorm. Child Psychol. 26*:221-236.

Cooper, D. H., Farran, C. D. (1988). Behavioral risk factor in kindergarten. *Early Childhood Res. Quart. 3*:1-19.

Douglas, V. A. (1984). The psychological processes implicated in ADD. In: *Attention Deficit Disorder: Diagnostic, Cognitive, and Therapeutic Understanding.* Bloomingdale, L. M., ed. Jamaica, NY: Spectrum.

Duane, D. D. (1988). The classroom clinicians role in finding the cause of ADD/ LD. *Learn. Disabil. Focus 4(1)*:6-8.

Dykman, R. A., Ackerman, P. T., Clements, S. D., Peters, J. E. (1971). Specific learning disabilities: An attentional deficit syndrome. In: *Progress in Learning Disabilities,* Vol 2. Myklebust, H. R., ed. New York: Grune and Stratton, pp. 56-93.

Dykman, R. A., Ackerman, P. T., Holcomb, P. J. (1984). *Reading disabled and ADD children: Similarities and differences.* Paper presented at the Annual Convention of the American Psychological Association, August 1984. Toronto.

Fairfield-Suison, CA, Unified School District (OCR) (1989). *Ed. Handicapped Law Rep.* (Suppl. 242) *353*:205.

Famularo, R., Fenton, T. (1987). The effect of methylphenidate on school grades in children with attention deficit disorder without hyperactivity: A preliminary report. *J. Clin. Psychi. 48(3)*:112-114.

Federal Register (1977). 42 (163), 42478.

Federal Register (1981). 46, 3866.

Glasser, W. (1965). *Reality Therapy: A New Approach to Psychiatry.* New York: Harper and Row.

Goyette, C. H., Conners, C. K., Ulrich, R. F. (1978). Normative data on the revised Conners parent and Teacher Rating Scales. *J. Abnorm. Child Psychol. 6*:221-236.

Gruber, H. (1989). Why an association for learning disabilities should be concerned with ADD/ADHD. *ACLD Newsbriefs 24(1)*:12.

Hammill, D. D., Larsen, S. C., Leigh, J., McNutt, G. (1981) A new definition of learning disabilities. *Learn. Disabil. Quart. 4*:336-342.

Kaufman, A. S. (1975). Factor analysis of the WISC-R at eleven age levels between 6½ and 16½ years. *J. Consult. Clin. Psychol. 43*:135-147.

Kendall, P. C. and Braswell, L. (1985). *Behavioral Therapy for Impulsive Children.* New York: The Guilford Press.

Kinsbourne, M. (1984). Beyond attention deficit: Search for the disorder in ADD. In: *Attention Deficit Disorder: Diagnostic, Cognitive, and Therapeutic Understanding.* Bloomingdale, L. M., ed. Jamaica, NY: Spectrum.

Kirby, E. A., Grimley, L. K. (1986). *Understanding and Treating Attention Deficit Disorder.* New York: Pergamon Press.

Kneedler, R. D., Hallahan, D. P. (1981). Self-monitoring of on-task behavior with learning-disabled children: Current studies and directions. *Except. Ed. Quart. 2 (3)*:73-82.

Krupski, A. (1985). Variations in attention as a function of classroom task demands in learning handicapped and CA-matched nonhandicapped. *Except. Child. 52(1)*: 52-56.

Lahey, B. B., Hynd, G. W., Stone, P. A., Piacentini, J. C., Frick, P. J. (1989). Neuropsychological test performance and the attention deficit disorders: Clinical utility of the Luria-Nebraska Neuropsychological Battery-Children's Revision. *J. Consult. Clin. Psychol. 57(1)*:112-116.

Landau, S., Milich, R. (1988). Social communication patterns of attention-deficit-disordered boys. *J. Abnorm. Child Psychol. 16(1)*:69-81.

Levine, M. D. (1987). Attention deficits: The diverse effects of weak control systems in childhood. *Pediatric Ann. 16(2)*:117-131.

Lufi, D., Cohen, A. (1985). Using the WISC-R to identify attentional deficit disorder. *Psychol. Schools 22*:40-42.

Lyon, R., Watson, B. (1981). Empirically derived subgroups of learning disabled readers: Diagnostic characteristics. *J. Learn. Disabil. 14(5)*:256-261.

Manning, B. H. (1988). Application of cognitive behavior modification: First and third graders self-management of classroom behaviors. *Am. Ed. Res. J. 25(2)*: 193-212.

McGee, R., Williams, S., Silva, P. A. (1985). Factor structure and correlates of ratings of inattention, hyperactivity and antisocial behavior in a large sample of 9-year-old children from the general population. *J. Consult. Clin. Psychol. 53(4)*: 480-490.

McKinney, J. D. (1989). Longitudinal research on the behavioral characteristics of children with learning disabilities. *J. Learn. Disabil. 22(3)*:141-150.

McNallis, K. L. (1987). In search of the attentional deficit. In: *Handbook of Cognitive, Social, and Neuropsychological Aspects of Learning Disabilities,* vol. 2. Ceci, S. J., ed. Hillsdale, NJ: Lawrence Erlbaum, pp. 63-81.

Meichenbaum, D. (1977). *Cognitive Behavior Modification: An Integrative Approach.* New York: Plenum.

Novak, J. D., Gowan, D. B. (1984). *Learning How to Learn.* New York: Cambridge University Press.

New York State Education Association (1987). Case no. 11873 (1987-88). *Ed. Handicapped Law Rep. 509*:129.

O'Brien, M. A., Obrzut, J. E. (1986). Attention deficit disorder with hyperactivity: A review and implications for the classroom. *J. Spec. Ed. 20(3)*:281-297.

Pehrsson, R. S., Denner, P. R. (1989). *Semantic Organizers: A Study Strategy for Special Needs Learners.* Rockville, MD: Aspen Publishers.

Pelham, W. E. (1986). The effects of psychostimulant drugs on learning and academic achievement in children with attention deficit disorder and learning disabilities. In: *Psychological and Educational Perspectives on Learning Disabilities.* Torgesen, J. K., Wong, B. Y. L., eds., pp. 259-296.

Pelham, W. E., Bender, M. E. (1981) In: *Advances in Learning and Behavioral Disabilities.* Gadow, K. D., Bialer, I., eds. Greenwich, CT: Jai Press.

Public Law 94-142. Education for all handicapped. Sec. 602(15)

Reid, D. K. (1988). *Teaching the Learning Disabled: A Cognitive Developmental Approach.* Boston: Allyn and Bacon.

Rialto, CA, Unified School District (OCR) (1989). *Ed. Handicapped Law Rep.* (Suppl. 241) *353*:201.

Satz, P., Morris, R. (1981). Learning disability subtypes: A review. In: *Neuropsychological and Cognitive Processes in Reading.* Piorozzolo, F. J., Wittrock, M. C., eds. New York: Academic Press.

Sawyer, W. E. (1989). Attention deficit disorder: A wolf in sheep's clothing . . . again. *Read. Teach. 42(4)*:310-312.

Shure, M. B., Spivack, G. (1978). *Problem-Solving Techniques in Childrearing.* San Francisco: Jossey-Boss.

Silver, L. B. (1984). *The Misunderstood Child: A Guide for Parents of Learning Disabled Children.* New York: McGraw-Hill.

Sleater, E. K. (1986). Diagnosis. In: *Attention Deficit Disorder.* Sleater, E. K., Pelham, W. E., Jr., eds. Norwalk, CN: Appleton-Century-Croft.

Slenkovich, J. E. (1983). *PL94-142 as Applied to DSM III Diagnosis: An Analysis of DSM-III Diagnoses vis-à-vis Special Education Law.* Cupertino, CA: Kinghorn Press.

Smith, M. M. (1970). *Patterns of Intellectual Abilities in Educationally Handicapped Children.* Unpublished doctoral dissertation. Claremont College, CA.

Snow, J. H., Cohen, M., Holliman, W. B. (1985). Learning disability subgroups using cluster analysis of the WISC-R. *J. Psychoed. Assess. 4*:391-397.

Sutter, E., Bishop, P., Battin, R. R. (1987). Psychometric screening for attention deficit disorder in a clinical setting. *J. Psychoed. Assess. 3*:227-235.

Ullman, R. K., Sleator, E. K., Sprague, R. L. (1984). A new rating scale for diagnosis and monitoring of ADD children. *Psychopharmacol. Bull. 21*:915-20.

Vrana, F. V., Pihl, R. O. (1980). Selective attention deficit in learning disabled children: A cognitive interpretation. *J. Learn. Disabil. 13(7)*:42-46.

Wechsler, D. (1974). *Wechsler Intelligence Scale for Children—Revised.* New York: Psychological Corporation.

Zentall, S. S. (1988). Production deficiencies in elicited language but not in the spontaneous verbalizations of hyperactive children. *J. Abnorm. Child Psychol. 16(6)*: 657-673.

Zentall, D. D., Gohs, D. E. (1984). Hyperactive and comparison children's response to detailed vs. global cues in communication tasks. *Learn. Disabil. Quart. 7*:77-87.

12

Microcomputer Software in the Treatment of Attention Deficit Hyperactivity Disorder

Larry W. Desch

University of Missouri, Columbia, Missouri

> "Children do not learn by sitting passively in their seats listening to the teacher, any more than they learn to swim by sitting in rows on a wharf watching grown-up swimmers in the water."
>
> [Pulaski]

During the last decade there have been two areas of activity that have led to the increasing use of microcomputer software in the treatment of attention deficit hyperactivity disorder (ADHD). First, the recent advancements in special education services are, perhaps, most responsible for what is currently being done. Second, the progress made by neuropsychologists working with head-injury patients using microcomputer software as part of rehabilitation is contributing to the use of similar software for ADHD.

There is an additional, if indirect, factor also at work to increase the use of microcomputer programs with children with ADHD: the decreasing cost of home computers. Families have often obtained microcomputers with the hope of working with their child who has attention and learning problems specifically to improve the child's learning and academic skills. This situation is occurring in a haphazard fashion, and often the child's teacher is unaware of the child's work with a microcomputer at home.

Despite the rapid advances in microcomputer technology and the development of software, there remain many questions regarding the effectiveness of microcomputer instruction of children with attentional difficulties. This chapter will focus on the information currently available regarding computer programs designed to help children with *primary* ADHD—that is, an attentional disorder *not* secondary to head injury or other acquired etiologies.

MICROCOMPUTER POSSIBILITIES

For years special education teachers have searched for methods to improve education of children with learning disabilities (LD). There has been increasing research which has shown that many types of computer-assisted instruction (CAI) can be very effective as a teaching tool for LD children [Goldman and Pellegrino, 1987]. Educators have also tried microcomputer software programs with children who have attention deficits or "hyperactivity." Research on the use of these programs with this specific population remains very limited.

Since the early days of microcomputer software development for classroom instruction it has been felt that such programs might be very helpful in improving attention and concentration and enhancing task persistence in ADHD children. Such software, including computer games, are usually visual-spatial in nature and may thus help to improve eye-hand coordination. For most children the visually stimulating impact of microcomputer software is both interesting and motivating and provides the possibility for over-learning to achieve mastery in situations such as ADHD and LD. A computerized lesson can easily be repeated but with sufficient change so that it is not perceived as boring.

Since children with ADHD lack the ability to pay attention, in the early grades they are especially liable to miss the learning cues and strategies they need to learn. They usually have difficulty attending in just those situations in which academic problem-solving techniques are required.

Although at the present time there is little hard evidence regarding the use of CAI with children who have attentional difficulties, there are a number of features of CAI that logically support their utility. Some of these features are based on what previous research studies have shown in regard to the learning processes of children. Most children, including those who have poor attention and task persistence, seem to be fascinated by computers. The use of color and graphics and especially computer generated animation can be very useful in holding the student's attention longer. However, there is also evidence that too much of these attractive elements may actually serve as distractors from the learning that should take place.

In a relevant study by Douglass and Parry [1983], which used reinforcers other than CAI to enhance learning, it was shown that those reinforcements that were too powerful might become over-arousing and actually interfere with the learning process. In a study by Chiang [1983], LD children were found to have significant difficulties in a word-to-picture matching game when there were sound effects in the program; learning the correct answers took significantly less trials when no sound effects were used. Unfortunately, no mention was made in this report about whether or not any of the subjects also had ADHD. Lathrop [1982] concluded that inappropriate or extreme sound effects were disruptive even for children without attentional problems and represented one of the "ten commandments" for rejecting a particular piece of CAI.

Children with attentional difficulties, especially if they also have concomitant learning difficulties, often feel frustrated with new situations, especially new learning situations. Learning disabled students often find microcomputer software a very "safe" way to learn since they do not have to face any ridicule from others when they give wrong answers [Terwilliger, 1986]. In addition, computers exhibit the "ultimate patience": software programs are usually written so that the computer will wait indefinitely for an answer to be entered. Microcomputer software generally offers material in a self-paced individualized manner with the student progressing at his or her speed [Desch, 1986].

Perhaps most important, however, is the fact that computer software programs often will present the correction of a mistake immediately so that continuous uninterrupted feedback on the student's learning is provided. Previous research on reinforcement schedules in children with hyperactivity have demonstrated that these children work best under just such a system of continuous reinforcement, while intermittent or negative reinforcement actually can worsen the behaviors [Parry and Douglas, 1983]. Unfortunately, with an ADHD child, traditional instruction by a teacher, in a regular classroom setting, does *not* allow for this continuous reinforcement—and there is often actually an excess of negative feedback.

In summary, there are a number of aspects of CAI that are promising for children with attention deficit disorders. It appears, at least superficially, that these aspects of microcomputer software programs may actually help compensate for some of the problems seen with a child who has ADHD. A well-designed program controls the pace of learning and provides immediate feedback. If a wrong answer is impulsively given by an ADHD student, he or she has a chance to reflect on the problem, get the right answers, and allow the program to continue. A computer is also extremely patient and will wait for an answer despite the students taking longer than necessary because of distractions. The use of microcomputer also can provide a socially comfortable way to learn since there is neither ridicule nor other negative human responses. Finally, the intrinsic nature of the visual experience can help motivate any child.

The following section will address and critique some of the aspects of currently available software, especially in light of these unproven potentials of CAI. Specifically, the use of CAI with young elementary school-aged children with attentional problems will be reviewed.

MICROCOMPUTER REALITIES

It is somewhat surprising, in light of all the potential of CAI for teaching ADHD children, that so little research has been done. That is not to say there are not a large number of anecdotal or extremely limited studies that overwhelmingly endorse CAI for such children. Stowitschek [1984] strongly criticized the fact that, despite recent marked increases in school computer usage, especially with children with learning problems, the research continues to be minimal on the efficacy of these CAI programs. This is true for software developed for the regular as well as the special education classroom. In the studies that have been done, there are numerous methodological difficulties—such as not controlling for the previous information learned between each test group or not controlling for the specifics of each of the treatment conditions, for example, time spent with the microcomputer. Often only short-term CAI effects are analyzed, and whether any of the positive effects are long lasting is not even addressed.

Fitzgerald and colleagues [1986] compared the efficacy of CAI to that of traditional instruction in 9 students with attentional difficulties (mean age, 10.2 years). In this study *no* differences were found between the traditional instruction and CAI based on learning a number of spelling words when the results for each student were compared to the "no instruction" condition. Although, this research seemed to yield negative results, two important points need to be made. First, CAI methods were at least as effective as the teacher-conducted traditional spelling instruction: the ADHD did *not* interfere with the children's effective use of the microcomputer program. Second, and perhaps more important, however, is the fact that during the time that some of the children used the CAI program the teacher was free to give more individualized instruction to those students who were not using the microcomputer. This "liberation" of the teacher's time may actually prove to be the most significant aspect of CAI's effectiveness.

Fitzgerald and colleagues [1986] concluded that perhaps the best method of instruction for children with attention difficulties would be to combine traditional teacher instruction with periods of independent work using CAI. Although this particular study was better controlled than most, further studies are definitely needed to delineate the effectiveness variables for CAI with ADHD children. Unfortunately, there is no straight forward way to generalize the impact of one CAI program to other software programs that might become available.

COGNITIVE RETRAINING SOFTWARE

During the last decade neuropsychologists and others who deal with children and adults with head-injury sequelae have investigated the use of microcomputer software for "cognitive retraining" [Lynch, 1983]. Research on the use of this software for the cognitive retraining of people who have suffered head injuries has, for the most part, been more methodologically correct than CAI in special education settings. However, even though such cognitive rehabilitation programs may be proven in the future to be useful for primary ADHD, at the present time this software often focuses on rehabilitation of visual-spatial or memory skills, which do not seem to be that critically important for the young ADHD child. In addition, these software programs were intended to be used within a broader remediation program that involves occupational therapists, neuropsychologists, and others working with the head-injured population. Therefore, extending the use of cognitive retraining software to other populations, especially without the concomitant involvement of qualified therapists, reflects, at best, faulty reasoning, but may actually be harmful. On the one hand, carefully controled research using these cognitive rehabilitation software programs with primary ADHD is currently nonexistent. On the other hand, there are many similarities between the CAI programs developed for special education of ADHD and LD children and the software programs for cognitive retraining after head injury. Cognitive retraining software may soon be shown to be appropriate for use with young ADHD children.

ASSESSMENT ISSUES

As with any therapeutic intervention for ADHD children, it is important that proper assessment be done prior to the initiation of the therapy. Many young children with ADHD have associated difficulties with fine motor or visual perception, and these will need to be taken into account. Initial screening for any associated problems is best followed by any indicated diagnostic evaluations. A multi-, or intra-, or transdisciplinary approach with active involvement from a skilled occupational therapist is often needed to plan appropriate measures. Any associated learning disability should also be appropriately addressed.

The needs of the younger child with ADHD, especially in the earlier elementary grades, are unique. At this age, although children may be extremely motivated by the use of microcomputers, careful attention should be given to prevent overstimulation or over-reinforcement. For these youngsters it is important that sound effects be eliminated or minimized to prevent increased distractibility. Most CAI software programs involve the use of a computer keyboard. For the younger student this may be inappropriate since alphabet skills as well as keyboarding skills may be inadequately developed. Associated disabilities such as visual-perceptual or fine-motor difficulties significantly influence the use of a keyboard for input. There are some CAI programs that do not use keyboard interactions, and others make allowances for faulty visual motor integration. Large keypads are available as well as adapted joy-sticks that can be used in place of the keyboard [Desch, 1986]. Some of these software programs are adapted primarily for children with significant motor control problems such as cerebral palsy. Again, minimal or no research has been done to determine their inappropriateness or effectiveness with ADHD children.

The assessment process, however, should not end after a CAI program is initiated, especially since the data on effectiveness of CAI with ADHD remains so minimal. Perhaps, the most important part of any CAI intervention should be periodic ongoing reappraisals of efficacy similar to the way in which trials of stimulant medication are often carried out.

Based on the limited information available, there is little to be concerned about as far as causing harm when using CAI with ADHD children. At the present time, therefore, a reasonable approach might be for the regular education teacher and/or special education teacher to work with the ADHD child in a multiple baseline learning program: the child would alternate work on traditional instruction with trials of CAI. The learning curves of these two methods could then be compared, and if the child appears not to learn well with CAI, by both objective and subjective measures, then either another CAI program could be used or the traditional instruction would be used alone until a later point in time when CAI might be tried again.

Careful observations of the child during his or her interactions with a CAI program can often be very helpful in determining what difficulties are occurring. Once specific problems are identified (e.g., too much distraction from sound effects) then other more appropriate software may be used.

There is an important caveat that should be emphasized at this point: CAI should *not* be used only as a reward for "good behavior." This has been done too often in the past with children who have attentional and behavioral problems. CAI has the potential to be an appropriate adjunctive learning tool only if it is used as a learning tool and not as a behavioral management device. Otherwise the child will be given the impression that CAI is a toy rather than something that might help him to learn better.

GENERAL PRINCIPLES OF SOFTWARE SELECTION

There are several principles involved in selecting a specific computer software program. Many of these principles are appropriate both for ADHD children (with or without learning disabilities) as well as for regular classroom instruction. Special education teachers and those persons interested in helping special education teachers decide on specific software packages should find this checklist helpful (Table 1).

Colleagues can offer opinions about software programs prior to their use within a curriculum. This will give at least some idea of what to expect. In addition, software companies often will lend trial copies of software programs or can sometimes be persuaded to allow the purchaser to try out the program before buying. In fact, the purchaser should be wary of any software company that does not allow the program to be used on some form of trial basis before purchasing.

As with any microcomputer software program, it is important that instructions be simple and clear and that clearly written manuals be available. It is also helpful for the program to have "on-line help" available so that if something happens within the program, instructions or information to assist appear on screen. Some software programs are available free or with very low cost but have minimal or no accompanying instructions. These programs may be appropriate for use but should not be used unless a skilled person is available who is knowledgeable about the program.

Revisions of the software should be available at little or no cost from the company, since it is important to have software that works as well as possible and problems are often fixed between one version and the next. Many software programs come on copy-protected disks; these should be avoided if possible, since the program would become unavailable if something should happen to the only copy of the master program disk.

More important, the type of program and specific features of the program should be looked at carefully before purchase. Some programs are part of a larger integrated package of programs and may not be appropriate if used individually. Since ADHD children have problems with distractability, features within the program such as use of color or animation should be carefully assessed. Sound effects should be nonexistent or minimal and appropriate for child with ADHD. Also, ADHD children may experience frustration

Table 1 Aspects to Consider When Evaluating Microcomputer Software for Children with ADHD

Aspects of the Child	Aspects of the Software	Aspects of the Hardware
Age and developmental level	Appropriateness to current curriculum	Appropriateness of the hardware for use with the desired software
Grade level	Quality of documentation	Adaptability of hardware (alternate input and output devices available)
Physical disabilities	Availability of assistance from the company	Durability and maintenance concerns
Learning disabilities	Single versus integrated program	Portability (use at home)
Visual-motor abilities	Availability of optional input (e.g., large keyboard, touch screen, etc.)	Personal versus shared with others
Attentional control	Minimal or no sound effects	Cost of equipment and maintenance
Parent's perceptions and expectations	Control over pace of instructional presentation	
Availability of microcomputer at home	Cost versus perceived benefits	

and poor self-esteem with a program that gives negative feedback. Finally, the most important consideration of all is whether this CAI program fits in with the rest of the curriculum. If the usual instructional methods are far different than the methods in the software program, then it would be inappropriate to try to integrate such CAI into the curriculum.

Obtaining funding for computer software as well as microcomputers themselves will continue to be frustrating for many school districts unless existing inequities between schools are somehow resolved. Fortunately, there is a provision within public law 94-142, the Education for Handicapped Children Act, which specifically indicates that funding should be made available for "technological" devices, including software, to help children with special education needs. Although there is this provision within this public law, difficulties in funding will continue. Cooperative efforts between philanthropic agencies, school systems, and parents may offer the best solution for adequate funding. Parent groups for children with special education needs may be able to effectively lobby for other sources of funding as well as convince schools of the need for appropriate microcomputers and computer software. It is unfortunate that in many school districts microcomputers continue to be provided mainly for gifted and talented students, while those with learning difficulties or ADHD have minimal or no time allocated to spend with microcomputers.

For those persons who will not be actively involved in the selection of software, there remains an important advocacy role that could be developed. Professionals who deal with ADHD children are beginning to realize the importance of a multimodal approach as the best therapeutic methodology. The ultimate aim of intervention with ADHD children is to make them more functional and independent as children and later as adults. This is not just the province of medicine or education or some other single area. A given physician or special education teacher cannot be expected to be always up-to-date on all new research and technology. Knowing who and what is available that can help is far more important. Fortunately, more readily available sources of information about the latest uses of CAI programs for children with special needs have been developed. Sources such as Special Net, run by the National Directors of Special Education Association and State Technological Assistance in Education Services, are available in most states.

Table 2 provides a brief selection of several potentially useful commercially available software packages, and a list of useful resources can be found in the Appendix to this chapter.

THE FUTURE OF MICROCOMPUTERS IN ADHD

The generalizability of the skills learned through CAI or cognitive rehabilitation software to other areas of learning and problem solving will require

Table 2	Examples of Commercially Available Software Packages

Special Education Software

Memory—First Steps in Problem Solving* (10 programs; approx. $300)
Sunburst Communications
39 Washington Ave.
Pleasantville, New York 10570-2898

Spelling Machine*
SouthWest EdPsych Services, Inc.
P.O. Box 1870
Phoenix, Arizona 85001

Logic Builders
Scholastic Inc.
P.O. Box 7502
2931 East McCarty Street
Jefferson City, Missouri 65102

Rocky's Boots (approx. $70)
The Learning Company
6493 Kaiser Drive
Fremont, California 94555

Cognitive Rehabilitation Software

Captain's Log: Cognitive Training System (three modules; approx. $600)
Network Services
Huguenot Professional Center
1915 Huguenot Road
Richmond, Virginia 23225

Cognitive Rehabilitation Series ($200-$500)
Hartley Courseware, Inc.
123 Bridge Street
Box 419
Dimondale, Michigan 48821

Journal of Cognitive Rehabilitation: A Publication for the Therapist, Family, and
   Patient (free printed programs)
655 Carrollton Avenue
Indianapolis, Indiana 46220

*Some limited research has been done using this software with children who have ADHD.

much research. Computer learning must be validated by demonstration of improved academic skill development in the classroom. Otherwise microcomputers will have limited practical application in the education of a child, especially a child with learning difficulties or attention deficit problems.

There remain many aspects of ADHD that CAI has not even begun to address. For example, at the present time, CAI has little to offer in the development of verbal interaction skills. While there are some computer programs that have synthetic voice output, which can be helpful for the nonreader, voice input is essentially still a methodology that is perhaps decades in the future. Social skill development is critically important in the life course of a child with ADHD; however, this is probably an area that will never be helped much by CAI, since it is more appropriately taught by individual communications and small-group interactions. However, the increase in videodisk and microcomputer interactive technology might yet produce some role-playing applications to help children with ADHD learn the basics of better interaction. This method would again have the distinct advantage of being able to be carried out in a protected environment so that learning could take place without fear of ridicule from others. Some work is ongoing with these types of interactive video programs, especially for older children and for children with other developmental disorders such as mental retardation [Thorkildsen, 1979].

Since the United States populace is becoming increasingly technological in its day-to-day experiences, many individuals have begun to look to technology as a "cure" for a multitude of problems [Desch, 1986]. While CAI has an appropriate role in treating the problems that children with ADHD exhibit, it does not necessarily follow that the more technology used with these children, the better will be the outcome. Even if evidence accumulates that demonstrates the effectiveness of computer programs with ADHD children, it will still be important to realize that the presence of a good teacher and other therapists remains essential to ensure that the software is used appropriately. Teachers are necessary to help the children understand what is expected from the use of CAI, to guide them through the learning process, and to be available to help them in areas not amenable to CAI. There will always be many tasks that are better taught through interpersonal relationships rather than through a computer.

Since it appears inevitable that CAI and cognitive rehabilitation will be increasingly used with children with ADHD, it is important that involved professionals have some basic knowledge about what to look for when selecting appropriate software. Because there is a definite lack of evidence regarding the effectiveness of these programs, the best approach remains a well-planned trial that compares the effectiveness of traditional instructional methods to those of the software programs.

APPENDIX

Closing the Gap
P.O. Box 68
Henderson, Minnesota 56044
(612) 248-3294

Minnesota Education Computing Consortium (MECC)
3490 Lexington Ave., N.
St. Paul, Minnesota 55112
(612) 481-3500

Center for Special Education Technology
Council for Exceptional Children
1920 Association Dr.
Reston, VA 22091
(800) 873-TALK

ERIC
Educational Resources Information Center
2440 Research Blvd., Ste. 550
Rockville, MD 20850
(800) 873-3742

Special Education Software Center
LINC Resources, Inc.
4820 Indianola Ave.
Columbus, Ohio 43214
(614) 885-5599

Special Net
National Association of State Directors of Special Education
2021 K ST., NW, Suite 315
Washington, D.C. 20006
(202) 296-1800

Technical Resource Center
3200 1201 5th St., SW
Calgary, Alberta
Canada, P2R 0Y6
(403) 262-9445

REFERENCES

Chiang, B. (1984). Overuse of sound effects in a microcomputer program and its impact on the performance of students with learning disabilities. In: *Discovery 1983: Computers for the Disabled Conference Papers.* Roehl, J. E., ed. Menomonie, WI: University of Wisconsin—Stout, p. 55.

Desch, L. W. (1986). High technology for handicapped children: A pediatrician's viewpoint. *Pediatrics 77*:71.

Douglass, V. I., Parry, P. (1983). Effects of reward on the delayed reaction time task performance of hyperactive children. *J. Abnorm. Child Psychol. 11*:313.

Fitzgerald, G., Fick, L., Milich, R. (1986). Computer-assisted instruction for students with attentional difficulties. *J. Learn. Disabil., 19*:376.

Goldman, S. R., Pellegrino, J. W. (1987). Information processing and educational microcomputer technology—Where do we go from here? *J. Learn. Disabil., 20*: 144.

Lathrop, A. (1982). The terrible ten in educational programming. *Ed. Comput. 2*: 34.

Lynch, W. J. (1983). Cognitive retraining using microcomputer games and commercially available software. *Cognit. Rehabil. 2*:19.

Parry, P., Douglas, V. I. (1983). Effects of reinforcement on concept identification in hyperactive children. *J. Abnorm. Child Psychol. 11*:327.

Pulaski, M. A. B. (1971). *Understanding Piaget.* New York: Harper & Row Publishers, p. 197.

Stowitschek, J., Stowitschek, C. (1984). Once more with feeling: The absence of research on teacher use of microcomputers. *Excep. Educ. Qart. 4*:13.

Terwilliger, C. (1986). The child with attention deficit disorder: Finding a safe place to learn problem solving. In: *Proceedings of the Conference on Computer Technology in Special Education and Rehabilitation.* Harry, J., ed. Northridge: University of California, p. 325.

Thorkildsen, R. J., Bickel, W. K., Williams, J. G. (1979). A microcomputer/videodisc CAI system for the moderately mentally retarded. *J. Spec. Educ. Tech. 2*:45.

13

Psychostimulant Medication: The Pharmacotherapy of Attention Deficit Hyperactivity Disorder

Jill D. Morrow

St. Louis University School of Medicine, St. Louis, Missouri

> *"No rational knowledgeable individual can dispute the efficacy of short-term stimulant treatment in the management of hyperkinetic children."*
>
> [Gittleman-Klein et al., 1976]

HISTORICAL PERSPECTIVES

Psychostimulant medications belong to the family of drugs that includes sympathomimetic amines and their derivatives. Their use dates back at least five thousand years to ancient China: an herb called *"ma huang"* (Ephedra vulgaris) has many medicinal uses and is the source of the sympathomimetic ephedrine that was widely used for relief of bronchial asthma in the 1920s [Leake, 1958]. Attempts to synthesize ephedrine in the laboratory resulted in the discovery of amphetamine, trade name Benzedrine. Although amphetamine was initially used for asthma, Alles [1933] reported that it also had stimulating effects on the central nervous system (CNS). Amphetamine not only counteracted the CNS depressant effects of barbiturates but also increased alertness and sensitivity to stimuli.

While amphetamines proved to be an effective CNS stimulant, the question of whether or not they improved behavioral and academic performance remained. Bradley [1937] studied the effects of amphetamine on behavioral disordered children and found the drug had positive effects on hyperactivity, emotional lability, and classroom behavior. It also enhanced academic performance in arithmetic, but not spelling. Around the same time as Bradley's pioneer observations another group of researchers studied the amphetamine effects on juvenile delinquents in a state residential facility. Using performance on a standardized achievement test in a double-binded study, Molitch and Sullivan [1937] showed that the treated group outperformed the placebo group. Later studies of CNS stimulants in the 1950s and 1960s concentrated on whether or not they could enhance performance on measures of attention and memory and concluded that performance could be improved by CNS stimulants [Kornetsky, 1975; Sprague and Sleator, 1977].

Prior to the 1950s, drug treatment of behavior disorders consisted almost exclusively of amphetamine and dextroamphetamine (DA). Developed in the 1950s, methylphenidate (MPH) soon became the drug of choice [Gadow, 1986]. Other drugs have since been used with some success. In the 1960s the tricyclic antidepressants were first recommended for attentional disorders. One of these, imipramine, has been increasingly used since 1965 [Baren, 1989]. New forms of psychostimulants have also been added to the armamentarium for ADHD: sustained-release dextroamphetamine (DA-SR) and methylphenidate (MPH-SR) were developed, and pemoline, a long-acting CNS stimulant structurally different from DA or MPH, has been approved for use in the United States since 1975. Other classes of drugs such as neuroleptics, anxiolytics, and benzodiazepines have also been tried with varying rates of success (Table 1).

In the early 1960s medication played only a minor role in the treatment of attention deficit disorder (ADD). Over the next two decades the use of drugs has steadily increased to where it has become the dominant component in the treatment of ADD [Shaywitz and Shaywitz, 1984]. While there is currently a confusing multiplicity of drug options, recent studies have indicated a disproportionate increase in the use of psychostimulants such as MPH. In 1971, 40% of all children receiving medication for ADD were given MPH, 36% received DA, and the remaining 24% were on nonstimulants [Safer and Krager, 1984]. In 1983, 93% received MPH, while only 5% were on DA, 2% on pemoline, and 3% on nonstimulants [Safer and Krager, 1988]. Increases in psychostimulant medication use have occurred not only in elementary school children, but also in middle, junior high, and senior high school students between 1971 and 1987 (Figure 1). The trend toward the almost exclusive use of MPH in the treatment of ADD in the 1980s is marked. Thus, in

Table 1   A Brief History of Psychostimulant Medication

3000 BC	*Ma huang* (ephedra vulgaris) used in Chinese herbal medicine
1920s	Ephedrine (derived from ephedra vulgaris) used for asthma
1920s	Amphetamine synthesized in an attempt to make ephedrine in the laboratory
1933	Alles reported effects of amphetamine on central nervous system
1937	Bradley described improved behavior in behavior-disordered children
1937	Molitch and Sullivan showed improved academic achievement scores in juvenile delinquents treated with amphetamine
1950s	Methylphenidate synthesized
1960s	Studies of psychostimulants concentrated on performance effects
1965	First use of imipramine for ADHD
1975	Pemoline approved for use to treat ADHD
1980s	Use of methylphenidate to treat ADHD escalates

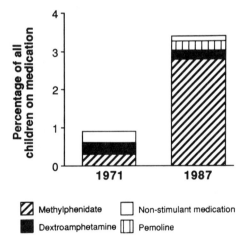

Figure 1   History of use of medication for ADHD in school children in Baltimore County.

the 40 years since the first recognition of the CNS stimulating effects of amphetamines, they and their derivatives have become an unavoidable fact in the management of children with ADD.

INDICATIONS FOR USE
Diagnosis

The initial population of children who were noted to respond behaviorally to psychostimulants was described as hyperactive, impulsive, and disruptive in the classroom [Shaywitz and Shaywitz, 1984]. Since these early studies, researchers have attempted to more clearly define the population on which stimulants might have a positive effect (Table 2). DSM-IIIR [1987] describes children with attention deficit hyperactivity disorder (ADHD) as inattentive, impulsive, and hyperactive to the point that it interferes with daily functioning not only at school, but also at home and in the neighborhood. The response of the inattention and hyperactivity to psychostimulants is dramatic in the majority of children who fit this classic "hyperkinetic" picture [Baren, 1989].

In recent years another group of inattentive children has been described. These children, while inattentive, are not hyperactive: they are more learning disabled with a fluctuating attention span. Many of these children are also now being treated with stimulants, a change that accounts for some of the increase in stimulant use. While the long-term results of the stimulant treatment of such children are uncertain, these drugs are noted to improve attention, grade level and the amount of school work completed [Shafer and Krager, 1988].

Other uses of psychostimulants are less straightforward and not well accepted. They have been advertised to improve reading in some learning-disabled children, but these studies make no mention of the presence or absence of concomitant attentional disorder with or without hyperactivity [Ashman and Schroeder, 1986]. The use of psychostimulant drugs in learning-disabled children without an attentional component is not recommended.

Table 2 Relative Indications for Psychostimulant Medication

Attention deficit hyperactivity disorder	+ + +
Learning disabilities with attention problems	+ +
Mental retardation	
Educably mentally handicapped	+
Trainably mentally handicapped	+ / −
Severely to profoundly mentally handicapped	−

+, Generally responds to medication; −, generally does not respond to medication.

Psychostimulant therapy has also been tried in the mentally retarded population, usually to control such undesirable behaviors as self-mutilation, hyperactivity, aggressiveness, and stereotypic motor activity. While limited data suggest that psychostimulants may sometimes be effective to control hyperactivity in mildly retarded children, this effect has not been well studied. Studies in trainable mentally handicapped children show a variable response to stimulants. With severely-to-profoundly retarded children stimulants have produced undesirable drug side effects without any therapeutic behavioral effects. Although psychostimulants may be effective in mildly retarded children and perhaps in selected individuals with more severe cognitive impairment, their use in the mentally retarded should be approached with caution.

Age

The beneficial effects of psychostimulants have been most evident in prepubertal school-age children. Stimulants produce positive behavioral changes in approximately 70% of children with ADHD in this age group [Gadow, 1986]. There is growing evidence, however, that psychostimulants can also benefit adolescents and adults with ADD even though the changes may not be as striking. In a double-blind, crossover trial of (MPH) and placebo in ADHD adolescents aged 12 to 19 years, both parent and teacher ratings showed a decrease in inattention, overactivity, and noncompliance in response to MPH [Klorman et al., 1987]. As the benefits to older children are becoming more widely recognized, the use of psychostimulants in students in middle schools and junior high schools is increasing at a greater rate than that in elementary schools [Safer and Krager, 1984]. In adults with ADD, residual type, MPH has been shown to produce a positive response analagous to that of children with ADHD. Clinical observation confirms that continued use of psychostimulants may be beneficial in a segment of this adult ADHD population. Wender [1987] found that 57% of adults with a childhood history of ADHD still responded to MPH (Figure 2). Further research is needed to better delineate which adults are likely to benefit from psychostimulant medication.

At the other end of the age spectrum, psychostimulants have not proved very useful with preschoolers under age 6 years. While drug effects are often present, they tend to be more variable, less predictable [Conners, 1976], and cover a much smaller range of behaviors. Even when positive, the behavioral effects are often less dramatic in preschool-age children. Preschoolers also seem to be less tolerant of the side effects of high doses, with negative effects on mood, causing sadness, increased irritability, a decrease in social play and social interaction, and an increase in solitary play [Schleifer, 1975]. Although the effects of stimulant medication on preschoolers are erratic,

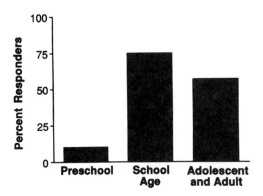

Figure 2 Percentage of patients who respond to psychostimulants, based on age group.

medication can be considered in conjunction with behavior management therapy and an appropriate preschool placement if the latter two alone are not successful. Such cases often represent the more severely affected children who seriously endanger themselves by their impulsivity despite behavioral interventions. Medication, despite its variable effects, can sometimes be useful in ameliorating these children's behavior and may be tried in selected preschoolers.

CLINICAL APPLICATIONS

Psychostimulant medication is available in many forms. MPH is the most commonly used drug, although pemoline has been increasingly used in older children and adolescents. The key to appropriate pharmacologic treatment of ADHD is to determine the dosage of psychostimulant that produces the maximum therapeutic effect with a minimum of side effects. This means tailoring the medication dosage to the individual patient. The dose used should be based on clinical response and not on dose-body weight nomograms [Taylor, 1986]. There are, however, some helpful dosage-level guidelines for each drug (Table 3). The endpoint of pharmacologic treatment is a dramatic improvement in behavior and attention span. The continuation of psychostimulant treatment in the absence of such a dramatic response is unwarranted because of potential side effects.

Dextroamphetamine

Dextroamphetamine sulfate (Dexedrine) (DA) (Figure 3) was one of the first compounds used to treat ADHD. It is still in use today, but represents only

Table 3 Types and dosages of psychostimulant medication

Chemical Name	Product Name	How Supplied (mg)	Dosage, mg/kg body weight (frequency)
Dextroamphetamine (DA)	Dexedrine	5,10	0.15-0.50(q4h)
Dextroamphetamine-sustained release (DA-SR)	Dexedrine spansule	5,10,15	0.15-0.50(q8h)
Methylphenidate (MPH)	Ritalin	5,10,20	0.3-0.8(q4h)
Methylphenidate-sustained release (MPH-SR)	Ritalin-SR	20	0.3-0.8(q8h)
Pemoline	Cylert	18.75,37.5,75	0.5-3.0(q12-24h)

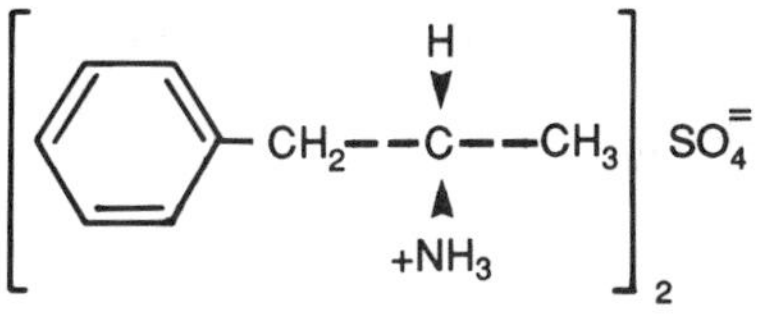

Figure 3 Dextroamphetamine sulfate (Dexedrine) (DA).

about 5% of the legal psychostimulant market [Gadow, 1986]. Although a CNS stimulant, DA is often described as exerting a "paradoxical" effect on the behavior of ADHD children because it decreases restlessness and hyperactivity. However, the pattern of lengthening attention span, increasing vigilance, and suppressing irrelevant information is similar to the effect of small amphetamine doses reported in normal subjects [Alles, 1933]. This is attributed to the increase of available catecholamine in the synapse: DA is known to block the enzyme that degrades catecholamines, prevent reuptake inactivation of catecholamines, and increase presynaptic release of catecholamines. This interpretation does not, however, require ADHD to represent a CNS catecholamine deficiency. While catechole-deficient rats exhibit hyperactivity, no such central catecholamine deficiency has been documented in ADHD children. Studies of catecholamine metabolites in ADHD children taking stimulant medication actually show a decrease in the concentration of catecholamine metabolites [Raskin et al., 1984].

While questions remain about the exact mechanism of action of DA in the brain of ADHD individuals, the clinical pharmacology of the drug is well-documented. The action of DA begins 30 minutes after ingestion and peaks in 30 to 60 minutes. Although DA has a half-life of 6 to 10 hours, its clinical duration of action is 4 to 6 hours [Wender, 1987]. The behavioral effects are observable shortly after starting the medication. The range of single doses of DA is 0.15 to 0.5. mg/kg of body weight. The dosage is titrated to produce the best behavioral effects with the fewest side effects.

Because DA has relatively more severe side effects than the other psychostimulants, it is often relegated to a second-line drug. However, up to 20% of children who fail to respond to other psychostimulants may benefit from DA. It is sometimes used with children under 5 years of age because it is available in a liquid form (elixer) and may be given in doses as small as 1.25 mg. It may also be used with patients with a history of tics since its primarily noradrenic activity may be safer than the dopaminergic effects of other medications [Baren, 1989].

Methylphenidate

MPH is a piperadine derivative of amphetamine with a structure similar to DA (Figure 4) [Taylor, 1986]. Biochemically MPH stimulates the release of dopamine from reserpine sensitive pools. Clinically MPH produces a smoother response and is easier to manage than DA. Although MPH is a weaker CNS stimulant than DA, it has been shown to ameliorate the symptoms of ADHD as effectively as DA and with fewer side effects (less appetite suppression and decreased cardiovascular stimulation) [Kornetsky, 1975].

The most widely used psychostimulant, MPH [Safer and Krager, 1988] is a short-acting drug, taking effect 30 minutes after ingestion and with a duration of action of 4 to 6 hours. Because of these characteristics, a trial of medication to determine the drug efficacy in a given patient is easily performed. Medication trials can begin with a small dose of MPH (5 mg for young school-age children or 10 mg for older school-age children and adolescents) once a day for 4 to 5 days. If there is no behavioral response and no reported side effects (especially appetite suppression), then the dosage can be increased by 5-mg increments until either a significant behavioral response

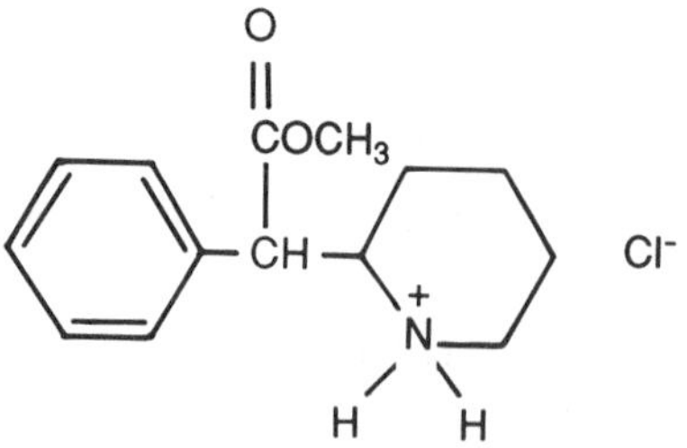

Figure 4   Methylphenidate hydrochloride (Ritalin).

or appetite suppression occurs. Very few, if any, ADHD children will respond positively to a dose of MPH higher than that which causes moderate appetite suppression. If a dose of 25 mg produces no behavioral response, then it is unlikely that MPH will be effective with that particular patient, and one of the other psychostimulants may be considered [Baren, 1989].

While a lack of response to the medication is a treatment failure, some authors would argue that a positive response may not be specific to the effects of the drug. Ulmann and Sleator [1985] advocate a blinded placebo evaluation for each child, as they have found as many as 18% of the responders to stimulant medication may be responding to the drug's nonspecific effects. However, they do point out some differences in the response to the medication between the true responders and the placebo responders. There is an improvement in handwriting in the true responders that is not present in the others. There also is an improvement in the children's feelings about themselves and their interactions with their peers. Blinded placebo trials are necessary in research and in determining the magnitude of action of the drug being studied. In clinical practice where each patient may choose a different pharmacy based on location and insurance, however, setting up a placebo trial with each patient is an impractical goal. Improvements in attention, hyperactivity, and handwriting will continue to be the measure of response to an appropriate dose of medication.

The typical dose of MPH ranges between 0.3 and 0.7 mg/kg/dose [Dulcan, 1985]. There is no one dosage that is optimal for all cognitive function. Sprague and Sleator [1977] showed that the dosage for the best performance on memory and attentional tasks was 0.3 mg/kg but that motor and social behavior continued to improve linearly with dosage increases up to 1.0 mg/kg. Similarly, Connors and Solanto [1984] studied the effects of three dosage levels (0.3, 0.6, and 1.0 mg/kg) on children with ADHD using each child as their own control. They compared the dose-response curves for cognitive and motor behaviors and found that cognitive/memory responses exhibited peak performance at a dose of 0.3 mg/kg, while motor activity and social behavior continued to improve up to the 1.0 mg/kg dosage. Other research has shown that performance on both cognitive and behavioral tasks improves linearly with increasing doses in the range of 0.3 to 0.8 mg/kg [Shaywitz and Shaywitz, 1984]. Tannock et al. [1989] reported positive effects on both behavior and academic tasks at a 0.3 mg/kg dose with the behavioral response continuing to improve up to 1.0 mg/kg. Academic performance in this study improved with MPH but did not vary with the dose.

Pemoline

Pemoline is a recent long-acting psychostimulant used in the treatment of ADHD. A mild CNS stimulant, pemoline, is structurally different from either DA or MPH (Figure 5). It is thought to work by a dopaminergic me-

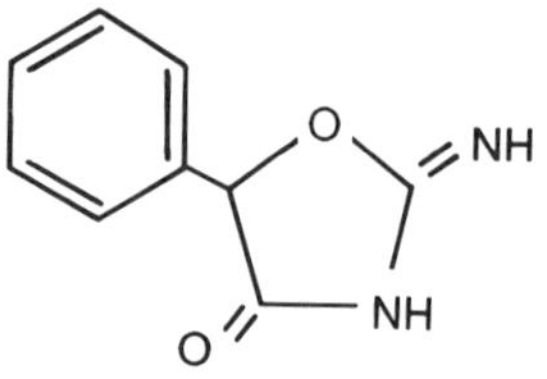

Figure 5   Pemoline (Cylert).

chanism like that of MPH but with fewer sympathomimetic effects. Its behavioral and side effects are similar to those of the other psychostimulants. However, the incidence and severity of those side effects are both much less than with DA or MPH. In rare cases pemoline has also been known to cause hepatotoxicity manifested by jaundice or epigastric pain. Although it is recommended that liver functions be monitored during long-term therapy with pemoline [Wender, 1986], asymptomatic hepatotoxicity is unlikely.

The pharmacokinetics of pemoline are very different from those of either DA or MPH. Pemoline has a half-life of 4 to 16 hours [McDaniel, 1986]. The drug reaches steady-state levels in 2 to 3 days. However, the peak behavioral effect does not correlate with this attainment of a steady-state blood level, and the onset of behavioral effects is gradual, often appearing only after 3 to 6 weeks of therapy. Rarely, improvement can occur as early as 1 to 2 weeks after the initiation of treatment.

Pemoline is given once a day with a daily dosage range of 0.5 to 3.0 mg/ kg [Dulcan, 1985]. A course of pemoline is usually begun after a trial of one of the shorter-acting stimulants has identified the child as a positive responder. Patients who respond to MPH are often switched to pemoline because it can be given once a day and produces a smoother behavioral result. Occasionally the effects of pemoline will wear off during the day or side effects will occur at the peak of the dose. In this event the dose can be divided into two half doses to be taken twice a day. Pemoline is manufactured in multiples of 18.75 mg which is 75% of 25 mg. A trial begins with 18.75 or 37.5 mg depending on the weight of the patient. Younger children are started on the smallest dose. Adolescents and adults can begin on the largest dose. If no behavioral or side effects are present after 4 weeks of treatment, the dose can be increased by 18.75 every 2 weeks until improved behavior, appetite suppression, or other side effects occur. The maximum dose is 112.5 mg.

Long-Acting Formulas

Both MPH and DA have relatively short durations of action lasting at the most 4 to 6 hours [Brown et al., 1985]. Multiple daily dosing is thus required for behavioral effects to last throughout the school day. To avoid this inconvenience, three forms of longer-acting CNS stimulants can be used: sustained-released methylphenidate (MPH-SR) and dextroamphedamine (DA-SR) and pemoline. MPH-SR and DA-SR contain the equivalent of two doses of the immediate release forms of these drugs. Thus, MPH-SR is available only in a 20 mg tablet that contains the equivalent of two 10 mg doses of short-acting MPH [Whitehouse et al., 1984]. In this form the MPH is absorbed more slowly to give a longer therapeutic effect, usually lasting about 8 hours. Bioavailability studies measuring a urinary metabolite of MPH show that the extent of absorption of MPH-SR is similar to that of the immediate release form, and serum levels of MPH confirm that the biochemical absorption of MPH-SR is equivalent to that of immediate release MPH [Patrick et al., 1985]. However, the therapeutic equivalence of these two forms of MPH has not been adequately studied. In clinical practice the treatment effects of sustained release preparations are noticeably erratic [Baren, 1989]. While this option has the advantage of avoiding the administration of a medication dose at school, the somewhat unpredictable effects of the sustained-release formulation make its use problematic.

DA-SR is available in a capsule form called a "spansule." Each spansule contains an initial dose that is released immediately and a second dose that is released gradually over a prolonged period of time—usually the length of a school day. DA-SR is not superior in efficacy to the immediate release form, but does reduce the need for multiple dosing, avoiding the need for a school-time dose of medication.

As noted above, pemoline only comes in a long-acting form; but it has several advantages over the other long-acting compounds. A single dose appears to be able to affect behavior for closer to a 24-hour period, thus impacting on behavior at home as well as in school. In addition it does not usually exhibit the erratic behavioral responses that the other sustained release formulations frequently produce.

Second-Line Drugs

Both short-acting and long-acting CNS stimulants are considered first-line drugs for the treatment of ADHD. However, not all children respond favorably to these psychostimulants. Therefore alternative classes of drugs have sometimes been used with variable success. These second-line drugs include tricyclic antidepressants such as imipramine or noripramine. Imipramine has been used since 1965 and has been noted to have generally beneficial effects in controlled trials. Unfortunately, the initial response is often not maintained and many children develop tachyphylaxis to the drug [Brown et al., 1985]. Serious cardiotoxic side effects and a lowering of the seizure threshold have been described with imipramine. The incidence of adverse side effects can be as high as 40% [Kornetsky, 1975]. Other classes of medication such as neuroleptics (e.g., stellazine), sedatives (e.g., hydroxyzine), and anxiolytics (e.g., diazepam) have been used with some success. Neuroleptics should be used cautiously since they have a much higher rate of serious side effects than stimulants and often precipitate a lowering of cognitive functioning. Hydroxyzine has questionable, if any, effects on ADHD, but has been used at bedtime to help induce sleep. Diazepam has exhibited some limited success in younger children who respond poorly to psychostimulants. Combination therapy of (a) MPH and stellazine, (b) MPH and imipramine, or (c) imipramine and stellazine has been successful in rare cases.

INITIATION OF THERAPY

Psychostimulant medication should be used only after a complete medical, psychological, educational, and social evaluation has determined whether the attentional problems are caused by disorders requiring other modes of treatment such as a language disorder or covert physical, sexual, or psychological abuse. In addition, it is important to recognize the learning disabilities that accompany attention deficit in 50 to 75% of cases [Accardo, 1989, personal communication]. Children with concomitant learning disorders need to have these adequately diagnosed and treated in order to obtain an optimal response to stimulant medication therapy. It is preferable that medication be started only after an appropriate school placement [Shaywitz and Shaywitz, 1984] and behavioral management program are in place. The school placement takes many forms. Mild learning disabilities may require consultation with a learning disabilities specialist to make appropriate classroom modifications for that student or resource room services. Children with more severe learning problems may need more intensive help such as a self-contained classroom or a residential placement. The advantage of a self-contained classroom is that the small class size addresses the treatment of attention problems as well as learning problems. The diagnosis of multiple family problems in addition to attention and learning problems may preclude adequate treatment of the child's problems in the present situation. Instead, a residential placement is usually recommended. In addition to an appropriate school placement, the initiation of a behavior management program prior to beginning medication is recommended. This consists not only of a therapist working with the whole family on discipline techniques, but also a teacher in school working with the classroom teacher and the student on techniques to control behavior and complete school work. In general, medication should rarely, if ever, be the sole mode of treatment. Instead, it needs to be part of a comprehensive treatment plan.

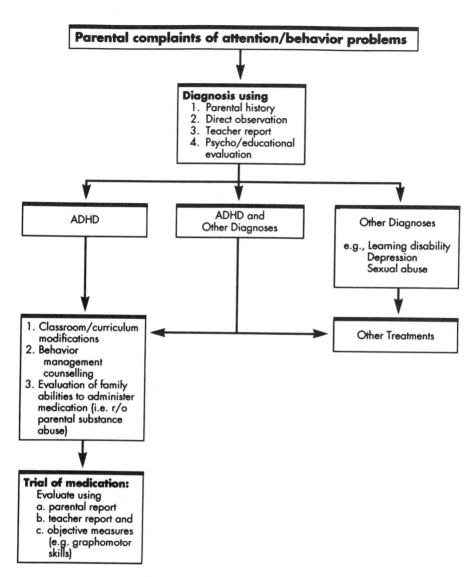

Figure 6   Steps in initiating psychostimulant therapy for ADHD.

TIMING

Once an adequate dose of MPH or DA is determined, then one must decide how many times a day to give the medication. This decision is often based on when during the day the child most needs to have a good attention span. Younger children may be managed with two doses, one in the morning and an equal or slightly smaller dose at noon. In this case the drug is only in effect during school. A third dose can be added in the late afternoon if it is needed for homework and evening activities or if a child has problems with severe impulsivity. Many practitioners treat children only during the school day on school week, but not on evenings, weekends, or holidays [Baren, 1989]. However, an argument can be made for treating children on weekends and evenings as well because important learning takes place at home and during play and other extracurricular activities, as well as at school. The social learning that occurs in these settings is critically important to the attention deficit child who often inadvertently alienates peers and family members because of poor impulse control, short attention span, and hyperactivity.

The long-acting duration and once-a-day timing of pemoline make the dosage schedule of this drug very easy. No decisions need to be made about treating on weekends and holidays. Pemoline works not only during the day but also at night and on weekends, benefiting learning in all settings.

The best time to initiate stimulant medication is during a time when there are no other major changes occurring in the child's environment [Shaywitz and Shaywitz, 1984]. Medication should not be started coincident with beginning a new school year or with movement into a novel classroom setting (e.g., with initiation of special classes for learning disability). One needs to give the child time to adjust to the new environment; this not only allows the establishment of a baseline of behavior, but also helps separate any medication effect from the impact of environmental changes. In most cases it is important to withhold medication until after appropriate school placement.

An alternative to starting medication after major environmental changes is to begin it prior to the onset of change. This approach is particularly helpful with children who have been on stimulant medication in the past and have demonstrated that this medication has made such transitions easier and resulted in a more positive attitude in both the student and the teachers.

If the medication is no longer effective after dosage adjustments that allow for the patient's growth, then it should be discontinued. There is, however, no medical reason to halt stimulant medication with continued effectiveness and the absence of serious side effects. This is contrary to the widely followed practice of automatically stopping medication at puberty in the belief that children outgrow ADHD. There is growing evidence that stimulant medication continues to have beneficial effects not only into adolescence, but also into adulthood [Klorman et al., 1987; McDaniel, 1986]. If the magnitude of beneficial behavioral and cognitive effects exceeds the disadvantages of daily pills, then the medication should be considered a viable treatment option regardless of the patient's age.

In the management of psychostimulant treatment it is important to periodically assess the continued efficacy of the drug. This can be accomplished by using a drug holiday or drug-free period. A patient must usually be off the medication at least several weeks to allow adequate clearance of the drug from the body. The drug holiday can also be used to determine whether or not the present dosage is effectively treating the attentional problems. In cases where there is minimal effect of medication withdrawal, an increased dosage can be tried. If that has no effect, the medication may be discontinued. Caution must be used in evaluating the behavioral effect immediately after discontinuing the medication. There can be an acute but temporary worsening of behavior when the medication is stopped. This usually resolves in a short period of time. The ideal time to implement a drug holiday is during summer vacation. The drug-free period may also include the first 4 to 6 weeks of the new school year, allowing the new teacher to become familiar with the student and to ascertain how well the student does without medication [Shaywitz and Shaywitz, 1984]. If continued medicaton is needed, then the teacher has a familiarity with the student's baseline behavior and learning and can better evaluate the effects of medication.

Management of stimulant medication requires frequent follow-up and monitoring not only of drug effects and side effects, but also of the school and behavior management interventions. An exacerbation of behavioral problems is not always due to improper medication dosage, but often to problems in school placement or lack of follow-through or an adequate behavior management program. Patients on stimulant medication should be seen every 3 to 4 months [Baren, 1989; Dulcan, 1985]. Monitoring should include height, weight, blood pressure, and pulse. An interim history will help identify any problems with medication or dosing and allow changes to be made.

RESPONSE TO TREATMENT

In 1937 Bradley described the effects of amphetamine on children with behavior disorders: "[T]o see a single daily dose of benzedrine produce a greater improvement in school performance than the combined efforts of a capable staff working in a most favorable setting would have been all but demoralizing to the teachers, had not the improvement been so gratifying from a practical viewpoint." These dramatic behavioral observations were only the beginning of the study of the complex effects of stimulants on behavior, cognition, and motor performance. The goal of treating behavior disorders in children generally includes modifying a number of factors in order to improve the child's functioning at school and at home. In discussing the positive effects on behavior (including attention, impulsivity, hyperactivity, and conduct), cognition, learning, and motor performance, it should be remembered that the effects in one area tend to overlap with and improve those in other areas.

Historically, the symptom most commonly targeted with stimulants was hyperactivity. Children with ADHD exhibit higher levels of motor activity when compared to children without ADHD [Ottenbacher and Cooper, 1983; Ullmann and Sleator, 1986]. Stimulant medication has been shown to decrease the level of motor activity in ADHD children. It appears to be most effective when used in structured stiuations like the classroom, but it has a similar effect in the home environment as well. This "paradoxical calming" effect of stimulants enables the child with ADHD to better sit still in the classroom.

Another cardinal feature of ADHD is inattention. Stimulant medication facilitates three basic aspects of attentional behavior: (a) focusing attention, (b) maintaining attention, and (c) shifting attention to a new stimulus at the appropriate time. When treated with stimulant medication, ADHD children improve their performance on measures of sustained attention such as the Children's Checking Task, which requires the comparison of two sets of numbers—one auditory and one visual. Their reaction time, a common measure of selective attention, is also bettered [Ashman and Schroeder, 1986; Shaywitz and Shaywitz, 1984]. Thus stimulant medication improves both selective and sustained attention in ADHD children.

Impulsivity is another feature of ADHD that is positively affected by stimulant medication. Responses of ADHD children to tests such as the Matching Familiar Figures Test are more reflective when they are on stimulant medication. In this test a line drawing of an object is presented among seven similar drawings and one identical drawing of the same item. The children must identify the stimulus drawing's match. As opposed to impulsivity, active reflection results in more correct answers. This active reflection suggests better inhibition of impulses in other situations.

While conduct problems are not always associated with ADHD, children who are inattentive, impulsive, and hyperactive often develop conduct disorders in part because of these characteristics. Disturbing others, noncompliance, misinterpreting social cues, getting in fights, and wandering around the classroom are all ADHD behaviors that are potentially ameliorated by medication. A child who "stops, looks, and listens" is less likely to get into trouble in school or at home. Barkley and Cunningham [1979] have shown that ADHD children treated with stimulants obey better, have less off-task behavior, and are more compliant. This change in behavior results in changes in their parents' reaction to them and leads to more positive parent-child interactions. Teacher-child interactions are improved in a similar manner [Whalen and Henker, 1976; Gadow, 1986]. Peer relations, on the other hand, are not improved by medication alone, but there is some evidence that social skills training in combination with medication may help normalize peer interactions.

Psychostimulants can effect learning and cognitive behaviors; however, the magnitude and character of these effects remain controversial. While some studies have shown improvement in scores on intelligence tests due to medication, others document changes only in parent and teacher ratings of scholastic achievement and not in objective measures [Shaywitz and Shaywitz, 1984]. In the last decade, the focus of this research has shifted from the product to the process of learning. This involves studying the use of learning strategies and the child's organization of information in complex problem solving. Based on differences in performance measures of processing and in using both new and old information in MPH versus placebo trials, MPH has been shown to increase the efficiency of information processing but not to affect strategic behavior, planning, or organization of information [Ashman and Schroeder, 1986]. While stimulant medication clearly affects classroom behavior in terms of attention and activity levels, further study is needed to elucidate its effects on learning and cognition.

An additional area where stimulant medication has demonstrated positive effects is performance on gross and fine motor tasks. MPH has been shown not only to improve gross motor functions like balance, but also to facilitate the acquisition of such skills [Wade, 1976]. Stimulants have also shown positive effects on fine motor skills. Handwriting improved in 52% of ADHD children on stimulants as compared to 2% of children on placebo; those children maintained on stimulants continued to make improvements in handwriting over a period of months [Lerer et al., 1977]. Improved performance on other fine motor tasks requiring motor steadiness, speed, and coordination has also been documented. Such improvement is not only helpful for school and sports, but may also be useful in assessing the efficacy of stimulant medication in the individual patient.

The instrument often used to measure the efficacy of drug therapy is similar or identical to those used for diagnosis. Behavioral questionnaires are standardly used and employ the observations of teachers as well as parents. These questionnaires usually measure behavioral and social functioning of the child [Ottenbacher and Cooper, 1983]. Questionnaires vary in length and require that the parent be able to read and comprehend the questions in order to respond appropriately with their appraisal of the child's behavior

Table 4 Behavioral Questionnaires Used in
the Diagnosis of ADHD and the Assessment of
Medication Response*

Questionnaire	Items, no.
ANSER Parent Questionnaire	245
ANSER Teacher Questionnaire	87
Auchenbach Child Behavior Checklist	138
Conners Parent Rating Scale	93
Conners Parent Rating Scale— Revised	48
Conners Teacher Rating Scale	39
Conners Teacher Rating Scale— Revised	28
DSMIII-R criteria	14
Yale Children's Inventory	63

*Adapted from Blondis et al. [1989].

(Table 4). One disadvantage in using questionnaires is that they do not directly measure a child's performance. Instead they tap the parent's and teacher's subjective impressions of the child. Such measurements are subject to a halo effect in which the evaluator's preconceptions of the child exaggerate a disruptive child's negative behaviors. There is also a practice effect that causes an apparent improvement in the child's behavior based only on the repetition of the measurement [Safer and Krager, 1989]. Even though these disadvantages make the use of questionnaires less than ideal for follow-up, these instruments can supply useful information about the effects of medication in school and at home. Using such objective measures of behavior to complement a follow-up history provides a more complete body of information to evaluate drug effectiveness [Ottinger et al., 1985].

While behavioral questionnaires are the most widely used measurement of stimulant efficacy, perceptual motor assessments represent a commonly employed alternative or complementary method. These assessments range from standardized drawing tests such as the Bender Visual-Motor Gestalt test [Bender, 1938] to "pure motor activities" such as movement recordings from ankle or wrist actometers [Ottenbacher and Cooper, 1983]. Lerer and others [1977] have suggested comparing serial handwriting samples off and on medication to document positive drug effects. These improvements (smoother movements, better rhythm and flow of writing, gains in speed and accuracy, and reduced effort) became apparent shortly after starting the medication and deteriorated rapidly with its discontinuation. Although improvements in handwriting do not always correlate with improvements in behavior and attention, comparison of handwriting samples and other graphomotor skills can be used as a quick, easy adjunct to behavioral questionnaires and interval history in managing stimulant medication.

SIDE EFFECTS

All stimulant medications used to treat ADHD have similar side effects involving the central and autonomic nervous systems (Table 5). The most common CNS side effects are anorexia and insomnia [Gadow, 1986; Ottinger et al., 1985]. The temporary supression of weight and height growth that has been described is probably secondary to the anorexia. *Appetite suppression* is a problem especially with the short-acting stimulants MPH and DA. This common side effect occurs in most patients as the therapeutic dose is approached and it can be used to titrate the medication. Anorexia is greatest at the peak activity of the medication and decreases as the medication wears off. Mild appetite suppression cannot always be eliminated, but children can be encouraged to eat during periods when the medication has either worn off or not yet taken effect. A good breakfast and an evening snack can help make up for any calories missed at lunch and dinner because of decreased appetite. Most children develop a tolerance of this side effect and do not have significant weight loss. If, however, the appetite suppression is causing

Table 5 Side Effects of Stimulant Medication

Central Nervous System
    Anorexia
    Apathy
    Depression
    Dizziness
    Dysphoria
    Emotional lability
    Headache
    Insomnia
    Irritability
    Psychosis
Autonomic Nervous System
    Abdominal pain
    Hypertension
    Nausea
    Tachycardia
Other
    Decreased growth
    Tic disorder

weight loss or lack of appropriate weight or height gain, then the dose of medication can be decreased to ameliorate the side effect but maintain the behavioral effect. Alternatively, pemoline may be used as it has a very mild effect on appetite.

Insomnia is a common complaint with ADHD children even before starting stimulant medication. These children have trouble falling asleep at night, and a late afternoon dose of medication to help them complete their homework can contribute to a rebound effect that will often exacerbate their insomnia. There are two ways to approach this problem. One is to delete the late afternoon dose. However, this leaves such problems as not finishing homework and problematic home behaviors. The other option is to give a small dose of stimulant medication (5 or 10 mg) prior to bedtime. The latter approach seems to help children fall asleep more easily and works better than the use of traditional sleep aids such as diphenhydramine that quickly exhibit tachyphylaxis. An alternative to the two options listed above is to place older children and adults on long-acting pemoline, which has less negative effects on sleep.

Other CNS side effects that occasionally occur are restlessness, dizziness, and irritability. Mood changes such as weepiness or, more rarely, psychosis have been described. Stimulants also produce autonomic side effects such as increased heart rate, hypertension, nausea, or abdominal discomfort [McDaniel, 1986]. Use of stimulant medication has been associated with the onset or exacerbation of tic disorders, especially Gilles de la Tourette syndrome [Barabas, 1988a,b], and has been alleged to increase the frequency of seizures in ADHD children with concurrent seizure disorders [Feldman et al., 1989]. While these side effects are troublesome, most of them can be easily managed or avoided.

The severity of side effects in the use of stimulant medication is generally dose-related, with the higher doses producing more severe side effects. Thus, many of the side effects can be controlled with adjustments in the dosage or the schedule of administration. Rarely are the side effects associated with the typical dosages very severe. Denhoff [1973] and others have concluded that properly prescribed stimulant medication has not evidenced harmful long-term side effects.

Changes in mood including dysphoria, depression, fearfulness and irritability, while less commonly described, occur with some frequency [McDaniel, 1986; Gadow, 1986]. Apathy and withdrawal are more prevalent in preschool children treated with stimulant medication but can occur in older children and adults [Baren, 1989]. *Dysphoria,* a feeling of unhappiness, is a well-recognized problem. Taylor [1986] and others reported dysphoria in 2 out of 38 children on stimulant medication. Both children were noted to become tearful. One developed fears of monsters, while the other became preoccupied with how bad he had been. While it remains uncertain exactly what causes these reactions, it is possible that on the medication these children gain some sudden and overwhelming insight into what effect they have on the world around them as they begin to perceive what they had been missing because of their short attention span. This insight may cause them to be unhappy and appear tearful, weepy, and easily upset. The dysphoria can be treated by decreasing the dose of the medication slightly until the symptoms disappear. Then the medication can later be slowly increased to a more effective dose [Barabas, 1988a,b].

Rarely a *psychotic-like syndrome* has been precipitated in association with stimulant medication [Baren, 1989]. It is thought to be an indication of an underlying and previously existing psychotic process or an unrelated event. Such symptoms usually disappear when the medication is stopped.

Autonomic side effects, such as increased heart rate and blood pressure, are often present with stimulant therapy. The magnitude of this increase is usually quite small, and not significant in the short-term in a healthy child with a normal cardiovascular system. There are no long-term studies into adulthood on the cardiovascular function in ADHD patients treated with long-term stimulants. Other autonomic side effects such as abdominal discomfort, palpitations, flushing, nausea, or dry mouth are present occasionally, but children quickly develop a tolerance to these symptoms [Wender, 1986].

The potential side effects discussed so far are short-term and ameliorated by decreasing the dose of medication. *Growth suppression,* on the other hand, is a potential complication of chronic long-term use of stimulant medication. In the 1970s, Safer and his colleagues [1972] studied the effects of stimulant medication on growth and concluded that there was a significant growth suppressive effect. In 1979, the Pediatric Subcommitee of the FDA Psychopharmacologic Drugs Advisory Commitee reviewed the literature relevant to possible growth suppression associated with stimulant medication. They concluded that there is reasonable evidence of a moderate suppression of weight growth in prepubescent children treated with stimulants and that this effect is more apparent in children treated with higher doses. In addition, there may be mild suppression of height growth, but evidence that this suppression occurs to a significant degree is less convincing. Height growth suppression secondary to stimulant medication makes a very small contribution to ultimate height. The effects of stimulant medication on height and weight growth during puberty and adolescence is unknown.

The reported suppression of weight and height growth is 0.5 kg/year and 0.4 to 0.9 cm/year, respectively. Suppression appears to occur over the first 1 to 3 years of treatment. However, after 6 years of treatment there is little or no difference in height and weight growth, indicating a possible tolerance to the effect [Roche, 1979]. Safer and others [1975] found that growth rates of ADHD children tend to increase during periods off medication (drug holidays) and produce catch-up growth. Although this catch-up is often incomplete, by adulthood there is no evidence of the early growth suppression. Because these studies contained so few patients, it is uncertain what the risk of larger effects on height and weight may be in a small number of children. Therefore, close monitoring of height and weight, especially in children with short stature, is recommended and the risks and benefits of such treatment should be carefully considered and discussed with the family before it is begun.

A little-discussed problem in the use of psychostimulants is the treatment of ADHD children with concomitant *seizure disorder* [Feldman, 1989]. Use of MPH in these children has been strongly discouraged by one drug manufacturer on the grounds that the drug may exacerbate known seizure disorders or potentially cause seizures in the absence of a known seizure disorder. While there are clinical case reports suggesting that MPH lowers the seizure threshold, potentially causing seizures, there is little objective evidence to confirm this hypothesis [Tannock et al., 1989]. A recent study of 10 children who had seizure disorders and fit DSM-III criteria for ADHD showed that there was no increase in frequency of seizures or major EEG changes when the children were treated with MPH. These results are similar to those in a study by McBride et al. [1986] which noted that children with well-controlled seizure disorders on anticonvulsants had no increase in seizures during MPH treatment. In addition those children who continued to take psychostimulants after the study period remained free of seizures. Despite these small sample sizes, the data support that MPH may be used safely in children with seizure disorders without precipitating an increase in the frequency of seizures.

Another recognized side effect of stimulant medication with potential long-term consequences is an increased incidence of tics [Lowe et al., 1982]. It is estimated that 3% of the general pediatric population will exhibit tics at some time during life and 1.3% of children receiving MPH for ADD will develop motor tic symptoms. While most of these tics are transient, a small number of these children will develop *Gilles de la Tourette's syndrome* (TS) [Golden, 1988]. TS has specific symptoms that are persistent and chronic. In patients with TS the tics appear between 2 and 15 years of age, are both motor and vocal, wax and wane in severity, change in nature over time, and must be present for at least 1 year [Barabas, 1988a,b]. TS is more common in males with an estimated 30 to 50% of cases being familial and reflecting a pattern of autosomal dominance with variable penetrance. The nonfamilial cases of TS are thought to be sporadic. While TS is a relatively rare disorder with an estimated 100,000 cases in the United States [Sleator, 1980], there is a high incidence of ADHD symptoms in this population. These ADHD symptoms are more severe in patients with more severe TS and more common in male patients with TS [Matthews, 1988; Sverd et al., 1988].

The significant association of ADHD and TS and the exacerbation of TS symptoms by stimulant medication have created a controversy in the pharmacologic treatment of children with ADHD in the presence of tics or a family history of tics. In a study by Denkla and colleagues [1976] of 1529 children with ADD, none of those children who developed motor tics developed TS. However, in patients with TS who received stimulant medication, 6% had onset of TS while taking medication and 53% had marked, but usually transient, exacerbation of their tics. The increase in tic symptoms associated equally with MPH, DA, and pemoline is postulated to be due to a facilitation of dopaminergic activity. TS symptoms have also been noted to be associated with other drugs like phenothiazines, which alter the sensitivity of dopamine receptors or endogenous levels of dopamine [Barabas, 1988a,b].

The frequency of ADHD in TS and the risk of precipitation of tics with the use of stimulant medication poses a dilemma to the clinician treating these patients. In the case of a positive family history of tics, many practitioners do not use stimulant medication [Shaywitz and Shaywitz, 1984]. Behavior management and curriculum modification should be tried first in these children. However, if these are not successful and the severity of the ADHD becomes the limiting factor in the child's functioning and development, then stimulant medication should be considered. Case studies of TS children who continue to have significant problems with inattention and hyperactivity despite adequate treatment of their tic disorder demonstrate that concomitant use of stimulant medication in some patients can significantly improve their behavior [Comings and Comings, 1984].

Adequate information about the risk of tic development versus the benefits of stimulant medication should be given to both the parents and the child prior to the initiation of a therapeutic regimen. If tics occur in a child, then the medication should be discontinued and the situation reassessed. Currently, new drugs are being developed to treat both tics and attentional behavior in children with TS. Clonidine has been used with some success, and drug combinations such as haloperidol and MPH have been tried. Imipramine or other tricyclic antidepressants may prove useful in children with ADHD and TS or a tic disorder.

CONTRAINDICATIONS TO STIMULANT MEDICATION

MPH, DA, and pemoline are all CNS stimulants classified by the Drug Enforcement Administration of the United States under the Controlled Substances Act as Schedule II drugs. These drugs are defined as having a high abuse potential in addition to an accepted medical use. Abuse with these drugs leads to severe psychological or physical dependence. Because of this abuse potential, these drugs should be used cautiously, taking into consideration as much information about the patient, family, and household as is available. The American Medical Association [Ballin, 1980] recommends the consideration of two factors in addition to an appropriate medical indication for the use of stimulants in any patient: the first is the patient's and family's reliability in administering the medication; and the second, the dependence liability of the drug with regard to the patient's susceptibility to abuse. Extrapolating these factors to fit children, it is important to ascertain that the child's parent or guardian is capable of consistently administering the proper dosage on the correct schedule and able to recognize and report any side effects. Besides the ability to give the medication appropriately, the parent or guardian must be able to cooperate and follow through with the total treatment plan, as stimulant medication in the absence of an appropriate school placement and behavior management program has not been proven to be effective long-term.

While these criteria are often initially difficult to establish without an in-depth multidisciplinary evaluation of the child and family, there are some clues to inappropriate use of medication during treatment. Patients who consistently run out of their medication early may not be giving it appropriately or may be using it for other purposes. New patients who come into the office requesting inappropriately large doses of MPH or DA should be suspect, as should children who have a demonstrable response to medication, but then suddenly stop responding possibly because they are no longer receiving their medication. In conclusion, stimulant medication is used as an adjunct to behavioral and educational treatment in ADHD. Because of its potential for abuse, the patient's family and their ability to responsibly administer the medication must be considered before initiating a regimen of medication. Use of medication is contraindicated in any family that generates reasonable doubt that the medication will be used appropriately. The presence of relatives in the home with a known history of substance abuse should be considered a serious contraindication to the use of stimulant medication.

Another relative contraindication to stimulant medication is the presence of TS. As previously discussed, stimulant medication has been associated with a provocation or exacerbation of TS. While the association has not been proven causative and the timing of the precipitation of TS in relation to the administration of stimulant medication remains unclear, caution should be used in treating such children with stimulant medication. Conservative use of stimulant medication in conjunction with adequate counseling of the parents and child and in the presence of appropriate school placement may help the child function more adequately. Use of medication is strongly advocated in the situation where the limiting factor in the TS child's development is ADHD, but medication should be tried only after behavior management and an appropriate school program are in place.

MISCONCEPTIONS ABOUT THE ROLE OF PSYCHOSTIMULANTS

Historically stimulant medication has had a well-documented and often strikingly positive effect on behavior in patients with inattention, impulsivity, and poor behavioral and social functioning. Because of this dramatic response, the use of stimulant medication has escalated and has become the major mental health intervention for children in the 1980s. As previously noted, the percentage of elementary school children on stimulant medication in Baltimore County alone has increased fivefold in recent years [Safer and Krager, 1988]. While this rate of treatment is one of the highest in the nation, the trend of increased use is reflected nationwide. This trend has spurred a movement questioning and attempting to discredit the use of stimulant medication despite its proven effectiveness. Protests against the use of stimulants have appeared in national and local media and produced a reluctance on the part of many parents, physicians and other professionals to recommend medication. Although some of the allegations against stimulant usage have an element of truth, many are erroneous distortions (Table 6).

One of the common misconceptions about stimulant medication is that it acts as a "chemical straight-jacket" that schools and teachers advocate in order to sedate problem children and make them easier to manage. On the contrary, the goal of stimulants is to facilitate a defective attention mechanism and a decrease in motor hyperactivity, but not to sedate. If a child on stimulants is described as lethargic, zombie-like, or glassy-eyed, then either the dosage of the medication is too high or the initial diagnosis of ADHD is in error.

Another misconception is that stimulant medication causes children to abuse drugs and alcohol and get into trouble with the law. While children treated with stimulants have a higher incidence of substance abuse and delinquency, this is related to their underlying syndrome of impulsivity and inattention. Their lack of success in school and poor self-esteem lead to these behaviors. Use of stimulants improves behavior in school and at home and can lead to improved self-esteem. This actually tends to *discourage* substance abuse and delinquency. The goal of early treatment with medication as well as behavior management and school placement is to prevent delinquent and criminal behaviors by making life a more positive experience [Baren, 1989].

Other concerns with regard to medication side effects include permanent brain damage, severe emotional stress, depression, psychosis, and TS. The

Table 6 Myths about Stimulant Medication

Always work
Never work
Safe
Dangerous
Foster dependency
Addictive
No side effects
Placebos
Always indicated
Never indicated
Should be used alone
Cannot be used alone
Only child indicators
Sedative
Tranquilizer
Diagnostic
No effect on learning
A form of child abuse
Replace psychotherapy
Replace educational intervention
Decrease child responsibility
Decrease parent responsibility
Decrease school responsibility
Treat learning disability
Treat behavior disorder
Treat family psychopathology
Induce dwarfism
Induce psychosis
Obligatory holidays
Obligatory questionnaires
Chemical straitjacket
Antidepressant
Differential SES usage
Only for school

implication that these associations are caused primarily by stimulant usage is fallacious. The correlation between TS and stimulant medication probably represents an earlier onset of symptoms that would have appeared in any case [Baren, 1989]. Psychotic-like reactions are not clearly caused by the medication and readily resolve after it is discontinued.

While TS and psychosis, though rare, have documented associations with stimulant medication, the other alleged side effects are not related to stimulant medication. There is absolutely no scientific evidence linking brain damage, transient or permanent, to stimulant medication usage in appropriate doses for ADHD [Baren, 1989]. Nor does stimulant medication directly cause severe emotional problems. Although emotional problems and depression often coexist with ADHD, these are often part of or secondary to the disorder and its mismanagement and not the result of medication. It should be noted that childhood depression can mimic ADHD and in such cases stimulant therapy would not be appropriate. Depression has not been shown to be caused by stimulants. This scenario should, however, result in a failure of stimulant medication to ameliorate symptoms with a subsequent reevaluation of the diagnosis and treatment. Occasionally, even if stimulant therapy is the appropriate treatment, the dosage may be too high and the child may appear depressed. In this case a lower dose should correct the lethargy and sedation. Thus an appropriate dose of stimulant medication in an ADHD child does not cause depression, emotional problems, or permanent brain damage.

Despite attempts to discredit their use, stimulants have a half-century record of success as a significant adjunct in the treatment of ADHD. Side effects are, for the most part, dose related and easily managed. Those that are not dose related often disappear after discontinuation of the medication. The use of stimulants in the rare instance of TS or a risk for its development should be approached with caution, carefully weighing the benefits of treatment against its risks. Although improper use of stimulant medication occurs, there are too many cases of its appropriate and successful use to ignore.

CONCLUSION

The group of patients characterized by inattention and impulsivity, whose behavior interferes with their functioning at home, school, and work make up 5 to 10% of the population. Up to 75% of these patients have shown dramatic positive responses to stimulant medication resulting in improved attention and decreased impulsivity and hyperactivity. Although stimulant medication, like any other drug, has side effects, these are mostly dose related and short term. Therefore, for most ADHD patients, the benefits of treatment far outweigh the risks.

Proper use of stimulants requires an accurate diagnosis. A careful evaluation of each individual with regard to problems and behaviors at home, school, and other situations is essential. This evaluation is best done with a multidisciplinary team, but can be accomplished if necessary in tandem with the aid of behavioral questionnaires and separate medical and psychoeducational evaluations. Careful diagnosis to rule out pathology that can mimic ADHD, such as sexual abuse or depression, and to identify associated deficits, such as learning disorders or TS, strengthens the decision to try stimulants. Evaluation of a family's ability to give and use the medication as directed as well as to cooperate in a total management program is also important.

While stimulants have been shown to have short-term effects, it remains unclear what the long-term effects of appropriately used stimulants are. Stimulant medication alone has certainly not been very effective either short or long term. However, it remains to be seen what the long-term effects of stimulants will be as an adjunct to a full treatment plan including behavior management, appropriate school services for both behavior disorders and learning disorders, and psychotherapy when needed.

REFERENCES

Alles, G. A. (1933). The comparative physiological actions of d,l-beta-Phenylisopropylamines. *J. Pharmacol. Exp. Therap. 47*:339.

American Psychiatric Association (1987). *Diagnostic and Statistical Manual of Mental Disorders* (DSM-III R). 3rd Ed., Rev. Washington, D.C.: APA.

Ashman, A., Schroeder, S. R. (1986). Hyperactivity, methylphenidate, and complex human cognition. In: *Advances in Learning and Behavioral Disabilities. Vol. 5,* 10th Ed. Greenwich, CT: JAI Press, pp. 295-316.

Ballin, J. C. (1980). *AMA Drug Evaluations.* Chicago: American Medical Association, pp. 18-24.

Barabas, G. (1988a). Tourette Syndrome: An overview. *Pediatric Ann. 17*:391.

Barabas, G. (1988b). Tourettism. *Pediatric. Ann. 17*:422.

Baren, M. (1989). The case for Ritalin: A fresh look at the controversy. *Contemp. Pediatric 6*:16.

Barkley, R. A., Cunningham, C. E. (1979). The effects of methylphenidate on mother-child interactions of hyperactive children. *Arch. Gen. Psychi. 5*:351.

Bender, L. (1938). A visual-motor gestalt test and its clinical use. New York: American Orthopsychiatric Association.

Blondis, T. A., Accardo, P. J., Snow, J. H. (1989a). Measures of attention deficit: Part I, Questionnaires. *Clin. Pediatric 28*:222.

Blondis, T. A., Accardo, P. J., Snow, J. H. (1989b). Measures of attention deficit: Part II, Clinical perspectives and test interpretation. *Clin. Pediatric 28*:268.

Bradley, C. (1937). The behavior of children receiving benzedrine. *Am. J. Psych. 94*:577.

Brown, G. L., Ebert, M. H., Minichiello, M. D. (1985). Biochemical and pharmacologic aspects of attention deficit disorder. In: *Attention Deficit Disorder: Identification, Course and Treatment Rationale.* Bloomingdale, L. M., ed. Spectrum Publications, Inc., City, pp. 93-130.

Comings, D. E., Comings, B. G. (1984). Tourette's Syndrome and attention deficit disorder with hyperactivity: Are they genetically related? *J. Am. Acad. Child Psychol. 23*[2]:138.

Connors, C. K. (1976). Rating scales for use in drug studies with methylphenidate. In: *ECDEU* Assessment Manual. Guy, W., ed. Rockville, MD: US Department of Health, Education, and Welfare, pp. 330-332.

Connors, C. K., Solanto, M. V. (1984). The psychophysiology of stimulant drug response in hyperkinetic children. In: *Attention Deficit Disorder: Diagnostic, Cognitive and Therapeutic Understanding.* Bloomingdale, L. M., ed. Spectrum Publications, Inc., pp. 191-204.

Denhoff, E. (1973). The natural life history of children with minimal brain dysfunction. *Ann. New York Acad. Sci. 205*:188.

Denckla, M. B., Bemporad, J. R., MacKay, M. C. (1976). Tics following methylphenidate administration. *JAMA 235*:1349.

Dulcan, M. K. (1985). Attention deficit disorder: Evaluation and treatment. *Pediatric Ann. 14*:383.

Feldman, H., Crumrine, P., Handen, B. L., Alvin, R., Teodori, J. (1989). Methylphenidate in children with seizures and attention-deficit disorder. *AJDC 143*: 1081.

Gadow, K. D. (1986). *Children on Medication. Vol. 1: Hyperactivity, learning disabilities and mental retardation,* Boston: Little, Brown and Company, pp. 31, 143-185.

Gittleman-Klein, R., Klein, D. F., Abikoff, H., Katz, S., Gloisten, A. C., Kates, W. (1976). Relative efficacy of methylphenidate and behavior modification in hyperkinetic children: An interim report. *J. Abnorm. Child Psychol. 4*:361.

Golden, G. (1988). The relationship between stimulant medication and tics. *Pediatric Ann. 17*(6):405.

Klorman, R., Coons, H., Borgstedt, A. (1987). Effects of methylphenidate on adolescents with a childhood history of attention deficit disorder: I. Clinical findings. *J. Am. Acad. Child Adolesc. Psychi. 26*(3):363.

Kornetsky, C. (1975). Minimal brain dysfunction and drugs. In: *Perceptual and Learning Disabilities in Children volume 2, Research and Theory.* Vol. 2. Cruickshank, W. M., Hallahan, D. P., eds. Syracuse, NY: Syracuse University Press, pp. 446-481.

Leake, C. D. (1958). *The Amphetamines.* Springfield, IL: Charles C. Thomas.

Lerer, R. J., Lerer, M. P., Artner, J. (1977). The effects of methylphenidate on the handwriting of children with minimal brain dysfunction. *J. Pediatric 91*[1]:127.

Lowe, T. L., Cohen, D. J., Detlon, J., Kremenitzer, M. W., Shaywitz, B. A. (1982). Stimulant medications precipitate Tourette Syndrome. *JAMA 247*[8]:1168.

Matthews, W. (1988). Attention deficits and learning disabilities in children with Tourette Syndrome. *Pediatric Ann. 17*[6]:410.

McBride, M. C., Wang, D. D., Torres, C. F. (1986). Methylphenidate in therapeutic doses does not lower seizure threshold. *Ann. Neurol. 20*:428 (abstr. 130).

McDaniel, K. D. (1986). Pharmacologic treatment of psychiatric and neurodevelopmental disorders in children and adolescents: Part 1. *Clin. Pediatric 25*[2]:65.

Molitch, M., Sullivan, J. P. (1937). Effect of benzedrine sulfate on children taking New Stanford Achievement Test. *Am. J. Orthopsychi. 7*:519.

Ottenbacher, K. J., Cooper, H. M. (1983). Drug treatment of hyperactivity in children. *Dev. Med. Child Neurol. 25*:358-366.

Ottinger, D. R., Halpin, B., Miller, M., Demian, L., Hannemann, R. (1985). Evaluating drug effectiveness in an office setting for children with attention deficit disorders. *Clin. Pediatric 24*[5]:245.

Patrick, K. S., Ellington, K. R., Breese, G. R., Kilts, C. D. (1985). Methylphenidate: Sustained-release vs. immediate-release. *J. Chromatogr. Biomed. Appl. 343*:329.

Pauls, D. L., Cohen, D. J., Heimbuch, R., Detlor, J., Kidd, K. K. (1981). Familial pattern and transmission of Gille de la Tourette syndrome and multiple tics. *Arch. Gen. Psychi. 38*:1091.

Pauls, D. L., Leckman, J. F. (1986). The inheritance of Gilles de la Tourette's Syndrome and Associated behaviors. *N. Engl. J. Med. 315*:993.

Pollack, M. A., Cohen, N. L., Friedhoff, A. J. (1977). Gille de la Tourette's Syndrome. *Arch. Neurol. 34*:630.

Raskin, L. A., Shaywitz, S. E., Shaywitz, B. A., Anderson, G. M., Cohen, D. J. (1984). Neurochemical correlates of Attention deficit disorder. *Pediatric Clin. North Am. 31*[2]:387.

Roche, A. F., Lipman, R. S., Overall, J. E., Hung, W. (1979). The effects of stimulant medication on the growth of hyperkinetic children. *Pediatric 63*[6]:847.

Safer, D., Allen, R., Barr, E. (1972). Depression of growth in hyperactive children on stimulant drugs. *N. Engl. J. Med. 287*:217.

Safer, D., Allen, R., Barr, E. (1975). Growth rebound after termination of stimulant drugs. *Pediatric 86*:113.

Safer, D. J., Krager, J. M. (1984). Trends in medication therapy for hyperactivity: National and international perspectives. In: *Advances in Learning and Behavioral Disabilities Vol. 3*. Gadow, K. D., ed. Greenwich, CT: JAI Press, pp. 125-149.

Safer, D. J., Krager, J. M. (1988). A survey of medication treatment for hyperactive/ inattentive students. *JAMA 260*[15]:2256.

Safer, D. J., Krager, D. M. (1989). Hyperactivity and inattentiveness: School assessment of stimulant treatment. *Clin. Pediatric 28*[5]:216.

Schachar, R., Taylor, E., Wieselberg, M., Thorley, G., Rutter, M. (1987). Changes in family function and relationships in children who respond to methylphenidate. *J. Am. Acad. Child Adolesc. Phychi. 26*[5]:728.

Schleifer, M., Weiss, G., Cohen, N., Elman, M., Cvejic, H., and Kruger, E. (1975). Hyperactivity in preschoolers and the effect of methylphenidate. *Am. J. Orthopsychi. 45*:38-50.

Shaywitz, B. A. (1984). Pharmacokinetic, neuroendocrine, and behavioral substrates of ADD. In: *Attention Deficit Disorder: Diagnostic, Cognitive and Therapeutic Understanding*. Bloomingdale, L. M., ed. Spectrum Publications, pp. 179-188.

Shaywitz, S. E., Shaywitz, B. A. (1984). Diagnosis and management of attention deficit disorder: A pediatric perspective. *Pediatric Clin. North Am. 31*[2]:429.

Sleator, E. K. (1980). Deleterious effects of drugs used for hyperactivity on patients with Gilles de la Tourette Syndrome. *Clin. Pediatric 19*[7]:453.

Sprague, R. L., Sleater, E. K. (1977). Methylphenidate in hyperactive children: Differences in dose effect on learning and social behavior. *Science 198*:1274-1276.

Sverd, J., Curley, A. D., Jandorf, M. A., Volkersz, L. (1988). Behavior disorder and attention deficit in boys with Tourette Syndrome. *J. Am. Acad. Child Adolesc. Psychi. 27*[4]:413.

Tannock, R., Schachar, R. J., Carr, R. P., Logan, G. D. (1989). Dose-response effects of methylphenidate on academic performance and overt behavior in hyperactive children. *Pediatrics 84*[4]:648.

Taylor, E. A. (1986). The basis of drug treatment. In: *The Overactive Child.* Taylor E. A., ed. Philadelphia: Spastico International Medical Publications, pp. 192-218.

Ullmann, R. K., Sleator, E. K. (1985). Attention deficit disorder children with or without hyperactivity: Which behaviors are helped by stimulants? *Clin. Pediatric 24*:547.

Ullmann, R. K., Sleator, E. K. (1986). Responders, nonresponders, and placebo responders among children with attention deficit disorder: Importance of a blinded placebo evaluation. *Clin. Pediatric 25*:594.

Wade, M. G. (1976). Effects of methylphenidate on motor skill acquisition of hyperactive children. *J. Learn. Disabil. 9*:443-447.

Wender, P. H., Wood, D. R., Reimherr, F. W. (1985). Pharmacological treatment of attention deficit disorder, residual type ["ADD-RT", "Minimal Brain Dysfunction", "Hyperactivity"] in adults. *Psychopharmacol. Bull. 21*[2]:222.

Wender, P. H. (1987). The hyperactive child, adolescent, and adult: Attention deficit disorder throughout the lifespan. New York: Oxford University Press.

Whalen, C. K., Henker, B. (1976). Psychostimulants and children: A review and analysis. *Psychol. Bull. 83*:1113.

Whitehouse, D., Shah, U., Palmer, F. B. (1984). *J. Clin. Psychi. 48*:282.

14

Antidepressants in the Treatment of Attention Deficit Hyperactivity Disorder and Comorbid Disorders

Jean M. Thomas

St. Louis University School of Medicine, St. Louis, Missouri

> *"It is . . . striking . . . that until very recently research findings have not been analyzed in ways that take account of comorbidity."*
>
> [Rutter, 1989]

This chapter focuses on the use of antidepressants in the treatment of children and adolescents with attention-deficit hyperactivity disorder (ADHD) while addressing the complexities of early diagnosis and treatment. The treatment of complex, constantly developing young people with disturbing biological, psychological, and social problems requires a multidisciplinary science and multimodal clinical interventions. A pragmatic clinician seeks an artistic blend of scientific truth and clinical sensitivity to suit individual differences and needs. But pragmatism must avoid oversimplification of investigation and treatment. This chapter examines current questions of diagnoses of ADHD and ADHD with comorbid disorders (ADHD +) in an effort to shed light on the complexity of presentation and the use of antidepressants as adjunctive therapy.

The American Psychiatric Association's *Diagnostic and Statistical Manual of Mental Disorders, 3rd Ed.* (DSM-III) [APA, 1980] and DSM-III-R (DSM-III-Revised) [APA, 1987] have attempted to standardize, operationalize, and refine the diagnostic criteria for the biopsychosocial disorder we currently call attention-deficit hyperactivity disorder. These efforts represent significant steps in a most elusive half-century task of defining ADHD and understanding etiologic factors. Low levels of professional agreement about diagnosis and etiology are the rule. Most experts agree, however, that past and present diagnostic efforts describe a heterogeneous group of similarly symptomatic children. This heterogeneity within the diagnostic category appears to confound much relevant study.

> Until one knows how to classify the subjects into homogeneous groups, there is no hope of finding either unique biological or environmental causes, to say nothing of the transactional causative networks that . . . are the most likely explanatory systems for such complex behavioral manifestations. [Conners and Wells, 1986]

The current uncertainty of scientific truths with respect to ADHD greatly increases the expectable complexity of child and adolescent psychiatric evaluation and intervention. Clinicians must inquire about the patient's biological, psychological, and social contexts. What are the genetic and the physical predisposing and precipitating factors? What are the child's cognitive abilities? What are the child's intrapsychic structures? What are the chronic and acute stressors at home and at school? How do family histories repeat themselves and get played out in dysfunctional family systems? What are parental expectations that preclude "goodness of fit" [Thomas and Chess, 1984]? After the formulation and the diagnosis, how do we select and integrate the interventions suggested by each context—the biological, the psychological, and the social? How do we help reframe the problem for parents who have been consistently concerned but lost hope that their child, and, that they as parents, can get relief? How do we facilitate "repair of mismatch" in the parent-child relationship [Tronick and Gianino, 1986]? How do we re-empower the child and the family to facilitate normal development of trust, autonomy, initation, industry, identity [Erikson, 1950]? How, in the face of the 1980s and 1990s financial cutbacks in medical care, can we accomplish this complex task pragmatically?

Psychopharmacologic treatment recommendations must be consistent with the general treatment goals of children and adolescents with psychiatric symptoms and signs. Medication may serve to externalize children's and families' loci of control and, in so doing, may impede progress toward normal development including the fostering of trust and autonomy [Erikson, 1950] and the generalization of behavioral gains over situation and time. Psychopharmacologic intervention with children is a greater risk than with adults, given the increased number of biological unknowns. Because of the likelihood of increased externalization of control and the many biological unknowns, psychoactive medication is used with caution and as an adjunct to interventions that promote an internalization of control. Medications are used only when these primary interventions do not help enough or do not help fast enough.

TOWARD A UNIFIED UNDERSTANDING AND DEFINITION OF ADHD

Historical Context

A brief history documents the diversity and uncertainty of scientific endeavors to define and understand the complexities of the ADHD. Although the disorder was described in German folklore more than 100 years ago [Weiss and Hechtman, 1979], the serendipitous discovery by Bradley [1937] of behavioral and attentional improvements in a heterogeneous group of behaviorally disordered children treated with (d,l) amphetamine brought the disorder to medical attention. In 1957, Laufer, a child psychiatrist, and Denhoff, a pediatric neurologist, described the essential feature of the hyperkinetic syndrome as hyperactivity and included learning and concentration deficits thought to be associated with a subcortical brain dysfunction. They attributed additional symptoms to secondary psychological mechanisms. They recommended treatment integrating education, psychotherapy, and medication and expressed concern that psychotherapy might be neglected since stimulant medication was so attractive [Laufer and Denhoff, 1957]. In 1966, the concept of "minimal brain dysfunction" described "deviations of functions of the central nervous system. . . . [that] may manifest themselves by various combinations of impairment in perceptions, conceptualization, language, memory, and control of attentions, impulse, or motor function" [Clements, 1966]. In 1968, the APA's *Diagnostic and Statistic Manual* (DSM-II) used the label "hyperkinetic reaction of childhood" and described it as "a disorder characterized by overactivity, restlessness, distractibility, and short attention span." Etiology was not specified. In 1980, DSM-III used the label "attention deficit disorder with hyperactivity" to denote the switch in conceptualization to the central feature of inattention. In 1987, DSM-III-R used the label "attention-deficit hyperactivity disorder" to denote the dual centrality of both inattention and hyperactivity. In DSM-III and DSM-III-R, as in DSM-II, definitions are explicitly empirical; no etiology is implied.

Historical Dichotomy of Internalizing
and Externalizing Symptoms

DSM-II, employing the classical dichotomy, separated childhood disorders into those characterized by internalizing symptoms (neurotic) and those characterized by externalizing symptoms (acting out). DSM-III, acknowledging the complex co-occurrence of categorical psychiatric disorders with developmental disorders, with personality disorders, with medical disorders, and with environmental stressors, created a multiaxial diagnostic system. DSM-III operationalized criteria from three symptom clusters: inattention, impulsivity, and hyperactivity. DSM-III identified the core deficit as inattention and required the addition of impulsivity but attention deficit disorder could present with hyperactivity (ADDH) or without hyperactivity (ADD). An important set of research based on the DSM-III dichotomy of ADD with and without hyperactivity emerged. Lahey et al. [1987] demonstrated that the subgroup of ADD children without hyperactivity had significantly more codiagnoses of anxiety and affective disorders than did the subgroup with hyperactivity. The ADDH children, on the other hand, had significantly more codiagnoses of conduct disorder than did those without hyperactivity. Lahey et al. [1988] suggest an analysis of empirically derived clusters of symptoms corresponds better with the DSM-III three symptom clusters than with the newer DSM-III-R unidimensional definition. However, the DSM-III subgrouping of ADD children essentially paralleled the classical dichotomy of internalizing versus externalizing disorders and, in oversimplifying, distracted attention from an emerging body of data suggesting that internalizing and externalizing symptoms frequently coexist.

Overlap of Internalizing and Externalizing Symptoms

The overlap of internalizing and externalizing symptoms within individual children has been demonstrated across age groups in multiple studies. Rutter et al. [1970] in the Isle of Wight Study identified 21% of psychiatrically disturbed children and 27% of psychiatrically disturbed boys with "mixed disorders" of conduct and mood. Carlson and Cantwell [1980] studied 102 children and adolescents in a psychiatric population to determine the prevalence of depressive symptoms and depressive disorder. They concluded that "in some children with hyperactivity, aggressive behavior, and some antisocial behavior, a depressive disorder coexists." To an alert physician, the depression will not be "masked" by the more salient behavioral disturbance. Chiles et al. [1980] found that 23% of boys ages 13-15 who were admitted to a correctional facility were diagnosed with major depression by Research Diagnostic Criteria (RDC) [Spitzer et al., 1978]. Puig-Antich [1982] made an unexpected discovery that one-third of the preadolescent boys fitting RDC criteria for major depression met DSM-III criteria for conduct disorder. Marriage et al. [1986] demonstrated DSM-III conduct disorder in one-third of children with DSM-III affective disorder.

The use of factor analysis has spawned a number of studies demonstrating the overlap of internalizing and externalizing symptoms in children and adolescents. Rescorla [1986] demonstrated that the co-occurence of "aggressive/destructive behavior and feelings of anxiety, sadness and emotional insecurity" within individual preschool-age children was the rule rather than the exception. Sixteen percent of the children were "high on the anxious/ depressed factor and low on the aggressive/destructive factor (i.e., 'pure' internalizers).'' Twenty-five percent of boys and 18% of girls were "high on the aggressive/destructive factor and low on the anxious/depressed factor (i.e., 'pure' externalizers).'' Thirty-six percent of boys and 37% of girls were high on both factors. Employing factor analysis of the Conners Parent Questionnaire, Conners and Wells [1986] empirically derived five clusters of parent reported symptoms to define natural subdivisions of 316 children who presented at an outpatient clinic and 365 normal children from his sample. They concluded that parent reported symptom patterns empirically cluster into groups that more closely define clinically occuring subtypes than did the earlier dichotomy differentiating internalizing versus externalizing symptomatology. They believe that the early dichotomy characterizing hyperkinetics as externalizers and neurotics as internalizers is incompatible with subgroupings more empirically derived by factor analysis.

HETEROGENEITY OF ADDH/ADHD

Increased Clarity with Codiagnoses

"It is . . . striking . . . that until very recently research findings have not been analyzed in ways that take account of comorbidity" [Rutter, 1989]. Kashani et al. [1987] found that children and adolescents who present for psychiatric evaluation qualify, on the average, for 2.4 Axis I, DSM-III diagnoses each. (Axis I lists primary psychiatric diagnoses.) Recent studies documenting the comorbidity of ADDH/ADHD with neuromaturational disorders, conduct, and oppositional disorders, affective disorders and anxiety disorders demonstrate that comorbidity is expectable [Munir et al., 1987; Szatmari et al., 1989a,b]. These studies strengthen earlier studies suggesting the close association of developmental disorders and ADDH/ADHD. The importance of the comorbidity of conduct disorders and "hyperkinetic/attention deficit syndromes" and of conduct disorder and depressive disorders highlighted in "Isle of Wight Revisited" [Rutter, 1989] is of special interest here in our consideration of interventions that include the use of antidepressants.

Cormorbidity in ADDH/ADHD Is "The Rule"

Szatmari et al. [1989b], in the Ontario Child Health Study, conclude that a major finding with regard to ADDH is that multiple diagnoses seem to be "the rule rather than the exception." They found that 53% of male ADDH patients ages 4 to 11 have at least one other diagnosis; 9.2% have two other diagnoses.

Structured interview techniques have facilitated the identification of multiple diagnoses in child psychiatric patients. Munir et al. [1987] studied 22 boys with a primary diagnosis of ADD from consecutive referrals to the Pediatric Psychopharmacology Clinic and the Child Psychiatry Service. Using structured parent interviews, all DSM-III diagnoses were made and reported as lifetime prevalences for every subject. According to Munir et al., 21 (96%) of the ADD patients received more than one Axis I diagnosis; 18 (82%) of the patients received more than two Axis I diagnoses. When compared with a matched normal control group derived from a pediatric primary care service, ADD patients had "significantly higher rates of conduct disorder . . . oppositional disorder . . . major affective disorder . . . tics (non-Tourette) . . . language disorder/stuttering . . . encopresis . . . and attendance in special class in school." To further characterize the ADD patients, four non-mutually exclusive subgroups were formed. These groups included ADD with co-occurring

1. conduct or oppositional disorders (CD/OPD)
2. major affective disorder (MAD)
3. anxiety disorder (ANXD)
4. neuromaturational disorders (NMD)

Compared with controls, (a) the rate of neuromaturational disorder was higher in the ADD patients with co-occurring CD/OPD; (b) the rates of conduct and oppositional disorders were higher in the ADD groups with co-occurring MAD, ANXD, and NMD; and (c) the rate of major affective disorders was higher in the ADD groups with co-occurring ANXD and CD/OPD but not in ADD patients with co-occurring NMD. The authors conclude that "subgrouping ADD patients may lead to identification of more homogeneous groups of patients with common course, outcome, family history, biological markers, and response to treatment."

Developmental Problems

Developmental problems, even after controlling for poor school performance, were most closely associated with ADDH among those variables significant in the analyses of data collected from parent reports in the large Ontario

Child Health Study. Other variables significant at the same level included family dysfunction and parental mental health problems [Szatmari et al., 1989a].

Behavioral and cognitive subtypes of ADHD were defined in a large sample of school children ages 5 to 14 years. All children (n = 1038) in grades K through 7 attending two suburban schools were rated by teachers on the revised Conners Teacher Rating Scale [Goyette et al., 1978]. Ninty-five students (9.2%) were identified as ADHD on the Hyperactivity Index of this scale. Of the ADHD students, 20% with reading disorders were labeled "cognitive ADHD"; 80% without reading disorders were labeled "behavioral ADHD." In the behavioral ADHD group, those with the most significant problems with impulsivity, overactivity, and aggressivity "did not qualify as reading disabled but showed weaknesses on test of short-term memory similar to those observed in reading disabled students." These results indicate that in many ADHD children, comorbid reading disorders may be the primary cause of poor school achievement. The authors further suggest that situational factors determining the degree of internal regulation of behavior and of compliance with external demands may contribute to poor performance in those both with and without reading disabilities [August and Garfinkel, 1989].

Children with language disorders and high psychosocial stress appear to be at significant risk for psychiatric disorders, both behavioral and emotional. In a study of linguistically disordered children Baker and Cantwell [1987] found that behaviorally disordered and psychiatrically well children differed on a number of factors including developmental disorders, language diagnoses (comprehension, expression, processing), psychosocial stress, and maleness. Interestingly, emotionally disordered children differed from psychiatrically well children on factors including disorders of language (comprehension, expression, and processing), psychosocial stress, and femaleness. Developmental delay and sex were the only factors that differentiated the behaviorally and emotionally disordered children.

Conduct/Oppositional Disorders

Comorbidity studies document the frequent overlap of ADDH/ADHD and conduct/oppositional disorders. Approximately 40% of ADDH children also have a diagnoses of conduct disorder, according to the Ontario Child Health Study [Szatmari et al., 1989b]. Werry et al. [1987] reviewed studies comparing ADDH, conduct disorder (CD), and anxiety disorder (ANXD), all using DSM-III criteria. They suggest as do others [Szatmari et al., 1989a] that ADDH may be a cognitive disorder, possibly of neurodevelopmental origin. Werry et al. [1987] suggest that CD, on the other hand, is a disorder of social relationships and of psychosocial origin. These studies conclude that when the two disorders coexist, the degree of disability is increased [Werry et al., 1987; Szatmari et al., 1989a]. Reeves et al. [1987] in their outpatient sample of 99 children ages 6 to 13 years found that CD most often occurred in the presence of ADDH. They found that ADDH children with CD were more socially handicapped than children with ADDH alone. The ADDH and ADDH + CD groups were most differentiated by severe adverse family backgrounds. Barkley et al. [1989] also document that aggressive ADHD children have "more impaired family situations" than nonagressive ADHD children.

Family history studies by Biederman et al. [1987a] used the same subjects and controls as Munir et al. [1987], detailed above. In Biederman et al. 14 (64%) of the ADD boys met DSM-III criteria for conduct or oppositional disorder (CD/OPD +), 8 (36%) did not (CD/OPD −). The rate of ADD in relatives of both CD/OPD + and CD/OPD − probands was significantly higher than the rate of ADD in relatives of non-ADD controls. The rate of antisocial disorders and OPD in relatives of CD/OPD + probands was significantly higher than in relatives of CD/OPD − probands. The rates of major depressive disorder (MDD) and overanxious disorder in relatives of CD/OPD + were significantly higher than in relatives of CD/OPD − and in relatives of controls. Family history studies suggest a familial componet in the origins of ADD, CD/OPD + , MDD, and ANXD. Given the increased positive family history of mood and anxiety disorders in ADD children with CD/OPD + , clinicians should be alert for an increased likelihood of internalizing disorders in these most behaviorally difficult ADD children.

Affective/Mood Disorders

According to the Ontario Child Health Study, up to 50% of ADDH children and adolescents are also diagnosed with emotional disorder. The group with the highest rate of comorbid emotional disorders was ADDH girls ages 12 to 16 years; the group with the lowest rate was the ADDH girls ages 4 to 11 years. ADDH boys had an intermediate proportion of comorbid emotional disorders [Szatmari et al., 1989a]. As reported above, ADD patients, compared with controls, have appreciably higher rates of conduct disorder, oppositional disorder and affective disorder [Munir et al., 1987]. The rate of affective disorder was higher, in comparison with controls, in the ADD groups with co-occurring anxiety disorder and with co-occurring CD/OPD. Using the same population, Biederman et al. [1987b] report the rate of MDD in ADD probands to be 32%, the rate of MDD in relatives of ADD probands to be 27%, and the rate of MDD in relatives of controls to be 6%.

Children with ADDH and children with MDD have overlapping externalizing and internalizing symptoms even when codiagnoses cannot be made. Jensen et al. [1988] employed structured interviews of parents and subjects consisting of 24 boys ages 9 to 18 consecutively admitted to an outpatient child and adolescent psychiatry clinic. Patients were included if, on structured interview, they had one diagnosis only, either ADDH or MDD. Those on stimulants were withdrawn from medication 3 days prior to testing; those on antidepressants were withdrawn from medication 2 weeks prior to testing. Eleven controls, ages 8 to 18, were matched for sex but not SES. Using the Child Depression Rating Scale (CDRS) [Poznanski et al., 1979,1984], ADDH boys scored significantly higher than controls on "social withdrawal," "guilt," "weeping," and "depressed affect." On these items, no significant difference was found between MDD and ADDH boys. Employing the Jesness Inventory Manifest Aggression Scale (JIMAS) [Jesness and Wedge, 1984], MDD boys scored significantly higher than controls on "bad thoughts," "families argue too much," "sometimes rather be in trouble," and "gets angry quickly." On the JIMAS, controls scored significantly lower; however, "ADDH and MDD boys could not be differentiated." Jensen et al. [1988] concluded that boys with ADDH (without codiagnosis) frequently demonstrate significant depressive symptoms and that boys with MDD (without codiagnosis) frequently demonstrate significant conduct symptoms. Similar overlap of externalizing and internalizing symptoms had been reported previously [Carlson and Cantwell, 1980; Puig-Antich, 1982; Marriage et al., 1986].

Affective and anxiety symptoms may temper externalizing symptoms of children comorbid for both externalizing and internalizing disorders. Nevertheless, parents of these cormorbid children identify more externalizing than internalizing symptoms. In a recent study of psychiatrically hospitalized children ages 4 to 14, of 35 who received at least one behavior diagnosis, 51% were comorbid for behavior and affective/anxiety disorders by DSM-III-R criteria. The behavior diagnoses included CD, Oppositional Defiant Disorder, and ADHD. The affective/anxiety diagnoses included major depressive or dysthymic disorders and adult anxiety disorders. Seventeen patients had a behavior diagnosis without an affective/anxiety diagnosis (Behavior Group); 18 patients had both a behavior and an affective/anxiety diagnosis (Behavior and Affective/Anxiety Group). Both groups had "particular difficulties expressing themselves and coping with difficult social situations" [Woolston et al., 1989]. Children in the mixed group did not show less adaptive functioning as hypothesized. It is suggested that affective/anxiety symptoms may have tempered the disruptive behavior in the mixed group. Nevertheless, for both the Behavior Group and the Behavior and Affective/

Anxiety Group, caregivers reported significantly more externalizing than internalizing behaviors [Woolston et al., 1989].

UNDERREPORTING AND UNDERRECOGNITION OF INTERNALIZING SYMPTOMS

Both parents and children underreport internalizing symptoms. Parents report more externalizing than internalizing symptoms in children comorbid for externalizing and internalizing disorders [Kashani et al., 1989; Woolston et al., 1989]. Because in comorbid presentation the behavior symptoms are more conspicuous than the depressive symptoms, the depressive symptoms may be overlooked [Carlson & Cantwell, 1980]. In addition, children with mixed disorders may appear more adapted than children with externalizing disorders only. Therefore, mixed disorders may more likely be missed [Woolston et al., 1989]. Children and adolescents are more aware of their symptoms of anxiety and depression than are their parents [Rutter et al., 1976; Berg and Fielding, 1979; Kashani et al., 1989]. Furthermore, children 6 years old or older are considered to be accurate historians [Herjanic et al., 1975]. Nevertheless, young children frequently lack the conceptual and verbal skills to identify and report feeling states. Behaviorally disordered children with and without internalizing symptoms have specific difficulties expressing themselves [Woolston et al., 1989]. In addition, children, especially those aged 6 to 12 years, are highly self-critical [Shaffii and Shaffii, 1982] and, therefore, highly self-protective, avoiding negative self-critique. Consequently, many children brought for psychiatric evaluation will, like their parents, underreport or minimize feelings or symptoms suggesting sadness or anxiety. Healthy children are predictably defensive about divulging symptoms they perceive as weaknesses [Shaffii and Shaffii, 1982]; emotionally disturbed children are typically more defensive [Zimet and Farley, 1987].

Zimet and Farley [1987] have attempted to elucidate what emotionally disturbed children report about their competencies and self-esteem. One hundred and two prepubescent children in a psychiatric day treatment center were asked to rate themselves in four areas of perceived competence: cognitive, social, physical, and general. In comparison with a matched sample of children without identified psychiatric disorders, the disordered children perceived their competencies more globally and less multidimensionally. Furthermore, among the day treatment subjects who were unable to make age-appropriate differentiations about their competencies, 75% of the children were self-aggrandizing. Farley and Zimet [1985] found that in disturbed children, the more competent they perceived themselves to be, the less urinary cortisol they secreted. Stress hormone secretion was decreased in association with increased perceived competence; stress hormone secretion was not signi-

Table 1 ADHD Symptoms Can Be Markers of Anxiety, Depression, and Defensiveness

ADHD Symptom	Disorder/Defense	Origin of Symptom
Inattention	Anxiety	Hypervigilence
		Poor concentration
		Poor frustration tolerance
	Depression	Poor concentration
		Decreased interest
		Decreased motivation
		Low energy
	Defense	Avoidance of potential failure
Hyperactivity/Impulsivity	Anxiety	Disorganization
		Agitation/fidgitiness
		Increased impulsivity
	Depression	Increased psychomotor activity
		Agitation
	Defense	Turning passive into active
		Impulsive acting out of feelings
Externalizing Behaviors	Anxiety	Increased impulsivity
		Poor frustration tolerance
	Depression	Irritability
		Decreased hopefulness and trust
	Defense	Denial of responsibility
		Externalization of responsibility
		Identification with the aggressor
		Acting out of feelings

ficantly correlated with measured ability. This data suggests that not only do disturbed children have difficulty perceiving and reporting unfavorable self-characteristics, but, in addition, biology strongly reinforces this tendency to minimize painful perceptions.

Internalizing symptoms and associated defensive behaviors are often both underreported and clinically underrecognized. Symptoms of inattention, hyperactivity, impulsivity, and externalizing behaviors are frequently markers of anxiety, depression, and defensiveness (see Table 1). The more vulnerable the child, the more anxiety, depression, and defensiveness is expected. Inattention to an assigned task may signal hypervigilence associated with anxiety, decreased concentration associated with depression, or defensive avoidance of potential failure. Hyperactivity and impulsivity may signal a child's disorganizing anxiety and/or overactivity as a defense against feeling passive and helpless. Externalizing behaviors and deteriorating family or peer relationships may signal irritability associated with depression and/or defensive externalization of responsibility often presenting with impulsive acting out of those feelings. Inability to verbalize feelings of vulnerability, anxiety and depression may signal defensive denial especially common in children ages 6 to 12 [Shafii and Shaffii, 1982].

Clinicians must use all the information available including histories taken from parents, parent substitutes, teachers, and children and including observations of mood and defensiveness. The child's report, notably lacking in many studies of ADDH/ADHD children, is required for accurate reporting of internalizing symptoms. In addition, clinical observations augment histories. Just as low mood may be inferred from observing a child's dysphoric affect [Poznanski et al., 1985], low self-esteem, anxiety, and defensive behaviors may be inferred from observing a child's interactions with the family and with the examiner and from observing a child's play.

MULTIPLE TREATMENT MODALITIES SUGGESTED BY MULTIPLE DIAGNOSES

One major contribution of comorbidity studies in ADDH/ADHD is that specific interventions can be tailored to specific diagnoses [Puig-Antich, 1982; Anderson et al., 1987; Pliszka, 1987; August and Garfinkel, 1989; Szatmari et al., 1989a; Woolston et al., 1989]. Laufer and Denhoff [1957] recommended treatment integrating education, psychotherapy, and medication and expressed concern that psychotherapy might be neglected since stimulant medication was so attractive. Mental health professionals who treat children and adolescents must, in addition to reducing symptoms, work toward promoting normal development [Rutter, 1981; Satterfield et al., 1987], including fostering of trust and autonomy, [Erikson, 1950] and generalization of behavioral gains across situation and time. Multimodal treatment of hyperactive boys has been associated with "unexpectedly good outcome" [Satterfield et al., 1979] and, over time, has been "a cost effective treatment approach" [Satterfield et al., 1987].

Identifying reading or language problems points the way toward specific educational interventions. When teachers and parents are alert to a specific disability, opportunities not only for communication but also for empathic exchanges are increased. If more than 50% of children presenting with language and speech problems have psychiatric problems, [Baker and Cantwell, 1987] and if reciprocal communication is fundamental to the formation of healthy relationships [Tronick and Gianino, 1986] it is likely that much psychiatric morbidity can be prevented if communication at home and school is facilitated. "He doesn't listen" is a frequent presenting complaint of parents bringing an ADHD child for psychiatric evaluation. When these same parents understand that the problem begins in language processing or comprehension, their anger and frustration often give way to empathy and patience which, in addition to the use of specific communication tools, can readily facilitate "repair of mismatch" [Tronick and Gianino, 1986] in the parent-child relationship.

ADHD children comorbid for CD have decreased social skills, increased severe family adversity and increased affective symptoms and disorders [Szatmari et al., 1989a]. Strayhorn and Weidman [1989] have shown that "parent-child interaction training" has reduced attention deficit and internalizing symptoms in low-income preschool children. The critical issue is the fostering of relationships in which trust and internalized rules can be developed. In their work with adults with antisocial personality disorder, Gerstley et al. [1989] have documented a significant association between the patient's ability to form a therapeutic alliance and positive treatment outcome. Such a therapeutic alliance with the child or adolescent patient and with the parents, who have an increased probability of being affectively or personality disordered themselves [Biederman et al., 1987a], is likely to be associated with a more positive treatment outcome for the child or adolescent.

Satterfield et al. [1987] provided individualized multimodal treatments to address the problems of decreased social skills, increased family adversity, and mood problems in hyperactive youths and their families. Such multimodal treatment, extending 2 to 3 years, was associated with significantly decreased morbidity. Multimodal treatment consisted of stimulant medication plus intensive psychotherapies, including individual and group psychotherapy for the boys and family therapy, parent training, and marital therapy for the families. Treatment plans were designed for individual patients and families and on the average included 3.5 visits per month for each family. The control groups received stimulant medication and monthly counseling only. Attrition rates were comparable for both groups with 30% in the drug treatment only group and 27% in the multimodal treatment group. Multimodal treatment patients who remained in treatment less than 2 years had modest decreases in delinquency; those remaining in treatment 2 to 3 years had the greatest reduction in delinquency. Groups did not differ in arrests for minor offenses; however, arrests for felonies were significantly decreased. The number of institutionalizations decreased 33% for the multimodal treatment group as compared with the drug treatment only group. Improved academic performance was also found in the multimodal-treatment group seen over 2 to 3 years [Satterfield et al., 1987].

Earlier, Satterfield et al. [1979] reported improved social relationships at home and at school, improved academic performance, and improved self-concepts in addition to decreased antisocial behavior in hyperactive boys with multimodal treatments. From this earlier study group, those receiving multimodal treatment for 2 to 3 years showed significantly better outcomes at 3-year and at 9-year follow-ups than did those with multimodal treatment for less than 2 years. "This suggests that a fairly lengthy period of childhood treatment is crucial to an optimal treatment" and that medication used to improve impulse control may facilitate the process and outcome of psychotherapeutic interventions [Satterfield et al., 1987]. In addition, medication may provide immediate symptom improvement that can enhance the establishment of a therapeutic alliance [Schowalter, 1989], central to positive treatment outcome [Gerstly et al., 1989].

BIOCHEMICAL THEORIES OF ADDH/ADHD

Medication Studies May Lead to Greater Understanding

The complexity of diagnosing and understanding ADHD has been matched by the complexity of biochemical theories and data resulting from medication trials. Efforts to understand the mechanism of action, especially of stimulants but also of antidepressants and of newer medications, have generated several important theories. Currently a nonspecific catecholamine hypothesis, including the indolamine serotonin, appears most promising for guiding clinical research and treatment. Understanding more about how different medications impact on ADDH/ADHD may lead to greater understanding of the symptoms and the disorder itself.

Three Neurotransmitter Hypotheses

The dopamine hypothesis suggests that diminished activity of brain dopamine may underlie the primary symptoms of ADDH and that medications that decrease ADDH symptoms such as stimulants may, in effect, provide increased dopamine to the brain. Shaywitz et al. [1976] demonstrated that in neonatal rats with chemically destroyed CNS dopamine neurons there was a significant rise in motor activity, which was effectively reduced by stimulant medication. The authors concluded that in a subset of hyperactive children, dopamine depletion may be associated with supersensitive postsynaptic dopamine receptors. Given that the dopamine system in normal children is slow to mature and apparently vulnerable, it seems feasible that prenatal and early childhood insults might easily upset dopamine mediated controls of motor and cognitive functions [Coyle, 1987; Teicher and Baldessarini, 1987].

The noradrenergic hypothesis proposes that in ADDH there is a pathological hyperfunctioning of the noradrenergic system. In rats, even at birth, it can be demonstrated that increased norepinephrine (noradrenalin) can produce increased locomotor activity [Teicher and Baldessarini, 1987]. Norepinephrine mediates the expression of anxiety and also appears to mediate shifts in cognition from external focus in vigilence to internal focus in problem solving, as summarized by Hunt et al. [1985]. Norepinephrine turnover is decreased by medications that ameliorate the symptoms of ADDH including stimulants, tricyclic antidepressants (TCAs), monoamine oxidize inhibitors (MAOIs), and clonidine. Noradrenergic mechanisms also appear central to the antidepressant effect of TCAs and MAOIs and to the antihypertensive effect of clonidine [Zametkin and Rapoport, 1987; Hunt et al., 1985].

The serotonergic hypothesis emanates from studies in which increased activity and aggression are seen in serotonin depleted animals [Zametkin and Rapoport, 1987]. In addition, Heffner and Seiden [1982] have demonstrated that overactivity caused by dopamine depletion in neonatal rats and ameliorated by ampetamine appears to be mediated by serotonergic mechanisms.

The Multiple Neurotransmitter Hypothesis

A hypothesis that predicts the interaction of multiple neuronal systems and multiple neurotransmitters in ADHD is more tenable. Dopamine is a precursor of norepinephrine synthesis; norepinephrine regulates the synthesis of dopamine. Furthermore, dopamine can directly influence adrenergic neurons, though its potency is less than that of norepinephrine. Stimulant medications are known to affect dopaminergic, noradrenergic, and serotonergic systems. Some studies suggest that inattention may be selectively mediated by dopaminergic mechanisms, while other ADDH symptoms may be mediated by noradrenergic mechanisms [Zametkin and Rapoport, 1987].

Nonstimulant medications that ameliorate ADHD symptoms are known to affect many neuronal systems. Antidepressants affect noradrenergic, serotonergic, and, to a lesser extent, dopamine systems [Zametkin and Rapoport, 1987]. MAO inhibitors whose substrates include norepinephrine, serotonin, and dopamine all provide immediate ADHD symptom improvement similar to that with stimulants [Zametkin et al., 1985]. Recent work by Stoff et al. [1989] demonstrates that MAO, normally decreased during childhood, is elevated in association with high impulsivity tested in prepubescent boys. He suggests that high MAO in these children may be a biological substrate predisposing these children to externalizing, impulsive behaviors and that environmental factors are needed for the full expression of behavior disorders marked by problems with impulsity. Clonidine directly inhibits nora-

Table 2 Medications with Documented Clinical Usefulness in the Treatment of ADDH/ADHD

Stimulants
  Short acting
    Methylphenidate (Ritalin)
    Dextroamphetamine (Dexedrine)
  Long acting
    Pemoline (Cylert)
Antidepressants
  Tricyclic antidepressants
    Imipramine (Tofranil)
    Desipramine (Norpramin)
    Clomipramine (Anafranil)
  Nontricyclic antidepressants
    Bupropion (Wellbutrin)
  Antiepileptic/mood stabilizer
    Carbamazepine (Tegretol)
Antihypertensive
  Clonidine (Catapres)
Neuroleptics[a]
  More sedating
    Chlorpromazine (Thorazine)
    Thioridazine (Mellaril)
  Less sedating
    Haloperidol (Haldol)

---

[a]Neuroleptics are the drugs of last choice because of side effects.

drenergic activity and has a secondary modulating effect on dopamine activity [Hunt et al., 1985]. A closer look at the medications that demonstrate usefulness in ADHD lends some further credance to the various hypotheses, especially the multiple neurotransmitter hypothesis.

MEDICATIONS USEFUL IN ADDH/ADHD (see Table 2)
Stimulants in the Treatment of ADDH/ADHD
Concern about Overuse of Stimulants

Growing concern about the overuse of stimulant medication in children with ADHD has been repeatedly publicized in the popular media. These current concerns reflect earlier concerns of Laufer and Denhoff [1957] who predicted that psychotherapy might be neglected since stimulant medication was so attractive. Multimodal treatment, including medication as an adjunct to educational and psychotherapeutic interventions, is documented as highly preferable to medication alone, especially with treatment extending for more than 2 years. [Satterfield et al., 1979; Satterfield et al., 1987]. Although early studies neglected to include multimodal treatment, in recent ADDH/ADHD medication studies, multimodal treatment is standard [Garfinkel et al., 1983; Biederman et al., 1989a,b]. Multimodal treatment using medication adjunctively is most consistent with the general goals of treatment that focus on facilitation of normal development as well as on symptom relief.

Stimulants: Limitations and Untoward Effects

Lack of response to stimulants in up to 30% of symptomatic children [Barkley, 1977] and significant side effects, including worsened behavior, preclude the use of stimulants in many cases. Transient side effects include increased sympathetic tone manifested in increases in heart rate and increases in systolic and dyastolic blood pressure. Associated gastrointestinal symptoms include anorexia, weight loss, stomach aches, nausea, vomiting, constipation, and diarrhea. Untoward CNS effects include rebound symptoms of increased restlessness, overstimulation, dysphoria, mood lability, and irritability. Significant concern has been expressed about the addictive or street-value potential of stimulants used by adolescents with ongoing symptoms of ADDH. Of additional concern is the precipitation or exacerbation of psychosis and of involuntary motor symptoms including stereotypies, tics, and Tourette's disorder. Although some authors conclude that stimulants do not trigger or accelerate the development of movement disorders [Shapiro and Shapiro, 1981], most suggest that in children who have preexisting tics or a family history of tics or Tourette's, stimulants are contraindicated [Campbell et al., 1985].

Long-term effects of additional concern include suppression of growth in weight and height. In a 1979 review of data on growth suppression, the Pediatric Subcommittee of the Food and Drug Administration Psychopharmacologic Drugs Advisory Committee concluded that with stimulant doses equivalent to methylphenidate 20 mg/day that moderate weight and less significant height suppression, not evident in adulthood, occurred [Roche et al., 1979]. Mattes and Gittelman [1983], however, found that in 86 hyperactive boys on average doses of 40 mg/day for up to 4 years, height percentile decreases, not significant over the first year, decreased to 18.1% after 4 years.

Antidepressants in the Treatment of ADDH/ADHD

Antidepressants: Drug of Second Choice, Drug of First Choice

Antidepressants have been considered the drug of second choice since the 1960s for treatment of symptoms of the hyperkinetic reaction of childhood and of ADDH. Pliszka [1987] reviews the literature up through 1985 on the use of tricyclic antidepressants in these disorders. He concludes that stimulants, overall, appear to be superior to TCAs but that in a subgroup of children who have significant anxiety and depressive symptoms in association with ADDH, TCAs may be the treatment of first choice, "a novel idea" according to Campbell and Spencer [1988]. More recent studies, theoretical considerations and clinical experience suggest that further study of and experience with antidepressants in the treatment of ADHD is warranted.

Early Studies of TCAs in the Treatment of Hyperactivity

Early studies suggested the possible efficacy of TCAs in the treatment of hyperactivity and behavior disorders. Rapoport [1965] administered imipramine (10-40 mg/day), over 6 to 24 months, to 41 behaviorally and learning disordered patients ages 5 to 21. Parents reported 33 (80.5%) improved. Rapoport observed that "as tension is reduced, the ability to concentrate and remember improves, thus facilitating the learning process." Winsberg et al. [1972] administered imipramine (75-150 mg/day), dextroamphetamine (15-30 mg/day) and placebo, each over 7-10 days, to 32 neuropsychiatrically impaired, hyperactive, aggressive children and adolescents referred primarily for hyperactivity and aggressiveness. Parents rated more children improved on imipramine (69%) than on dextroamphetamine (44%). Waizer et al. [1974] administered imipramine (mean dose, 173.7 mg/day), over 8 weeks followed by 4 weeks of placebo, to 19 hyperactive children. According to ratings by psychiatrists, teachers, and parents, as compared with placebo, "significant improvement was observed in hyperactivity, defiance, inattentiveness and sociability."

Placebo-Controlled Drug Comparison Studies (see Table 3)

More recent placebo-controlled drug comparison studies include a double-blind study by Rapoport et al. [1974] who compared imipramine (mean dose, 80 mg/day) and methylphenidate (mean dose, 20 mg/day) over 6 weeks in 76 hyperactive boys ages 6 to 12. Both drugs produced improvements (decreased impulsivity and hyperactivity) on Conners' rating scales for teachers and parents. The "degree of enthusiasm for medication varied considerably between rater groups," with teachers more consistently favoring methylphenidate over imipramine than did parents. Although teachers rated hyperactivity more improved (decreased) with methylphenidate than with imipramine, parents rated hyperactivity equally or more improved (decreased) with imipramine than with methylphenidate. Cognitive test scores were more improved with methylphenidate than with imipramine. However, psychologists rated attention equally improved with methylphenidate and imipramine. Children demonstrating the greatest cognitive change on imipramine were those seen by psychiatrists as most anxious and inhibited. The authors report that their discomfort with raising imipramine does to levels used in other studies limited the comparability of the drugs studied.

Table 3 Placebo-Controlled Drug Comparison Studies

Symptom	Study Group	Ratings of Medications as Reported by	
		Teacher	Parent/Childcare Worker
Conduct/Aggression	Q[a]	I = M > N	M = I = N
	W[b]	I = M = P	I > M, I > P
	G[b]	M > C, M > D	M = C, M > D, M > P
		M > P, C = D > P	C > D, C > P, D > P
Hyperactivity	R[b]	M > I > P	I = M > P
	Q[a]	I = M > N	M = I = N
	W[b]	M = I = P	I > M, I = P
Impulsivity	G[b]	M > D = C = P	M = C, M > D, M > P
			C > D, C > P, D > P
Evening Disturbance (activity, attention, cooperactivity)	G[b]		D > M, D > P, D = C
			C > M, C > P
Attention/ Concentration Deficit	G[b]	M > D, M > P M > C	M > C, M > D, M > P C > P, D > P
Depressed/Angry Mood	G[b]	C > D, C > P C > > M	C = M, C > P, C > D
Lowered Self-Esteem	G[b]	C > M, C > D C = P, P = D	D > M, D > C, D > P

Only statistically significant data reported. When ratings are statistically equal (=), order denotes greater magnitude (>) without significant difference. Medications: Stimulant: methylphenidate (M); TCAs: imipramine (I), clomipramine (C), desipramine (D); Placebo (P); No treatment (N). Studies: Rapoport et al., 1974 (R); Quinn and Rapoport, 1975 (Q); Werry et al., 1980 (W); Garfinkel et al., 1983 (G).
[a]Long-term (1 year) study.
[b]Short-term (3-6 weeks) study.

A 1-year follow-up of these 76 boys by Quinn and Rapoport (1975) found equal improvement in those who continued the treatment on either imipramine or methylphenidate. "The good responders to imipramine and the good responders to methylphenidate did not differ in any measure at one-year follow-up." Teachers reported that boys in both treatment groups showed significant improvement in classroom behavior and hyperactivity over boys who had discontinued treatment. On similar scales, parents reported significant improvements in all groups as compared with baselines (see Table 3). Long-term treatment appears to equalize the differential effects of stimulants and TCAs. Nevertheless, "the striking clinical impression at one-year follow-up was that boys in all three groups continued to have difficulties." A further investigation of treatment over more than 1 year is pertinent. In addition, the authors report greater compliance with methylphenidate than with imipramine. Less compliance with TCA treatment may reflect the authors' discomfort with imipramine side effects as reported in this study and in that by Rapoport et al. [1974].

Werry et al. [1980] in a double-blind, placebo-controlled, crossover study with imipramine and methylphenidate "unexpectedly" demonstrated superiority of imipramine. They studied 30 children ages 5 to 12 with a parent-identified, prolonged history of inattention and impulsivity at home and at school. Over 3-4 weeks for each drug, they compared the efficacy of two doses of imipramine (1.0 and 2.0 mg/kg/day) with that of a standard dose of methylphenidate (0.4 mg/kg/day). The child psychiatrist's synthesis of data "unexpectedly" demonstrated "greatest benefit accruing from imipramine." Teacher ratings showed neither drug resulted in significant improvements in conduct and hyperactivity on Conners' scales. Parent ratings, on the other hand, showed imipramine resulted in greatest improvement on those two scales. Tests of attention showed effects of methylphenidate and of imipramine to be equal. Tests of cognition showed effects of methylphenidate to be superior to those of imipramine. The authors concluded that imipramine's pattern of effect paralleled that of methylphenidate: "physiological measures, learning performance, motor overflow, motor steadiness, and social effects were all consistent with a stimulant type of effect." They also suggested that the apparent superiority of imipramine might be due to the clinical assessment of the psychiatrist relying heavily on the parent reports, which reflect the advantage of imipramine's longer-acting symptom control continuing during family time.

Garfinkel et al. [1983] demonstrated that teachers rating school activities prefer stimulants, while parents and childcare workers rating evening activities prefer TCAs for ADD children. In a double-blind, placebo-controlled, crossover study, they compared 12 boys ages 5 to 11 with ADD (without co-existing psychiatric disorders) for 3 weeks with each drug, methylphenidate, clomipramine, and desipramine, and placebo. Multimodal treatments were provided for all treatment groups. The mean dose of methylphenidate was 0.75 mg/kg/day; the mean dose of TCAs was 3.5 mg/kg/day. No medication was given on weekends. In comparison with placebo, teachers rated daytime global disturbance decreased with methylphenidate (24%), with clomipramine (11.1%), and with desipramine (8.2%). Cognitive scores were most improved on methylphenidate. On the Conners scales, parent and childcare workers rated methylphenidate equal or superior to TCAs. Parents and childcare workers rated evening motor activity, attention to the activity at hand, and cooperation most improved with TCAs. Both teachers and parents rated depressive/affective symptoms and self-esteem most improved with TCAs (see Table 3).

Garfinkel et al. [1983] concluded that the stimulant produced more side effects than did the TCAs because of marked sleep deterioration with methyphenidate, that improvements with methylphenidate were not associated with improvements in mood and self-esteem, and that, in fact, methylphenidate produces irritability and dysphoria in some children. On the other hand, TCAs did improve mood and self-esteem. The reported advantages of TCAs in this study are more remarkable given that the TCAs were discontinued on weekends and that failure to maintain blood levels may decrease toward effects and increase untoward effects.

Adolescents with ADD May Find Advantages with TCAs

In adolescents, decreased effectiveness of stimulants and the potential of abuse lead Gastfriend et al. [1984] to explore the usefulness of TCAs in this population. They treated 12 adolescent outpatients with ADD in an open trial with desipramine over a 6-12 month period. Eight of these adolescents had Axis II diagnoses (specific learning disorders), 2 had additional Axis I diagnoses, and 2 had significant Axis III diagnoses (medical disorders). Doses were titrated up to 5 mg/kg/day. Dose requirements varied as much as 10-fold among patients; 4 of 12 obtained optimal benefit with doses of 3.5 mg/kg/day or above. Eleven of 12 adolescents showed decreased inattention, impulsivity, and hyperactivity after 4 weeks of treatment. Of 10 treated over 6-12 months, 9 showed "much" or "very much" improvement sustained over the treatment time. Multimodal treatment was systematically provided before and after the first 4-week trial to minimize the confounding of data with nondrug interventions. Side effects, most apparent in the first 4 weeks of treatment and eliminated in all cases with dose adjustment, included the following: drowsiness (50%), postural dizziness (25%), weight loss or decreased appetite (25%), headache (16%), insomnia (16%) and racing thoughts (8%). The work of Gastfriend et al. [1984] suggests the advantages and minimal disadvantages of TCAs in adolescents with ADD, a population in which the value of stimulant therapy is "somewhat more limited than . . . among prepubertal ADD children" [Klorman et al., 1987].

Controlling for Coexisting Psychiatric Disorder

Most recently, Biederman et al. [1989a], in a double-blind placebo-controlled trial with desipramine, treated 62 children and adolescents ages 6 to 17. Patients and controls were matched for presence of frequently coexisting psychiatric disorders, including learning disorders, conduct disorders, and oppositional disorders. Patients were drawn from an outpatient clinic and met DSM-III diagnosis for ADD, had symptoms in at least two of three settings, and a score of at least 15/30 on Conners Abbreviated Questionnaire.

Desipramine (mean dose, 4.6 mg/kg/day) was given for 3 to 6 weeks. Differencies in efficacy of desipramine over placebo were not observed until weeks 3 and 4. Desipramine-treated patients showed significant improvement over placebo-treated patients in ratings by clinician, parents, and teachers, but no significant improvement or worsening was seen in short-term laboratory measures of cognition. As rated by patient and mother, desipramine-treated patients showed a marked reduction in depressive symptoms compared with placebo-treated patients, a finding similar to that of Garfinkel et al. [1983]. This suggests that dysphoria and other symptoms of depression and anxiety frequently associated with ADD [Biederman et al., 1987b; Munir et al., 1987; Pliszka, 1989; Szatmari et al., 1989a] and often secondary to stimulant treatment [Quinn and Rapoport, 1975; Garfinkel et al., 1983; Pliszka, 1987] are reduced with desipramine treatment. Clinical improvement for adolescents paralleled that for younger children.

Other Pharmacological Approaches in ADDH/ADHD

Neuroleptics

Campbell et al. [1985] reviewed the literature on the usefulness of neuroleptics in aggressive, destructive children and suggest that in ADDH, neuroleptics "should be considered only for those patients who failed to respond to treatment with stimulants." Werry and Aman [1975] targeted symptoms of hyperactivity and aggressiveness in children of normal intelligence and found that haloperidol in low doses (0.025 mg/kg/day) and high doses (0.05 mg/kg/day) effectively decreased behavioral symptoms; cognitive performance was worse on the higher dose. Both more-sedating neuroleptics, such as chlorpromazine (Thorazine) and thioridazine (Mellaril), and less-sedating neuroleptics, such as haloperidol (Haldol), have been widely used in institutionalized children and in the mentally retarded [Werry et al., 1966]. Diminished coignitive functioning, sedation, and risk of extrapyramidal symptoms, including dystonias and dyskinesias, has restricted the usefulness of neuroleptics [Campbell et al., 1985].

Clonidine

Clonidine is a "safe, effective medication for a subgroup of children with symptoms of ADDH" [Hunt et al., 1985]. It "may be preferable" to stimulants for children who have stimulant-rebound symptoms, insomnia, anorexia, growth retardation, or chronic tics. Clonidine, known best as an antihypertensive [Manheim et al., 1982] and more recently as an inhibitor of opiate withdrawal [Gold et al., 1980], is an alpha-adrenergic stimulating agent that acts presynaptically to inhibit noradrenergic activity. It has been shown effective in Tourettes disorder in decreasing tics, increasing attention, and in decreasing behavioral symptoms including hyperactivity and impulsivity [Cohen et al., 1980].

In a double-blind, placebo-controlled, crossover study, Hunt et al. [1985] treated 10 ADDH children ages 8 to 13 with clonidine for 8 weeks and placebo for 4 weeks. Dosage, beginning with 0.05 mg/day, was increased to 4-5 μg/kg/day, given in four divided doses. Teachers, parents, and clinicians rated children significantly improved in hyperactivity and conduct. Clonidine improved performance on some neuromaturational tests but not to a significant level. Sleepiness, the main side effect, subsiding after 3 weeks, limited usefulness in one child. Mean blood pressure decreases of 10% and occasional postural hypotension did not limit treatment. Affective symptoms increased in one child with previous symptoms of depression. The potential usefulness of this medication in ADHD deserves attention.

Non-TCA Medications with Antidepressant Efficacy

Other pharmacologic approaches to ADHD include medications that have been used for mood disorders and for behavioral dyscontrol. MAO inhibitors, selective MAO A, MAO B, and mixed MAO A and B, all have immediate effects on classroom behavior and attention that approximate effects of stimulants [Zametkin et al., 1985]. Side effects, including dietary restrictions required to avoid hypertensive crises, limit the usefulness of MAO inhibitors in children and adolescents. Campbell et al. [1984] in a double-blind, placebo-controlled study demonstrated that lithium decreased symptoms of conduct disorder as well as did haloperidol but with fewer side effects. The hyperactivity observed in some of these children was decreased with lithium. DeLong and Aldershof [1987] concluded that only ADD children with coexisting mood symptoms (38%) improved on lithium; the rest worsened. In a recent case study, Licamele and Goldberg [1989] reported that a 7-year-old boy with symptoms of ADDH, irritability, sadness, and explosiveness improved more with combined methylphenidate and lithium treatment than with either alone. Evans et al. [1987] reported successful treatment of an 8-year-old boy with ADDH, learning disability, explosive outbursts, and right temporal lobe epiletiform activity with carbamazepine 400-600 mg/day. Serum levels of >8.0 mEq were associated with most marked improvement. In addition, Simeon et al. [1986] found some success in treating hyperactive children with the new antidepressant bupropion (Wellbutrin). Simeon's success suggests the investigation into the usefulness of other non-TCA antidepressants such as fluoxetine (Prozac). The efficacy of non-TCA antidepressants in ADDH/ADHD suggests that the association of ADHD and mood symptoms needs further investigation.

ANTIDEPRESSANT VERSUS STIMULANT TREATMENT
OF ADHD/ADDH

TCAs, Accepted Second-Choice Medication

When stimulants are contraindicated or have failed, TCAs are the accepted, second-choice medication. Tics or Tourette's disorder in the child or adolescent or a family history of the same are widely, but not consistently, considered a contraindication for stimulant medication. Of significant concern in adolescents is the abuse potential of stimulant medication. In addition, stimulants are intermittently abused by parents. Interference with growth, especially linear growth, is a relative contraindication. Although compensatory growth apparently occurs when stimulants are discontinued, there is some concern about treatment of adolescents in whom the closing of epiphises may preclude attainment of potential height.

TCA and Stimulant Advantages Reassessed

Although stimulants have in most studies been considered more effective than TCAs, a reassessment of TCA and stimulant advantages is warranted. Werry et al. [1980] suggest that, except for variations in degree, imipramine's action "mirrors" that of the stimulants in the treatment of hyperactive children. Depending on which symptoms are studied and who is reporting, very different conclusions may be drawn (see Table 3). Although teachers usually rate stimulants higher than TCAs, parents and childcare workers usually rate TCA's higher [Winsberg et al., 1972; Rapoport et al., 1974; Werry et al., 1980; Garfinkel et al., 1983]. Short-term studies suggest that stimulants are more effective than TCA's [Rapoport et al., 1974; Garfinkel et al., 1983]; long-term studies suggest that stimulants and TCA's may be equally efficacious [Quinn and Rapoport, 1975]. With these differences in reported efficacy with rater preferences and treatment length in mind, let us look more closely at the differential effects on target symptoms and function (see Table 3).

Externalizing Symptoms

Teacher and parent reports of children's externalizing symptoms often differ [Rutter, 1989]. In most short-term drug comparison studies, teachers rate stimulants more effective than TCAs for reducing externalizing symptoms (conduct/aggression, hyperactivity, and impulsivity) [Rapoport et al., 1974; Garfinkel et al., 1983]. In the same studies and others, parents and childcare workers rate TCAs equally effective or more effective than stimulants for reducing externalizing symptoms [Winsberg et al., 1972; Rapoport et al.,

1974; Werry et al., 1980; Garfinkel et al., 1983]. Biederman et al. [1989a] suggest there is no testable change with TCAs for 3 to 4 weeks. After a year of treatment, the differences between stimulants and TCAs disappear [Quinn and Rapoport, 1975].

Attention and Cognition

Attention is often considered best treated with stimulants but in some studies TCAs are considered equally effective. Teachers and parents rated stimulants more effective than TCAs for problems with attention [Garfinkel et al., 1983]. On the other hand, psychologists globally rated stimulants and TCAs equally effective for inattention and both drugs more effective than placebo [Rapoport et al., 1974].

Cognitive test scores show stimulants often, but not always, superior to TCAs; both drugs are superior to placebo [Werry et al, 1980; Garfinkel et al., 1983]. Although Rapoport et al. [1974] report that stimulants improve "achievement," improved cognitive function associated with stimulant treatment does not appear to be associated with increased performance on achievement tests [Conners and Taylor, 1980]. Early concern about TCAs diminishing cognitive performance appears dispelled by multiple studies [Quinn and Rapport, 1975; Werry et al., 1980; Garfinkel et al., 1983; Biederman et al., 1989a].

Internalizing Symptoms

Mood and self-esteem, as rated by teachers and parents, are improved more with TCAs than with stimulants [Garfinkel et al., 1983]. Stimulants are well known to produce dysphoria as a common side effect [Pliszka, 1987; Biederman et al., 1989a]. Pliszka [1987, 1989] concluded TCAs may be the drug of first choice in ADDH children who have overlapping anxiety and depressive symptoms.

Social Interaction

Social interaction is more improved with stimulants according to teacher reports and more improved with TCAs according to parent reports [Rapoport et al., 1974; Werry et al., 1980; Garfinkel et al., 1983]. After longer treatment, improvements on stimulants and TCAs by teacher and parent report become indistinguishable [Quinn and Rapoport, 1975]. Improved family function is demonstrated with methylphenidate when dosage is flexible to the needs of parents [Schachar et al., 1987]. The repeated finding that parents prefer longer-acting medications such as TCAs and pemoline [Winsberg et al., 1972; Werry et al., 1980; Garfinkel et al., 1983; Conners and Taylor, 1980] suggests that improved family function may be facilitated by longer-acting medications. Studies of the differential effects of various stimulants and TCAs on family function similar to the studies of Schachar et al. [1987] and Barkley [1988, 1989] need to be done.

Side Effects

Side effects of most concern with both drugs are those affecting the cardiovascular system. According to the well-controlled comparison study of Garfinkel et al. [1983], stimulants and TCAs demonstrated similar elevations of diastolic blood pressure at mean doses of 18 mg/day of methylpnenidate (0.75 mg/kg/day) and 85 mg/day for TCAs (3.5 mg/kg/day). Doses of TCAs above 3.5 mg/kg/day require blood level and ECG monitoring [Puig-Antich et al., 1987; Biederman et al., 1989a,b].

Overall, the stimulant "produced more marked side effects than the TCAs" because of marked sleep deterioration produced by methylphenidate [Garfinkel et al., 1983]. This conclusion is more remarkable since TCAs were not administered on weekends; abrupt stopping of TCAs frequently precipitates sleep disturbance, headache, abdominal discomfort, and malaise. Of additional concern are stimulant side effects of rebound overactivity during afterschool/evening hours, dysphoria, increased risk for tics/Tourettes, risk of abuse/addiction, and growth retardation.

When Are TCAs the Drug of First Choice?

TCAs are the drug of first choice when ADDH/ADHD patients are comorbid for anxiety and depressive disorders. TCAs may also be the drug of first choice when ADDH/ADHD patients have significant symptoms of anxiety and depression even without frank disorder (see Table 1) or need medication during afterschool/evening hours [Werry et al., 1980; Garfinkel et al., 1983; Biederman, 1986; Pliszka, 1987, 1989]. Recently Pliszka [1989] demonstrated that ADHD children comorbid for anxiety disorder respond less well to stimulants than do those with ADHD without anxiety disorder. Improvement in anxiety and mood symptoms and symptom relief during afterschool/evening hours may be reasons why parents and childcare workers rated TCAs better than stimulants in several studies [Werry et al., 1980; Garfinkel et al., 1983]. The potential for TCAs improving anxiety and mood symptoms and the quality of family relationships are primary indications for their use.

GUIDELINES FOR THE USE OF ANTIDEPRESSANTS

Which Antidepressant Is Recommended?

Once the decision has been made to use an antidepressant for a child with ADHD, which medication is optimal? A track record in adults is advisable prior to use in children. During the interuterine period of development and the first 2 years of life, the rate of synaptogenesis is much greater than that in later years. The rate of synaptogenesis gradually decreases and by age 2 to 3 years is more similar to the rate in the adult than to the rate in the fetus. Treatment of children less than 3 years old carries significantly more risks, given the increased rate of neural development and the increased biological vulnerability in this period. After age 3, however, toxicity is likely more similar to that in adults [Popper, 1987]. Although there are no established guidelines for the introduction of new medications in children, "it may be prudent to wait perhaps 3 to 5 years for a minor chemical innovation . . . or 10 to 15 years before using a new category or class of pharmacological agents in children." However, "If a psychotropic drug has major technical advantages over previous treatments . . . rapid introduction . . . may be advisable" [Popper and Spiegel, 1987].

During the first 3 years of life, not only is neurotoxicity a relative unknown, but also, pharmacokinetic factors change rapidly. The greater percentage of water in a child's body in comparison with an adult's means the volume of distribution is greater and larger doses may be needed. Although kidney function is similar in children and adults, liver function is proportionately greater in children. This means that in a drug primarily metabolized by the liver, like TCAs, metabolism is proportionately increased and, therefore, availability is decreased. Finally, smaller body compartments require more precise dosing. Given these many unknowns, it is advisable to use one or two agents that have been well studied—for example, imipramine and desipramine—and to build clinical experience and confidence with those drugs [Popper and Spiegel, 1987].

Imipramine (Tofranil) is by far the most studied and most used TCA for child and adolescent patients. Desipramine (Norpramin), though without FDA approval for children, is an active metabolite of imipramine. Imipramine has a balanced reuptake blockade of norepinephrine and serotonin, whereas desipramine has a more pure reuptake blockade of norepinephrine. Imipramine is more sedative and desipramine more activating. Imipramine, because of its serotonin blockade, may be more helpful especially with obsessive-compulsive symptoms and with anxiety symptoms including panic attacks. Imipramine has more anticholinergic effects than does desipramine and may therefore cause more drying of the mouth and blurring of vision, though both are rare complaints in young patients. Recent studies suggest that cardiovascular side effects may be less with desipramine than with imipramine [Schroeder et al., 1989; Biederman et al., 1989b]; this warrants further investigation as do the side-effect profiles of newer antidepressant treatments.

Garfinkel et al. [1983] compared methylphenidate with clomipramine and desipramine. Clomipramine, previously available in the United States only experimentally, has a primary serotonin reuptake blockade as compared with desipramine's primary norepinephrine reuptake blockade and imipramine's more balanced serotonin and norepinephrine reuptake blockade. Toward and untoward effects of imipramine would be expected to be intermediate to those of clomipramine and desipramine. Garfinkel et al. [1983] demonstrated that by teacher and parent report, subjects had significantly fewer depressive/affective symptoms with clomipramine than with desipramine. By parent report, desipramine increased self-esteem more than other drugs. Both TCAs improved depressive/affective and self-esteem scores better than did methylphenidate. On teacher report of global improvement in behavior, children on methylphenidate did best, but those on clomipramine did better than those on desipramine. Sleep deterioration was far greater with the stimulant than with TCA treatment. In short, clomipramine- and desipramine-treated children demonstrated improvement over stimulant-treated children in scores of mood and self-esteem and with regard to sleep. Clomipramine may show a slight advantage over desipramine in global classroom behavior and mood. Since imipramine effects are likely intermediate

Table 4 Guidelines for Administering TCAs Imipramine (Tofranil) and Desipramine (Norpramin)

Generics: equally reliable.

Table sizes (mg): 10, 25, 50, 75, 100, 150.

Clinical response: expected after 3-4 weeks, may be earlier.

Duration of treatment: 4-6 months after symptoms resolve.

Half-life: 20-24 hours (adult), 6-15 hours (prepubescent child).

Initial dose: 25 mg if patient $\geq$ 50 lbs; 10 mg if patient < 50 lbs.

Dose frequency: if tolerated, pm dose only; younger children often require BID dosage.

Dose timing: pm dose given 1 hour before bedtime may potentiate sleep; dosage after meals for young children may decrease chance of gastrointestinal symptoms.

Dose increases: 25 mg every 3 days if patient $\geq$ 50 lbs; 10 mg every 3 days if patient < 50 lbs; increases may be more rapid if patient is in hospital.

Dose decreases: 25 mg every 2-4 weeks if patient $\geq$ 50 lbs; 10 mg every 2-4 weeks if patient < 50 lbs.

Dose range: 2.5-3.5 mg/kg/day (approximately 1.0-1.5 mg/lb/day); some require up to 5 mg/kg/day.

Plasma levels: therapeutic range is extrapolated from studies of adults and children treated for mood disorders; dose needed to establish therapeutic levels varies among individuals 10- to 30-fold; blood sample collected 8-12 hours after last dose. Imipramine: sum of imipramine plus desipramine equals 150 to 225 (300) ng/ml. Desipramine: desipramine equals 150 to 225 (300) ng/ml.

ECG warranted: before treatment; if doses $\geq$ 3.5 mg/kg/day; if plasma level $\geq$ 150 ng/ml; if cardiac disease, additional evaluation required.

ECG safety limits: maintain HR < 130 beats/minutes; maintain PR < 200 msec; maintain QRS < 120 msec.

between clomipramine and desipramine, and since desipramine is a significant active metabolite of imipramine, the differences in toward and untoward effects are likely to be small.

Administration of Antidepressants (see Table 4)

The Power of Nondrug Interventions

Nondrug, predrug, and placebo treatments have demonstrated efficacy in children with externalizing and internalizing symptoms. "Parent-child interaction training" significantly improved "parent ratings of attention-deficit and internalizing symptoms" in preschool children of low-income families [Strayhorn and Weidman, 1989]. Intensive evaluation of depressed children presenting for drug trials resulted in the recovery, before drug treatment, of 20% [Puig-Antich et al., 1987]. Placebos have been demonstrated effective a third or more of the time [Schowalter, 1989] and have been demonstrated effective in multiple studies with children [Conners and Taylor, 1980; Puig-Antich et al., 1987]. Puig-Antich et al. [1987] documented greater success of placebo over TCA treatment of depressed children. These authors suggest that the power of placebo may be greater in children than in adults. "Freud wrote that the 'state of mind in which expectation is coloured by hope and faith is an effective force with which we all have to reckon, strictly speaking, in all our attempts at treatment and cure' " [Schowalter, 1989]. The expectation of hope as communicated in clinician-child/parent relationships may provide significant efficacy with or without medication.

The Meaning of Medication

What is the meaning of medication to the patient and to the parents? Does it mean the patient or family has failed or that they have appropriately sought help for a serious concern? Does it mean control is externalized or outside help is needed to support a child in his or her attempts to increase self-control? The more the child and parents understand about the problem and the reasons for certain treatment interventions, the greater is the chance they will feel empowered. The more they know, the greater is the chance they will experience increased internalized control. Prior to the use of medication, parents are fully informed and give informed consent either verbally or in writing. The child is informed—age appropriately—and gives his or her "assent" [Popper and Spiegel, 1987]. The informed consent of the parents and the informed assent of the child potentially increase the parents' and the child's sense of control and likely the compliance and the efficacy. Noncompliance is the "most common reason for medication failure" [Schowalter, 1989].

Essential to the educative process and to the healing process is the framing of medication as adjunctive to psychotherapeutic interventions. When the patient (and parents) know that medication can only help calm the patient who must make the necessary changes himself or herself, expectations are appropriate and an internalized locus of control is fostered. One 6-year-old boy, having heard this explained, returned to school and, as reported by his teacher, changed his own behavior and taught his peers how to better control themselves and avoid being "timed-out." This child's ADHD symptoms resolved without medication as did the symptoms of the preschool children in the study of Strayhorn and Weidman [1989].

Empowering the parent, who has felt helpless and with little hope, is as central as empowering the patient. Parents want to know how they can help. Identifying parental concern and help-seeking as an appropriate first step, supporting previous effective parental efforts, and acknowledging the complexity and seriousness of the problem all help the parent to feel accepted and appreciated. Asking the parents' collaboration as part of the treatment team for both psychotherapeutic and pharmacologic interventions is essential. Explaining the toward and untoward effects of medication and the details of appropriate administration further empower the parent with a sense of being able to understand and contribute to the child's treatment.

Expected Duration of Treatment

Clinical response has in some studies been noted immediately and in others after 3-4 weeks [Biederman et al., 1989a]. The earlier response appears to overlap the period of early side effects seen with antidepressants in the treatment of mood disorders. The later response appears to overlap the period of antidepressant effect. These overlaps suggest possible mechanisms of action that remain to be understood. It is helpful to share these unknowns with patients and parents so that they understand immediate effects may be experienced but greater effects are expected after a consistent blood level at therapeutic dose has been achieved over about 3 weeks. The patient and parents need to know that over time they will note more improvement with the medication, especially as the patient is gradually able to make more and more constructive decisions about his or her behavior. In fact, Prien and Kupfer [1986] found that continuation of TCAs after symptoms remit can be beneficial; clinical experience reinforces this finding. So the patient and parents are told that for optimal advantage, antidepressant medication is continued for 4-6 months after symptoms disappear. TCAs are discontinued slowly. The dosage is decreased by 25 mg (10 mg in a child of 50 lbs or less) every 2-4 weeks to allow for smooth transitions and careful monitoring of symptoms.

Frequency and Time of Dosage

Parents and especially patients are pleased with once or twice-a-day dosage of TCAs because schooltime administration with associated embarrassment can be avoided. A single dose is adequate in adults given the half-life of approximately 20-24 hours. In preadolescent children the half-life is 6-15 hours [Puig-Antich et al., 1987] and, therefore, twice-a-day dosage may be preferred. Adolescents seem to tolerate once-a-day dosage somewhat better than preadolescents. Compliance is likely facilitated with once-a-day dosage. Bedtime is usually the best administration time, especially since medication may cause sedation especially as the dosage is first begun and gradually increased. In order to potentiate sleep in children with initial insomnia, administration an hour or more before bedtime is preferred. If excessive sleepiness occurs in the morning, the evening dose may be too large and splitting the daily dosage may be preferable. If anorexia is a problem, as it is more frequently with young children, then administration of medication after a meal is preferred.

Titration of Appropriate Dose

Both imipramine and desipramine may be initiated with a 25 mg dose unless, as in a child of under 50 lbs, the total daily dose is expected to be less than 50 mg; then a 10 mg dose is initiated. The dose may be increased by 25 mg (10 mg in a child of 50 lbs or less) every 3 days, or faster if the patient is hospitalized. Increases are continued until the total dose is between 2.5 and 3.5 mg/kg/day (in the English system this approximates 1 to 1.5 mg/lb/day). Garfinkel et al. [1983] demonstrated good results with doses up to 3.5 mg/kg/day. Gastfriend et al. [1984] and Biederman et al. [1986, 1989a] documented good results and doses up to 5 mg/kg/day. These latter doses were used over 4-52 weeks with "moderate" or "marked" improvement in 80% of patients. There was no evidence of response inhibition at higher doses [Gastfriend et al., 1984].

Because of individual differences (10- to 30-fold) in steady-state plasma levels in physically healthy individuals [Preskorn et al., 1989], titration by plasma level is advisable whenever financially feasible and especially when titration by clinical response proves difficult. Plasma samples are collected 8-12 hours after the last dose. For imipramine levels, the sum of reported levels of imipramine and desipramine, an active metabolite, should ideally be within the therapeutic range. Therapeutic blood levels of 150-225 ng/ml, empirically demonstrated for antidepressant efficacy with adults, have been extrapolated for use with children and adolescents. Puig-Antich et al. [1987] showed that for affectively disordered preadolescent children, plasma levels greater than 150 ng/ml were associated with 85% response, whereas those less than 150 ng/ml were associated with only 30% response. They further documented that in affectively disordered children, plasma level predicts response linearly, which greatly facilitates titration. Therapeutic plasma levels for treatment of ADHD have not been established. Those demonstrated for treatment of affective or mood disorder may be useful guidelines, since doses and plasma levels apparently effective in ADHD are in the same range as doses effective for mood disorder [Biederman et al. 1989a,b]. Biederman et al. [1989b] suggest serum levels of desipramine "in the 100- to 300-ng/ml range are probably adequate and relatively safe for most ADDH patients, but some may require daily doses above 3.5 mg/kg to attain these levels."

Precautions

Adverse effects, even with doses in the range of 5.0 mg/kg/day, were "mild and only slightly more common in association with DMI [desipramine] than with placebo" [Biederman et al., 1989a]. In this study, adverse side effects for desipramine versus placebo were: "dry mouth (32.3% vs. 19.4%), decreased appetite (29.0% vs. 12.9%), headache (29.0% vs. 9.7%), abdominal discomfort (25.8% vs. 19.4%), tiredness (25.8% vs. 12.9%) dizziness (22.6% vs. 9.7%), and trouble sleeping (22.6% vs. 6.5%)." Side effects appeared during dosage increases and were readily managed with dosage adjustment. Similar side effect frequencies were reported by Gastfriend et al. [1984]. Biederman et al. [1989a] observed in one patient a rash that did not preclude treatment. Cutaneous reactions to standard antidepressants are reported in 2% to 4% of adult patients, are usually transient, and can be managed conservatively [Warnock and Knesevich, 1988]. Worth mentioning to patients and parents is the advisability of careful tooth care with the increased risk of dental caries apparently secondary to dryness of mouth with antidepressant medication [BTP, 1987].

Cardiovascular side effects with TCA treatment can be more serious but seldom preclude their usefulness. Biederman et al. [1989a,b] report statistically significant rises in diastolic blood pressure, heart rate, and conduction times. Serum levels above 150 ng/ml were associated with increased heart rates and more conduction abnormalities and warranted monitoring of ECGs. Puig-Antich et al. [1987] carefully monitored cardiovascular effects in prepubertal children given imipramine for affective disorder. Blood levels and ECGs were obtained serially with dose increases to 1.5, 3, 4, and 5 mg/kg/day. These authors suggest the following guidelines: heart rate was considered safe up to 130 beats/min, PR interval (usually not increased above 0.18 sec in their study) was considered "quite safe" up to 0.21 sec. Cardiovascular side effects limited dosage in only 4 of 30 children treated with imipramine. One child had heart rate increased to 130 beats/min at rest; 2 had orthostatic hypotension; 1 had chest pain [Puig-Antich et al., 1987]. Puig-Antich et al. [1987] and Biederman et al. [1989a,b] recommended blood level and ECG monitoring in patients with known cardiac problems and for all children and adolescents with TCA doses of 3.5 mg/kg/day or above. Pretreatment ECG is advised.

Schroeder et al. [1989] demonstrated that imipramine and desipramine have similar cardiovascular side effects in children ages 5 to 12 years. Comparing the two drugs, they suggest the change in heart rate appears the same. There may, however, be less effect on PR interval and corrected QT interval with desipramine than with imipramie. At doses of 5.0 mg/kg/day, "more potentially severe ECG abnormalities such as atrioventricular block, QRS prolongation, arrythmias were not observed . . . despite careful ECG and Holter monitoring through the study." Cardiovascular side effects may be less with desipramine than with imipramine [Schroeder et al., 1989; Biederman et al., 1989b] but further study is warranted.

Because TCA overdose can be lethal, it is advisable to limit the number of pills dispensed whenever depression is severe and suicide is a potential. Parents must understand the dangers of overdose. When danger to the patient or to other children is possible, it is advisable to dispense only a 1-week supply of medication and carefully instruct parents to prevent access to medication of those in potential danger. In adult patients 1 g of TCA is potentially lethal; a significantly smaller amount would be lethal in a child. Because of the danger of inappropriately high doses of TCAs, parents are instructed not to double the dose if a previous dose is missed but to call if a missed dose creates discomfort. One-third to one-half of the dose missed is then prescribed, depending on the size of the total dose.

SUMMARY AND CONCLUSIONS
Comorbidity in ADDH/ADHD Is Expectable

Comorbidity in ADDH/ADHD is the "rule rather than the exception" [Szatmari et al., 1989b]. Up to 96% of ADD patients have more than one psychiatric diagnosis [Munir et al., 1987]. Identification of disorders presenting cormorbidly with ADHD has facilitated both diagnostic subgrouping of the heterogeneous ADHD population and multimodal intervention pertinent to the multiple problems of these children and their families. Treatment of comorbid externalizing and internalizing symptoms with antidepressants as a part of long-term, multimodal intervention is both pragmatic and preventive.

Underreporting and Underrecognition of Internalizing Symptoms

Underreporting and underrecognition of internalizing symptoms and associated defensive behaviors impede identification of comorbid disorders. Internalizing disorders copresent with ADHD up to 50% of the time [Anderson et al., 1987; Szatmari et al., 1989a]. This figure may underrepresent the comorbidity of ADHD and internalizing disorders because internalizing symptoms are frequently underreported by parents and by children and adolescents [Zimet and Farley, 1987; Kashani et al., 1989; Woolston et al., 1989] and underrecognized clinically. Although it is easier to collect data from teachers and parents, it is essential to ask the children and adolescents directly about internalizing symptoms. By the age of 6 years, children are able to report quite accurately [Herjanic et al., 1975]. Children and adolescents are more in touch with their internal states than parents or teachers can be [Rutter et al., 1976; Berg and Fielding, 1979; Kashani et al., 1989]. However, eliciting data from children is complicated by their relatively limited world view, their limited verbal skills, and their vulnerability.

Internalizing symptoms and associated defensive behaviors are not only underreported but also often underrecognized clinically. Symptoms of inattention, hyperactivity, impulsivity, and externalizing behaviors are frequently markers of anxiety, depression, and defensiveness. For example, inattention may be secondary to decreased concentration associated with depression; increased activity and impulsivity may be secondary to anxiety; and increased externalizing behaviors may be secondary to irritability associated with depression and externalization of responsibility associated with defensiveness (see Table 1). In addition to collecting histories from parents, teachers, and the child, clinicians must carefully observe the child for dysphoric affect as a marker for low mood [Poznanaski et al., 1985] and for symptoms of ADHD as markers for anxiety, depression, and defensiveness.

Oversimplification of Research Paradigms Obfuscates Complexity

Just as eliciting more complete data from children will change our understanding of ADHD, so too will changes in research study design. For example, in short-term studies stimulants appear more pragmatic than TCAs. In long-term studies their efficacy appears equal. If we look at teacher ratings, stimulants appear more pragmatic. If we look at parent ratings, TCAs appear equally or more pragmatic. If we look at activity and attention over the short term, stimulants appear better. If we look at mood and self-esteem over the short term, TCAs appear better (see Table 3). If we look for a single diagnosis, we will see and treat the externalizing symptoms. If we look for comorbidities and find developmental disorders, conduct and oppositional disorders, or anxiety and mood disorders, we will treat the multiple pertinent symptoms and signs. If we look only at symptoms and signs, we will miss the child or the adolescent, the complex biological, psychological, and social self that is vulnerable and suffering.

Knowledge dictates pragmatics, but pragmatics must not dictate knowledge. Short-term studies are most useful when they are the beginning of long-term studies. Rapoport et al. [1974] demonstrated efficacy of stimulants in reducing inattention and overactivity; Quinn and Rapoport [1975] showed the equal efficacy of long-term stimulants and TCAs in reducing these symptoms. Satterfield et al. [1979] documented that multimodal treatment was more efficacious than drug treatment alone. Follow-up studies showed multimodal treatment over 2 to 3 years was more efficacious than the same treatment for less than 2 years. Nine-year follow-up studies demonstrated much more—decreased numbers of felonies and institutionalizations. Not only did symptoms resolve better but development in a significant number of patients proceded more normally.

Long-term prospective studies usually do not seem pragmatic but can yield knowledge that facilitates pragmatics. Thomas and Chess [1984] in the New York Longitudinal Study first hypothesized that a young child's temperament was an index of his or her biological tendancy to develop behavioral problems. They concluded that behavior problems emerge from the interaction of a child's biological characteristics and the environment, especially as influenced by parental patterns of functioning. Thomas and Chess [1984] proposed that the "goodness of fit" between what parents expect of a child and the child's actual capacities facilitates optimal functioning and prevents maladaptive behavior patterns from developing. This "goodness of fit" may be related to what Werner [1988] understood to be the family's ability to buffer risk. Among children with biological neonatal risk, those who were resilient had nurturing relationships with persons who "accepted them unconditionally" and helped them "encounter graduated challenges that enhance[d] their competence and confidence" [Werner, 1988].

Codiagnoses Reframe the Problem and Define Pragmatic Interventions

Educating parents and children about the complexity of cormorbid symptoms and disorders often helps reframe the problem so the parent and child are able to adjust expectations and choose behaviors that improve "goodness of fit" [Thomas and Chess, 1984]. In working with ADHD children and parents, identification of occult anxiety, depressive symptoms or major depression helps to reframe the child as needing concern, not just creating problems. One frustrated, impatient father brought his 10-year-old son for evaluation of "hyperactivity." As the father began to understand that the boy was depressed and that his increased irritability and decreased impulse control were associated with his depression, the father's eyes moistened. At the moment the father was able to show his tears, the boy understood the father's true concern, previously covered by anger and impatience. Initial "repair of mismatch" [Tronick and Gianino, 1986] in this relationship lead to further communication and reciprocity. Such "repair" helps resolve symptoms and normalize development in general.

What we are aiming for in our interventions with ADHD and ADHD+ children is the fostering of normal development, which implies that a child is acquiring an increased sense of self-effectance in social, academic, and physical competencies. Multiple diagnoses are a most useful beginning in providing a knowledge base that leads to pragmatic interventions for multiple problems including those of attention, hyperactivity, impulsivity, reading, language, conduct, anxiety, mood, self-esteem, social skills, and family function.

Psychological and Biological Interventions Synergize

As we learn more about how psychology and biology work together, we are developing treatments that take advantage of the synergy of psychological and biological interventions. The meaning of medication can be more powerful than the medication itself [Schowalter, 1989]. Placebos can at times appear more effective than medications [Puig-Antich et al., 1987]. Placebos can also create side effects [Garfinkel et al., 1983; Gastfriend et al. 1984; Biederman et al., 1989a]. Medication may increase compliance with other treatments as well. The clinician can make use of all these tools, including, of course, the toward effects of medications themselves (see Table 2).

Stimulants and TCAs Are Equal Over the Long-Term

Stimulants and TCAs are equally effective in ADHD when treatment is long-term [Quinn and Rapoport, 1975]. DSM-III-R criteria for ADHD requires at least 6-months duration; one would expect that a disorder associated with chronic dysfunction would require treatment over months. If quick symptom relief is needed, stimulants may be an advantage. A two-tiered approach such as that used for panic disorder may be advisable. For panic disorder benzodiazepines can be used to decrease acute symptoms before TCAs take full effect. For ADHD, methylphenidate may be used to decrease acute symptoms before TCAs take full effect if TCAs are preferred to treat concurrent anxiety or mood symptoms or to avoid untoward effects of stimulants.

TCAs, First-Choice Drugs in ADDH/ADHD with Internalizing Symptoms

TCAs are the drug of first choice when ADDH/ADHD patients are comorbid for anxiety and depressive disorders. TCAs may also be the drug of first choice when ADDH/ADHD patients have concurrent anxiety or mood symptoms without frank disorder (see Table 1) or need medication during after-school/evening hours. Stimulants do not improve self-esteem; in fact, they often create or exacerbate dysphoria [Garfinkel et al., 1983; Biederman, 1986; Pliszka, 1987, 1989]. Given that up to 26% of ADD children have coexisting anxiety disorders, that up to 50% of ADDH children have affective disorder [Anderson et al., 1987; Szatmari et al., 1989a], and that internalizing symptoms are underreported and underrecognized, TCAs may be the drug of first choice more often than previously recognized. Even in children with ADDH alone, symptoms of dysphoria are common [Jensen et al., 1988]. These symptoms may be associated with ADDH primarily or secondarily because of frustration with primary symptoms or because of the side effects of stimulants. Anxiety, dysphoria and low self-esteem, whatever their origin, may not be as disruptive as externalizing symptoms but can hardly be considered trivial. In addition, TCAs, with their long duration of action, may be the drug of first choice when symptoms of ADHD, anxiety, dysphoria, and/or low self-esteem interfere with family relationships during afterschool/evening hours.

Avoiding Risks and Potentiating Normal Development

Choice of TCA or stimulant medication may be made to avoid side effects of either drug. Major liabilities of stimulants include dysphoria, insomnia, growth retardation, possible precipitation or exacerbation of tics, and potential addiction. Major liabilities of TCAs include lethality in overdose and the potential for cardiac conduction block and arrythmias in susceptible children. Careful dosage and monitoring is, of course, paramount (see Table 4).

Use of medications may obfuscate associated morbidities. This has been the greatest liability of stimulants. Stimulants eliminate the most salient symptoms and may preclude further evaluation and detection of more profound difficulties, such as reading or language disorders, anxiety or mood disorders, poor social skills, or severe family adversity. Full evaluation and identification of all diagnoses are the keys to planning treatment interventions that do not merely treat symptoms but also potentiate normal development. As we provide multimodal interventions that facilitate a child's or adolescent's acceptance, social effectance, and competence, we will foster normal development and above all trust in others and in self.

REFERENCES

American Psychiatric Association (1968). *Diagnostic and Statistical Manual of Mental Disorders,* 2nd Ed. Washington, D.C.: APA.

American Psychiatric Association (1980). *Diagnostic and Statistical Manual of Mental Disorders,* 3rd Ed. Washington, D.C.: APA.

American Psychiatric Association (1987). *Diagnostic and Statistical Manual of Mental Disorder,* 3rd Ed.—Rev. Washington, D.C.: APA.

Anderson, J. C., Williams, S., McGee, R., Silva, P. A. (1987). DSM—III disorders in preadolescent children: Prevalence in a large sample from the general population. *Arch. Gen. Psychiatry 44*:69-76.

August, G. J., Garfinkel, B. D. (1989). Behavioral and cognitive subtypes of ADHD. *J. Am. Acad. Child Adolesc. Psychiatry 28(5)*:739-748.

Baker, L., Cantwell, D. P. (1987). Comparison of well, emotionally disordered, and behaviorally disordered children with linguistic problems. *J. Am. Acad. Child Adolesc. Psychiatry 26(2)*:193-196.

Barkley, R. A. (1989). Hyperactive girls and boys: Stimulant drug effects on mother-child interactions. *J. Child Psychol. Psychiatry 30(3)*:379-390.

Barkley, R. A., McMurray, M. B., Edelbrock, C. S., Robbins, K. (1989). The response of aggressive and nonaggressive ADHD children to two doses of methylphenidate. *J. Am. Acad. Child Adolesc. Psychiatry 28(6)*:873-881.

Barkley, R. A. (1988). The effects of methylphenidate on the interactions of preschool ADHD children with their mothers. *J. Am. Acad. Child Adolesc. Psychiatry 27(3)*:336-341.

Barkley, R. (1977). A review of stimulant drug research with hyperactive children. *J. Child Psychol. Psychiatry 18*:137-165.

Berg, I., Fielding, D. (1979). An interview with a child to assess psychiatric disturbance: A note on its reliability and validity. *J. Abnorm. Child Psychol. 7*:83-89.

Biederman, J., Baldessarini, R. J., Wright, V., Knee, D., Harmatz, J. S. (1989a). A double-blind placebo controlled study of desipramine in the treatment of ADD: I. Efficacy. *J. Am. Acad. Child Adolesc. Psychiatry 28(5)*:777-784.

Biederman, J., Baldessarini, R. J., Wright, V., Knee, D., Harmatz, J. S., Goldblatt, A. (1989b). A double-blind placebo controlled study of desipramine in the treatment of ADD: II. Serum drug levels and cardiovascular findings. *J. Am. Acad. Child Adolesc. Psychiatry 28(6)*:903-911.

Biederman, J., Munir, K., Knee, D. (1987a). Conduct and oppositional disorder in clinically referred children with attention deficit disorder: A controlled family study. *J. Am. Acad. Child Adolesc. Psychiatry 26(5)*:724-727.

Biederman, J., Munir, K., Knee, D., Armentano, M., Autor, S., Waternaux, C., Tsuang, M. (1987b). High rate of affective disorders in probands with attention deficit disorder and in their relatives: A controlled family study. *Am. J. Psychiatry 144*:330-333.

Biederman, J. (1986). Desipramine in attention deficit disorder. *Biol. Therap. Psychiatry 9(8)*:1, 31-32.

Bradley, C. (1937). The behavior of children receiving benezedrine. *Am. J. Psychiatry 94*:577-585.

Campbell, M., Spencer, E. K. (1988). Psychopharmacology in child and adolescent psychiatry: A review of the past five years. *J. Am. Acad. Child Adolesc. Psychiatry 27(3)*:269-279.

Campbell, M., Green, W., Deutsch, S. (1985). Child and adolescent psychopharmacology. In: *Developmental Clinical Psychology and Psychiatry,* Vol. 2. Beverly Hills, CA: Sage Publications, pp. 71-92.

Campbell, M., Perry, R., Green, W. H., et al. (1984). Behavioral efficacy of haloperidol and lithium carbonate: A comparison in hospitalized aggressive children with conduct disorder. *Arch. Gen. Psychiatry 41*:650-656.

Carlson, G. A., Cantwell, D. P. (1980). Unmasking masked depression in children and adolescents. *Am. J. Psychiatry 137*:4.

Chiles, J., Miller, M., Cox, G. (1980). Depression in an adolescent delinquent population. *Arch. Gen. Psychiatry 37*:179-183.

Clements, S. D. (1966). *Task Force One: Minimal Brain Dysfunction in Children.* Washington, D.C.: National Institute of Neurological Diseases and Blindness Monograph No. 3, DHEW.

Cohen, D. J., Detlor, J., Young, J. G., Shaywitz, B. A. (1980).Clonidine ameliorates Gilles de la Tourette syndrome. *Arch. Gen. Psychiatry 34*:1350-1357.

Conners, C. K., Wells, K. C. (1986). Hyperkinetic children: A neuropsychosocial approach. In: *Developmental Clinical Psychology and Psychiatry,* Vol. 7. Beverly Hills, CA: Sage Publications, pp. 1-160.

Conners, C. K., Taylor, E., (1980). Pemoline, methylphenidate, and placebo in children with minimal brain dysfunction. *Arch. Gen. Psychiatry 37*:922-930.

Coyle, J. T. (1987). Biochemical development of the brain: Neurotransmitters and child psychiatry. In: *Psychiatric Pharmacosciences of Children and Adolescents,* Popper, C., ed. Washington, D.C.: American Psychiatric Press, pp. 1-26.

Delong, G. R., Aldershof, A. L. (1987). Long-term experience with lithium treatment in childhood: Correlation with clinical diagnosis. *J. Am. Acad. Child Adolesc. Psychiatry 26(3)*:389-394.

Erikson, E. (1963). *Childhood and Society.* 2nd Ed. New York: Norton.

Evans, R. W., Clay, T. H., Gualtieri, C. T. (1987). Carbamazepine in pediatric psychiatry. *J. Am. Acad. Child Adolesc. Psychiatry 26(1)*:2-8.

Farley, G. K., Zimet, S. G. (1985). Cortisol excretion of emotionally disturbed children in relation to stress, anxiety, and competence. Unpublished paper. Denver: University of Colorado Health Sciences Center.

Freud, S. (1953). *Psychical (or Mental) Treatment,* Stand. Ed. Vol 7. London: Hogarth Press, pp. 283-302.

Garfinkel, B. D., Wender, P. H., Sloman, L., O'Neill, I. (1983). Tricyclic antidepressant and methylphenidate treatment of attention deficit disorder in children. *J. Am. Acad. Child Psychiatry 22(4)*:343-348.

Gastfriend, D. R., Biederman, J., Jellinek, M. S. (1984). Desipramine in the treatment of adolescents with attention deficit disorder. *Am. J. Psychiatry 141*:906-908.

Gelenberg, A. J. (ed.) (1987). Antidepressants, cavities, and children. *Biol. Therap. Psychiatry 10(7)*:29.

Gerstley, L., McLellan, A. T., Alterman, A. I., Woody, G. E., Luborsky, L., Prout, M. (1989). Ability to form an alliance with the therapist: A possible marker of prognosis for patients with antisocial personality disorder. *Am. J. Psychiatry 146*:508-512.

Gold, M. S., Pottash, A. L., Sweeney, D. R., Davies, R. K., Kleber, H. D. (1980). Clonidine decreases opiate withdrawal-related anxiety: Possible opiate noradrenergic interaction in anxiety and panic. *Subst. Alcohol Act. Misuse 1*:239-246.

Goyette, C. H., Connors, C. K., Ulrich, R. F. (1978). Normative data on revised Connor parent and teacher rating scales. *J. Abnorm. Child Psycholo. 6*:221-236.

Heffner, T. G., Seiden, L. S. (1982). Possible involvement of serotonergic neurons in the reduction of locomotor hyperactivity caused by amphetamine in neonatal rats depleted of brain dopamine. *Brain Res. 244*:81-90.

Herjanic, B., Herjanic, M., Brown, F., Wheatt, T. (1975). Are children reliable reporters? *J. Abnorm. Child Psychol. 3*:41-48.

Hunt, R. D., Minderaa, R. B., Cohen, D. J. (1985). Clonidine benefits children with attention deficit disorder and hyperactivity: Report of a double-blind placebo crossover therapeutic trial. *J. Am. Acad. Child Psychiatry 24(5)*:617-629.

Jensen, J. B., Burke, N., Garfinkel, B. D. (1988). Depression and symptoms of attention deficit disorder with hyperactivity. *J. Am. Acad. Child Adolesc. Psychiatry 6*:742-747.

Jesness, C. F., Wedge, R. F. (1984). Validity of a revised Jesness inventory I-level classification with delinquents. *J. Consult. Clin. Psychol. 52*:999-1010.

Kashani, J. H., Goddard, P., Reid, J. C. (1989). Correlates of suicidal ideation in a community sample of children and adolescents. *J. Am. Acad. Child Adolesc. Psychiatry 28(6)*:912-917.

Kashani, J. H., Beck, N. C., Hoeper, E. W., Fallahi, C., Corcoran, C. M., McAllister, J. A., Rosenberg, T. K., Reid, J. (1987). Psychiatric disorders in a community sample of adolescents. *Am. J. Psychiatry 144*:584-589.

Klorman, R., Coons, H., Borgstedt, A. D. (1987). Effects of mehtylphenidate on adolescents with a childhood history of attention deficit disorder: I. Clinical Findings. *J. Am. Acad. Child Adolesc. Psychiatry 26(3)*:363-367.

Lahey, B. B., Schaughency, E. A., Hynd, G. W., Carlson, C. L., Nieves, N. (1987). Attention deficit disorder with and without hyperactivity: Comparison of behavioral characteristics of clinic-referred children. *J. Am. Acad. Child Adolesc. Psychiatry 26(5)*:718-723.

Lahey, B. B., Pelham, W. E., Schaughency, E. A., Atkins, M. S., Murphy, H. A., Hynd, G., Russo, M., Hartdagen, S., Lorys-Vernon, A. (1988). Dimensions and types of attention deficit disorder. *J. Am. Acad. Child Adolesc. Psychiatry 27(3)*: 330-335.

Laufer, M. W., Denhoff, E. (1957). Hyperkinetic impulse disorder in children. *J. Pediatrics 50*:463-474.

Licamele, W. L., Goldberg, R. L. (1989). The concurrent use of lithium and methylphenidate in a child. *J. Am. Acad. Child Adolesc. Psychiatry 28(5)*:785-787.

Manheim, P., Paalzow, L., Hokfelt, B. (1982). Plasma clonidine in relation to blood pressure, catecholamines, and renin activity during long-term treatment of hypertension. *Clin. Pharmacol. Ther. 31*:445-451.

Marriage, K., Fine, Stuart, Moretti, M., Haley, G. (1986). Relationship between depression and conduct disorder in children and adolescents. *J. Am. Acad. Child Adolesc. Psychiatry 25(5)*:687-691.

Mason, S. T. (1980). Noradrenaline and selective attention: A review of the model and the evidence. *Life Sci. 28*:617-631.

Mason, S. T., Iversen, S. D. (1978). Reward, attention and the dorsal noradrenergic bundle. *Brain Res. 150*:135-148.

Mattes, J., Gittelman, R. (1983). Growth of hyperactive children on maintenance methylphenidate. *Arch. Gen. Psychiatry 40*:317-321.

Munir, K., Biederman, J., Knee, D. (1987). Psychiatric comorbidity in patients with attention deficit disorder: A controlled study. *J. Am. Acad. Child Adolesc. Psychiatry 26(6)*:844-848.

Newcorn, J. H., Halperin, J. M., Healey, J. M., O'Brien, J. D., Pascualvaca, D. M., Wolf, L. E., Morganstein, A., Vanshdeep, S., Young, G. J. (1989). Are ADDH and ADHD the same or different? *J. Am. Acad. Child Adolesc. Psychiatry 285*: 734-738.

Pliszka, S. R. (1989). Effect of anxiety on cognition, behavior, and stimulant response in ADHD. *J. Am. Acad. Child Adolesc. Psychiatry 28(6)*:882-887.

Pliszka, S. R. (1987). Tricyclic antidepressants in the treatment of children with attention deficit disorder. *J. Am. Acad. Child Adolesc. Psychi. 28(2)*:127-132.

Popper, C. (1987). Medical unknowns and ethical consent: Prescribing psychotropic medications for children in the face of uncertainty. In: *Psychiatric Pharmacosciences of Children and Adolescents*, Popper, C. (ed.). Washington, D.C.: American Psychiatric Press, pp. 127-161.

Poznanski, E., Hartmut, B. M., Grossman, J., Freeman, L. N. (1985). Diagnostic criteria in childhood depression. *Am. J. Psychi. 142*:1168-1173.

Poznanski, E., Grossman, J., Buschsbaum, Y., et al. (1984). Preliminary studies of the reliability and validity of the children's depression rating scale. *J. Am. Acad. Child Psychi. 23*:191-197.

Poznanski, E., Cook, S. C., Carroll, B. J. (1979). A depression rating scale for children. *Pediatrics 64*:442-450.

Preskorn, S. H., Bupp, S. J., Weller, E. B., Weller, R. A. (1989). Plasma levels of imipramine and metabolites in 68 hospitalized children. *J. Am. Acad. Child Adolesc. Psychi. 28(3)*:373-375.

Prien, R. F., Kupfer, D. J. (1986). Continuation drug therapy for major depressive episodes: How long should it be maintained? *Am. J. Psychi. 143*:18-23.

Puig-Antich, J., Perel, J. M., Lupatkin, W., Chambers, W. J., Tabrizi, M. A., King, J., Goetz, R., Davies, M., Stiller, R. L. (1987). Imipramine in prepubertal major depressive disorders. *Arch. Gen. Psychi. 44*:81-89.

Puig-Antich, J. (1982). Major depression and conduct disorder in prepuberty. *J. Am. Acad. Child Psychi. 21(2)*:118-128.

Quinn, P. O., Rapoport, J. L. (1975). One-year follow-up of hyperactive boys treated with imipramine or methylphenidate. *Am. J. Psychi. 132*:3.

Rapoport, J., (1965). Childhood behavior and learning problems treated with imipramine. *Int. J. Neuropsychi.*

Rapoport, J. L., Quinn, P. O., Bradbard, G., Riddle, D., Brooks, E. (1974). Imipramine and methylphenidate treatments of hyperactive boys. *Arch. Gen. Psychi. 30.*

Reeves, J. C., Werry, J. S., Elkind, G. S., Zametkin, A. (1987). Attention deficit, conduct, oppositional, and anxiety disorders in children: II. Clinical characteristics. *J. Am. Acad. Child Adolesc. Psychi. 26*:144-155.

Rescorla, L. A. (1986). Preschool psychiatric disorders: Diagnostic classification and symptom patterns. *J. Am. Acad. Child Psychi. 25(2)*:162-169.

Roche, A. F., Lipman, R. A., Overall, J. E., Hung, W. E. (1979). The effects of stimulant medication on the growth of hyperkinetic children. *Pediatrics 63*:847-850.

Rutter, M. (1989). Isle of Wight revisited: Twenty-five years of child psychiatric epidemiology. *J. Am. Acad. Child Adolesc. Psychi. 28(5)*:633-653.

Rutter, M. (1981). *Longitudinal studies: A Psychiatric Perspective Longitudinal Research—An empirical basis for the primary prevention of Psychosocial Disorders.* Oxford: Oxford University Press.

Rutter, M., Graham, P., Chadwick, O. F. D., Yule, W. (1976). Adolescent turmoil: Fact or fiction? *J. Child Psychol. Psychi. 17*:35-56.

Rutter, M., Tizard, J., Whitmore, K. (1970). *Education, Health and Behavior.* London, Longmans.

Satterfield, J. H., Satterfield, B. T., Schell, A. M. (1987). Therapeutic interventions to prevent delinquency in hyperactive boys. *J. Am. Acad. Child Adolesc. Psychi. 26(1)*:56-64.

Satterfield, J. H., Cantwell, D. P., Satterfield, B. T. (1979). Multimoldality treatment. *Arch. Gen. Psychi. 36*:965-974.

Schachar, R., Taylor, E., Wieselberg, M. B., Thorley, G., Rutter, M. (1987). Changes in family function and relationships in children who respond to methylphenidate. *J. Am. Acad. Child Adolesc. Psychi. 26(5)*:728-732.

Schowalter, J. E. (1989). Psychodynamics and medication. *J. Am. Acad. Child Adolesc. Psychi. 28(5)*:681-684.

Schroeder, J. S., Mullin, A. V., Elliott, G. R., Steiner, H., Nichols, M., Gordon, A., Paulos, M. (1989). Cardiovascular effects of desipramine in children. *J. Am. Acad. Child Adolesc. Psychi. 28(3)*:376-379.

Shafii, M., Shafii, S. L. (1982). *Pathways of Human Development: Normal Growth and Emotional Disorders in Infancy, Childhood and Adolescence.* New York, NY: Thieme-Stratton, Inc., pp. 56-58.

Shapiro, A. K., Shapiro, E. (1981). Do stimulants provoke, cause or exacerbate tics and Tourette's syndrome? *Comp. Psychi. 22(3)*:265-273.

Shaywitz, B. A., Klopper, J. H., Yager, R. D., Gordon, J. W. (1976). Paradoxical response to amphetamine in developing rats treated with 6-hydroxydopamine. *Nature 261*:153-155.

Simeon, J. G., Ferguson, H. B., Van Wyck Fleet, J. (1986). Bupropion effects in attention deficit and conduct disorders. *Can. J. Psychi. 31*:581-585.

Spitzer, R. L., Endicott, J., Robins, E. (1978). Research diagnostic criteria: Rationale and reliability. *Arch. Gen. Psychi. 35*:773-782.

Stoff, D. M., Friedman, E., Pollock, L., Vitiello, B., Kendal, P. C., Bridger, W. H. (1989). Elevated platelet MAO is related to impulsivity in disruptive behavior disorders. *J. Am. Acad. Child Adolesc. Psychi. 28(5)*:754-760.

Strayhorn, J. M., Weidman, C. S. (1989). Reduction of attention deficit and internalizing symptoms in preschoolers through parent-child interaction training. *J. Am. Acad. Child Adolesc. Psychi. 28(6)*:888-896.

Szatmari, P., Offord, D. R., Boyle, M. H. (1989a). Correlates, associated impairments and patterns of service utilization of children with attention deficit disorder: Findings from the Ontario child health study. *J. Child Psychol. Psychi. 30(2)*: 205-217.

Szatmari, P., Offord, D. R., Boyle, M. H. (1989b). Ontario child health study: Prevalence of attention deficit disorder with hyperactivity. *J. Child Psychol. Psychi. 30(2)*:219-230.

Teicher, M. H., Baldessarini, R. J. (1987). Developmental pharmacodynamics. In: *Psychiatric Pharmacosciences of Children and Adolescents,* Popper, C., ed. Washington, D. C: American Psychiatric Press, pp. 45-80.

Thomas, A., Chess, S. (1984). Genesis and evolution of behavioral disorders: From infancy to early adult life. *Am. J. Psychi. 141*:1-9.

Tronick, E. Z., Gianino, A. (1986). Interactive mismatch and repair: challenges to the coping infant. Zero to Three. *Bull. Nat. Cent. Clin. Infant Prog. 6(3)*:1-6.

Waizer, J., Hoffman, S. P., Polizos, P., Engelhardt, D. M. (1974). Outpatient treatment of hyperactive school children with imipramine. *Am. J. Psychi. 131*:5.

Warnock, J. K., Knesevich, J. W. (1988). Adverse cutaneous reactions to antidepressants. *Am. J. Psychi. 145*:425-430.

Weiss, G., Hechtman, L. (1979). The hyperactive child syndrome. *Science 205(28)*: 1348-1353.

Werner, E. E. (1988). Individual differences, universal needs: A 30-year study of resilient high risk infants. Zero to Three. *Bull. Nat. Cent. Clin. Infant Prog. 8(4)*:1-5.

Werry, J. S., Reeves, J. C., Elkind, G. S. (1987). Attention deficit, conduct, oppositional, and anxiety disorders in children: I. A review of research on differentiating characteristics. *J. Am. Acad. Child Adolesc. Psychi. 26(2)*:133-143.

Werry, J. S., Aman, M. G., Diamond, E. (1980). Imipramine and methylphenidate in hyperactive children. *J. Child Psychol. Psychi. 21*:27-35.

Werry, J. S., Aman, M. G. (1975). Methylphenidate and haloperidol in children: Effects on attention, memory, and activity. *Arch. Gen. Psychi. 32*:790-795.

Werry, J. S., Weiss, G., Dourglas, V., Martin, J. (1966). Studies on the hyperactive child: III. The effect of chlorpromazine upon behavior and learning ability. *J. Am. Acad. of Child Psychi. 5*:292-312.

Winsberg, B. G., Bialer, I., Kupietz, S., Tobias, J. (1972). Effects of imipramine and dextroamphetamine on behavior of neuropsychiatrically impaired children. *Am. J. Psychi. 128*:11.

Woolston, J. L., Rosenthal, S. L., Riddle, M. A., Sparrow, S. S., Cicchetti, D., Zimmerman, L. D. (1989). Childhood comorbidity of anxiety/affective disorders and behavior disorders. *J. Am. Acad. Child Adolesc. Psychi. 28(5)*:707-713.

Zametkin, A. J., Rapoport, J. L., (1987). Neurobiology of attention deficit disorder with hyperactivity: Where have we come in 50 years. *J. Am. Acad. Child Adolesc. Psychi. 26(5)*:676-686.

Zametkin, A. J., Rapoport, J. L., Murphy, D. L., et al. (1985). Treatment of hyperactive children with monoamine oxidase inhibitors: II. Plasma and urinary monamine findings after treatment. *Arch. Gen. Psychi. 42*:969-973.

Zimet, S. G., Farley, G. K. (1987). How do emotionally disturbed children report their competencies and self-worth? *J. Am. Acad. Child. Adolesc. Psychi. 26(1)*: 33-38.

tions followed accepted pharmaceutical standards by classifying as irrational almost all drug combinations. In later editions the language was tempered, but the principle stands. Most current other therapies are mixtures of bits and pieces of earlier disproven myths. Such individualized mixtures are virtually impossible to replicate and evaluate and thus provide a temporary haven safe from the winds of reason. This nonalcoholic brand of mixology claims to bring the brain-damaged child "from comatose to superman."

Adherents of other therapies often prefer the descriptor *alternative* as if there were really something approaching equivalent options. This would also imply further underlying assumptions of competence, expertise, and lack of bias, none of which are usually fulfilled. If the "alternative" is supposed to suggest some kind of balance between the choices, then they should be in some way comparable, of the same order of magnitude, be rooted in compatible systems of logic, or at least originate on similar planets. In fact, the only "alternative" actually offered is between (1) the existence of a permanent central nervous system impairment, which, although it cannot be cured, can with time and effort be effectively managed by a variable combination of family and behavioral therapy, medication, classroom placement, and curriculum modifications; and (2) pseudoreligious mythology with fuzzy tenets that when put into practice will reinforce the delusional belief in their effectiveness all the while the family's energies and resources are squandered and the child's problems actually worsen. The failure of this prochoice movement favoring such alternatives to produce more mayhem than it actually does among the pediatric ADHD population results from a combination of factors: misdiagnosis (and the resulting treatment of many children who would not be diagnosed by experienced clinicians), a focus on the milder (and always more numerous) end of the spectrum, and the implementation of other therapeutic components (along with inconsistent follow-up and dropping out of even the most "successful" cases). The problems and difficulties inherent in measuring long-term outcomes for dramatically successful short-term stimulant therapy are neither recognized nor understood— much less measured—by the proponents of alternative therapies.

From what has been said thus far the derivation of other modifiers for these other therapies can be seen to logically include *questionable* (many questions, few answers), *controversial* (but with no commonly accepted system of discourse for debate), *fringe* (located at the far outskirts of commonsense where they can intersect and join forces with many other oddball conceits), *fallacious* (an unfair charge in the absence of inductive or deductive logic), *unsafe* (but then life is unsafe, and it is a common ploy to calculate the risks only for traditional therapies: the "Evel Knievel gambit"), *holistic* (a faddish term that a short decade ago was to renew the face of the therapeutic globe but has since exhibited premature senility—a fate not uncommon to shallow progressivist claims), *silly* (we have here many candidates for a new *Natural History of Nonsense* to be compiled in the next millennium), and *metaphysical* and *mystical* (two words that in their strictly defined philosophical and theological denotations represent some of the noblest achievements of humanity but are often prostituted by purveyors of nostrums and the occult sciences to electroplate their base ideas). And yes, reference has been made to *quackery* but this is too technical an area of medical history to be pursued in this brief chapter [Holbrook, 1962; Young, 1967].

MAPPA MUNDI

Any attempt to map out the territorial claims of the numerous other therapies is a priori doomed to frustration. They simply do not permit rational boundaries to be drawn. While clinicians and researchers in the field of ADHD are always sensitive to issues of accurate diagnosis and subject selection, nothing could be of less concern to these other therapists. They will accept almost anybody's claim that the child has whatever condition and will not see any need to support this "diagnosis" by even considering possible alternatives, whether from the spectrum and continuum of central nervous system dysfunction or from the point of view of child and family psychopathology. Rather than interpret this as blissful diagnostic ignorance they will simply view their treatment approach as effective for any possible diagnosis and of benefit to the healthy. Whenever objective measures are utilized, they are typically those with the weakest reliability and validity parameters. Table 2 attempts to categorize some of the more common "other therapies." It will be readily seen that no attempt has been made to exclude treatments from the more severe end of the neurodevelopmental spectrum. Most "other" therapists have neither the clinical acumen nor the desire to make such distinctions. Their magical keys are meant to unlock the potential of any child. The underlying theoretical substrate to many of these approaches is such a confused mixture of guesses, assumptions, presumptions, and odd if misunderstood facts that they frequently intersect with the result that each theory uses the unproved claims of the others to increase its verisimilitude. Thus, for example, subclinical nystagmus is a key marker for sensory integration under "General Physical" and both the vestibular dysfunction theories under "Ear" and in the optometric training under "Eye" under "Special Physical." The minimal factual basis for these claims is simply that diffuse brain damage will often impair eye muscle coordination (producing at the extreme end of the spectrum the strabismus that is common in cerebral palsy) and sometimes affect cerebellar pathways or produce labyrinthine dysfunction. The multiple sensory inputs to the complex oculomotor control system can

Table 2   Other Therapies in Developmental Disabilities

General Physical
  Guggenbuhl's fresh air treatment for cretinism
  Seguin's physical exercise programs for the retarded
  Doman Delacato patterning
  Kephart's kinesthetic training
  Chiropractic
  Frostig's visual perceptual training
Special Physical
  Ear
    Vestibular training
    Antimotion sickness drugs
      Meclazine
      Diphenhydramine
      Cyclizine
  Eye
    Optometric training
    Irlen lenses
    (fluorescent lighting)
  Hormones
    Thyroid
    Turkel's "U" series (48 compounds)
    Sicca cell therapy
Diet
  Supplement
    Orthomolecular therapy
    Megavitamin therapy
    Amino acid therapy
      Glutamic acid
      Mashed animal brains
    Bronson's GTC 3 formula
    Trace elements
  Elimination
    Feingold diet
      Salicylates
      Dyes
      Preservatives
      Colors
    Glucose/sucrose
    Cott hypoglycemia diet
    "Caveman"
    Gluten
    Mold

also be distorted. But true subclinical nystagmus is virtually undetectable by the techniques employed by these therapists, and even if more accurate measurements were readily available (a condition contrary to fact), their treatments to remediate this peripheral outcome have consistently been demonstrated to be ineffective [Ottenbacher and Short, 1985].

Reviewing the historical evolution of many of these other therapies, one is struck by their longevity. In various dress they can probably be traced back to Chaldean and Pythagorean rituals and beliefs. It remains to be seen whether their faddish recurrences represent true immortality or merely vampire like simulacra. Closer examination of the patterns of their development suggests a historical "law" of cyclical reappearance. If one were to apply this law to a piece of silliness like fenfluramine therapy for autism, one would predict the following historical evolution:

> Anecdotal case reports document striking improvement with fenfluramine treatment in a few children with autism.
>
> Hypothesis: successful fenfluramine therapy suggests that autism is a unique biochemical disorder with the potential of a lock-and-key response (magical cure) and not a frustrating, treatment-resistant, diffuse, brain-damage syndrome with strong ties to mental retardation and severe communication disorders.
>
> This hypothesis receives "support" from platelet serotonin studies that unfortunately have been related to just about everything under the sun except brain serotonin neurotransmitter levels.
>
> The larger and better designed the next wave of research studies, the less frequent are the miracle cures seen. The lay press continues, however, to report testimonial cases of "belief" in the drug's efficacy to normalize autistic behavior.
>
> Soon anecdotal case reports surface of the nearly magical effect that fenfluramine has in the treatment of attentional disorders.
>
> The cycle repeats with the early research reflecting dramatic confusion and the later papers documenting frustration and confusion.
>
> One by one, the members of the entire spectrum of developmental disabilities are briefly cured by fenfluramine, and each series of scientific reports reinforces the need to expand the treatment horizons for this amazing drug. [Dreyfus, 1988]

If and when all the central nervous system diagnoses and symptoms are exhausted, a sufficient number of years will have passed that fenfluramine can be rediscovered and tried again with revised and updated diagnostic criteria for autism. Or its limited (actually nil) effectiveness can be bolstered by combining it with other treatment components of similar efficacy. Any drug that can work an occasional miracle is perceived as magical and can act so again if only the right patient, the right disorder, or the right set of circumstances are found. Gualtieri's [1986] critique of fenfluramine studies was interpreted as suggesting a halt to further research on the drug. Professionals were aghast at this unwarranted intrusion of commonsense into the sacrosanct confines of "Aren't we all entitled to pursue research funding into the silliest areas? After all who would have thought of antibiotics from bread mold?" (This is the old—and moldy—Galileo, or preferably Christopher Columbus, gambit.) The fact is that fenfluramine is a cruel hoax on its way to becoming a tiny component in a larger and older myth. Its future contribution to the history of mankind's delusions is only made inevitable by its link with a debased science. In a refusal to accept the permanent nature of organic brain deficits, parents and researchers grasp at straws.

And the foolishness does not stop there; it never does. Table 3 represents but a small selection of some of the saner entries in Walker [1978] who inexplicably omitted iridology [Simon et al., 1979]. Many such as acupuncture have a recognized place in the treatment of fairly specific conditions, but their weak and often unscientific theoretical frameworks allow if not encourage exaggerated claims, self-delusions, and entrepreneural charlatanism. Their practitioners have limited-to-no diagnostic skills in the field of developmental disabilities, and their claims to have objective results that should be given credibility by the scientific community cannot be taken seriously.

Table 3 More Other Therapies in Developmental Disabilities

Acupuncture
Art therapy
Astrology
Aversion therapy
Electrotherapy
Exorcism
Herbalism
Homeopathy
Hormone therapy
Hydrotherapy
Hypnosis
Kinesio therapy
Massage therapy
Music therapy
Occupational therapy
Physical therapy
Sex therapy
Scientology
Cosmetic surgery

Thus any attempt to investigate the reported association between Down Syndrome risk and astrological signs must be categorically classified as a waste of time and energy. While we have declined to recommend requested exorcisms, we have encountered a number of ADHD children who have been victims of exorcistic rituals performed by fundamentalist ministers.

The extraordinary record of other therapies has been reviewed and criticized elsewhere [Aman and Singh, 1988; Brown, 1987; Cohen, 1986; Golden, 1984; Silver, 1975, 1986; Spitz, 1986; Starrett, 1991; Storm, 1983]. The present chapter will use but one of these schools of treatment, dietotherapy, to exemplify the fundamental unreason and danger of such approaches.

THE MYTH OF HOMO GASTRONOMICUS

Since nutrition is necessary for organic life, the surrounding of eating with ritualistic associations and taboos throughout human history is not unexpected. Attempts to validate such customs with rationalizations—the clean and the unclean, the cooked and the raw—are also not new, and the past century has witnessed a marked proliferation of nutritional pseudoscience [Fellman and Fellman, 1981]. Genuine scientific breakthroughs such as the treatment of pernicious anemia by liver or vitamin B_{12}, the prevention of the mental retardation associated with phenylketonuria by a restrictive diet, and vitamin supplementation for scurvy, pellagra, rickets and beriberi—all these have achieved the status of myths in the popular mind (and its unthinking mirror, the media) to suggest a system of analogies run wild. Outdistancing such competition as ancient sympathetic magic practices and Freudian dream interpretation, the free associations in the dietotherapy literature give new meaning to both dissociative and wishful thinking.

The influence of diet on behavior and learning is variably attributed to subclinical deficiency states, toxicity from excess of unnatural poisons, food allergy, and that disorder with a thousand faces—hypoglycemia. Each of these etiological factors combines a smidgen of medical fact with a teaspoon to a tablespoon of folk wisdom, and adds a dash of paranoia to an industrial strength gallon of credulity to create a "system" of dietary advice and prohibitions that begin to make ancient religious taboos seem reasonable by comparison. By the middle of the nineteenth century neurochemistry documented a high phosphorus content in the human brain. This was combined with the anecdotal observation that fisherman were smarter than farmers (pre IQ test era) to identify high phosphorus fish as "brain food." The myth persists into our own century but with a modernized (amino acid) rationalization, but it's just another fish story.

Postulate: A moving target is more difficult to hit than a fixed one. The dietotherapy target moves by virtue of the fact that the impact of research negating, for example, the influence of allergy on behavior is discounted because it did not control for hypoglycemia. Dietotherapeutics becomes a veritable Bermuda triangle in which reason and commonsense frequently disappear. But eventually even the most primitive folk healing attempts to imitate the structure of orthodox medicine and set up its own counter system [Whorton, 1987], so we will try to examine each prop of this New Age approach.

The idea of a *subclinical deficiency state* (especially as applied to vitamins) ignores two critical factors. First, the body's physiological homeostasis should be able to self-correct for such mild imbalances—otherwise they are not mild. (That this is not just a small verbal criticism requires more than a small amount of critical acumen.) Second, when one blames signs and symptoms of a disease process on a mild deficiency state, it would be considered reasonable to expect those signs and symptoms to be milder versions of the ones associated with the more severe clinically diagnosed full-blown deficiency state. That is, after all, the analogical basis for interpreting minimal brain dysfunction as a milder variant of maximal brain dysfunction rather than kidney or liver disease. Yet except for those signs and symptoms attributable to general malaise and "being sick," no such attenuation of findings is observed compared to recognized vitamin deficiency syndromes.

Lemma: If something is good for you, then more is better. Vitamins are good for you—some are even essential—therefore, megavitamins are a panacea for all the ills that the human frame is heir to. The fact that one could substitute many other subjects in the major premise of this invalid syllogism to generate patently absurd conclusions seems to tax the commonsense of many otherwise educated persons. The tendency to perceive vitamins as magical is so universal that it must be suggested that perhaps pediatricians should routinely caution parents *against* the routine use of vitamin supplements in children as a necessary component of patient education.

An interesting alternative syllogism to consider would suggest that if very large amounts of a substance can be toxic, then lesser amounts can also be toxic—possibly in fairly subtle ways so as even to affect the next generation. The older lesson of diethystilbesterol and the more recently described retinoic acid embryopathy (central nervous system deficits, microtia, and cardiac defects) should stand as warnings to all additive prone therapists. But the potential toxicity of such seemingly benign substances [Haslam et al., 1984; Shaywitz et al., 1977] is routinely ignored (Table 4). For the 20 dietary additives commonly recommended to improve behavior, cognition, and general health as well as to treat supposed subclinical disease and otherwise offset the evils of civilization, 17 can cause adverse effects in humans and at least 9 have been associated with human deaths. Allergic reactions including fatal anaphylaxis should probably be considered a universal risk for either the

Table 4 Potential Toxicity of Common Additives

Additive	Identified Deficiency	Toxicity
A (retinol)	Xerophthalmia	+
B$_1$ (thiamine)	Beriberi	+
B$_2$ (riboflavin)	+	−
B$_3$ (nicotinic acid)	Pellagra	+
B$_6$ (pyridoxine)	+	+
B$_{12}$ (cyanocobalamin)	Pernicious anemia	−
C (ascorbic acid)	Scurvy	+
D (calciferol)	Rickets	+
E (tocopherol)	+	−
Biotin	+	−
Folic acid	Megaloblastic anemia	+
Pantothenic acid	+	+
PABA	(Achromotrichia)	+
Calcium	Rickets/tetany	+
Chromium	+	+
Copper	+	+
Magnesium	+	+
Manganese	−	+
Selenium	+	+
Zinc	+	+

additive itself or for the medium in which it is delivered. While some of the reported toxicity occurs only at extremely high dosages such as in industrial exposures, the point to this table is that these "natural" substances can be poisonous when taken in non-natural ways. The potentially fatal eosinophilic myalgia syndrome (EMS) has recently been associated with ingestion of the naturopathic essential amino acid L-tryptophane, with onset often occurring long after exposure to this harmless food additive has been discontinued.

The megavitamin mania started with the treatment of schizophrenia where it was soon documented to be completely ineffective. But the fact that it had once been rumored to help that disorder was considered sufficient justification to try it on defenseless children with ADHD and learning disabilities [Cott, 1971; Cott et al., 1985]. And if you are going to have a panacea, you might as well treat everything including the common cold [Pauling, 1970]. As evidence accumulated that megavitamins were ineffective and potentially dangerous, the professional warnings of the American Academy of Pediatrics [1976] and the American Psychiatric Association were ludicrously countered by pronouncements from the "Academy of Orthomolecular Psychiatry" [Harley, 1980]—as if the later body had any other than media credibility.

The involved professional groups were treated as, and reduced to the status of, priest magicians vying for popular credulity and free newspaper copy. Nobelist Linus Pauling [1974a,b] did not do his scientific reputation any credit with his flippant nonsequitors about research design and medical ethics. Harrell et al. [1981] ignore or violate every conceivable rule of research design methodology ranging from subject selection through statistical analysis of data. Published as an equivalent to a paid advertisement, this paper is an example of how *not* to do research. One of the leading dietotherapists in recounting his conversion experience [Smith, 1977] commented that he "once believed that if a doctor gave vitamin injections he was a quack or at least bilking the public." Dietotherapy is composed of half truths and the first half of Smith's sentence represents the half that's true.

Starting from an allergic background Feingold [1975] suggested a non-allergy mediated behavioral effect for certain *food additives* or low molecular weight chemicals such as salicylates, artificial colors, flavors, and preservatives. The wave of popular enthusiasm that greeted this hypothesis virtually overwhelmed the research establishment, which then scurried about and assigned a much greater contribution to this phenomenon than the data ever warranted [National Institute of Allergy, 1982]. Anecdotal and uncontrolled success rates rapidly dwindled from press releases of 90% to 50% as controlled studies [Thorley, 1984] could document no effects to a barely 5% success rate and then only in very selected children in very narrow and very young age groups and along very limited parameters—a very long way to go for very little to nothing [Conners, 1980]. The best current consensus is that there is no causal relationship between food additives and hyperactivity and related disorders [Wender, 1986].

Food allergy is a genuine but relatively rare medical condition and one not reliably implicated in behavioral pathology. But when Speer [1954] defined the allergic tension fatigue syndrome, he commented on the possibility of cerebral allergy and a neuropathic diathesis whose symptoms could include fretfulness, insomnia, irritability, alternating lethargy and restlessness, and intense temper outbursts. First, it should be noted that these symptoms bear only the most superficial resemblance to ADHD. Second, for Speer allergic tension fatigue syndrome also required, in addition to the above behavioral symptoms, the further presence of signs of allergic disease, such as nasal stuffiness, pallor, hyperhidrosis, infraorbital edema with dark coloring, and increased salivation. Later writers [Crook, 1975; Crook and Stevens, 1987] have not exercised nearly as much caution and restraint in their claims for this nebulous entity. The absence of an increased incidence of learning disorders and behavioral problems in well-defined atopic populations [McLoughlin et al., 1983] along with the academic overachievement of some of the most severely allergic children [Wright et al., 1979] are observations difficult to reconcile with the existence of any significant contribution of allergy to neurobehavioral disorders. The further probability that food sensitivities are overdiagnosed, less prevalent than generally thought, and extremely inconsistent over time [Bock, 1987] does nothing to prop up this already weak hypothesis. The impression that allergies are so important to behavior receives its strongest behavioral reinforcement from the overprescription of formula changes in infancy to treat maternal anxiety thus planting the seed of a pernicious idea when the mother is most vulnerable.

As with most fallacious treatments one needs to be concerned whether the limited diagnostic skills of its enthusiasts are actually causing harm by missing significant other diagnoses. Hyperactivity, ADHD and learning disorders do not simply represent an open field for any therapeutic fad to waltz into; these are difficult and complex diagnostic challenges. Egger et al. [1985] report a high incidence of headaches, abdominal pains, and limb aches in their hyperkinetic children successfully treated by an allergy diet. Their prevalence rate for this symptom triad is striking, especially since an experienced pediatric clinician would consider this triplet as almost diagnostic of psychosomatic disorder [Apley, 1959; Apley and MacKeith, 1968] and recommend a comprehensive family assessment before stalking the elusive allergy etiology. The possibility that much of the "success" of hypoallergenic and other diets is attributable to indirect effects on pathologic parent-child interactions receives further support from such incidental observations as "abnormal thirst" in allergic hyperactive children [Barnes and Colquhon, 1984]. That milder degrees of psychogenic polydipsia (excessive water drinking) can reflect inadequate nurturance has been reported [Accardo et al., 1989b]. Focusing on allergy diets can be a good way to avoid coming to grips with the main problem. The difficulty here is that parents and pseudotherapists are jumping the gun to treatment when neither are competent in the area of diagnosis.

Hypoglycemia is another genuine medical condition whose severe forms can produce brain damage but whose milder forms are exceedingly difficult to document. If a fraction of the suspicions raised by Runion [1980] had any basis in fact, then all children with ADHD, hyperactivity, and learning disabilities should receive an extensive biomedical evaluation since there exist close to 100 specific disease conditions that can present with varying degrees of hypoglycemia [Sauls, 1974]. If it is present, hypoglycemia needs to be considered a marker for serious underlying organic pathology and in need of an indepth diagnostic assessment. But the facts are that sugar levels do not have much of an effect on activity level [Kruesi et al., 1987] and that most of the vague symptomatology that anxious, depressed, and hypochondriacal adults attribute to "hypoglycemia" has a psychogenic cause [Jaspan, 1989].

If diet of any sort has a specific effect on behavior and activity it is minimal. Medication produces much more striking improvement [Williams et al., 1978], and medication is never meant to be used alone. Even studies that support a positive effect of diet conclude that "not a single parent believed that participation in this study had transformed their child into an easy to manage person" [Kaplan et al., 1989]—but it did improve their halitosis. Prinz [1985] reviewed the levels of causation for diet-behavior interactions and reduced them to four hypotheses:

1. All hyperactivity is primarily due to diet.
2. Some hyperactivity is primarily due to diet.
3. Hyperactivity is due to diet in combination with nondietary factors.
4. Hyperactivity is influenced but not caused by diet.

There is a sufficient accumulation of research data to discard 1 and 2 and to make 3 extremely improbable. The fourth hypothesis is probably true but also trivial. Its truth is reflected in the truism that "sugar makes kids hyperactive." Whatever baseline level of activity a child or an adult exhibits, sugar, especially in the form of chocolate, supplies a quick energy boost and allows the child or adult to increase their activity level. Also much of the hyperactivity that parents associate with increased candy intake is coincident with holidays and special occasions such as birthdays when children's behavior is typically under less control, and the children are more excitable due to the time of year rather than the specific food intake.

In the sixteenth and seventeenth centuries the apothecaries guild fought the company of grocers over the right to sell gingerbread and bananas [Mathison, 1958]. The pharmacists tried to assert a monopoly on these two products because they were classified as drugs. The grocers eventually prevailed, and over the next three centuries medicine worked on clarifying the distinction between a food and a drug. Dietotherapy, however, would like to turn back the clock and make iced gingerbread available to children only by a "doctor's" prescription [Accardo, 1985], while at the same time it recommends poisoning the child's system with near toxic levels of pharmaceutically packaged supplements—and all this is done in the name of "nature." This pathologic inversion, the medicalization of food, is part of the modern world's desacralization of eating rituals—sacramental banquets—the meaning and significance of which goes far beyond any dietotherapist's delusions [Capon, 1969, 1979]. This whole movement represents simply the most recent rehash of a much older piece of foolishness: over two millennia ago the Athenian city state was plagued by therapists working overtime to turn food into a tasteless medication for the disease called life [Plato, Republic]. Then as now such mental aberrations were reflective of social pathology [Szasz, 1974]; we could labor to emulate the classic Greeks in more productive areas.

MEDICINE AND SCIENCE

Diethotherapy like homeopathy preaches the toxicity/efficacy of extremely small or infinitesimal dosages; its therapeutic reasoning by vague analogy further recalls Hahnemann's *similia similibus* [Gevitz, 1987]. In his classic essay on "Homeopathy and its kindred delusions" [1891] an amiable Oliver Wendell Holmes [1809-1894] questioned whether it was fair of him to scathingly criticize the unassuming pretentions and harmless errors of homeopathy, to perform what can only be characterized as an "uncalled for aggression upon an unoffending doctrine and its peaceful advocates." After reviewing some of the more fanciful and senseless extravagances in the history of medicine, he described the underlying tenets of Hahnemann's philosophy as a "mingled mass of perverse ingenuity, of tinsel erudition, of imbecile credulity, and of artful misrepresentation." He then concluded that "it always does very great harm to the community to encourage ignorance, error or deception in a profession which deals with the life and health of our fellow-creatures."

Quackery and charlatanism flourish because physicians fail to practice good medicine. It is an inadequate response for organized medicine to actively oppose other therapies [Holohan, 1987]. Families and children with ADHD and other developmental disorders must have access to physicians with expertise in the diagnosis and management of these neurobehavioral syndromes. The bumbling agreement and implied approval of the untrained and inexperienced practitioner—"Well, I guess it couldn't hurt to try it"—when parents voice their decision to employ diet or physiological retraining or Irlen lenses, needs to be recognized for exactly what it is—applied scientific ignorance and medical malpractice—with significant ethical implications [Accardo, 1989].

If this seems to be a bit too personal or *ad hominem,* it should be noted that many of the popular publications on the naturopathic triad of allergy, diet and vitamin/mineral supplements either directly or indirectly paint a portrait of the preferred pediatrician, a modern version of the wise old family doctor who made house calls. The identifying stigmata vary and like most of the other ingredients in this irrational brew they do not often exhibit coherence: they seem to have been decided upon by a committee whose principal goals were more in the fields of advertising and public relations (Table 5). Historically few things seem to date more quickly than those faddish items characterized as "progressive."

While it is imperative for even the primary care provider to locate the terms of this debate with other therapies in the framework of science and antiscience, the opposite extreme must also be avoided. Medicine is not a

Table 5 The Pediatric Prescriber

Progressive Pediatrician	True Pediatrician
Stresses preventive medicine through the role of diet and vitamin supplements and nutritional counseling.	Stresses preventive medicine through anticipatory guidance, family and behavioral counseling, accident prevention, immunizations, and nutritional counseling.
Praises "natural" foods and wastes much of the routine visit spouting tirades deploring the degenerate eating habits of most children (as well as the decline of civilization and moral standards in general).	Does not attempt to impose personal philosophy on the state of civilization when communicating to parents medically acceptable ranges of eating and other behaviors of children.
Sees allergies everywhere, causing everything—if only one looks and believes hard enough.	Recognizes allergic diatheses as very common and multifaceted but nevertheless sufficiently clearly defined to be able to be ruled out without expensive testing or risky elimination diets.
Is a living museum of all the popular and faddish treatments, old wives' tales, and home remedies of the previous generation—and century.	Lives and thinks in the present; does not usually have a practical working knowledge of antiquated nostrums, herbs, and witches' brews.
Claims or at least suggests that proposed treatment regimens do not simply heal but represent the key to superior if not superhuman function, longevity if not immortality, and probably a good complexion.	Recognizes that life and civilization are not diseases (pace Freud) and that the treatment of behavior disorders is meant only to allow (and not magically guarantee) the child to achieve his full potential.
Accepts nutrition as a fully developed science.	See the science of nutrition as in its infancy and confused with much nonsense.
Skillfully manipulates parental susceptibility to guilt over hesitation to employ any and all means to assure their offspring's success.	Accepts parental freedom of choice with regard to lifestyle and limited parental responsibility for child's future; restricts guilt promoting criticisms to parental actions that have a proven negative impact on the child.
Willing to endorse vitamin and nutritional supplement dosages far in excess of recommended safe levels.	Reluctant to hazard child's health and safety on personal whim.
Distinguishes infant cries.	Declines to grandstand and overawe parents with unprovable interpretations of infant behavior.

(continues)

Table 5 (Continued)

Progressive Pediatrician	True Pediatrician
Focuses on externals such as diet changes and magic vitamin pills. (The evil is out there and you can magically control it.)	Focuses on internals such as modified expectations, altered behavioral interactions, and structured classroom settings. (There is no evil out there; there are only perceptions of evil and the evil that we do.)
Impresses colleagues and community with skillful financial practice management.	Is consulted by colleagues on difficult cases; is asked to treat children of other health care professionals.
Does not interrupt sacrosanct parent consultations with calls from stockbroker.	Does not have a stockbroker.

Some of the sillier items in the first column are unattributed direct quotations.

science, but it is scientific. It is applied science and a practical art [Accardo, 1987]. In his critique of the commercialization of science popularization Burnham [1987] contrasted the "gee whiz!" school of science reportage with the patient methodology of true science (Table 6). There is concern that not only science popularization but science itself may be moving over toward the magic column in the area of public education. It should also be noted that the dichotomy of naturalistic versus organic is artificial, and that positivistic philosophy does not have an exclusive hold on science proper. Indeed in its extreme forms such a philosophy may even precipitate a wholesale migration to column two. If science lies down with bad philosophy, it will get up with more than fleas.

An item that might be expected to be included in column one, evolution, is ironically almost a hallmark for fringe therapies; their pseudoscientific supporters long ago recognized the utility and attractiveness of explanatory hypotheses that defy disproof. As a general rule of thumb, whenever the evolutionary *deus ex machina* is brought in to support a proposed relationship between diet and brain function, one's index of suspicion needs to be raised. People overly susceptible to this kind of romantic mythologizing rarely notice the paradoxical implications of their creed: if food really does affect how people think, then should not the simple vegetarian diet of protohominid food gatherers limit our thought patterns to those of prehuman simpletons? Modern man seems to be having serious difficulty choosing between socratic anguish and swinish tranquility.

In our informational age a growing cultural illiteracy is being equalled by a growing scientific illiteracy [Hendee and Loeb, 1988]. For a technological society to allow this trend to continue is suicidal. The roots of the current disenchantment and disillusionment with science stem in part from a translation

Table 6   Science Versus Magic

Science	Magic and Superstition
Rational	Irrational
Objective	Subjective
Methodological	Enthusiastic
Skeptical	Credulous
Inductive	Analogical
Theory	Fact
Coherence	Isolated observation
Process	Product
Progressive	Static, reactionary
Institutional	Anti-institutional
Civilization	Nature
Traditional	Nontraditional
Orthodox	Unorthodox
Classic	Romantic
Intellectual stance	Life style
Naturalistic	Organic
Materialist, atomist	Idealist
Reductionist	Holistic
Positivist	Naturopathic
Mechanistic	Metaphysical, mystical
Education	Propaganda
Peer-review	Lay press/popular media
Disciplined self-sacrifice	Consumerism/profit motive

of science into scientism, an investment of scientific medicine with all the attributes of a religion with a priesthood [Nisbet, 1975]. The short-term gain in prestige from this conversion is more than offset by its long-term disastrous consequences. Patients are led to expect magical cures that they don't have to work at or understand, and when medicine can't deliver them, other therapies can (at least promise to). That technological toys could serve as narcotics and as an opiate for people and help turn science itself into the ultimate superstition is not a novel phenomenon [deUnamuno, 1984]. More than half a century ago Chesterton [1931] observed the breakdown of the paired ideas of reason and authority:

> [people] have not only grown to doubt the quack, but the doctor who denounces the quack. Everything has become a matter of opinion, or, rather, a matter of taste; and larger and larger crowds of people simply have a taste in quacks. They move about in a mesmerized and mechanical condition, talking and thinking merely on the authority of somebody who is not an authority.

Science contributes to this sad state of affairs when its practitioners pretend to a generalization of expertise and pontificate on topics having no conceivable relationship to their training and research. The end result is that most popular science (that is, most of the literature on other therapies) is popular but contains no science [Jaki, 1986].

If on the one side (pseudo) scientists and (pseudo) therapists play to the crowd, on the more abstract side of scientific theory there prevails a pampered solipsist epistemology that disclaims any objective knowledge of the real world. This posture is totally destructive to the enterprise of scientific medicine and concedes the equation of scientific therapists with any magi or gurus that can appeal to the masses [DeMille, 1980; Feyerabend, 1975]. It is no accident that even apart from the Church of Scientology (Dianetics) most other therapies gravitate toward a (pseudo) religious quality in their rationalizations, the structure of their support groups, and their proselytizing. There are limits to the debunking of this sort of thing; the one boundary that cannot be crossed is to attempt to fight them on their own ground by assuming the religious mantle.

REFERENCES

Accardo, P. (1985). The myth of Homo Gastronomicus: Your child is not what he eats. *Missouri Medicine 82*:72-74.

Accardo, P. J. (1987). *Diagnosis and Detection.* Rutherford, NJ: Fairleigh Dickenson University Press.

Accardo, P. J. (1989). Dante and medicine: The circle of malpractice. *South. Med. J. 82*:624-628.

Accardo, P. J., Blondis, T. A., Capute, A. J. (1989a). Developmental disorders in childhood. *Comp. Therapy. 15*:3-10.

Accardo, P. J., Caul, J., Whitman, B. Y. (1989b). Excessive water drinking—a marker of caretaker interaction disturbance. *Clin. Pediatrics 28*:416-418.

Aman, M. G., Singh, N. N. (1988). Vitamins, mineral, and dietary treatments. In: Aman, M. G. Singh, N. N., eds. *Psychopharmacology of the Developmental Disabilities.* New York: Springer-Verlag, pp. 168-196.

American Academy of Pediatrics, Committee on Nutrition (1976). Megavitamin therapy for childhood psychoses and learning disabilities. *Pediatrics 58*:910-911.

AMA Council on Drugs (1971). *AMA Drug Evaluations.* Chicago: American Medical Association.

Apley, J. (1959). *The Child with Abdominal Pains.* Oxford: Blackwell Scientific Publications.

Apley, J., MacKeith, R. (1968). *The Child and His Symptoms: A Comprehensive Approach.* Philadelphia: F. A. Davis.

Barnes, B., Colquhon, I. (1984). *The Hyperactive Child: What the Family Can Do.* Thorsons Publishing Group.

Bock, S. A. (1987). Prospective appraisal of complaints of adverse reactions to foods in children during the first 3 years of life. *Pediatrics 79*:683-688.

Brown, G. W. (1987). Controversial therapy. In: *Textbook of Developmental Pediatrics* Gottlieb, M. I., Williams, J. E. New York: Plenum Press, pp. 431-450.

Burnham, J. C. (1987). *How Superstition Won and Science Lost: Popularizing Science and Health in the United States.* New Brunswick: Rutgers University Press.

Capon, R. F. (1969). *The Supper of the Lamb: A Culinary Entertainment.* New York: Doubleday and Company.

Capon, R. F. (1979). *Party Spirit: Some Entertaining Principles.* New York: William Morrow.

Chesterton, G. K. (1931). On twilight sleep. In: *Come to Think of It . . .* New York: Dodd, Mead & Company, pp. 158-163.

Cohen, M. W. (1986). Controversies continue in the treatment of learning disabilities and attention deficit disorder. *Am. J. Dis. Child. 140*:986-987.

Conners, C. K. (1980). *Food Additives and Hyperactive Children.* New York: Plenum Press.

Cott, A. (1971). Orthomolecular Approach to the Treatment of Learning Disabilities. *Schizophrenia 3*:95-105.

Cott, A., Agel, J., Boe, E. (1985). *Dr. Cott's Help for Your Learning Disabled Child: The Orthomolecular Treatment.* New York: Times Books.

Crook, W. G. (1975). Food allergy—the great masquerader. *Pediatric Clin. North Am. 22*:227-238.

Crook, W. G., Stevens L. J. (1987). *Solving the Puzzle of Your Hard-to-Raise Child.* New York: Random House.

DeMille, R. (1980). Ethnomethodallegory: Garfinkeling in the wilderness. In *The Don Juan Papers: Further Castaneda Controversies,* DeMille R., ed. Santa Barbara: Ross-Erikson Publishers, pp. 68-90.

deUnamuno, M. (1984). *The Private World: Selections from the Diario Intimo and Selected Letters 1890-1936.* Transl., Kerrigan, A., Lacy, A., Nozick, M. Princeton: Princeton University Press, p. 151.

Dreyfus, J. (1988). *A Remarkable Medicine Has Been Overlooked.* New York: Dreyfus Medical Foundation.

Egger, J., Graham, P. J., Carter, C. M. Gumley, D., Soothill, J. F. (1985). Controlled trial of oligoantigenic treatment in the hyperkinetic syndrome. *Lancet 1*: 540-545.

Feingold, B. (1975). *Why Your Child Is Hyperactive.* New York: Random House.

Fellman, A. C., Fellman, M. (1981). *Making Sense of Self: Medical Advice Literature in Late Nineteenth Century America.* Philadelphia: University of Pennsylvania Press.

Feyerabend, P. (1975). *Against Method.* London: New Left Books.

Finocchiaro, M. A. (1973). *History of Science as Explanation.* Detroit: Wayne State University Press.

Gevitz, N. (1987). Sectarian Medicine. *J. Am. Med. Assoc. 257*:1636-1640.

Golden, G. (1984). Controversial therapies. *Pediatric. Clin. North Am. 31*:459-469.

Gualtieri, C. T. (1986). Fenfluramine and autism: Careful reappraisal is in order. *J. Pediatrics 108*:417-419.

Harley, J. P. (1980). Dietary treatment of behavioral disorders. In: *Advances in Behavioral Pediatrics,* Vol I, Camp, B. W., ed. Greenwich, CT: JAI Press, pp. 129-151.

Harrell, R. F., Capp, R. H., Davis, D. R., Peerless, J., Ravitz, L. R. (1981). Can nutritional supplements help mentally retarded children? An exploratory study. *Proc. Natl. Acad. Sci. USA 78*:574-578.

Haslam, R. H. A., Dalby, J. T., Rademaker, A. W. (1984). Effects of megavitamin therapy in children with attention deficit disorder. *Pediatrics 74*:103-111.

Hendee, W. R., Loeb, J. M. (1988). Science literacy and the role of the physician. *J. Am. Med. Assoc. 260*:1941-1942.

Holbrook, S. H. (1962). *The Golden Age of Quackery.* New York: Collier Books.

Holmes, O. W. (1891). Homoeopathy and its kindred delusions. In: *Medical Essays 1842-1882.* Boston: Houghton Mifflin, pp. 1-102.

Holohan, T. V. (1987). Referral by default: The medical community and unorthodox therapy. *J. Am. Med. Assoc. 257*:1641-1643.

Jaki, S. L. (1986). Antagonist of scientism. In: *Chesterton, A Seer of Science.* Urbana: University of Illinois Press, pp. 29-53.

Jarvis, W. (1986). Helping your patients deal with questionable cancer treatments. *CA-A Cancer J. Clin. 36*:293-301.

Jaspan, J. B. (1989). Hypoglycemia: Fact or fiction. *Hosp. Prac. 24(3)*:11-14.

Kaplan, B. J., McNicol, J., Conte, R. A., Moghadam, H. K. (1989). Dietary Replacement in Preschool-Aged Hyperactive Boys. *Pediatrics 83*:7-17.

Keillor, G. (1989). The Current Crisis in Remorse. In: *We Are Still Married: Stories & Letters.* New York: Viking, pp. 22-26.

Kruesi, M. J. P., Rapoport, J. L., Cummings, E. M., Berg, C. J., Ismond, D. R., Flament, M., Yarrow, M., Zahn-Waxler, C. (1987). Effects of sugar and aspartame on aggression and activity in children. *Am. J. Psychiatry 144*:1487-1490.

Kuhn, T. S. (1970). *The Structure of Scientific Revolutions.* Chicago: University of Chicago Press.

Markowitz, H. J. (1989). Autism and authority. *Hosp. Prac. 24*:221-222.

Masland, R. L. (1966). Unproven methods of treatment. *Pediatrics 37*:713-714.

Mathison, R. R. (1958). *The Eternal Search: The Story of Man and His Drugs.* New York: G. P. Putnam's Sons.

McLoughlin, J., Nall, M., Isaacs, B., Petrosko, J., Karibo, J., Lindsey, B. (1983). The relationship of allergies and allergy treatment to school performance and student behavior. *Ann. Allergy 51*:506-510.

National Institute of Allergy and National Institute of Child Health and Human Development (1982). Concensus conference: Defined diets and childhood hyperactivity. *J. Am. Med. Assoc. 248*:290-292.

Nisbet, R. (1975). Knowledge dethroned. *New York Times Magazine.* September 28:34-46.

Ottenbacher, K., Short, M. A. (1985). Sensory integrative dysfunction in children: A review of theory and treatment. In *Advances in Developmental and Behavioral Pediatrics,* Vol 6, Wolraich, M., Routh, D. K., eds. Greenwich, CT: JAI Press, pp. 287-329.

Pauling, L. (1970). *Vitamin C and the Common Cold.* San Francisco: W. H. Freeman and Company.

Pauling, L. (1974a). Dr. Pauling comments on the comments. *Am. J. Psychiatry 131*:1405-1406.

Pauling, L. (1974b). On the orthomolecular environment of the mind: Orthomolecular theory. *Am. J. Psychi. 131*:1251-1257.

Plato. The Republic, Book III. In: *The Works of Plato.* Vol 2. Transl., Jowett, B. New York: Tudor, pp. 114-118.

Prinz, R. J. (1985). Diet-behavior research with children: Methodological and substantive issues. In: *Advances in Learning and Behavioral Disabilities,* Vol. 4, Gadow, K. D., ed. Greenwich, CT: JAI Press, pp. 181-199.

Runion, H. I. (1980). Hypoglycemia—Fact or fiction. In: *Approaches to Learning* Cruickshank, W. M., ed. Syracuse: Syracuse University Press, pp. 111-122.

Sauls, H. S. (1974). Hypoglycemia in infancy and childhood. In: *Metabolic, Endocrine and Genetic Disorders of Children*: Vol 2, Kelley, V. C., Limbeck, G. A., eds. Hagerstown, MD: Harper & Row, pp. 683-732.

Shaywitz, B. A., Siegel, N. J., Pearson H. A. (1977). Megavitamins for minimal brain dysfunction: A potentially dangerous therapy. *J. Am. Med. Assoc. 238*:1749-1750.

Silver, L. B. (1975). Acceptable and controversial approaches to treating the child with learning disabilities. *Pediatrics 55*:406-415.

Silver, L. B. (1986). Controversial approaches to treating learning disabilities and attention deficit disorder. *Am. J. Dis. Child. 140*:1045-1052.

Simon, A., Worthen, D. M., Mitas, J. A. II (1979). An evaluation of iridology. *J. Am. Med. Assoc. 242*:1385-1389.

Smith, L. H. (1977). *Improving Your Child's Behavior Chemistry.* New York: Pocket Books.

Speer, F. (1954). The allergic tension-fatigue syndrome. *Pediatric Clin. North Am.* 1:1029-1037.

Spitz, H. H. (1986). *The Raising of Intelligence: A Selected History of Attempts to Raise Retarded Intelligence.* Hillsdale, NJ: Lawrence Erlbaum Associates.

Starrett, A. (1991). Nonstandard therapies. In *Developmental Disorders in Infancy and Childhood.* Capute, A. J., Accardo, P. J., eds. Baltimore: Paul H. Brookes, pp. 219-233.

Storm, G. (1983). Alternative therapies. In: *Developmental-Behavioral Pediatrics.* Levine, M. D., Carey, W. B., Crocker, A. C., Gross, R. T., eds. Philadelphia: W. B. Saunders, pp. 1160-1167.

Szasz, T. (1974). Food abuse and foodaholism: From soul watching to weight watching. In: *Ceremonial Chemistry: The Ritual Persecution of Drugs, Addicts, and Pushers.* New York: Anchor Press, pp. 105-121.

Thorley, G. (1984). Pilot study to assess behavioral and cognitive effects of artificial food colours in a group of retarded children. *Dev. Med. Child Neurol. 26*: 56-61.

Walker, B. (1978). *Encyclopedia of Metaphysical Medicine.* London: Routledge and Kegan Paul.

Wender, E. H. (1986). The food additive-free diet in the treatment of behavior disorders: A review. *J. Dev. Behav. Pediatrics 7*:35-42.

Whorton, J. C. (1987). Traditions of folk medicine in America. *J. Am. Med. Assoc. 257*:1632-1635.

Williams, J. I., Cram, D. M., Tausig, F. T., Webster, E. (1978). Relative effects of drugs and diet on hyperactive behavior: An experimental study. *Pediatrics 61*: 811-817.

Wright, L., Schaefer, A. B., Solomons, G. (1979). Asthma, in *Encyclopedia of Pediatric Psychology*. Baltimore: University Park Press, pp. 65-76.

Young, J. H. (1967). *The Medical Messiahs: A Social History of Health Quackery in Twentieth-Century America*. Princeton: Princeton University Press.

Appendix: National Resources for Parents of Children with Attentional Problems

ADDA — Attention Deficit Disorders Association
National ADD Support Group Directory
1-800-487-2282
Contact person: Linda Philips

CHADD — Children with Attention Deficit Disorders
1859 North Pine Island Road, Suite 185
Plantation, FL 33322
(305) 587-3700

— Challenge
A Newsletter on Attention-Deficit Hyperactivity Disorder
P.O. Box 2001
West Newburg, MA 01985
(508) 462-0495

ERIC — Clearinghouse on Handicapped Gifted Children
CEC — Council for Exceptional Children
1920 Association Drive
Reston, VA 22091-1589
(703) 620-3660

LDAA — Learning Disabilities Association of America
4156 Library Road
Pittsburgh, PA 15234
(412) 341-1515

NCLD   — National Center for Learning Disabilities
            99 Park Avenue
            New York, NY 10016
            (212) 687-7211

NICHCY — National Information Center for Handicapped Children
            Children and Youth
            7926 Jones Branch Drive
            McLean, VA 22101
            (703) 893-6061

SDP   — Society for Developmental Pediatrics
            P.O. Box 23836
            Baltimore, MD 21203
            (301) 522-5420

Index